Bigelow's Drive and Memory Troubleshooting Pocket Reference

Stephen J. Bigelow

McGraw-Hill

New York   San Francisco   Washington, D.C.   Auckland   Bogotá
Caracas   Lisbon   London   Madrid   Mexico City   Milan
Montreal   New Delhi   San Juan   Singapore
Sydney   Tokyo   Toronto

Library of Congress Cataloging-in-Publication Data

Bigelow, Stephen J.
  Bigelow's drive and memory troubleshooting pocket
reference/Stephen J. Bigelow.
        p.   cm.
    ISBN 0-07-135453-0
    1. Computer storage devices—Repairing.   2. Data disk
drives—Repairing.   I. Title.
  TK7895.M4 B48   2000
  621.39'7'0288—dc21   99-059391
          CIP

McGraw-Hill

A Division of The McGraw·Hill Companies

1 2 3 4 5 6 7 8 9 0   DOC/DOC   9 0 4 3 2 1 0 9

0-07-135453-0

*The sponsoring editor for this book was Michael Sprague, the edit-
ing supervisor was Penny Linskey, and the production supervisor
was Claire Stanley. It was set in Century Schoolbook by Don
Feldman of McGraw-Hill's Professional Book Group composition
unit, in cooperation with Spring Point Publishing Services.*

Printed and bound by R. R. Donnelley & Sons Company.

Disclaimer
and Cautions

It is *important* that you read and understand the following information. Please read it carefully!

PERSONAL RISK AND LIMITS OF LIABILITY

The repair of personal computers and their peripherals involves some amount of personal risk. Use *extreme* caution when working with ac and high-voltage power sources. Every reasonable effort has been made to identify and reduce areas of personal risk. You are instructed to read this book carefully *before* attempting the procedures discussed. If you are uncomfortable following the procedures that are outlined in this book, do *not* attempt them—refer your service to qualified service personnel.

NEITHER THE AUTHOR, THE PUBLISHER, NOR ANYONE DIRECTLY OR INDIRECTLY CONNECTED WITH THE PUBLICATION OF THIS BOOK SHALL MAKE ANY WARRANTY EITHER EXPRESSED OR IMPLIED, WITH REGARD TO THIS MATERIAL, INCLUDING, BUT NOT LIMITED TO, THE IMPLIED WARRANTIES OF QUALITY, MERCHANTABILITY, AND FITNESS FOR ANY PARTICULAR PURPOSE. Further, neither the author, publisher, nor anyone

Contents

List of Symptoms

1

Memory Modules

Memory holds the program code and data that are processed by the CPU, and it is this intimate relationship between memory and the CPU that forms the basis of computer performance. Larger and faster CPUs are constantly being introduced, and more complex software is regularly developed to take advantage of the processing power. In turn, the more complex software demands larger amounts of faster memory. With the explosive growth of Windows (and more recently Windows 98), the demands made on memory performance are more acute than ever. These demands have resulted in a proliferation of memory types that go far beyond the simple, traditional DRAM. Cache (SRAM), extended data output (EDO) memory, video memory (VRAM), synchronous DRAM (SDRAM), flash BIOS, and other exotic memory types (such as RAMBUS) now compete for the attention of PC technicians. These new forms of memory also present some new problems. This chapter will provide you with an understanding of memory types, configurations, installation concerns, and troubleshooting solutions.

Memory Types

In order for a computer to work, the CPU must take program instructions and exchange data directly with memory. As a consequence, memory must keep pace with the CPU (or make the CPU wait for it to catch up). Now that processors are so incredibly fast (and getting faster every few months), traditional memory architectures are being replaced by specialized memory devices that have been tailored to serve specific functions in the PC. As you upgrade and repair various systems, you will undoubtedly encounter some of the memory designations explained below (listed alphabetically):

BEDO (burst extended data output RAM).   This powerful variation of EDO RAM reads data in a burst, which means that after a valid address has been provided, subsequent data addresses can be read in only one clock cycle each. The CPU can read BEDO data in a 5-1-1-1 pattern (5 clock cycles for the first address, then 1 clock cycle for subsequent addresses). While BEDO offers an advantage over EDO, it is currently only supported by the VIA chipsets: 580VP, 590VP, and 680VP. Also, BEDO seems to have difficulty supporting motherboards over 66 MHz.

CDRAM (cached DRAM).   Like EDRAM, the CDRAM from Mitsubishi incorporates cache and DRAM on the same IC. This eliminates the need for an external (or L2) cache and has the extra benefit of adding cache whenever RAM is added to the system. The difference is that CDRAM uses a "set-associative" cache approach that can be 15 to 20 percent more efficient than the EDRAM cache scheme. On the other hand, EDRAM appears to offer better overall performance.

DDR SDRAM (double data rate SDRAM).   One limitation of SDRAM is that the theoretical limitation of the design is 125 MHz (though technology advances may allow up to 133-MHz operation), and bus speeds will need to increase well beyond that in order for memory bandwidth to keep up with future processors. There are several competing standards on the horizon; however, most of them require special pinouts, smaller bus widths, or other design considerations. In the meantime, DDR SDRAM allows output operations to occur on both the rising and falling edges of the clock. Currently, only the rising edge signals an event to occur, so the DDR SDRAM design can effectively double the speed of operation up to at least 200 MHz. There is already one Socket 7 chipset that has support for DDR SDRAM, and more will certainly follow if manufacturers decide to make this memory available.

DRAM (dynamic random-access memory). DRAM was first utilized in early personal computers. It achieves a good mix of speed and density, while being relatively simple and inexpensive to produce—only a single transistor and capacitor are needed to hold a bit. Unfortunately, DRAM contents must be refreshed every few milliseconds, or the contents of each bit location will decay. DRAM performance is also limited because of relatively long access times. Today, a few low-end video boards continue to use DRAM SIMMs to supply video memory. DRAM remains the most recognized and common form of computer memory, and we often use the term *DRAM* to refer to other types of RAM (though that's technically inaccurate).

A typical DRAM memory access would occur as follows: the row address bits are placed onto the address pins. After a period of time, the RAS (Row Address Select) signal falls, which activates sense amps and causes the row address to be latched into the row address buffer. When the RAS signal stabilizes, the selected row is transferred onto the sense amps. Next, the column address bits are set up, and they are then latched into the column address buffer when the CAS signal falls. At that point, the output buffer is also turned on. When the CAS (Column Address Select) signal stabilizes, the selected sense amp feeds its data to the output buffer.

EDO RAM (extended data out RAM). EDO RAM is a well-established variation of DRAM which extends the time during which output data are valid—thus the data's presence on the data bus is "extended." This is accomplished by modifying the DRAM's output buffer to prolong the time during which *read data* is valid. The data will remain valid until a motherboard signal to release them is received. This eases timing constraints on the memory and allows a 15 to 30 percent improvement in memory performance with little real increase in cost. Because a new external signal is needed to operate EDO RAM, the motherboard must use a chipset designed to accommodate EDO. Intel's Triton chipset was one of the first to support EDO, though now most chipsets (and most current motherboards) do so. EDO RAM can be used in non-EDO motherboards, but there will be no performance improvement.

EDRAM (enhanced DRAM). This is another, lesser-known variation of the classic DRAM developed by Ramtron International and United Memories. First demonstrated in August 1994, EDRAM eliminates an external cache by placing a small amount of static RAM (cache) into each EDRAM device itself. In essence, the cache is distributed *within* the system RAM, and as more memory is added to the PC, more cache is effectively added as well. The internal construction of an EDRAM allows it to act like page-mode memory—if a subsequent read requests data that are in the EDRAM's cache (known as a *hit*), the data are made available in about 15 ns (roughly equal to the speed of a fair external cache). If the subsequent read requests data that are not in the cache (called a *miss*), the data are accessed from the DRAM portion of memory in about 35 ns, which is still much faster than ordinary DRAM.

FPM DRAM (fast-page-mode DRAM). This is a popular twist on conventional DRAM. Typical DRAM access is accomplished in a fashion similar to reading from a book—a memory "page" is accessed first, and then the contents of that page can be located. The problem is that every access requires the DRAM to relocate the page. The *fast-page mode* overcomes this delay by allowing the CPU to access multiple pieces of data on the same page without having to relocate the page every time—as long as the subsequent read or write cycle is on the previously located page, the FPM DRAM can access the specific location on that page directly.

For a time, FPM was the most widely used access method for DRAMs, and it is still used on many older systems. The general benefit of FPM memory is reduced power consumption (since sense and restore current is not necessary during page-mode access). Though FPM was a major innovation, there are still some drawbacks. The most significant limitation is that the output buffers turn off when CAS goes high. Also, the minimum cycle time is 5 ns before the output buffers turn off, which essentially adds at least 5 ns to the cycle time.

Today, FPM memory is one of the least desirable forms of memory. You should consider using FPM only if your system does not support any of the later memory types (such as a 486-based system). Typical timings are 6-3-3-3 (initial latency of 3 clocks, with a 3-clock page access). Because of the limited demand, you may find that FPM is actually more expensive than most of the faster memories now available.

PC100 SDRAM. When Intel decided to officially implement a 100-MHz system bus speed, it understood that most of the SDRAM modules available at that time would not operate properly above 83 MHz. In order to support 100-MHz bus speeds, Intel introduced the PC100 specification as a guideline to manufacturers for building modules that would function properly on their 100-MHz chipsets (e.g., the 440BX). With the PC100 specification, Intel laid out a number of guidelines for trace lengths, trace widths and spacing, the number of printed circuit layers, EEPROM programming specs, and so on.

There is still quite a bit of confusion regarding what a "true" PC100 module actually consists of. Unfortunately, there are quite a few modules that are being sold today as PC100, yet do not operate reliably at 100 MHz. While the chip speed rating is used most often to determine the overall performance of the chip, a number of other timings are very important—$tRCD$ (RAS-to-CAS delay), tRP (RAS precharge time), and CAS $latency$ all play a role in determining the fastest bus speed the module will operate at and still achieve a 4-1-1-1 timing.

PC100 SDRAM on a 100-MHz (or faster) system bus will provide a performance boost for Socket 7 systems of between 10 and 15 percent, since the L2 cache is running at system bus speed. Pentium II/III systems will not see as big a boost because the L2 cache is running at half the processor speed (with the exception of the cacheless Celeron chips, of course).

RDRAM (Rambus DRAM).   Most of the memory alternatives so far have been variations of the same basic architecture. Ramtron, Inc. (one of the developers of EDRAM) has created a new memory architecture called the RAMBUS Channel. A CPU or specialized IC is used as the master device, and the RDRAMs are used as slave devices. Data are sent back and forth across the RAMBUS channel in 256-byte blocks. With a dual 250-MHz clock, the RAMBUS channel can transfer data based on the timing of both clocks; this results in data transfer rates approaching 500 MB/s (roughly equivalent to 2-ns access time). The problem with RDRAM is that a RAMBUS channel requires an extensive redesign of the current PC memory architecture. PC makers have generally resisted this move, but as Intel embraces RAMBUS for use with the Pentium III, you will begin to see RDRAM in high-end systems.

SDRAM (synchronous or synchronized DRAM). Typical memory can transfer data only during certain portions of a clock cycle. The SDRAM modifies memory operation so that outputs can be valid at *any* point in the clock cycle. By itself, this is not really significant, but SDRAM also provides a "pipeline burst" mode which allows a second access to begin before the current access is complete. This "continuous" memory access offers effective access speeds as fast as 10 ns and data transfer at up to 100 MB/s. SDRAM is now quite popular on current motherboard designs, and is supported by the Intel VX (and later) chipsets, as well as by the VIA 580VP, 590VP, and 680VP (and later) chipsets. Like BEDO, SDRAM can transfer data in a 5-1-1-1 pattern, but it can support motherboard speeds up to 100 MHz, which is ideal for the 75-, 82-, and 100-MHz motherboards that are now so vital for Pentium II/III systems. Check out the references below for more information on SDRAM:

- *http://www.chips.ibm.com/products/memory/sdramart/sdramart.html*
- *http://www.fujitsu-ede.com/sdram/index.html*
- *http://www.ti.com/sc/docs/memory/brief.htm*

SRAM (static random-access memory). The SRAM is also a classical memory design—it is even older than DRAM. SRAM does not require regular refresh operations and can be made to operate at access speeds that are much faster than those achieved by DRAM. However, SRAM uses six transistors or more to hold a single bit. This reduces the density of SRAM and increases its power demands (which is why SRAM was never adopted for general PC use in the first place). Still, the high speed of SRAM has earned it a place as the PC's L2 (or external) cache. You'll probably encounter three types of SRAM cache schemes: asynchronous, synchronous burst, and pipeline burst.

- *Asynchronous static RAM (async SRAM or ASRAM).* This is the traditional form of L2 cache introduced with i386 systems. There's really nothing too special about ASRAM except that its contents can be accessed much faster (20, 15, or 12 ns) than those of DRAM. ASRAM does not have enough performance to be accessed synchronously and has long since been replaced by better types of cache.

- *Synchronous burst static RAM (sync SRAM or SBSRAM).* This is largely regarded as the best type of L2 cache for intermediate-speed motherboards (about 60 to 66 MHz). With access times of 8.5 and 12 ns, the SBSRAM can provide synchronous bursts of cache information in 2-1-1-1 cycles (i.e., 2 clock cycles for the first access, then 1 cycle per access—in time with the CPU clock). However, as motherboards pass 66 MHz (e.g., 75- and 83-MHz designs), SBSRAM loses its advantage to pipelined burst SRAM.

- *Pipelined burst static RAM (PB SRAM).* At 4.5 to 8 ns, this is the fastest form of high-performance cache now available for 75-MHz+ motherboards. PBSRAM requires an extra clock cycle for "leadoff," but it then can sync with the motherboard clock (with timing such as 3-1-1-1) across a wide range of motherboard frequencies. If you're interested in more technical details about PBSRAM, check out the ASUS site at *http://asustek.asus.com.tw/Products/TB/mem-0001.html.*

VRAM (video random-access memory). DRAM has been the traditional choice for video memory, but the ever-increasing demand for fast video information (e.g., high-resolution SVGA displays) requires a more efficient means of transferring data to and from video memory. Originally developed by Samsung Electronics, video RAM achieves speed improvements by using a dual data bus scheme. Ordinary RAM uses a single data bus—data enter and leave the RAM through a single set of signals. Video RAM provides an input data bus and an output data bus. This allows data to be read from video RAM at the same time new information is being written to it. You should realize that the advantages of VRAM will be realized only on high-end video systems such as 1024 × 768 × 256 (or higher), where you can get up to 40 percent more performance than from a DRAM video adapter. Below that, you will see no perceivable improvement with a VRAM video adapter.

WRAM (Windows RAM). Samsung Electronics has introduced WRAM as a new video-specific memory device. WRAM uses multiple bit arrays connected with an extensive internal bus and high-speed registers that can transfer data almost continuously. Other specialized registers support attributes such as foreground color, background color, write-block control bits, and true-byte masking. Samsung claims data transfer rates of up to 640 MB/s—about 50 percent faster than VRAM—yet WRAM devices are cheaper than their VRAM counterparts. While WRAM has received some serious consideration in the last few years, it has been largely ignored in favor of SDRAM for video systems.

Memory Characteristics

Memory has become far more important than just a place to store bits for the microprocessor. It has proliferated and specialized to the point where it is difficult to keep track of all the memory options and architectures that are available. This portion of the chapter outlines a selection of memory concepts that may help you better understand memory performance.

Memory speed and wait states

The PC industry is constantly struggling with the balance between price and performance. Higher prices usually bring higher performance, but low cost makes the PC appealing to more people. In terms of memory, cost cutting typically involves using cheaper (slower) memory devices. Unfortunately, when slower memory is used, the CPU must be made to wait until memory can catch up. All memory is rated in terms of speed— specifically *access time*. Access time is the delay between the time when data in memory are successfully addressed and the point at which the data have been successfully delivered to the data bus. For PC memory, access time is measured in nanoseconds (ns). Current memory offers access times of 50 to 60 ns; 70-ns memory is extremely common in older i486 systems.

SDRAM is an exception to this rule; it is typically rated in terms of *cycle time* rather than access time. Cycle time is the minimum amount of time needed between accesses. Cycle time for SDRAM averages around 12 ns, with 10-ns and faster SDRAM devices available.

It is almost always possible to use faster memory than the manufacturer recommends. The system should continue to operate normally, but there is rarely a performance benefit. As you will see in the following sections, memory and architectures are typically tailored for specific performance. Using memory that is faster should not hurt the memory or impair system performance, but it costs more and will not produce a noticeable performance improvement simply because the system is not equipped to employ the faster memory to its best advantage. The only time such a tactic would be advised is when your current system is almost obsolete, and you want the new memory to be usable on a new, faster motherboard if you choose to upgrade the motherboard later on.

A *wait state* orders the CPU to pause for one clock cycle in order to give memory additional time to operate. Typical PCs use one wait state, although very old systems may require two or three. The latest PC designs with high-end memory or aggressive caching may be able to operate with no (zero) wait states. As you might imagine, a wait state is basically a waste of time, so more wait states result in lower system performance. Zero wait states allow optimum system performance. Wait states let the system support old, slow memory (but the resulting system performance would be so poor that there would be little point in using the system in the first place).

There are three classical means of selecting wait states. First, the number of wait states may be fixed (common in old XT systems). Second, wait states may be selected with one or more jumpers on the motherboard (typical of i286 and early i386 systems). Finally, midrange and later systems (such as i486, Pentium, and Pentium II/III computers) place the *wait state* or *memory speed* control in the CMOS Setup routine. You may have to look in an *advanced settings* area to find the appropriate entry. When optimizing a computer, you should be sure to set the *minimum* number of wait states.

> **NOTE**: Setting too *few* wait states can cause the PC to behave erratically, or even prevent the system from starting.

Determining memory speed

It is often necessary to check SIMMs or DIMMs for proper memory speed (a.k.a. access time, or cycle time for SDRAM) during troubleshooting or when selecting replacement parts. Unfortunately, it can be very difficult to determine memory speed accurately based on part markings. Speeds are normally marked cryptically by adding a number to the end of the part number. For example, a part number ending in -6 often means 60 ns, a -7 is usually 70 ns, and an -8 can be 80 ns. SDRAM often uses markings such as -12 for 12-ns cycle time or -10 for 10-ns cycle time. Still, the only way of being absolutely certain of the memory speed is to cross-reference the memory part number with a manufacturer's catalog, and read the speed from the catalog's description (e.g., 4Mx32 50ns EDO).

Megabytes and memory layout

Now is a good time to explain the idea of bytes and megabytes. Very simply, a *byte* is 8 bits (binary 1s and 0s), and a *megabyte* (MB) is one million of those bytes (1,048,576 bytes to be exact, but manufacturers often round down to the nearest million or so). The idea of megabytes is important when measuring memory in your PC. For example, if a SIMM is laid out as 1M by 8 bits, it has 1 MB. If the SIMM is laid out as 4 M by 8 bits, it has 4 MB. Unfortunately, memory has not been laid out as 8 bits since the IBM XT.

More practical memory layouts involve 32-bit memory (for 486 and Overdrive processors) or 64-bit memory (for Pentium II/III processors). When memory is wider than 1 byte, it is still measured in megabytes. For example, a 1M × 32-bit (4 bytes) SIMM would be 4 MB (that is, the *capacity* of the device is 4 MB), while a 4M × 32-bit SIMM would be 16 MB. So when you go shopping for an 8-MB 72-pin SIMM, chances are you're getting a 2M × 32-bit memory module. Table 1.1 provides you with an index to help identify common 72-pin SIMMs and 168-pin DIMMs based on the number and type of RAM chips onboard. You can see the relationship between memory layout and overall capacity. Table 1.2 outlines standard part numbers for common memory modules.

TABLE 1.1 SIMM/DIMM Identification Guidelines

168-Pin Synchronous DIMMs

Type of component	Number of chips on board	Module type	DIMM capacity
2 × 8 TSOP SDRAM	8	2 MB × 64	16 MB
2 × 8 TSOP SDRAM	16	4 MB × 64	32 MB
4 × 4 TSOP SDRAM	32	8 MB × 64	64 MB
8 × 8 TSOP SDRAM	8	8 MB × 64 (noncomposite)	64 MB
8 × 8 TSOP SDRAM	9	8 MB × 72 (noncomposite)	64 MB
8 × 8 TSOP SDRAM	16	16 MB × 64 (noncomposite)	128 MB
8 × 8 TSOP SDRAM	18	16 MB × 72 (noncomposite)	128 MB

168-Pin PC DIMMs

Type of component	Number of chips on board	Module type	DIMM capacity
4 × 4 SOJ/TSOP DRAM	16	4 MB × 64	32 MB
4 × 4 SOJ/TSOP DRAM	18	4 MB × 72 ECC	32 MB
4 × 4 SOJ/TSOP DRAM	32	8 MB × 64	64 MB
4 × 4 SOJ/TSOP DRAM	36	8 MB × 72 ECC	64 MB
8 × 8 SOJ/TSOP DRAM	16	16 MB × 64	128 MB

72-Pin SIMM Modules

Type of component	Number of chips on board	Module type	SIMM capacity
1 × 4 SOJ	8	1 MB × 32	4 MB
1 × 16 SOJ	2	1 MB × 32	4 MB
1 × 4 / 1 × 1 SOJ	8 / 4	1 MB × 36	4 MB
1 × 4 SOJ	16	2 MB × 32	8 MB
1 × 16 SOJ	4	2 MB × 32	8 MB
1 × 4 / 1 × 1 SOJ	16 / 8	2 MB × 36	8 MB
4 × 4 SOJ/TSOP	8	4 MB × 32	16 MB
4 × 4 / 4 × 1 SOJ/TSOP	8 / 4	4 MB × 36	16 MB
4 × 4 SOJ	16	8 MB × 32	32 MB

TABLE 1.1   SIMM/DIMM Identification Guidelines (*Continued*):

4 × 4 / 4 × 1 SOJ	16 / 8	8 MB × 36	32 MB
16 × 1 SOJ	32	16 MB × 32	64 MB
16 × 1 SOJ	36	16 MB × 36	64 MB

TSOP—thin small-outline package
SOJ—small-outline "J"-lead package
ECC—Error Correction Code (a more powerful form of parity)
x 8, x 32, x 64—nonparity RAM
x 9, x 36, x 72—parity or ECC RAM

Presence detect (PD)

Another feature of modern memory devices is a series of physical signals known as the *presence detect* lines. If the appropriate conditions of the PD signals are set, it is possible for a computer to immediately recognize the characteristics of the installed memory devices and configure itself accordingly. Presence detect lines typically specify three operating characteristics of memory: size, device layout, and speed. Table 1.3 highlights many of the most commonly used signal combinations.

Understanding memory refresh

The electrical signals placed in each DRAM storage cell must be replenished (or *refreshed*) every few milliseconds. Without refresh, DRAM data will be lost. In principle, refresh requires that each storage cell be read and rewritten to the memory array. This is typically accomplished by reading and rewriting an entire row of the array at one time. Each row of bits is sequentially read into a sense/refresh amplifier (part of the DRAM IC), which basically recharges the appropriate storage capacitors, then rewrites each row bit to the array. In actual operation, a row of bits is automatically refreshed whenever an array row is selected. Thus, the entire memory array can be refreshed by reading each row in the array every few milliseconds.

TABLE 1.2 Typical Part Numbers for Common Memory Modules

168-Pin Standard DIMMs

| EDO | ECC | | Non-ECC | |
---	Buffered	Nonbuffered	Buffered	Nonbuffered
16 MB	KTM2x72VN82-60EG	KTM2x72VN44-60EG	—	KTM2x64VN61-60EG
32 MB	KTM4x72V82-60EG	KTM4x72VN44-60EG	—	KTM4x64VN42-60EG
64 MB	KTM8x72V84-64EG	KTM8x72VN84-60EG	—	KTM8x64VN84-60EG
128 MB	KTM16x72V44-60EG	KTM16x72VN84-60EG	—	KTM16x64VN84-60EG
256 MB	KTM32x72V44-60EG	—	—	

| FPM | ECC | | Non-ECC | |
---	Buffered	Nonbuffered	Buffered	Nonbuffered
16 MB	KTM2x72V82-60G	—	—	—
32 MB	KTM4x72V44-60G	—	—	—
64 MB	KTM8x72V84-60G	—	—	—
128 MB	KTM16x72V48-60G	—	—	—

TABLE 1.2 Typical Part Numbers for Common Memory Modules (Continued)

SDRAM	ECC		Non-ECC	
	66 MHz	100 MHz	66 MHz	100 MHz
16 MB	KTM66x72/16	—	KTM66x64/16	—
32 MB	KTM66x72/32	KGM100x72C#/32	KTM66x64/32	KGM100x64C#/32
64 MB	KTM66x72/64	KGM100x72C#/64	TM66x64/64	KGM100x64C#/64
128 MB	KTM66x72/128	KGM100x72C#/128	KTM66x64/128	KGM100x64C#/128

NOTE: For 100-MHz SDRAM DIMMs, substitute either a 2 or a 3 for the # to indicate CAS latency speed. The modules are interchangeable and can be mixed, but the system will run at the slower CAS latency 3 speed.

72-Pin Standard SIMMs

EDO		60 ns		70 ns	
		Nonparity	Parity	Nonparity	Parity
8 MB	Tin leads	KTM2x32L-60ET	KTM2x36L-60ET	KTM2x32L-70ET	—
	Gold leads	KTM2x32L-60EG	KTM2x36L-60EG	KTM2x32L-70EG	—
16 MB	Tin leads	KTM4x32L-60ET	KTM4x36L-60ET	KTM4x32L-70ET	—
	Gold leads	KTM4x32L-60EG	KTM4x36L-60EG	KTM4x32L-70EG	—

32 MB	Tin leads	KTM8x32L-60ET	KTM8x36L-60ET	KTM8x32L-70ET	—
32 MB	Gold leads	KTM8x32L-60EG	KTM8x36L-60EG	KTM8x32L-70EG	—
64 MB	Tin leads	KTM16x32LA-60ET	—	—	—
64 MB	Gold leads	KTM16x32LA-60EG	—	—	—
128 MB	Tin leads	KTM32x32LA-60ET	—	—	—
128 MB	Gold leads	KTM32x32LA-60EG	—	—	—

FPM		60 ns		70 ns	
		Nonparity	Parity	Nonparity	Parity
8 MB	Tin leads	KTM2x32L-60T	KTM2x36L-60T	KTM2x32L-70T	KTM2x36L-70T
8 MB	Gold leads	KTM2x32L-60G	KTM2x36L-60G	KTM2x32L-70G	KTM2x36L-70G
16 MB	Tin leads	KTM4x32L-60T	KTM4x36L-60T	KTM4x32L-70T	KTM4x36L-70T
16 MB	Gold leads	KTM4x32L-60G	KTM4x36L-60G	KTM4x32L-70G	KTM4x36L-70G
32 MB	Tin leads	KTM8x32L-60T	KTM8x36L-60T	KTM8x32L-70T	KTM8x36L-70T
32 MB	Gold leads	KTM8x32L-60G	KTM8x36L-60G	KTM8x32L-70G	KTM8x36L-70G
64 MB	Tin leads	KTM16x32L-60T	KTM16x36L-60T	KTM16x32L-70T	KTM16x36L-70T
64 MB	Gold leads	KTM16x32L-60G	KTM16x36L-60G	KTM16x32L-70G	KTM16x36L-70G
128 MB	Tin leads	KTM32x32L-60T	KTM32x36L-60T	—	—
128 MB	Gold leads	KTM32x32L-60G	KTM32x36L-60G	—	—

TABLE 1.3 Index of Presence Detect (PD) Signals

	72-Pin SIMM	Pin 67 (PD1)	Pin 68 (PD2)	Pin 69 (PD3)	Pin 70 (PD4)	Pin 71 (PD5)
Size (parity pinout)	256K × 32/36	GND	N/C	—	—	—
	512K × 32/36	N/C	GND	—	—	—
	1M × 32/36	GND	GND	—	—	—
	2M × 32/36	N/C	N/C	—	—	—
	4M × 32/36	GND	N/C	—	—	N/C
	8M × 32/36	N/C	GND	—	—	N/C
Size (ECC pinout)	256K × 32/36	GND	N/C	—	—	N/C
	512K × 32/36	N/C	GND	—	—	N/C
	1M × 32/36	GND	GND	—	—	N/C
	2M × 32/36	N/C	N/C	—	—	N/C
	4M × 32/36	GND	N/C	—	—	GND
	8M × 32/36	N/C	GND	—	—	GND
Speed (parity/ECC pinout)	60 ns	—	—	N/C	N/C	—
	70 ns	—	—	GND	N/C	—
	80 ns	—	—	N/C	GND	—
	100 ns	—	—	GND	GND	—
	120 ns	—	—	N/C	N/C	—

GND—Jumper installed

N/C—No jumper installed

The key to refresh is in the *way* DRAM is addressed. Unlike other memory ICs, which supply all address signals to the IC simultaneously, a DRAM is addressed in a two-step sequence. The overall address is separated into a row (low) address and a column (high) address. Row-address bits are placed on the DRAM address bus first, and the -RAS line is pulsed logic 0 to multiplex the bits into the IC's address decoding circuitry. The low portion of the address activates an entire array row and causes each bit in the row to be sensed and refreshed. Logic 0s remain logic 0s, and logic 1s are recharged to their full value.

Column address bits are then placed on the DRAM address bus, and the -CAS line is pulsed to logic 0. The column portion of the address selects the appropriate bits within the chosen row. If a read operation is taking place, the selected bits pass through the data buffer to the data bus. During a write operation, the read/write line must be logic 0, and valid data must be available to the IC before -CAS is strobed. New data bits are then placed in their corresponding locations in the memory array.

Even if the IC is not being accessed for reading or writing, the memory must *still* be refreshed to ensure data integrity. Fortunately, refresh can be accomplished by interrupting the microprocessor to run a refresh routine which simply steps through every row address in sequence (column addresses need not be selected for simple refresh). This row-only (or -RAS-only) refresh technique speeds the refresh process. Although refreshing DRAM every few milliseconds may seem like a constant aggravation, the computer can execute quite a few instructions before being interrupted for refresh. Refresh operations are generally handled by the chipset on your motherboard. Often, memory problems (especially parity errors) which cannot be resolved by replacing a SIMM can be traced to a refresh fault on the motherboard.

Memory techniques

Rather than incur the added expense of specialized memory devices, PC makers often use inexpensive, well-established memory types in unique architectures designed to make the most of low-end memory. There are three popular architectures that you will probably encounter in almost all systems: paged memory, interleaved memory, and memory caching.

Paged memory. This approach basically divides system RAM into small groups (or "pages") from 512 bytes to several kilobytes long. Memory management circuitry on the motherboard allows subsequent memory accesses on the same page to be accomplished with zero wait states. If the subsequent access takes place outside of the current page, one or more wait states may be added while the new page is found. This is identical in principle to fast-page-mode DRAM, explained above. You will find page-mode architectures implemented on high-end i286, PS/2 (models 70 and 80), and many i386 systems.

Interleaved memory. This is a technique which provides better performance than paged memory. Simply put, interleaved memory combines two banks of memory into one. The first portion is "even" and the second portion is "odd," so memory contents are alternated between these two areas. This allows a memory access in the second portion to begin before the memory access in the first portion has finished. In effect, interleaving can double memory performance. The problem with interleaving is that you must provide twice the amount of memory as matched pairs. Most PCs that employ interleaving will allow you to add memory one bank at a time, but interleaving will be disabled, and system performance will suffer.

Memory caching. This is perhaps the most recognized form of memory enhancement architecture. Cache is a small amount (anywhere from 8 KB to 1 MB) of very fast SRAM which forms an interface between the CPU and ordinary DRAM. The SRAM typically operates on the order of 5 to 15 ns, which is fast enough to keep pace with a CPU using zero wait states. A *cache controller* IC on the motherboard keeps track of frequently accessed memory locations (as well as predicted memory locations) and copies the contents of those locations into cache. When a CPU reads from memory, it checks the cache first. If the needed contents are present in cache (called a *cache hit*), the data are read at zero wait states. If the needed contents are not present in cache (known as a *cache miss*), the data must be read directly from DRAM at a penalty of one or more wait states. A small quantity of very fast cache (called *Tag RAM*) acts as an index, recording the various locations of data stored in cache. A well-designed caching system can achieve a hit ratio of 95 percent or more— in other words, memory can run *without* wait states 95 percent of the time.

There are two levels of cache in the contemporary PC. CPUs from the i486 onward have a small internal cache—known as *L1 cache*—and external cache (SRAM installed as DIPs or COAST modules on the motherboard), which is referred to as *L2 cache*. The i386 CPUs have no internal cache (although IBM's 386SLC offers 8 KB of L1 cache). Most i486 CPUs provide an 8-KB internal cache. Early Pentium processors are fitted with two 8-KB internal caches—one for data and one for instructions. Today's Pentium II/III Slot 1 CPU incorporates 256 to 512 KB of L2 cache into the processor cartridge itself.

Shadow memory. ROM devices (whether the BIOS ROM on your motherboard or a ROM IC on an expansion board) are frustratingly slow, with access times often exceeding several hundred nanoseconds. ROM access thus requires a large number of wait states, which slow down the system's performance. This problem is compounded because the routines stored in BIOS (especially the video BIOS ROM on the video board) are some of the most frequently accessed memory in your computer.

Beginning with the i386-class computers, some designs employed a memory technique called *shadowing*. ROM contents are loaded into an area of fast RAM during system initialization, then the computer maps the fast RAM into memory locations used by the ROM devices. Whenever ROM routines must be accessed during run time, information is taken from the shadowed ROM instead of from the actual ROM IC. The ROM performance can be improved by at least 300 percent.

Shadow memory is also useful for ROM devices that do not use the full available data bus width. For example, a 16-bit computer system may hold an expansion board containing an 8-bit ROM IC. The system would have to access the ROM not once but *twice* to extract a single 16-bit word. If the computer is a 32-bit machine, that 8-bit ROM would have to be addressed four times to make a complete 32-bit word. You may imagine the hideous system delays that can be encountered. Loading the ROM to shadow memory in advance virtually eliminates such delays. Shadowing can usually be turned on or off through the system's CMOS Setup routines.

Composite vs. noncomposite

Finally, you may see SIMMs and DIMMs referred to as composite or noncomposite modules. These terms are used infrequently to describe the technology level of the memory module. For example, a *composite* module uses older, lower-density memory, so more ICs are required to achieve the required storage capacity. Conversely, a *noncomposite* module uses newer memory technology, so fewer ICs are needed to reach the same storage capacity. In other words, if you encounter a high-density SIMM with only a few ICs on it, chances are that the SIMM is noncomposite.

Parity and Error Correction

As you might imagine, it is *vital* that data and program instructions remain error-free. Even one incorrect bit due to electrical noise or a·component failure can crash the PC, corrupt drive information, cause video problems, or result in a myriad of other faults. PC designers approached the issue of memory integrity by employing a technique known as *parity* (the same technique used to check serial data integrity).

The parity principle

The basic idea behind parity is simple: Each byte written to memory is checked, and a ninth bit is added to the byte as a checking (or parity) bit. When a memory address is later read by the CPU, memory-checking circuitry on the motherboard will calculate the *expected* parity bit and compare it to the bit *actually* read from memory. In this fashion, the PC can continuously diagnose system memory by checking the integrity of its data. If the read parity bit *matches* the expected parity bit, the data (and indirectly the RAM) are assumed to be valid, and the CPU can go on its way. If the read and expected parity bits *do not* match, the system registers an error and halts. Every *byte* is given a parity bit, so for a 32-bit PC, there will be 4 parity bits for every address. For a 64-bit PC, there are 8 parity bits, and so on.

Even vs. odd

There are two types of parity, even and odd. With *even parity*, the parity bit is set to 0 if there is an even number of 1s already in the corresponding byte (keeping the number of 1s even). If there is not an even number of 1s in the byte, the even parity bit will be 1 (making the number of 1s even). With *odd parity*, the parity bit is set to 0 if there is an odd number of 1s already in the corresponding byte (keeping the number of 1s odd). If there is not an odd number of 1s in the byte, the odd parity bit will be 1 (making the number of 1s odd).

Although even and odd parity are the opposite of each other, both schemes serve exactly the same purpose and have the same probability of catching a bad bit. The memory device itself does not care at all about what type of parity is being used—it just needs to have the parity bits available. The use of parity (and the choice of even or odd) is left up to the motherboard's memory control circuit.

The problems with parity

While parity has proven to be a simple and cost-effective means of continuously checking memory, it has two significant limitations. First, though parity can detect an error, it *cannot* correct the error because it has no way to tell *which* bit has gone bad. This is why a system simply halts when a parity error is detected. Second, parity is unable to detect multibit errors. For example, if a 1 accidentally becomes a 0 and a 0 accidentally becomes a 1 within the same byte, parity conditions will still be satisfied. Fortunately, the probability of a multibit error in the same byte is extremely remote.

Circumventing parity

Over the last few years, parity has come under fire from PC makers and memory manufacturers alike. Opponents claim that the rate of parity errors due to hardware (RAM) faults is very small, and that in a memory-hungry marketplace, the expense of providing parity bits just isn't justified anymore. There is some truth to this argument, considering that the parity technique is over 15 years old and has serious limitations.

As a consequence, some motherboard makers have begun removing parity support from their low-end motherboards, and others are providing motherboards that will function with or without parity (usually set in CMOS or with a motherboard jumper). Similarly, some memory makers are now providing nonparity and "fake"-parity memory as cheaper alternatives to conventional-parity memory. *Nonparity* memory simply forgoes the ninth bit. For example, a nonparity SIMM would be designated x8 or x32 (e.g., 4Mx8 or 4Mx32). If the SIMM supports parity, it will be designated x9 or x36 (e.g., 4Mx9 or 4Mx36). *Fake parity* is a bit more devious—the ninth bit is replaced by a simple (and dirt cheap) parity generator chip which looks like a normal DRAM IC. When a read cycle occurs, the parity chip on the SIMM provides the proper parity bit to the motherboard *all the time*. In effect, your memory is lying to the motherboard.

While there is a cost savings, your memory is left with no means of error checking at all. It's a little like driving a car without a speedometer—you can go for miles without a problem, but sooner or later you'll cross a speed trap. In actual practice, you can go on indefinitely without parity, but when an error *does* occur, having parity in place can save you immeasurable frustration. Unless the lowest cost is your absolute highest system priority, it is recommended that you spend the extra few dollars for parity RAM.

> **NOTE**: Most motherboards can be operated with nonparity RAM. It is also usually possible to mix parity and nonparity memory in the same system. But in either case, you will need to disable *all* parity checking features for the RAM.

Abuse and detection of fake-parity memory

Another potential problem with fake-parity memory is fraud. There have already been reported instances where someone purchased "parity" memory at full price—only to find that the parity ICs were actually parity generators. This was determined by dissecting the IC packages and finding that the IC die in the parity position did not match the IC dies in the other bit positions. The buyer doesn't know because parity generators are packaged to look just like DRAM ICs, and there is no obvious way to tell just by looking at the SIMM or other memory device. System diagnostic software also cannot detect whether parity memory or fake memory is present.

There are really only two ways to protect yourself from fake-memory fraud. First, industry experts indicate that many fake-parity ICs (the parity generators) are marked with designations such as "BP," "VT," "GSM," or "MPEC." If you find that one out of every nine ICs on your SIMM carries such a designation (or any other designation not matching the first eight), you may have a fraud situation. Of course, the first step in all justice is a "benefit of the doubt," so contact the organization you purchased the memory from—it may simply have sent the wrong SIMMs.

Second, you can check the IC dies themselves. Unfortunately, this requires you to carefully dissect several IC packages on the SIMM and compare the IC dies under a microscope—resulting in the destruction of the memory device(s). If the ninth die looks radically different from the other eight (usually much simpler), you've probably got fake parity. A nondestructive way to check the SIMM is to use a SIMM checker (if you have access to one) with a testing routine specially written to test parity memory. If the SIMM works but the parity IC test fails (i.e., the tester cannot *write* to the parity memory), chances are that you've got fake parity.

If you determine that you have been sold fake-parity memory in place of real-parity memory, and you cannot get any satisfaction from the seller, you are encouraged to contact the Attorney General in the seller's state and convey your information. After all, if you're being stiffed, chances are that a lot of other people are, too—and they probably don't even know it.

Alternative error correction

Although this book supports the use of parity, it is also quick to recognize its old age. In the world of personal computing, parity is an *ancient* technique. Frankly, it could easily be replaced by more sophisticated techniques such as *Error Correction Code* (ECC) or *ECC-on-SIMM* (EOS). ECC (which is now commonly employed in high-end PCs and file servers) uses a mathematical process in conjunction with the motherboard's memory controller, and appends a number of ECC bits to the data bits. When data are read back from memory, the ECC memory controller checks the ECC data read-back as well. ECC has two important advantages over parity. First, it can actually *correct* single-bit errors "on the fly" without the user's ever knowing that there's been a problem. In addition, ECC can successfully detect 2-bit, 3-bit, and even 4-bit errors, which makes it an incredibly powerful error detection tool. If a rare multibit error is detected, ECC is unable to correct it, but it will be reported and the system will halt.

It takes 7 or 8 bits at each address to successfully implement ECC. For a 32-bit system, you will need to use x39 or x40 SIMMs (e.g., 8Mx39 or 8Mx40) or x71 or x72 DIMMs (e.g., 2Mx72 ECC). These are relatively new designations, so you should at least recognize them as ECC SIMMs/DIMMs if you encounter them. As an alternative, some 64-bit systems use two 36-bit SIMMs, for a total of 72 bits—64 bits for data and 8 bits (which would otherwise be for parity) for ECC information. Table 1.2 illustrates the layout for typical ECC-compliant DIMMs (e.g., the 66-MHz, 16-MB KTM66x72/16 device).

EOS is a relatively new (and rather expensive) technology which places ECC functions on the memory module itself, but provides ECC results as parity—so while the memory module runs ECC, the motherboard continues to see parity. This is an interesting experiment, but it is unlikely that EOS will gain significant market share. Systems that use parity can be fitted with parity memory much more cheaply than with EOS memory.

Memory Organization

The memory in your computer is the result of evolution over several computer generations. Memory operation and handling is taken care of by your system's microprocessor, so as CPUs have improved, memory-handling capabilities have improved as well. Today's microprocessors such as the Intel Pentium Pro, Pentium II, and Pentium III are capable of addressing more than 4 GB of system memory—well beyond the levels of contemporary software applications. Unfortunately, the early PCs were not nearly so powerful. Older PCs could address only 1 MB of memory because of limitations of the 8088 microprocessor.

Since backward compatibility is so important to computer users, the drawbacks and limitations of older systems had to be carried forward into newer computers instead of being eliminated. Newer systems overcome these inherent limitations by adding different types of memory, along with the hardware and software to access the memory. This part of the chapter describes the typical classifications of computer memory: conventional, extended, and expanded memory. This chapter also describes high-memory concepts. Note that these memory types have nothing to do with the actual ICs in your system, but involve the way in which system software *uses* the memory.

Conventional memory

Conventional memory is the traditional 640 KB assigned to the DOS Memory Area (10000h to 9FFFFh, as shown in Figure 1.1). The original PCs used micro-

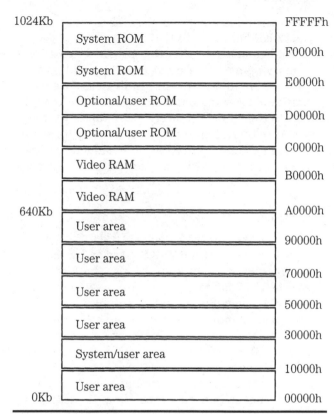

1024Kb		FFFFFh
	System ROM	
		F0000h
	System ROM	
		E0000h
	Optional/user ROM	
		D0000h
	Optional/user ROM	
		C0000h
	Video RAM	
		B0000h
	Video RAM	
640Kb		A0000h
	User area	
		90000h
	User area	
		70000h
	User area	
		50000h
	User area	
		30000h
	System/user area	
		10000h
	User area	
0Kb		00000h

Figure 1.1   Conventional and upper memory in a typical PC.

processors that could address only 1 MB of memory
(called *real-mode memory* or *base memory*). Out of that
1 MB, portions of the memory had to be set aside for
basic system functions. BIOS code, video memory, interrupt vectors, and BIOS data are only some of the areas
that require reserved memory. The remaining 640 KB
became available to load and run your application,
which can be any combination of executable code and
data. The original PC provided only 512 KB for the DOS
program area, but computer designers quickly learned
that another 128 KB could be added to the DOS area

while still retaining enough memory for overhead functions, so 512 KB became 640 KB.

Every IBM-compatible PC still provides a 640-KB "base memory" range, and most DOS application programs continue to fit within that limit to ensure backward compatibility with older systems. However, the drawbacks to the 8088 CPU were soon apparent. More memory *had* to be added to the computer for its evolution to continue. Yet memory had to be added in a way that did not interfere with the conventional memory area.

Extended memory

The 80286 processor introduced in IBM's PC/AT was designed to overcome the 640-KB barrier by incorporating a *protected mode* of addressing. The 80286 can address up to 16 MB of memory in protected mode, and its successors (the 80386 and later) can handle 4 GB of protected-mode memory. Today, virtually all computer systems provide several megabytes of *extended memory* (called XMS). Besides an advanced microprocessor, another key element for extended memory is *software*. Memory management software must be loaded in advance for the computer to be able to access its extended memory. Microsoft's later DOS versions (up to MS-DOS 6.22) provide an extended memory manager utility (HIMEM.SYS), but there are other off-the-shelf utilities as well.

Unfortunately, DOS itself cannot make use of extended memory. You may fill the extended memory with data, but the executable code making up the program remains limited to the original 640 KB of base memory. Some programs written with *DOS extenders* can overcome the 640-KB limit, but the additional code needed for the extenders can make such programs a bit clunky. A DOS extender is basically a software module containing its own memory management code which is compiled into the final application program.

The DOS extender loads a program into real-mode memory. After the program is loaded, it switches program control to the protected mode memory. When the program in protected mode needs to execute a DOS (real-mode) function, the DOS extender converts protected-mode addresses into real-mode addresses, copies any necessary program data from protected- to real-mode locations, switches the CPU to real-mode addressing, and carries out the function. The DOS extender then copies any results (if necessary) back to protected-mode addresses, and switches the system to protected mode once again, and the program continues to run. This back-and-forth conversion overhead results in less than optimum performance compared to strictly real-mode programs or true protected-mode programs.

With multiple megabytes of extended memory typically available, it is unlikely (but possible) that any one program will utilize all of the extended memory. Multiple programs that use extended memory must *not* attempt to utilize the same memory locations. If conflicts occur, a catastrophic system crash is almost inevitable. To prevent conflicts in extended memory, memory manager software can make use of three major industry standards: the *Extended Memory Specification* (XMS), the *Virtual Control Program Interface* (VCPI), or the *DOS Protected-Mode Interface* (DPMI). This chapter will not detail these standards, but you should know where they are used.

Expanded memory

Expanded memory (or EMS) is another popular technique used to overcome the traditional 640-KB limit of real-mode addressing. Expanded memory uses the same physical RAM chips, but it differs from extended memory in the way that physical memory is used. Instead of trying to address physical memory locations outside of the conventional memory range, as extended memory does, expanded memory blocks are switched into the base memory range where the CPU can access them in real mode. The original expanded memory specification [called the Lotus-Intel-Microsoft (LIM) or EMS specification] used 16-KB blocks of memory which were mapped into a 64-KB range of real-mode memory existing just above the video memory range. Thus, four "blocks" of expanded memory could be dealt with simultaneously in the real mode.

Early implementations of expanded memory utilized special expansion boards that switched blocks of memory, but later CPUs that support memory mapping allow expanded memory managers (EMMs or LIMs) to supply software-only solutions for i386, i486, Pentium, and later machines. EMS/LIM 4.0 is the latest version of the expanded memory standard; it handles up to 32 MB of memory. An expanded memory manager (such as the DOS utility EMM386.EXE) allows the extended memory sitting in your computer to emulate expanded memory. For most practical purposes, expanded memory is more useful than extended memory because its ability to map directly to the real mode allows support for program multitasking. To use expanded memory, programs must be written specifically to take advantage of the function calls and subroutines needed to switch memory blocks. Functions are completely specified in the LIM/EMS 4.0 standard.

Upper memory area

The upper 384 KB of real-mode memory are not available to DOS because they are dedicated to handling the memory requirements of the physical computer system. This is called the *High DOS Memory Range* or *Upper Memory Area* (UMA). However, even the most advanced PCs do not use the *entire* 384 KB, so there is often a substantial amount of unused memory existing in your system's real-mode range. Late-model CPUs like the i386 and i486 can remap extended memory into the range unused by your system. Since this "found" memory space is not contiguous with your 640-KB DOS space, DOS application programs cannot use the space, but small independent drivers and TSRs *can* be loaded and run from this UMA. The advantage of using this high DOS memory is that more of the 640-KB DOS range remains available for your application program. Memory management programs (such as the utilities found with DOS 5.0 and higher) are needed to locate and remap these memory blocks.

High memory

There is a peculiar anomaly that occurs with CPUs supporting extended memory—they can access one segment (about 64 KB) of extended memory *beyond* the real-mode area. This capability arises because of the address line layout on late-model CPUs. As a result, the real-mode operation can access roughly 64 KB *above* the 1-MB limit. Like high DOS memory, this "found" 64 KB is not contiguous with the normal 640-KB DOS memory range, so DOS cannot use it to load a DOS application, but device drivers and TSRs can be placed in high memory. DOS 5.0 (and later) has been intentionally designed so that its 40 to 50 KB of code can be easily moved into this high-memory area. With DOS loaded into high memory, an extra 40 to 50 KB or so will be available within the 640-KB DOS range.

Selecting and Installing Memory in PCs

Installing memory is not nearly as easy as it used to be. Certainly, today's memory modules just plug right in, but deciding which memory to buy, how much (or how little) to buy, and how to use existing memory in new systems presents technicians with a bewildering variety of choices. This part of the chapter illustrates the important ideas behind choosing and using memory.

Getting the right amount

"How much memory do I need?" This is an age-old question which has plagued the PC industry ever since Intel's 80286 CPU broke the 1-MB memory barrier. With more memory, the CPU can run additional programs and data at any given time—which indirectly helps to improve the productivity of the particular PC. The problem is cost. Today's SDRAM is running around $2/MB (U.S.), compared with about 1.25 cents/MB (about $12.50/GB) for hard-drive space. Consequently, memory is far more expensive than hard drive space, and so the goal of good system configuration is to install *enough* memory to support the PC's routine tasks. Installing *too much* memory means that you've spent money for PC resources that just remain idle. Installing *too little* memory results in programs that will not run (typical under DOS), or diminished system performance because of extensive swap file use (typical under Windows).

So how much memory *is* enough? The fact of the matter is that "enough" is an ever-changing figure. DOS systems of the early 1980s (8088/8086) worked just fine with 1 MB. By the mid-1980s (80286), DOS systems with 2 MB were adequate. Into the late 1980s (80386), Windows 3.0 and 3.1 needed 4 MB. As the 1990s got under way (80486), Windows systems with 8 MB were common (even DOS applications were using 4 to 6 MB of EMS). Today, with Pentium II/III systems and Windows 98, 32 MB is considered to be a minimum requirement, and 64- to 128-MB systems are readily available. For today, 32 MB is the minimum benchmark that you should use for general-purpose home and office systems. By early in the next decade, 256-MB systems will probably be the norm. And this is not to say that 256-MB systems are the pinnacle of performance. Today's file servers and industrial-strength design packages are employing 512 to 756 MB of RAM, and motherboard chipsets can often support up to 1GB of RAM or more.

Filling banks

Another point of confusion is the idea of a "memory bank." Most memory devices are installed in sets (or banks). The amount of memory in the bank can vary depending on how much you wish to add, but there must always be enough data bits in the bank to *fill* each bit position. Table 1.4 illustrates the relationship between data bits and banks for the range of typical CPUs. For example, the 8086 is a 16-bit microprocessor (2 bytes). This means that 2 extra bits are required for parity, giving a total of 18 bits. Thus, one bank is 18 bits wide. You may fill the bank by adding eighteen 1-bit DIPs or two 30-pin SIMMs. As another example, an 80486DX is a 32-bit CPU, so 36 bits are needed to fill a bank (32 bits plus 4 parity bits). If you use 30-pin SIMMs, you will need four to fill a bank. If you use 72-pin SIMMs, only one is needed. For a newer Pentium II or III CPU, you can fill a "bank" with only *one* 168-pin DIMM. Note that the size of the memory in megabytes does not really matter, so long as the *entire* bank is filled.

Bank requirements

There is more to filling a memory bank than just installing the right number of bits. Memory amount, memory matching, and bank order are three additional considerations. First, you must use the proper *memory amount* that will bring you to the expected volume of total memory. Suppose a Pentium system has 8 MB already installed in Bank 0, and you need to put another 8 MB into the system in Bank 1. Table 1.4 shows that two 72-pin SIMMs are needed to fill a bank, but each SIMM need be only 1 MB. Remember from the discussion of megabytes that a $1M \times 36$-bit (with parity) device is 4 MB. Since two such SIMMs are needed to fill a bank, the total would be 8 MB. When this is added to the 8 MB already in the system, the total would be 16 MB.

TABLE 1.4 CPUs vs. Memory Bank Size

CPU	Data width (with parity)	x MB by 1 DIPs	30-pin SIMMs	72-pin SIMMs	168-pin DIMMs
8088	9 bits	9	1	—	—
8086	18 bits	18	2	—	—
80286	18 bits	—	2	1 (2 banks)	—
80386SX, SL, SLC	18 bits	—	2	1 (2 banks)	—
80386DX	36 bits	—	4	1	—
80486SLC, SLC2	18 bits	—	2	1 (2 banks)	—
80486DX, SX, DX2, DX4	36 bits	—	4	1	—
Pentium	64 bits	—	8	2	1
Pentium II/III	64 bits	—	—	—	1

How about another example? Suppose the same 8 MB is already installed in your Pentium system, and you want to add 16 MB to Bank 1 rather than 8 MB (bringing the total system memory to 24 MB). In that case, you could use two 2-MB 72-pin SIMMs, where 2M × 36 is 8 MB (with parity) per SIMM. Two 8-MB SIMMs yield 16 MB, bringing the system total to 16 MB + 8 MB, or 24 MB.

Now for a curve. Suppose you want to outfit that Pentium as a network server with 128 MB of RAM. Remember that there's already 8 MB in Bank 0, which means that there's only Bank 1 available. Since the largest commercially available SIMMs are 8M × 36 (32 MB with parity), you can add only up to 64 MB to Bank 1 (for a system total of 72 MB). To get around this, you should *remove* the existing 1M × 36 SIMMs in Bank 0 and fill both Bank 0 and Bank 1 with 8M × 36 SIMMs, which would put 64 MB in Bank 0 and 64 MB in Bank 1, or 128 MB in total. You can review many of the recommended SIMM/DIMM combinations for a typical Pentium motherboard in Table 1.5.

Another bank requirement is *memory matching*— using SIMMs of the same size and speed within a bank. For example, when multiple SIMMs are added to a bank, each SIMM must be rated for the same access speed and share the same memory configuration (e.g., 2M × 36). This issue is not quite so critical with DIMMs, where only one device is needed to constitute a "bank."

Finally, you must follow the *bank order*. For example, fill Bank 0 first, then Bank 1, then Bank 2, and so on. Otherwise, memory will not be contiguous within the PC, and CMOS will not recognize the additional RAM.

Selecting and Completing BIOS Upgrades

The BIOS is a set of "firmware" routines recorded on the BIOS ROM chip located on your motherboard. Your

TABLE 1.5 Memory Combinations for a Typical Motherboard

Memory size	SIMM 1	SIMM 2	SIMM 3	SIMM 4	SIMM 5	SIMM 6	DIMM 1	DIMM 2
8 MB	1M × 32	1M × 32	—	—	—	—	—	—
8 MB	—	—	—	—	—	—	1M × 64	—
16 MB	2M × 32	2M × 32	—	—	—	—	—	—
16 MB	1M × 32	1M × 32	1M × 32	1M × 32	—	—	—	—
16 MB	—	—	—	—	—	—	2M × 64	—
16 MB	—	—	—	—	—	—	1M × 64	1M × 64
24 MB	1M × 32	1M × 32	2M × 32	2M × 32	—	—	—	—
24 MB	1M × 32	1M × 32	1M × 32	1M × 32	1M × 32	1M × 32	—	—
24 MB	—	—	—	—	—	—	1M × 64	2M × 64
32 MB	4M × 32	4M × 32	—	—	—	—	—	—
32 MB	2M × 32	2M × 32	2M × 32	2M × 32	—	—	—	—
32 MB	1M × 32	1M × 32	1M × 32	1M × 32	2M × 32	2M × 32	—	—
32 MB	—	—	—	—	—	—	4M × 64	—
32 MB	—	—	—	—	—	—	2M × 64	2M × 64
40 MB	1M × 32	1M × 32	4M × 32	4M × 32	—	—	—	—
40 MB	—	—	—	—	—	—	1M × 64	4M × 64
48 MB	2M × 32	2M × 32	4M × 32	4M × 32	—	—	—	—
48 MB	1M × 32	1M × 32	1M × 32	1M × 32	4M × 32	4M × 32	—	—
48 MB	2M × 32	2M × 32	2M × 32	2M × 32	2M × 32	2M × 32	—	—
48 MB	—	—	—	—	—	—	2M × 64	4M × 64
64 MB	8M × 32	8M × 32	—	—	—	—	—	—
64 MB	4M × 32	4M × 32	4M × 32	4M × 32	4M × 32	4M × 32	—	—
64 MB	2M × 32	2M × 32	2M × 32	2M × 32	4M × 32	4M × 32	2M × 64	—
64 MB	—	—	—	—	—	—	8M × 64	—

Total								
64 MB	—	1M × 32	—	8M × 32	8M × 32	—	—	4M × 64 · 4M × 64
72 MB	1M × 32	1M × 32	8M × 32	8M × 32	—	—	—	1M × 64 · 8M × 64
72 MB	—	—	—	1M × 32	—	—	—	—
80 MB	2M × 32	2M × 32	8M × 32	8M × 32	8M × 32	8M × 32	—	2M × 64 · 8M × 64
80 MB	1M × 32	1M × 32	1M × 32	1M × 32	—	—	—	—
80 MB	—	—	—	—	—	—	—	—
96 MB	4M × 32	4M × 32	8M × 32	8M × 32	8M × 32	8M × 32	—	4M × 64 · 8M × 64
96 MB	2M × 32	2M × 32	2M × 32	2M × 32	4M × 32	4M × 32	—	—
96 MB	4M × 32	4M × 32	4M × 32	4M × 32	—	—	—	—
96 MB	—	—	—	—	—	—	4M × 64	8M × 64
128 MB	16M × 32	16M × 32	8M × 32	8M × 32	8M × 32	8M × 32	—	8M × 64 · 8M × 64
128 MB	8M × 32	8M × 32	8M × 32	8M × 32	4M × 32	4M × 32	—	—
128 MB	4M × 32	4M × 32	4M × 32	4M × 32	8M × 32	8M × 32	—	8M × 64 · 8M × 64
128 MB	—	—	—	—	—	—	—	—
136 MB	1M × 32	1M × 32	16M × 32	16M × 32	16M × 32	16M × 32	—	—
144 MB	2M × 32	2M × 32	16M × 32	16M × 32	16M × 32	16M × 32	—	—
144 MB	1M × 32	1M × 32	1M × 32	1M × 32	1M × 32	1M × 32	—	—
160 MB	4M × 32	4M × 32	16M × 32	16M × 32	16M × 32	16M × 32	—	—
160 MB	2M × 32	2M × 32	2M × 32	2M × 32	2M × 32	2M × 32	—	—
192 MB	8M × 32	8M × 32	16M × 32	16M × 32	16M × 32	16M × 32	—	—
192 MB	4M × 32	4M × 32	4M × 32	4M × 32	4M × 32	4M × 32	—	—
192 MB	8M × 32	8M × 32	8M × 32	8M × 32	8M × 32	8M × 32	—	—
256 MB	32M × 32	32M × 32	—	—	—	—	—	—
256 MB	16M × 32	16M × 32	16M × 32	16M × 32	16M × 32	16M × 32	—	16M × 64 · 16M × 64
256 MB	8M × 32	8M × 32	8M × 32	8M × 32	8M × 32	8M × 32	—	—
256 MB	—	—	—	—	—	—	—	—

BIOS forms the vital link which allows operating systems to work with the many diverse combinations of hardware in the marketplace today. Ideally, a BIOS ROM should be viable for the life of a PC, and you should not need to update it. However, there are two compelling reasons to undertake a BIOS upgrade. First, a newer BIOS can add support for drives and devices that are not currently supported (or that require device drivers or TSRs). Two common examples of this are the inclusion of "bootable" CD-ROM drives (using the El Torito standard) and the addition of bootable LS-120 120-MB drives. Placing support for these drives on a BIOS ROM means that there is one less device driver demanding space in your system's memory. Second, BIOS ROM is fundamentally a piece of software. Like all software, it sometimes has defects or oversights (a.k.a. bugs) that cause problems with system operations. This is especially true when the same core BIOS code is OEMed into a variety of motherboards. For example, some motherboards may require a BIOS upgrade to better support the main chipset in use or to properly identify non-Intel CPUs. Bugs and compatibility problems virtually demand a BIOS upgrade.

Recognizing BIOS problems

Unfortunately, diagnosing a BIOS bug is not a simple task. There are no diagnostics to check BIOS operations. BIOS manufacturers rarely publicize their errors, so there is no centralized index of symptoms that you can refer to that suggest a faulty BIOS or incompatibility. However, BIOS problems tend to fall into several categories that might alert you to the possibility of BIOS trouble. You can then address the symptoms with the system or motherboard manufacturer directly, and obtain a BIOS update when it's available:

- *There is trouble with Windows 3.1 or Windows 95.* This is a problem typically found on older systems which appeared *before* the broad introduction of Windows 3.x, and it is usually related to drive access or keyboard operation problems. Some versions of BIOS intended to enhance Windows can cause certain older motherboard designs to crash or hang up intermittently. When the drives and keyboard check properly (and work just fine under DOS), a BIOS upgrade may be in order. You may also have to replace the keyboard controller IC. Note that BIOS upgrades may no longer be available for older systems. When this occurs, you'll need to upgrade the motherboard outright.

■ *There is trouble with floppy disk support.* Random disk errors may occur when a 720-KB diskette is used in a 1.44-MB drive, or the 1.44-MB drive may be unable to format 1.44-MB diskettes. Once again, this symptom is seen most frequently on older PCs (1988 to 1991, when 1.44-MB floppy drives were becoming commonplace in PCs). Floppy drive problems may be coupled to the mouse configuration. Older systems also may not support new floppy drive designs such as the Imation LS-120 ultra-high-density floppy drive.

■ *There is trouble with ATA (IDE) support.* The ATA drive interface standard (also known as Integrated Drive Electronics, or IDE) came to prominence in late 1989 and early 1990. Because of their unique timing requirements, early IDE devices were susceptible to such errors as data corruption, failure to boot, and so on. By the second quarter of 1990, most BIOS versions had streamlined their IDE support. When you encounter difficulties installing an ordinary IDE drive in an older PC, check its BIOS date. If the date is 1989 or earlier, consider a BIOS upgrade.

■ *There is no ATA-2 (EIDE) or Ultra-ATA (Ultra-DMA/33 or Ultra-DMA/66) support.* The mid-1990s saw hard drives move beyond 528 MB and employ advanced data transfer modes. The use of large, fast hard drives using the ATA-2 interface standard (called Enhanced IDE, or EIDE) required a BIOS which could "translate" more than 1024 cylinders and employ Logical Block Addressing when accessing the hard drive. Systems sold prior to the Pentium 133-MHz processor (prior to 1995) will need a BIOS upgrade to support EIDE hard drives, although new drive controllers will often provide their own on-board BIOS to overcome this problem. It is also possible to use overlay software such as *Disk Manager* or *EZ-Drive* to deal with this issue.

Current PCs provide support for Ultra-ATA hard drives which can support data transfer modes up to 33 MB/s (Ultra-DMA/33) or even 66 MB/s (Ultra-DMA/66). The hard drive, drive controller, and BIOS must all be capable of supporting Ultra-ATA in order to wring the highest performance from the drive. Otherwise, performance will fall back to ATA-2 speeds. If your current system does not support Ultra-ATA, you may be able to use a BIOS upgrade to support an Ultra-ATA hard drive, or upgrade the drive controller to one with a suitable on-board BIOS.

- *You can't successfully support hard drive partitions over 2 GB or 4 GB*. This is a symptom indirectly related to ATA-2 support. Even though ATA-2 supports hard drives beyond 8 GB in size using Logical Block Addressing, many BIOS makers have cut corners, limiting their BIOS to supporting only far smaller hard drives. There seem to be two distinct generations of this problem. The first seems to kick in at around 2 GB, and the second seems to occur around the 4-GB mark. In many cases, the drive will seem to partition properly, but the system will hang up during the reboot after using FDISK. You will need a BIOS upgrade to correct this problem.

- *There is trouble with network support*. In some circumstances, the PC will not work properly when it is integrated into a Novell Netware system (or some other network). This is often due to the inability of older Novell versions to work with PC user-defined drive types. ROM shadowing usually has to be enabled to allow user-defined drive types, and, unfortunately, not all older motherboard chipsets supported ROM shadowing. BIOS versions later than 1990 have generally corrected this problem.

- *There is trouble with one or both serial ports*. Older BIOS problems often manifest themselves as COM port difficulties under DOS or Windows (often when a mouse is installed). If the serial port circuitry checks properly under diagnostics, suspect a BIOS bug. Check with the BIOS manufacturer to find out if an upgrade or patch file is available.

- *You cannot disable on-board features to employ upgraded expansion devices*. Recent PC designs typically incorporate a number of key features (such as a video adapter and drive controller) directly on the motherboard. This provides the user with a distinct cost savings. To upgrade that existing controller, you need to disable it on the motherboard (through the CMOS Setup routine) before installing the upgrade device. Otherwise, a hardware conflict will result. Unfortunately, there are many motherboards in the marketplace which do *not* properly disable existing controllers. The result is that you cannot upgrade the particular feature. In some cases, a BIOS upgrade will be adequate to correct this problem. In other cases, this is a flaw in the design of the motherboard which will require you to replace the motherboard outright.

- *The system does not identify the particular CPU or bus speed properly*. Classic 486 motherboards used a jumper to "select" the installed CPU, but later systems use the CPUID feature incorporated into most new CPUs. In many cases, BIOS is released before the motherboard has been tested with non-Intel

CPUs (such as AMD or Cyrix chips) or new Intel chips. When these CPUs are employed on the motherboard, the BIOS cannot identify them or identifies them incorrectly (e.g., identifying a Pentium III CPU as a Pentium II). When the system does not identify the CPU or bus speed at startup, chances are you need a BIOS upgrade.

- *Key system features are not supported.* This often occurs in the very latest motherboard designs when the BIOS does not adequately support the features handled in the chipset. Typical examples of this are USB problems, SDRAM support or performance issues, or Plug-and-Play trouble. A BIOS upgrade should usually correct the problem, but be sure to check with the motherboard or system maker first to verify that a BIOS upgrade by itself will be enough to correct the problem.

- *You note BIOS checksum errors in the POST.* Normally, the POST scans all BIOS ICs located in the memory space and calculates a checksum for each one. That unique checksum is then compared against the checksum stored in the BIOS IC itself. If the two checksums match, the BIOS is assumed good, and the boot process can continue. Otherwise, an error is flagged. A BIOS checksum error is almost always fatal—the contents of that BIOS chip are corrupted, and a new BIOS IC is required to correct the problem.

> **NOTE**: There is no need to upgrade a BIOS indiscriminantly—attempt a BIOS upgrade only to correct a specific problem or to facilitate features that were not previously supported.

Gathering information

The BIOS upgrade process is not terribly difficult, but success depends on obtaining the *correct* replacement or upgrade. To ensure that you order (or download) the proper BIOS, it is important to collect some information about the system. In most cases, the following five specifications should help ensure an accurate upgrade:

- PC make and model

- Motherboard manufacturer and CPU (motherboard chipset also, if possible)

- Make and version of existing BIOS (shown on the display during initialization)

- Part number of the ROM IC itself (you may have to peel back the ROM label)

- Make, model, and part numbers of main motherboard chipset(s) (if any)

When you consider how closely BIOS is related to PC hardware, you can understand why this information is necessary. Today, most PC BIOS is recorded on flash ICs which can be reprogrammed in the field. If you find that you must replace the actual BIOS IC (because of a BIOS failure or corrupted flash process), upgrades can usually be purchased from a BIOS maker or the original system manufacturer. For your own protection, though, place orders only with firms that offer a reasonable return policy (in the event that the new BIOS does not work as expected).

Determining BIOS IC type

At one point or another, you'll probably need to determine the type of BIOS IC contained in your PC. Ordinarily, this should be specified in the system or motherboard documentation, but if the documentation isn't handy, you can tell by looking at the BIOS part number (keep in mind that you may need to peel back the sticker on the IC to read its part number):

28Fxxx	12-V flash
29Cxxx	5-V flash
29LVxxx	3-V flash (these are rare)

28Cxxx   EEPROM (similar to flash)

27Cxxx   EPROM (you'll see a quartz window)

Updating a flash BIOS

Flash BIOS represents the newest class of BIOS ROM ICs. It is typically found in fast i486 and virtually all Pentium-, Pentium II–, and Pentium III–based PCs. A flash BIOS is essentially an electrically erasable programmable read-only memory (EEPROM)—that is, the IC can be erased and reprogrammed right on the motherboard. Rather than worry about warehousing and shipping new BIOS ICs, a BIOS or motherboard manufacturer can provide updated BIOS code as a downloadable file. The name of the file is typically coupled to only a particular motherboard. For example, updating the flash BIOS on an AMI Atlas ISA/PCI Pentium motherboard requires a file named S721P.ROM. If this file name is not used, the BIOS will not be reprogrammed. The AMI Excalibur PCI-II ISA/PCI Pentium motherboard requires the filename S722P.ROM. When attempting a flash procedure, follow the steps below:

- First, you *must* have a flash BIOS IC in the computer. If the IC does not use flash technology, you won't be able to reprogram it. You'll need to replace the BIOS chip instead.

- Make a complete backup of your system hard drive(s) in the event of drive problems after the flash process is complete.

- Make a complete record of all CMOS Setup settings before flashing the BIOS. In many cases, you'll need to restore or tweak the CMOS Setup again after performing the flash upgrade. Pay particular attention to the hard drive geometry settings.

- Record the current BIOS version number and/or release date and verify that you do not already have this version running on your system.

- When downloading the flash file (usually several BIOS data files, a flashing utility, and brief documentation, all compressed into a single .ZIP file), be certain to download only the flash package for your exact PC make and model.

  NOTE: Downloading and flashing an *incorrect* BIOS upgrade can render your computer unbootable, forcing you to replace the physical BIOS IC.

- Create a "clean," bootable floppy disk with any version of DOS, or as a Windows 95/98 Startup Disk.

- Copy the downloaded .ZIP file containing your flash package to the diskette, and decompress the .ZIP file into its constituent files (usually an .EXE file as the flashing utility, a .BIN or .ROM file as the new BIOS data file, and one or more .TXT files as the documentation).

  NOTE: *Never* attempt to flash a BIOS by running the flash utility from a hard drive. Proceed from the floppy drive only.

- You may need to set a *Flash Enable* jumper on the motherboard. If so, turn off the PC, locate this jumper (refer to the documentation for your system), and set it.

- Reboot the PC and start your CMOS Setup to verify that the PC will boot from the floppy drive first. This is usually indicated as a *Boot Order* or *Boot Sequence* of *A:/C:*.

- Once the PC boots "clean" from the bootable diskette, start the flashing utility, such as

  ```
  A:\> awdflash    <Enter>
  ```

- When the flash program starts, it may ask you for the name of the .BIN or .ROM file you wish to use as an upgrade. Type in the *exact* name of this file when prompted to do so. In some cases, the flash utility will automatically use the only available source file.

- Many flash utilities will query whether you want to back up your current BIOS. If you have this opportunity, *do* make a backup copy of the current BIOS before proceeding. Enter the file name to save, and proceed. In some cases, the flash program will assign a backup file name automatically (e.g., BACKUP.BIN).

- You will then be asked if you are sure you wish to continue. Answer YES.

- Once the flash process begins, you'll usually see a progress indicator at the bottom of the display which will keep track of the flashing process.

   IMPORTANT NOTE: It is critical that you do *not* power down or reset the PC while the flash process is proceeding. Doing so will interrupt the flash process and leave your BIOS corrupt and unrecoverable.

- When the progress indicator has stopped (or the flash process has otherwise concluded), you'll probably see a message such as "Please cycle power or reset this machine."

- Turn your computer *completely off*—your new BIOS is installed and is ready to use.

- If you had to set a *flash enable* jumper on the motherboard, reset it now before restoring power to the PC.

- Remove the bootable diskette from the system.

- Restart the computer now—the new BIOS version will be shown on the display screen. You're done with the BIOS upgrade.

- In most cases, you'll need to restore your CMOS Setup parameters before you can utilize the PC.

Memory Troubleshooting

Unfortunately, even the best memory devices fail from time to time. An accidental static discharge during

installation, incorrect installation, a poor system configuration, operating system problems, and even outright failures due to old age or poor manufacture can
cause memory problems. This part of the chapter looks
at some of the troubles that typically plague memory
devices and offers advice on how to deal with them.

Repairing SIMM/DIMM sockets

If there is one weak link in the architecture of a SIMM
or DIMM, it is the *socket* that connects it to the motherboard. Ideally, the SIMM or DIMM should sit com-
fortably in the socket, then gently snap back, held in
place by two clips on either side of the socket. In actual practice, you really have to push that SIMM or
DIMM to get it into place. Taking it out again is just as
tricky. As a result, it is not uncommon for a socket to
break and render your extra memory unusable.

The best (a.k.a. textbook) solution is to remove the
damaged socket and install a new one. Clearly, there
are some problems with this tactic. First, removing the
old socket will require you to remove the motherboard,
desolder the broken socket, then solder in a new socket (which you can buy from a full-feature electronics
store such as DigiKey). In the hands of a skilled technician with the right tools, this is not so hard. But the
printed circuit runs of a computer motherboard are
extremely delicate, and the slightest amount of excess
heat can easily destroy the sensitive multilayer connections—ruining the motherboard entirely.

Fortunately, there are some tricks that may help
you. If either of the SIMM/DIMM clips has bent or broken, you can usually make use of a medium-weight
rubber band that is about 1 in shorter than the socket.
Wrap the rubber band around the SIMM/DIMM and
the socket; the rubber band should do a fair job of holding the memory module in place. If any part of the
socket should crack or break, it can be repaired (or at
least reinforced) with a good-quality epoxy. If you
choose to use epoxy, be sure to work in a ventilated

area, and allow plenty of time for the epoxy to dry. This does not fix the problem, but it does contain the damage and may allow the motherboard to have a long and reliable working life.

Contact corrosion

Corrosion can occur on SIMM/DIMM contacts if the module's contact metal is not the same as the socket's contact metal; this will eventually cause contact (and memory) problems. As a rule, check that the metal on the socket contact is the same as that on the SIMM/DIMM contacts (usually tin or gold). You may be able to get around the problem in the short term by cleaning corrosion off the contacts manually using a cotton swab and a good electronics-grade contact cleaner. In the meantime, if you discover that your memory and connectors have dissimilar metals, you may be able to get the memory seller to exchange your memory modules.

Parity errors

Parity errors constitute many of the memory faults that you will see as a technician. As you saw earlier in this chapter, *parity* is an important part of a computer's self-checking capability. Errors in memory will cause the system to halt rather than continue blindly along with a potentially catastrophic error. But it is not just faulty memory that causes parity errors. Parity can also be influenced by your system's configuration. Here are the major causes of parity problems:

- One or more memory bits is intermittent or has failed entirely.

- There are poor connections between the SIMM/DIMM and the socket.

- Too few wait states are entered in BIOS (memory is too slow for the CPU).

- An intermittent failure or other fault has occurred in the power supply.

- A bug, computer virus, or other rogue software is operating.

- A fault has occurred in the memory controller IC or BIOS.

When you are faced with a parity error after a memory upgrade, you should suspect a problem with wait states or memory type settings in the CMOS Setup routine, so check them first. If the wait states and other memory settings are correct, systematically remove each SIMM/DIMM, clean the contacts, and reseat the SIMM/DIMM. If the errors continue, try removing one bank of memory modules at a time (chances are that the memory is bad). You may have to relocate memory so that Bank 0 remains filled. When the error disappears, the memory you removed is likely to be defective.

> **NOTE**: Some full-service PC shops may have a SIMM/DIMM memory tester unit available. If so, the shop may be persuaded to test your suspect memory module(s) for a nominal cost (perhaps even for free).

When parity errors occur spontaneously (with no apparent cause), you should clean and reinstall each SIMM/DIMM *first* to eliminate the possibility of bad contacts. Next, check the power supply outputs—low or electrically noisy outputs may allow random bit errors. You may have to upgrade the supply if it is overloaded. Try booting the system "clean" from a write-protected floppy disk to eliminate the possibility of buggy software or computer viruses. If the problem persists, suspect a memory defect in the memory module.

Traditional AT memory errors

IBM's PC/AT was the leader of the 80286 generation. Since there was only one model (at the time), ATs use some specific error messages to pinpoint memory (RAM or ROM) problems on the motherboard, as well as in its standard memory expansion devices. The 200-series error codes represent system memory errors (Table 1.6). ATs present memory failures in the format: "AAXXXX YYYY 20x." The ten-digit code can be broken down to indicate the specific system bank and IC number, although the particular bit failure is not indicated. The first two digits (AA) represent the defective *bank*, and the last four digits (YYYY) show the defective *IC number*. It is then a matter or finding and replacing the faulty DIP IC. Table 1.7 shows a set of error codes for early AT-class computers. For example, suppose an IBM PC/AT displayed the error message "05xxxxxx 0001 201" (we don't care about the x's). That message would place the error in IC 0 of bank 1 on the AT's system memory.

Contemporary memory symptoms

With the rapid advances in computer technology, specific numerical (or "bank and bit") error codes have long since been rendered impractical in newer systems, where megabytes can be stored in just a few ICs. The i486, Pentium, Pentium II, and today's Pentium III computers use a series of generic error codes. The *address* of a fault is always presented, but no attempt is made to correlate the fault's address to a physical IC. Fortunately, today's memory systems are so small and modular that trial-and-error isolation can often be performed rapidly on just a few SIMMs or DIMMs. The symptoms below highlight many of the most common memory problems encountered in today's systems.

Symptom 1.1: You see the number 164 displayed on the monitor. This is a generic memory size error—the amount of memory found during the POST does not match the amount of memory listed in the system's

TABLE 1.6   200-Series Error Codes

201	Memory error (physical location will probably be displayed)
202	Memory address line 0–15 error
203	Memory address line 16–23 error; line 16–31 error (MCA)
204	Memory remapped to compensate for error (PS/2)
205	Error in first 128 KB (PS/2 ISA) of RAM
207	BIOS ROM failure
210	System board memory parity error
211	Error in first 64 KB of RAM (MCA)
212	Watchdog timer error
213	DMA bus arbitration time-out
215	Memory address error; 64 KB on daughter/SIP 2 failed (70)
216	Memory address error; 64 KB on daughter/SIP 1 failed (70)
221	ROM-to-RAM copy (shadowing) failed (MCA)
225	Wrong speed memory on system board (MCA)
230	Memory on motherboard and adapter board overlaps
231	Noncontiguous adapter memory installed
235	Stuck data line on memory module
241	Memory module 2 failed
251	Memory module 3 failed

CMOS setup. Run the CMOS Setup routine, and make sure that the listed memory amount matches the actual memory amount. If memory has been added to or removed from the system, you will have to adjust the figure in CMOS Setup to reflect that configuration change. If CMOS Setup parameters do not remain in the system after power is removed, try replacing the CMOS backup battery or CMOS/RTC IC.

NOTE: The latest CMOS Setup routines do not actually *list* the amount of RAM—it is detected automatically. However, you may simply have to enter the CMOS Setup, then immediately "save changes and exit" to reset the amount of detected RAM in your system.

Symptom 1.2: You see an Incorrect Memory Size error message. This message can be displayed if the CMOS system setup is incorrect, or if there is an actual memory failure that is not caught with a numerical 200-series or "164" codes.

TABLE 1.7 Classic AT Error Codes

"AAxxxx YYYY 20x": Memory Failure
AA Board Bank
00 01 02 03 Motherboard 0
04 05 06 07 Motherboard 1
08 09 128 KB memory expansion n/a
10 11 12 13 1st 512 KB memory adapter 0
14 15 16 17 1st 512 KB memory adapter 1
18 19 1A 1B 2d 512 KB memory adapter 0
1C 1D 1E 1F 2d 512 KB memory adapter 1
20 21 22 23 3d 512 KB memory adapter 0
24 25 26 27 3d 512 KB memory adapter 1
28 29 2A 2B 4th 512 KB memory adapter 0
2C 2D 2E 2F 4th 512 KB memory adapter 1
30 31 32 33 5th 512 KB memory adapter 0
34 35 36 37 5th 512 KB memory adapter 1
YYYY Failed IC YYYY Failed IC
0000 parity IC 0100 8
0001 0 0200 9
0002 1 0400 10
0004 2 0800 11
0008 3 1000 12
0010 4 2000 13
0020 5 4000 14
0040 6 8000 15
0080 7

- *Check the CMOS settings*. If the CMOS Setup is not updated to reflect memory additions (or removals), or if the overall memory size changes because of a memory failure, you may need to adjust or resave your CMOS Setup. If the error persists, there is probably a failure in some portion of RAM.

- *Isolate your memory*. Remove all expansion memory from the system, alter the CMOS Setup to reflect base memory (system board) only, and retest the system. If the problem disappears, the fault is in some portion of expansion memory.

- *Check the base memory*. If the problem still persists, you know that the trouble is probably in your base (system board) memory. Take a known-good SIMM or DIMM and systematically swap devices until you locate the defective device. If you have access to a

repair shop with a memory tester, the process will
be much faster.

- *Check the expansion memory*. If you successfully isolate the problem to a memory expansion board
(often found in older proprietary PCs), you can
adopt the same strategy for the board(s). Return one
board at a time to the system (and update the
CMOS Setup to keep track of available memory).
When the error message reappears, you will have
found the defective board. Use a known-good RAM
IC, SIMM, or DIMM, and begin a systematic swapping process until you have found the defective
memory device.

**Symptom 1.3: You see a ROM Error message displayed on
the monitor.** This may also appear as a *207* error on
some systems. To guarantee the integrity of system
ROM, a checksum error test is performed as part of the
POST. If this error occurs, one or more ROM locations
may be faulty. Your only alternative here is to replace
the system BIOS ROM(s) and retest the system (you
cannot flash older AT-class ROM).

**Symptom 1.4: New memory is installed, but the system
refuses to recognize it.** New memory installation has
always presented some unique problems, since different generations of PC deal with new memory differently.

- *Verify RAM identification*. The oldest PCs require
you to set jumpers or DIP switches in order to recognize new blocks of memory. The vintage i286 and
i386 systems (e.g., a PS/2) use a setup diskette to
tell CMOS about the PC's configuration (including
new memory). More recent i386 and i486 systems
incorporate an "installed memory" setting into a
CMOS Setup utility in BIOS which must be updated after the memory is installed or removed. Late-
model i486, Pentium, and Pentium II/III systems
actually "autodetect" installed memory each time

the system is booted (so it need not be entered in the CMOS Setup, although setup may need to "autodetect" the new RAM amount on first boot).

■ *Verify bank assignments*. Also check that a correct bank has been filled properly. The PC may not recognize any additional memory unless an entire bank has been filled and the bank is next in order (i.e., Bank 0, then Bank 1, and so on). You may wish to check the PC's user manual for any unique rules or limitations for the particular motherboard.

> **NOTE**: Many late-model Pentium II/III motherboards do *not* need banks filled in order, although that's usually the safest policy to follow when upgrading or troubleshooting any PC.

Symptom 1.5: New memory has been installed or memory has been replaced, and the system refuses to boot. Memory installations often proceed flawlessly, but when boot problems occur, you can usually narrow the problem down to several key areas.

■ *Check the power*. Always start by checking ac power, the system power switch, and power connections to the motherboard. Check that none of the system cabling was dislodged during the memory installation.

■ *Check the expansion devices*. See that all expansion boards are inserted evenly and completely in their expansion slots. Flexing the motherboard during memory installation may have pried one or more boards slightly out of their slots.

■ *Recheck the memory installation*. Your memory modules may not be inserted correctly. Take the modules out and seat them again, making sure that the locking arm is holding the module securely in place.

■ *Check the module type*. If the problem continues, you probably do not have the right memory module for that particular computer. Make sure that the memory module (SIMM or DIMM) is the correct part that is compatible with your PC.

- *Check the installation order.* Finally, check for any particular device order that may be required by the motherboard. Certain systems require that memory be installed in pairs or in descending order by size. Refer to the system or motherboard manual for specific details on your exact system.

Symptom 1.6: You see an XXXX Optional ROM Bad, Checksum = YYYY error message. Part of the POST sequence checks for the presence of any other ROMs in the system. When another ROM is located, a checksum test is performed to check its integrity. This error message indicates that an external BIOS ROM (such as an SCSI adapter BIOS or video card BIOS) has checked *bad* or that its address conflicts with that of another device in the system. In either case, system initialization cannot continue.

- *Check the ROM address setting.* If you have just installed a new peripheral device (e.g., an SCSI controller board) when this error occurs, try changing the new device's ROM address jumpers to resolve the conflict.

- *Check the new device.* Remove the peripheral board—the fault should disappear. Try the board on another PC. If the problem continues on another PC, the adapter (or its ROM) may be defective. If this error has occurred spontaneously, remove one peripheral board at a time and retest the system until you isolate the faulty board, then replace the faulty board (or just replace its ROM, if possible).

Symptom 1.7: You see a general RAM error with fault addresses listed. In actual practice, the error message may appear as any of the examples below, depending on the specific fault, where the fault was detected, and the BIOS version reporting the error:

- *Memory address line failure at XXXX, read YYYY, expecting ZZZZ*

- *Memory data line failure at XXXX, read YYYY, expecting ZZZZ*

- *Memory high-address failure at XXXX, read YYYY, expecting ZZZZ*

- *Memory logic failure at XXXX, read YYYY, expecting ZZZZ*

- *Memory odd/even logic failure at XXXX, read YYYY, expecting ZZZZ*

- *Memory parity failure at XXXX, read YYYY, expecting ZZZZ*

- *Memory read/write failure at XXXX, read YYYY, expecting ZZZZ*

Each of the errors shown above is a general RAM error message indicating a problem in base or extended/expanded RAM. The code *XXXX* is the failure segment address—an offset address may be included. The word *YYYY* is what was read back from the address, and *ZZZZ* is the word that was expected. The difference between these read and expected words is what precipitated the error. In general, these errors indicate that at least one base RAM IC (if you have RAM soldered to the motherboard) or at least one SIMM/DIMM has failed. A trial-and-error approach is usually the least expensive route to finding the problem. First, reseat each SIMM or DIMM and retest the system to be sure that each SIMM/DIMM is inserted and secured properly. Rotate a known-good SIMM/DIMM through each occupied SIMM/DIMM socket in sequence. If the error disappears when the known-good SIMM or DIMM is in a slot, the old device that was displaced is probably the faulty one. You can go on to use specialized SIMM troubleshooting equipment to identify the defective IC, but such equipment is rather expensive unless you intend to repair a large volume of SIMMs/DIMMs to the IC level.

If the problem remains unchanged even though every SIMM has been checked, the error is probably in the motherboard RAM or RAM support circuitry. Run a thorough system diagnostic if possible, and check for failures in other areas of the motherboard that affect memory (such as the interrupt controller, cache controller, DMA controller, or memory management chips). If the problem prohibits a software diagnostic, use a POST board and try identifying any hexadecimal error code. If a support IC is identified, you can replace the defective IC or replace the motherboard outright. If RAM continues to be the problem, try replacing the motherboard RAM (or replacing the entire motherboard) and retest the system.

Symptom 1.8: You see a Cache Memory Failure—Disabling Cache error. The cache system has failed. The tag RAM, cache logic (motherboard chipset), or cache memory on your motherboard is defective. Your best course is to replace the cache RAM IC(s) or COAST (Cache-on-a-Stick) module. If the problem persists, try replacing the cache logic or tag RAM (or replacing the entire motherboard). You will probably need a schematic diagram or a detailed block diagram of your system in order to locate the cache memory IC(s), so refer to the system or motherboard manual for detailed information.

Symptom 1.9: You see a Decreasing Available Memory error message. This is basically a confirmation message that indicates that a failure has been detected in extended or expanded memory, and that all memory *after* the failure has been disabled to allow the system to continue operating (although at a substantially reduced level). Your first step should be to reseat each SIMM/DIMM and ensure that it is properly inserted and secured. Next, take a known-good SIMM or DIMM and step through each occupied SIMM/DIMM slot until the problem disappears—the device that was removed is probably the faulty one. Keep in mind that you may have to alter the system's CMOS Setup parameters as you move memory around the machine (an incorrect setup can cause problems during system initialization).

Symptom 1.10: You are encountering a memory error with HIMEM.SYS under DOS. In many cases, this is a compatibility problem with system memory. For example, the Intel Advanced/AS motherboard is incompatible with two specific Texas Instruments EDO SIMMs (part numbers TM124FBK32S-60 and TM248 GBK32S-60). Other EDO SIMMs from TI and other vendors will not cause this error. Try a SIMM from a different manufacturer. Also, make sure that you're using the latest version of HIMEM.SYS.

Symptom 1.11: Memory devices from various vendors refuse to work together. The system experiences a "memory failure" during the memory count at start time. This is a very machine-specific problem. For example, Gateway Solo PCs can suffer this problem when customers use the same size memory modules (4, 8, or 16 MB) made by *different* vendors. Try matching memory modules from the same manufacturer (including part number and speed).

BIOS upgrade troubleshooting

Symptom 1.12: The PC does not boot after upgrading the BIOS. This is the classic problem that most frequently haunts technicians. When you've replaced the physical BIOS ICs, double-check the IC(s) for proper orientation and installation. Make sure that all of the pins are inserted into the socket and that none of the DIP pins have been bent under the IC's body. If you're replacing "even and odd" BIOS ICs, make sure that you have not accidentally transposed the even and odd IC locations. If the problem persists, try replacing the original BIOS ICs. If the original IC(s) work, you may have defective or improper replacement IC(s).

If you've flashed the BIOS, chances are that your problem is a little stickier. Either you've flashed the wrong BIOS version or the flash process failed for some reason. In either case, there's nothing you can do except to replace the BIOS IC or restore the BIOS "boot block" feature (and recover the original BIOS). You'll need to contact the system or motherboard manufacturer for a replacement BIOS chip.

Symptom 1.13: You accidentally reset or power down the PC during a BIOS flash, and now the PC won't start. The great weakness of flash BIOS is that it cannot be interrupted once the flash process is under way—if it is, the BIOS will be left partially programmed and totally corrupted. Your only course of action here is to replace the BIOS IC or to restore the BIOS "boot block" feature (and recover the original BIOS). You'll need to contact the system or motherboard manufacturer for a replacement BIOS chip.

Symptom 1.14: The BIOS upgrade proceeded properly, but now the system behaves erratically, or other errors appear. There are several potential causes here. Most of the time, either you've flashed the wrong BIOS version (probably for a system using an *almost* identical motherboard) or the BIOS was corrupted during the flash process. If you made a backup copy of the original BIOS file during the flash process, repeat the process and restore the original BIOS version. If the system works, you can verify that you downloaded the correct flash file (and repeat the upgrade if possible). If you cannot restore the original BIOS, or if the problems persist, replace the BIOS IC. If the problem occurs when replacing physical ICs, chances are that you've installed the BIOS for the wrong PC or motherboard, and you'll need to replace the original BIOS ICs until you get the proper replacements.

Symptom 1.15: The BIOS upgrade proceeded properly, but system performance seems poor. This is a frequent (but little-discussed) complaint with BIOS upgrades. In many cases, a new BIOS version will require you to restore or tweak your CMOS Setup for proper performance. If you recorded your original CMOS Setup contents before attempting your upgrade, you can enter the CMOS Setup and compare the current settings to the original ones—chances are that one or more performance-oriented settings have been disabled in favor of more conservative options. Here are some points for quick tweaking (remember that not all of these features may be available in all BIOS versions). For fastest booting:

- Set the *Boot Sequence* to *C:/A:*.

- Set the *Boot Up Floppy Drive Seek* to *DISABLED*.

- Set the *Boot Up System Speed* to *HIGH*.

- Set the *Quick Power-on Self Test* to *ENABLED*.

For highest overall system performance:

- Enable all shadowing unless you are using an adapter that absolutely requires that shadowing be disabled for a specified address. Video shadow will increase the video speed.

- Set *Auto Configuration* to *DISABLE*.

- Reduce all of the memory timings to their minimum values.

- Enable the *Turbo Read Lead Off*.

- Enable the *Speculative Lead Off*.

- Enable the *Turn Around Insertion*.

- Increase the ISA speed by setting *ISA Clock* to *PCI-CLK/3*.

- Lower 8- and 16-bit recovery times to 1 (one) each.

- Set the *System BIOS Cacheable* to *Enable*.

- Set the *Video BIOS Cacheable* to *Enable*.

- L2 cache cacheable size—if you are installing 64 MB of RAM or more, set to 512 MB (64 MB is the default).

- Pipeline cache timing—set to *FASTEST* if there is only 256 KB total pipeline cache (*FASTER* is the default).

    NOTE: When tweaking BIOS settings in the CMOS Setup, be sure to change only *one* parameter at a time, then retest the system's performance each time.

Symptom 1.16: After upgrading the BIOS, you see a message such as Update ESCD Successfully on boot-up. This is not really an error, but more of an informational message. The ESCD (Extended System Configuration Data) is a method that the BIOS uses to store resource information for both PNP and non-PNP devices. The reason it shows this message is because the system has at least one ISA card in it, and it is running Windows 95/98. The ESCD boot-up sequence arranged by Windows 95/98 is different from the ESCD boot-up sequence arranged by the BIOS. So on boot-up, the system BIOS will attempt to update the ESCD. This will in no way affect system performance.

Symptom 1.17: You just upgraded the BIOS, and now you can't boot from the A: drive. Otherwise, the A: drive seems to be working normally. In virtually all cases, the updated BIOS defaulted the CMOS Setup to a *Boot Sequence* of *C:/A:* instead of *A:/C:*, so the system isn't even checking the floppy drive at startup. Start your CMOS Setup and tweak the *Boot Sequence* to *A:/C:*, then save your changes and try the system again. Also verify that you actually have a working bootable floppy disk in the drive.

Symptom 1.18: After updating the BIOS, you get a message saying Incompatible BIOS translation detected—unable to load disk overlay. This typically happens when you upgrade a BIOS to support Logical Block Addressing (LBA), but the hard drive in your system is already using overlay software such as Disk Manager. Since overlay software and LBA are usually incompatible, you'll need to either disable LBA in the CMOS Setup or remove the overlay software from the hard drive. Since you probably upgraded the BIOS to support LBA anyway, chances are that you'll want to remove the overlay software:

- Back up the hard drive before proceeding.

- Boot the system from a bootable floppy disk.

- Run FDISK and delete all partitions on the hard drive.

- Reboot and check with FDISK to be sure that all the partitions on the drive have been removed.

- You can repartition and reformat the drive, then restore your files from a backup.

If you cannot remove all partitions from the hard drive with FDISK, you can use the procedure below to erase the master boot record (MBR) on the hard drive. You'll need the DEBUG utility on your bootable diskette before proceeding:

```
A:\> debug     <Enter>
F 200 L200 0
a 100
mov ax,301
mov bx,200
mov cx,1
mov dx,0080          ;Note: use 0081 for second
fixed disk
int 13
int 3
(enter a blank line here)
```

```
G=100

Q                              ;Quit
```

The drive should now have no partitions on it. Reboot and use FDISK to partition the drive and FORMAT to reformat each partition. You can then restore the operating system and recover files from your backup.

Windows-related memory errors

Symptom 1.19: Windows 95/98 Protection errors occur after adding SIMMs/DIMMs. Windows 95/98 stalls with *Windows Protection Errors* during boot, or randomly crashes with *Fatal Exception Errors* when opening applications. This is a known problem with the Intel Thor motherboard using the 1.00.01.CNOT BIOS after installing 32 MB of RAM. This issue is usually due to certain third party SIMMs operating at speeds faster or slower than 60 ns. The motherboard probably has tight memory specifications, and SIMMs which operate at the *correct* speed are required (not faster or slower, even if the SIMMs are marked properly). Some SIMM manufacturers mark the SIMMs at 60 ns, but the SIMMs actually run at 45 ns. Try some SIMMs from a different manufacturer. It is also possible that a BIOS upgrade may loosen timing enough to make the SIMMs usable.

Symptom 1.20: Windows returns a fault in the MS-DOS extender. This kind of error can occur in Windows 3.1, 3.11, 95, or 98, and usually happens in either of two formats: *Bad fault in MS-DOS extender* or *Fault outside of MS-DOS extender*. You may also see a stack dump with a format such as

```
Raw fault frame:

EC=0344  CS=031F  IP=85E2  AX=001D  BX=0005  CX=1800
DX=155F
```

```
SI=0178  DI=0178  BP=016E  DS=027F  ES=027F  SS=027F
SP=0166
```

An error such as *Bad fault in MS-DOS extender* generally occurs when the fault handler in DOSX.EXE (the
DOS extender) generates another cascaded fault while
trying to handle a protected-mode exception. This error
is usually caused by one of the following factors:

- HIMEM.SYS is unable to control the A20 line
  (which may indicate a motherboard problem).

- DOS=HIGH is not functioning properly (perhaps
  HIMEM.SYS is not loaded or is corrupt).

- Your RAM may be defective. You might try a RAM
  diagnostic to isolate any memory problems.

- You are not running MS-DOS (e.g., your system is
  running DR DOS).

- The third-party memory manager (e.g., 386MAX) is
  not configured correctly.

- A `EMM386.EXE  NOEMS  x=A000-EFFF` command
  line is missing from the CONFIG.SYS file.

- You have an old, out-of-date BIOS ROM which isn't
  supporting the DOS extender properly.

- Your memory-related CMOS Setup configuration is
  incorrect.

- Your Windows files are old or corrupted. Run
  ScanDisk to test for file problems, then reinstall
  Windows if necessary.

- Your system is infected with a computer virus
  (Form, Forms, Noint, and Yankee Doodle are known
  to cause this type of problem). Check the system
  with a current antivirus utility.

If you see *Standard mode fault outside MS-DOS
extender*, the Windows kernel may be generating a
processor exception during initialization (before it has
installed its own exception handlers) or when the

kernel determines that it cannot handle an exception. The underlying causes are almost always the same as those outlined above. The portion of the error display labeled *Raw fault frame* contains information generated by the 80286 or 80386 processor in response to the original fault. The meaning of these entries is outlined in Table 1.8.

Symptom 1.21: Windows returns a General Protection Fault (or GPF). There are several possible causes behind general protection faults under Windows 3.1x, 95, or 98. An x86-type CPU (from 80286 to Pentium III processors) can detect when a program encounters a problem. The most common problems include stack faults, invalid instructions (a.k.a. software bugs), divide errors (divide by zero or math errors), and general protection faults. These generally indicate non-standard code in a Windows application, in Windows itself, or in a Windows device driver:

Stack fault (a.k.a. Interrupt 12). There are several possible reasons for a stack fault. An instruction may try to access memory beyond the limits of the current stack

TABLE 1.8 DOS Extender Message Codes

Setting	Meaning
EC=xxxx	An exception code produced by the processor in response to the original fault.
*IP=xxxx	The program counter of the faulting instruction (8086 register "IP").
*CS=xxxx	The code segment of the fault instruction. If this is "0053" or "005B," the original fault was in DOSX.EXE.
FL=xxxx	The flag's image at the time of the original fault.
SP=xxxx	The stack pointer at the time of the original fault.
SS=xxxx	The stack segment at the time of the original fault. If this is "004B," the fault occurred on a stack belonging to DOSX.EXE.

*The CS and IP sections indicate the point in the program where the original problem was detected.

segment or to load the SS register with invalid information (though that shouldn't happen under Windows 95/98). Stack faults are always fatal to the current application in Windows, but Windows may not crash completely.

Invalid instruction (a.k.a. Interrupt 6). The CPU detects most invalid instructions and generates a software interrupt to report them. Invalid instructions are always fatal to the application. This should never happen, but it is usually caused by coding errors that accidentally execute data instead of code.

Divide error (a.k.a. Interrupt 0). This error is caused when the CPU's intended destination register cannot hold the result of a divide operation—it could be divide by zero or a divide overflow. In either case, the error is almost always due to a problem with the program.

General protection fault (a.k.a. Interrupt 13). Any protection violations that do not cause another exception cause a general protection exception because one of the following conditions is true:

- Exceeding a segment limit when using the CS, DS, ES, FS, or GS memory segments. This is a very common bug in programs, usually caused by miscalculating how much memory is required in an allocation.

- Transferring program execution to a segment of memory that is not executable (for example, jumping to a location that contains garbage).

- Writing to a read-only or code segment of memory.

- Loading a bad value into a segment register.

- Using a null pointer. A value of 0 is defined as a null pointer. In protected mode, it is always invalid to use a segment register that contains 0.

In virtually all cases, the solution to a protection fault is to try reloading the suspect program, driver, or

Windows module (run ScanDisk to check the disk file system for errors). If the suspect program or driver is buggy, it may be necessary to download and install a patch file to correct potential programming errors.

Symptom 1.22: You see a memory error such as Unable to control A20 line. This error is almost always related to the HIMEM.SYS driver. The A20 line controls access to the first 64 KB of extended memory (known as the *high memory area*, or HMA). The HIMEM.SYS device driver must control the A20 line in order to manage extended memory. The error message is reported by HIMEM.SYS if it *incorrectly* identifies the extended memory handling mechanism of the computer, or if the handling method in your PC's BIOS is unknown. There are two workarounds for this problem:

- *Set the Machine switch.* Add the /M:x (the machine type) switch to the HIMEM.SYS command line in your CONFIG.SYS file (where *x* is the machine number between 1 and 14 or 16). Shut down and then restart your computer. For example:

```
DEVICE=C:\DOS\HIMEM.SYS /M:1
```

> **NOTE**: An incorrect A20 machine handler may hang the system at boot-up. You should have an MS-DOS version 5.0 (or Windows 95/98) bootable floppy disk available to boot from before you experiment with different machine switches.

- *Check the BIOS version.* It may be necessary to upgrade your machine's BIOS or contact your system vendor for assistance in modifying your CMOS settings—you may need to disable a FastGate (or similar) option.

Symptom 1.23: You see a memory error such as Cannot setup EMS buffer or Unable to set page frame base address. This is a known problem with many Dell

Inspiron 7000 computers under Windows 98; and it appears when starting an DOS-based program which requires expanded memory (EMS) page frames. EMS page frames normally require 64 KB of upper memory, however, Dell Inspiron 7000-series computers can provide only 54 KB of upper memory. This is an issue with the Dell system design and generally cannot be corrected unless you turn off the program's use of EMS page frames (or run the program on another system).

Symptom 1.24: Memory contents are corrupted (or the PC halts) when entering a CPU power-down state under Windows 98.   If your system's power management settings are configured to allow the processor to enter a C3 power state on a computer supporting the Advanced Configuration and Power Interface (ACPI) standard, you may encounter symptoms such as corrupted memory after several minutes of inactivity, or the computer may stop responding after several minutes of inactivity.

This problem is due to an issue with the Intel 440BX chipset under Windows 98 (caused by Windows 98), which may allow memory contents to be corrupted when a CPU enters or leaves its power-down state. If that motherboard uses the Intel PIIX4-E IDE controller chipset, the computer might hang (known to occur if a bus mastering operation occurs while in the power-down state).

Until a patch is available for Windows 98, you can work around this issue by preventing the CPU from entering the C3 power state. To accomplish this, exit Windows and reboot the computer. Enter your CMOS Setup and set the *lvl3_latency* entry to a value greater than `0x3E8h` (1000 decimal)—if *lvl3_latency* is greater than `0x3E8h`, the Windows 98 ACPI driver does not enter the C3 state. You'll need to save your changes and reboot the PC for those changes to take effect.

Symptom 1.25: Windows 98 appears unstable after disabling virtual memory (the swap file). There is not enough RAM in the system. This can occur if you disable virtual memory with only 16 MB of RAM. Windows 98 has higher memory requirements than Windows 95, so while 16 MB may be the theoretical minimum for Windows 98, 32 MB of RAM or more would result in better system performance and stability. To resolve this problem, install more RAM in your computer or enable virtual memory (or both). To enable virtual memory:

- Restart your computer and hold down the <Ctrl> key until the Windows 98 *Startup* menu appears.

- Choose *Safe Mode* from the *Startup* menu.

- Click *Start*, highlight *Settings*, and then click *Control Panel*.

- Double-click *System*, click the *Performance* tab, and then click *Virtual Memory*.

- Click the option labeled *Let Windows manage my virtual memory settings*.

- Click *OK*, click *Close*, and then click *Yes* when you are prompted to restart your computer.

Symptom 1.26: You encounter a Windows 98 protection error involving NTKERN. This problem occurs when installing Windows 98 and restarting for the first time. You may see an error message such as

```
While   initializing   device   NTKERN:   Windows
Protection Error. You need to restart your com-
puter.
```

or you may receive an error message after the Windows 98 Setup is completed such as

```
Invalid  VxD  Dynamic  Link  Call  to  Device  3
Service B
```

or:

```
While   Initialing   Device   <filename>   Windows
Protection   Error.   You   need   to   restart   your
computer.
```

If you try to start in the safe mode, you may receive a message like:

```
Himem.sys  Has  Detected  Unreliable  XMS  Memory  at
<address>.
```

In virtually every case, there is defective memory (RAM) in your computer. You'll need to systematically remove or replace the SIMM(s) or DIMM(s) (or memory chips) in your computer to eliminate any bad memory. You can use any of the techniques below to try working around the memory problem until you can identify and replace the defective memory.

Limit RAM through SYSTEM.INI.   If your computer has more than 16 MB of memory, it may be possible to configure it to use only 16 MB of memory (factoring out any RAM above 16 MB):

- Use Notepad to open the SYSTEM.INI file in the *Windows* folder.

- Add the following line to the [386enh] section of the SYSTEM.INI file:

```
MaxPhysPage=01000
```

- Save this file and quit Notepad.

- Restart the computer, and then restart the Windows 98 Setup utility.

  NOTE: If you can't start in the safe mode, restart your computer and hold down the <Ctrl> key until the Windows 98 *Startup* menu appears, then choose *Command Prompt Only*. Use a DOS text editor like EDIT to update the \\Windows\\System.ini file as shown above.

Limit RAM through *System Configuration*. Use the *System Configuration* tool to limit the amount of memory (RAM) available to Windows 98:

- Restart your computer, hold the <Ctrl> key until the Windows 98 *Startup* menu appears, and choose *Safe Mode*.

- Click *Start*, highlight *Programs*, select *Accessories*, select *System Tools*, and then click *System Information*.

- On the *Tools* menu, click the *System Configuration* utility.

- On the *General* tab, click *Advanced*.

- Click the *Limit Memory To <n> MB* check box (where *<n>* is a number) to select it, and then set the memory limit value to *16 MB*.

- Click *OK*, click *OK* again, and then restart your computer.

Symptom 1.27: The Windows 95/98 system slows or locks up when playing MIDI files continuously. When a MIDI (Musical Instrument Device Interface or .MID) file is played repeatedly or continuously, your computer may lock up, or the computer may seem sluggish for a short time after you stop playing the MIDI file. Screen savers and games that use repeated MIDI playback are typically susceptible to this problem. The problem is caused by the Windows MIDI sequencer (MCISEQ.DRV), which loses a small amount of memory for each successive playback of a MIDI file.

This is a known problem with the MIDI sequencer in Windows 95 and Windows 98, so until a suitable update or patch file becomes available to correct the MIDI sequencer, you should avoid using the screen saver or game, or disable MIDI playback. Note that closing and then reloading a MIDI file releases the lost memory.

Symptom 1.28: After installation of Windows 98, the Device Manager may show a yellow exclamation mark next to the PC Card (PCMCIA) network adapter.   You may also see a status message such as *Error Code 10* in the adapter's *Properties*. This is known to occur on laptops such as the DEC HiNote Ultra II when the PC Card network adapter uses memory that the computer's BIOS has reserved. Windows 98 determines a free range of memory and then assigns that range to the network adapter for use, but the network adapter driver may not be able to use the assigned range if it is reserved by the BIOS. To get around this problem, try excluding the memory range that is being reserved by the BIOS so that Windows 98 will not use it:

- Click *Start*, highlight *Settings*, and click *Control Panel*.

- Double-click the *System* icon.

- Double-click *Computer* on the *Device Manager* tab.

- Click the *Reserve Resources* tab, and then click *Memory*.

- Click *Add*, type CA000 in the *Start Value* box, then type CB000 in the *End Value* box.

- Click *OK*, and click *OK* again.

- Click the *PC Card network adapter* to highlight it, and then click *Remove*.

- Click *OK*, and then click *Close*.

- Restart your computer. The network adapter will be redetected and reinstalled by Windows 98.

Symptom 1.29: You notice that Windows 98 system resources remain lower after quitting a program.   This is often referred to as *memory leakage*, when memory is not freed by a program after it quits.

- *Restart the PC*. Rebooting the PC from scratch should return any "leaked" memory. You can use this trick as a temporary workaround.

- *Be careful when exiting programs.* Memory leakage can occur if you start a program and then quit before it has completely started. Do not quit a program before it has completely started.

- *Patch the offending program(s).* Memory leakage is often caused by poorly coded or buggy software rather than by Windows itself. If you notice leakage with a particular program, check with the software maker's Web site to see if there is a downloadable patch or update which will correct the memory leakage.

Symptom 1.30: You see an error message such as Insufficient memory to initialize Windows even though there is plenty of RAM. The problem may be too much RAM. When attempting to install or start Windows 95/98 with over 768 MB of RAM (perhaps 1 GB or more), the system may return an erroneous "insufficient memory" message. This is generally regarded as a problem with Windows 95/98, but you can work around the problem by limiting the amount of RAM which Windows can use to 768 MB:

- Use Notepad to edit the SYSTEM.INI file.

- Add the following line in the [386Enh] section of the SYSTEM.INI file:

```
MaxPhysPage=30000
```

- Save the SYSTEM.INI file, and then restart your computer.

If this problem occurs during Windows Setup, start the system in the command prompt (a.k.a. DOS) mode and use the DOS-based EDIT utility to modify the SYSTEM.INI file. When you save the edited SYSTEM.INI file and reboot the PC, the Windows Setup should continue.

Symptom 1.31: When trying to format a hard drive under Windows 98, you see an error message such as Insufficient

memory to load system files. The format process will terminate. This error occurs if you attempt to format your hard disk using the `format c: /q /u /s /v` command at a command prompt, but there is not enough free conventional memory to use the `/s` switch. This error may also occur if you start your computer using the Windows 98 Startup Disk and *then* attempt to format your hard disk. This is a problem with Windows 98, but there are ways to work around the problem. First, do not use the `/s` switch with the `format` command—after the format process is finished, transfer the system files to the hard disk using the `SYS C:` command. If you're restarting your computer using the Windows 98 Startup Disk, choose *Start Computer With CD-ROM Support* on the Windows 98 *Startup* menu, and *then* use the `format` command to format your hard disk.

Symptom 1.32: Your Windows 95/98 system returns an internal stack overflow error. *Stacks* are small sections of reserved memory that programs use for processing hardware events. A stack overflow occurs when there is not enough space in memory to run the hardware interrupt routines. When Windows shows an internal stack overflow error, there is not enough space in memory (either set aside or available to handle the calls being made to the system hardware).

■ *Check stacks in CONFIG.SYS.* The CONFIG.SYS file may not be properly configured for the Windows installation. Try the following values: `STACKS= 64,512` (this is the maximum allowed), `FILES=60`, and `BUFFERS=40`.

■ *Check for old memory managers.* Examine the CONFIG.SYS file to determine if files such as Himem.sys or Emm386.exe are being loaded from a folder other than the Windows folder. If so, boot Windows using the *Safe Mode Command Prompt Only* (DOS) option. Rename the CONFIG.SYS file to

CONFIG.DOS, and the AUTOEXEC.BAT file to AUTOEXEC.DOS, and then restart the computer.

- *Eliminate TSRs.* Some TSRs may be interfering with Windows. Disable any nonboot device drivers in the CONFIG.SYS and AUTOEXEC.BAT files. If you are installing from Windows 3.x and getting a stack overflow error, check the WIN.INI and SYSTEM.INI files for non-Windows-based programs or drivers that may be loading.

- *Check for resource conflicts.* There may be an incompatible hardware configuration. Check the port and IRQ settings of any network card, sound card, and/or modem. Make sure that there are no COM2/COM4 or COM1/COM3 conflicts, and that no devices are sharing IRQs. Disable or remove conflicting devices.

- *Upgrade the BIOS.* The computer may need a BIOS upgrade. Check the BIOS version and contact the manufacturer of your computer for information about a BIOS upgrade.

Symptom 1.33: You encounter random fatal exception errors under Windows 95/98. You may also notice that there are more fatal exception errors under Windows 95/98 than under Windows 3.1x. The most common cause for these error messages is faulty physical memory (RAM) on the computer.

- *Check for drivers.* Try starting the system in safe mode. If the fatal exception errors disappear, the problem may be with one or more buggy or corrupted drivers loading in the normal mode. You may then need to systematically disable background software and drivers in order to isolate the offending software.

- *Check the CMOS Setup.* In some circumstances it may be possible to adjust the CMOS settings (such as changing memory wait states or disabling the motherboard's L2 cache) to stabilize Windows 95/98 successfully.

- *Check / replace the RAM*. To resolve "fatal exception" errors, it is often necessary to isolate and replace the defective RAM. In rare cases, the problem may be on the motherboard.

Symptom 1.34: An error indicates that there is not enough memory to start Windows 95/98 (or an application). This problem can occur if there is not enough real and virtual memory to start the Windows shell (or the particular program). Start your computer to the DOS prompt and free some space on the hard disk containing your swap file (virtual memory). Once you free some space on your hard disk, restart Windows normally and try to run the program again. If the problem persists (or you cannot free more space on the drive), try adding RAM to the system.

> **NOTE**: If you try to start a program on a PC with only 4 MB of free RAM and less than 8 MB of free space on the hard disk with a swap file, you may not be able to shut down and restart your computer normally. You must hit <Ctrl>+<Alt>+<Del> to open the *Close Program* dialog box, and then click *Shut Down* to shut down Windows.

Symptom 1.35: EMM386 refuses to load after installing Windows 98. This issue can occur if you load EMM386.EXE using the /Highscan switch. The /Highscan switch can interfere with hardware detection during setup, so it is disabled by Windows 98 Setup. You can reenable EMM386 using the following steps:

- Use Notepad to open the CONFIG.SYS file.

- Locate the line that loads Emm386.exe, and remove the following text from the beginning of the line:

```
rem - by Windows 98 setup -
```

- Save and close the CONFIG.SYS file.

- Restart the computer.

Symptom 1.36: General protection faults are generated after restarting a program in Windows 95/98. If you close a 16-bit program that is marked as *not responding* in the *Close Program* dialog box and then restart the program, you may receive a general protection fault (GPF) error. This happens because of the way the offending program was originally closed. When a program is closed normally, its dynamic link libraries (DLLs) are unloaded from memory. When you use the *Close Program* dialog box to close a program that is not responding, the program's DLLs are *not* unloaded (and are not reinitialized when you restart the program later). The only real solution here is to shut down the computer and then restart it from scratch.

Web Contacts

American Megatrends: *http://www.megatrends.com*

Autotime: *http://www.autotime.com*

Award: *http://www.award.com*

Cameleon Technology: *http://www.camusa.com*

CST, Inc: *http://www.simmtester.com*

IBM Memory Products: *http://www.chips.ibm.com/products/memory*

Innoventions: *http://www.simcheck.com*

Intel RAMBUS site: *http://developer.intel.com/design/chipsets/memory/rdram.htm*

Jaguar Marketing Group: *http://www2.inow.com/~degeorge/jaguar.htm*

Kingston: *http://www.kingston.com*

Memory Part Number Reference:
http://pdpsys.com/mem_man.htm

Micro Firmware: *http://www.firmware.com*

Microid Research: *http://www.mrbios.com*

PNY: *http://www.pny.com*

RAMBUS: *http://www.rimm.com/html/documentation.html*

Simmsaver Technology, Inc.: *http://www.simmsaver.com*

Unicore: *http://www.unicore.com*

Wim's BIOS page:
http://www.ping.be/bios/bios.shtml

2

Floppy Drives

The ability to exchange programs and data between various compatible computers is a fundamental requirement of almost every computer system. It is just this kind of file exchange compatibility that helped rocket IBM PC/XTs into everyday use and spur the personal computer industry in the early 1980s. A standardized operating system, file structure, and recording media also breathed life into the fledgling software industry. With the *floppy disk*, software developers could finally distribute programs and data to a mass market of compatible computer users. The mechanism that allowed this quantum leap in compatibility is the *floppy disk drive*. This chapter covers the characteristics, installation, testing, and troubleshooting of basic floppy drives.

Floppy Drive Layout and Characteristics

At the core of a floppy drive (Figure 2.1) is a *frame assembly* (15). It is the single, main structure for mounting the drive's mechanisms and electronics. Frames are typically made from die-cast aluminum to provide a strong, rigid foundation for the drive. The *front bezel* (18) attaches to the frame to provide a

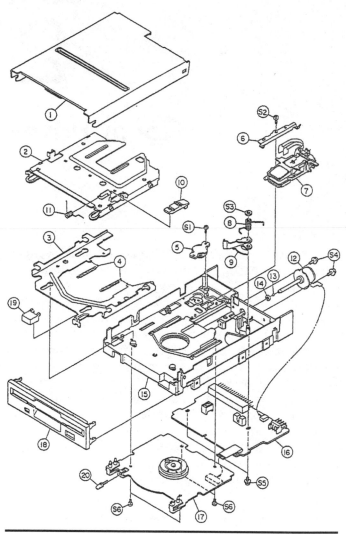

Figure 2.1 Exploded view of a floppy drive. *Teac America, Inc.*

clean, cosmetic appearance and to offer a fixed slot for disk insertion or removal. For 3.5-in drives, bezels often include a small colored lens, a disk ejection button hole, and a flap to cover the disk slot when the drive is empty. A *spindle motor assembly* (17) uses an outer-rotor dc motor fabricated onto a small PC board. The motor's shaft is inserted into a large hole in the frame. A disk's metal drive hub automatically interlocks to the spindle. The *disk activity LED* (20) illuminates through the bezel's colored lens whenever spindle motor activity is in progress.

Just behind the spindle motor is the drive's *control electronics* (16). It contains the circuitry needed to operate the drive's motors, read/write (R/W) heads, and sensors. A standardized interface is used to connect the drive to a floppy drive controller. The *read/write head assembly* (7), also sometimes called a *head carriage assembly*, holds a set of two R/W heads; head 0 is the lower head (underside of the disk), and head 1 is on top. A *head stepping motor* (12) is added to ensure even and consistent movement between tracks. A threaded rod at the motor end is what actually moves the heads. A *mechanical damper* (5) helps to smooth the disk's travel into or out of the drive.

When a floppy disk is inserted through the bezel, it is restrained by a *diskette clamp assembly* (2). To eject the floppy disk, you would press the *ejector button* (19), which pushes a *slider mechanism* (3). When the ejector button is fully depressed, the floppy disk will disengage from the spindle and pop out of the drive. Your particular drive may contain other miscellaneous components. Finally, the entire upper portion of a drive can be covered by a *metal shield* (1).

Drive sensors and electronics

A floppy drive's control electronics directs the drive's physical operations (i.e., spinning the diskette) and manages the flow of data into or out of the drive. These tasks are not nearly as simple as they sound, but the sleek, low-profile drives in today's computer systems are a far cry from the clunky, full-height drives found in early systems. Older drives needed a large number of ICs spanning several boards that had to be fitted to the chassis. However, the drive in your computer right now is probably implemented with only a few highly integrated ICs that are neatly surface-mounted on a single circuit board. This part of the chapter outlines the floppy drive's operating circuits. A complete block diagram for a Teac 3.5-in floppy drive is illustrated in Figure 2.2 (the figure is shown with a floppy disk inserted).

Write-protect sensors are used to detect the position of a disk's write-protect tab. For 3.5-in disks, the write-protect notch must be covered to allow both read and write operations. If the notch is open, the disk can only be read. Optoisolators are commonly used as write-protect sensors, since an open notch will easily allow light through, while a closed notch will cut off the light path.

Before the drive is allowed to operate at all, a diskette must be inserted properly and interlocked

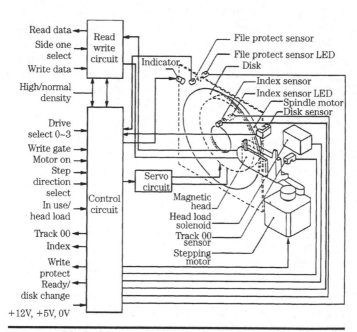

Figure 2.2 Block diagram of a Teac floppy drive. *Teac America, Inc.*

with the spindle. A *disk-in-place* sensor detects the presence or absence of a disk. Disk sensors are often mechanical switches that are activated by disk contact (although it is not unusual to find an optoisolator acting as a disk-in-place sensor). If drive access is attempted without a diskette in place, the operating system will report a *Disk Not Ready* error code/ message.

The electronics of a 3.5-in drive must be able to determine whether the diskette contains normal- ("double-") density or high-density media. A *high-density* sensor looks for the hole that is found near the top of all high-density disk bodies. A mechanical switch is typically used to detect the high-density hole, but a separate LED/detector pair may also be used. When the hole is absent (as with a double-density diskette), the switch is activated upon diskette insertion. If the hole is present (for a high-density diskette), the switch is not actuated. All switch conditions are translated into logic signals used by the drive electronics when reading from or writing to the diskette.

Before data can be read from or written to the diskette, the system must read the diskette's boot-sector information and File Allocation Table (FAT). While programs and data can be broken up and scattered all over a diskette, the FAT must *always* be located at a known location so that the drive knows where to look for it. The FAT is always located on track 00—the first track of diskette side 0. A *track 00* sensor provides a logic signal when the heads are positioned over track 00. Each time a read or write is ordered, the head assembly is stepped to track 00. Although a drive "remembers" how many steps should be needed to position the heads precisely over track 00, an optoisolator or switch senses the head carriage assembly position. At track 00, the head carriage should interrupt the optoisolator or actuate the switch. If the drive supposedly steps to track 00 and there is no sensor signal to confirm the position (or if the signal occurs *before* the drive has finished stepping), the drive assumes that a head positioning error has occurred. Head step counts and sensor outputs virtually always agree unless the sensor has failed or the drive has been physically damaged.

Spindle speed is a critically important drive parameter. Once the diskette has reached its running velocity (300 or 360 rpm), the drive *must* maintain that velocity for the duration of the disk access process. Unfortunately, simply telling the spindle motor to move is no guarantee that the motor is turning. A sensor is required to measure the motor's speed; this is the *index sensor*. Signals from the index sensor are fed back to the drive electronics, which adjusts spindle speed in order to maintain a constant rotation. Most drives use optoisolators as index sensors which detect the motion of small slots cut in a template or the spindle rotor itself. When a diskette is spinning, the output from an index sensor is a fast logic pulse sent along to the drive electronics. Keep in mind that some older index sensors are magnetic. A magnetic sensor typically operates by detecting the proximity of small slots in a template or the spindle rotor, but the pulse output is essentially identical to that of the optoisolator.

Physical interface

The drive must receive control and data signals from the computer and deliver status and data signals back to the computer as required. The series of connections between a floppy disk PC board and the floppy disk controller circuit is known as the *physical interface*. The advantage to using a standard interface is that various drives made by different manufacturers can be "mixed and matched" by computer designers. A floppy drive working in one computer will operate properly in another computer regardless of the manufacturer as long as the same physical interface scheme is being used.

Floppy drives use a physical interface that includes two cables, a power cable and a signal cable. Both cable pinouts are illustrated in Figure 2.3. The classical *power connector* is a 4-pin Molex connector, although many low-profile drives used in mobile computers (i.e., laptops or notebooks) may use much smaller connector designs. Floppy drives require two voltage levels: +5.0 V dc for logic and +12.0 V dc for motors. The return (ground) for each supply is also provided at the connector. The *signal connector* is typically a 34-pin *insulation displacement connector* (IDC) cable. Notice that all odd-numbered pins are ground lines, while the even-numbered pins carry active signals. Logic signals are all TTL-level signals.

In a system with more than one floppy drive, the particular destination drive must be selected before any read or write is attempted. A drive is selected using the

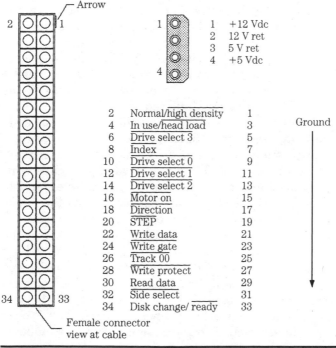

Figure 2.3 Diagram of a standard 34-pin floppy drive interface.

appropriate *Drive Select* line (Drive Select 0 to 3) on pins 10, 12, 14, and 6, respectively. For notebook or sub-notebook systems where only one floppy drive is used; only Drive Select 0 is used; the remaining select inputs may simply be disconnected. The spindle motor servo circuit is controlled through the *Motor ON* signal (pin 16). When pin 16 is logic 0, the spindle motor should *spin up* (approach a stable operating speed). The media must be spinning at the proper rate before reading or writing can take place.

To move the R/W heads, the host computer must specify the number of steps a head carriage assembly must move and the direction in which the steps must occur. A *Direction Select* signal (pin 18) tells the coil driver circuit whether the heads should be moved inward (toward the spindle) or outward (away from the spindle). The *Step* signal (pin 20) provides the pulse sequence that actually steps the head motor in the desired direction. The combination of *Step* and *Direction Select* controls can position the R/W heads over the floppy disk very precisely. The *Side Select* control pin (pin 32) determines whether head 0 or head 1 is active for reading or writing—only one side of the floppy disk can be manipulated at a time.

Two signals are needed to write data to a floppy disk. The *Write Gate* signal (pin 24) is logic 0 when writing is to occur and logic 1 when writing is inhibited (or reading). After the *Write Gate* is asserted, data can be written to the floppy disk over the *Write Data* line (pin 22). In reading, the data that are extracted from the floppy disk are delivered from the *Read Data* line (pin 30).

Each of the drive's sensor conditions is sent over the physical interface. The *Track 00* signal (pin 26) is logic 0 whenever the head carriage assembly is positioned over track 00. The *Write Protect* line (pin 28) is logic 0 whenever the floppy disk's write-protect notch is in place. Writing is inhibited whenever the *Write Protect* signal is asserted. The *Index* signal (pin 8) supplies a chain of pulses from the index sensor. Media type is indicated by the *Normal / High-Density* sensor (pin 2). The status of the disk-in-place sensor is indicated over the *Disk Change Ready* line (pin 34).

Floppy Drive Installation and Replacement

Unlike many of the peripherals and drives that are now available for a PC, floppy drives are almost universal in their design and features—there is usually very little to consider, since the drives are all the same. However, there are three issues that you must concern yourself with: available drive bay space, BIOS compatibility, and power connections. After you've selected the drive, installation should be very straightforward.

Drive bay space.   The trend toward smaller, low-profile enclosures has put a lot of pressure on available drive space. Given that many systems are already fitted with a floppy drive, hard drive, and CD-ROM drive, there is rarely a fourth bay available for even a second hard drive. One of the first problems when planning for a new floppy drive is to locate an external drive bay. If you do not have an external drive bay available, you may be able to move a hard drive to an internal drive bay. This relocates the hard drive and frees an external drive bay for another floppy drive. If you cannot free a drive bay for another floppy drive, you may need to consider a larger case (one with more external drive bays), use an external parallel-port floppy drive, or remove another unneeded drive to make space for the floppy.

BIOS compatibility.   One of the problems with the PC/AT (i286) and early i386 systems was that their BIOS often did not support the high-density 3.5-in drive format. The drive could be read from and written to properly, but the BIOS would allow diskettes to be formatted only to 720 KB (instead of 1.44 MB). The solution to this incompatibility has been to either upgrade the BIOS (to a version later than 11/85) or use the DRIVER.SYS utility in DOS to explicitly specify the physical drive as a high-density device. If you suspect that DRIVER.SYS is needed to support a 3.5-in high-density floppy drive on an older PC, open your CONFIG.SYS file and try a command line such as

```
device=c:\dos\driver.sys /D:1 /F:7
```

This command line creates a new "logical" floppy drive which is actually the same physical floppy drive specified by the /D switch (0 = A:, 1 = B:). The /F switch determines the type of drive to be created. In this case, a value of 7 indicates a 3.5-in, 1.44-MB drive. Check your DOS manual for additional parameters. This problem has been completely eliminated in virtually all BIOS releases after late 1985 and early 1986, but it can cause some confusion when dealing with very old PCs.

Power connections.   A power supply offers only a limited number of drive power connectors. In small systems, there may not be a free drive power connector for another floppy drive. When this occurs, you may use a "Y" splitter cable to add another power connector. However, place the Y cable in with the existing floppy drive (never split power from critical drives such as the hard drive). If you're simply replacing a defective floppy, just reuse the existing power connector.

Typical installation

In most cases, installing a second floppy drive is a three-step process: configure the drive jumper(s), mount and cable the drive, and configure the new drive in CMOS. While a floppy drive installation is often a quick and painless procedure (even for a novice), there are a few nuances that you should be aware of. When followed carefully, this process can typically be completed in under 30 min. If you're simply replacing an old or defective floppy drive, remove the old drive first, then follow the procedures below.

> **NOTE**: It's normally a good idea to perform a complete system backup of your hard drives before attempting any kind of drive work. While floppy installation should not affect your hard drives in any way, backups will protect your data and system configuration from accidental data loss.

> **NOTE**: Turn the system off and unplug it from the ac receptacle before proceeding—this both protects the new device and your personal safety.

Prepare the system.   Remove the screws holding down the outer cover, and put those screws in a safe place. Gently remove the PC's outer cover and set it aside (out of the path of normal floor traffic). You should now be able to look into the PC and observe the open drive bay, the motherboard, and any expansion boards and drives that are installed.

> **NOTE**: Remember to use an antistatic wrist strap whenever you are working inside a PC. This will prevent damage to the computer's delicate electronics caused by accidental static discharge.

Prepare the drive bay.   Once the outer cover has been removed, you should open the desired drive bay. In many cases, this is as simple as removing the plastic bezel covering an empty bay (the bezel will usually pop right out). If you must relocate an existing drive, things get a bit more complicated. First, decide where the drive (almost always a hard drive) will be relocated to—often an internal bay in the rear of the PC. You can then remove the mounting screws, disconnect the power and signal cables from the hard drive, and slide the hard drive out of the bay. Remount the hard drive in the internal bay, and gently secure each screw into place (be careful not to overtighten the screws). Reattach the power and signal cables to the hard drive. Pay particular attention when connecting the signal cable. If the cable is installed backward, the hard drive will not function. The red or blue stripe along one side of the ribbon cable always marks pin 1.

The procedure is a bit different when you are replacing an existing floppy drive. Unbolt the existing drive, then disconnect the power and signal cables. Slide the old drive out of the bay and set it aside carefully. If you have a good-quality antistatic bag available, seal the old drive in the antistatic bag. At this point, you should now have an open drive bay. Take a quick inventory and make sure that you have a floppy signal cable and power connector available—you may need a Y splitter connector in order to tap power from another drive.

> **NOTE**: When using a Y splitter to tap power from another drive, *never* split power from a hard drive. This can cause erratic drive (and system) operation.

Set the floppy jumpers.   Before installing the new drive, remove it from any protective packaging and locate any jumpers or DIP switches on the drive. A manual will be important here. It will be necessary to set at least four conditions: the drive select jumper, the disk change jumper, the media sensor jumper, and the terminating resistors.

The *drive select* (or DS) jumper allows the drive to be set as drive 0, 1, 2, or 3. Although most XT- and AT-type controllers support four floppy drives, each cable supports only two. As a general rule, you will set *both* the drives as B: (you'll see why below). However, interpreting the jumper selections is not always intuitive, because different manufacturers mark the jumpers differently. For example, instead of 0, 1, 2, and 3, drives may be labeled 1, 2, 3, and 4. Other variations include DS0 and DS1, or DS1 and DS2. As a rule of thumb, the lowest designation is generally considered to be drive A:, the next highest digit is considered drive B:, and so on. Since just about all floppy drive cables use a twist between the two floppy drive connectors,

both floppy drives can be set to the second jumper position (drive B:). As a consequence, the twist will automatically swap the *endmost* drive to A:. If you are in
doubt and there is a twist in the cable, set the drive
select jumpers to B:. If there is *no* twist in the floppy
cable (a very rare occurrence), be sure to set the endmost drive to A: and set the middle drive to B: (since
this is a daisy-chain configuration, you could actually
reverse this order, but it is not traditional).

Terminating resistors add another wrinkle to the
drive setup. As with many other daisy-chain cable
applications, terminating resistors are used at both
ends of the signal cable to establish ideal signal characteristics. Normally, floppy drives come with terminating resistors installed. Since most systems use a
single drive installed at the end of the cable (as drive
A:), this is generally a good default. When installing a
single drive, be sure that the drive has terminating
resistors installed. When installing a second floppy
drive as drive A:, be sure it has terminating resistors
in place, and check that the second drive (in the middle cable position) has no terminating resistors. When
installing a second floppy drive as drive B:, be sure
that the terminating resistors are removed.

> **NOTE**: While the middle (B:) floppy drive should have
> its terminating resistors removed or disabled, this is not
> always necessary because of the low-frequency signals
> on the floppy drive cable. In most cases, you can leave
> the terminating resistors of the middle (B:) floppy drive
> in place.

The *disk change* jumper is a vital part of almost all
contemporary drives. This signal tells the PC when a
diskette is removed so that when a new diskette is
inserted and read, the directory information will be
cached in the system. The disk change signal should be
enabled on all drives except for *old* 5.25-in, 360-KB
drives. Finally the *media sensor* (on 1.44- and 2.88-MB
drives) jumper should be *enabled* wherever possible—

the sensor allows the drive to detect whether a 760-KB, 1.44-MB, or 2.88-MB diskette is installed.

> **NOTE**: Today, virtually all commercial floppy drives are configured to serve as the A: drive (jumpered as B: but connected after the floppy cable twist) in a single-floppy system.

Mount the new floppy drive.   Now that the floppy drive is configured, slide it gently into the open drive bay. Line up the four mounting holes, and screw the drive in carefully. Be sure not to tighten the mounting screws excessively—this can warp the drive's frame and cause R/W problems or premature drive failure. Make it a point to use screws of the proper size and length to do the job.

Connect power and signal cables.   Once the drive is installed and mounted securely, connect the power and signal cables as required. The 4-pin power cable is relatively foolproof because of its keyed shape. For the signal cable, however, take care to install the card edge or IDC-type connector in the correct orientation—if the signal cable is installed backward, the drive will not work (the system may not even boot). The red or blue stripe along one side of the ribbon cable always represents pin 1.

Update CMOS settings.   If the previous steps have been performed correctly, the new floppy drive should now be fully installed. Before you can actually use the drive, however, you must update the system CMOS entries to accommodate the new drive. Make sure that any tools or extra hardware are removed from the system, reattach the ac cord to the power supply, then reboot the computer. As the system boots, start the CMOS Setup routine and adjust the configuration as needed for your new floppy drive. You'll need to specify whether a 5.25-in 360-KB, 5.25-in 1.2-MB, 3.5-in 720-KB, 3.5-in 1.44-MB, or 3.5-in 2.88-MB floppy drive is installed. If you have updated or replaced an old drive, make sure that the drive parameters reflect the *new* device. If you have added a second drive, enter the appropriate parameters for that new drive. When the settings are correct, save the system CMOS and reboot the system so that your changes can take effect.

Test the drive. Insert a known-good diskette in the drive. If the installation is correct, you should see the new drive designator under DOS, as an available option under the Windows File Manager, or as a new drive entry when double-clicking on *My Computer* on the Windows 95/98 desktop. Try writing a few files to and reading them from the drive. You might also try formatting a blank diskette in the new drive. If these tests are successful, you can be confident that the new drive is working properly. Be sure to remove any tools or hardware from the system, then reinstall the system's outer housings. Do not use excessive pressure to tighten the screws. Try the drive one more time, and return the system to service.

Reversing floppy drive assignments

In some instances, it may be necessary to reverse the letter assignments of your floppy drives. This is often the case when you wish to boot from a floppy drive which is not in a boot order supported by the BIOS. For example, you may want to change the boot order if you have a 5.25-in drive as A: and a 3.5-in drive as B:, and the boot order doesn't support booting from the B: drive. Fortunately, you can easily reverse the drive order by reversing the drives physically and logically. Remember to power down and unplug the computer before beginning.

Leave the drive jumpers in place. Remember that for most PCs, both floppy drives are jumpered as B: (it is the "flip" in the floppy drive cable that turns the endmost drive to A:). If your floppy drive cable does indeed have a flip, you can leave the floppy drives jumpered the way they are. The only time you'll need to reverse the drive's ID jumpers is when there is *no* flip in the cable, and each drive must be jumpered with a unique ID.

Exchange the floppy cable connections. Now reconnect the floppy drive cable, placing the middle drive at the end and the endmost drive at the middle. Depending on the way the drives are arranged in your system's case (and the amount of slack in the floppy cable), it may be necessary to actually exchange the floppy drives in the drive bays also. If this is the case, you should disconnect the power cables from the floppy drives, unbolt each drive, reinstall each drive in the opposite drive bay, then reattach the power and signal cables.

> **NOTE**: Now is a good time to check the floppy signal cable. If the cable is loose or appears damaged, it should be replaced.

> **NOTE**: If the middle drive had terminating resistors disabled, you may need to enable those terminating resistors when you place that drive at the end of the cable (A:), and to disable the terminating resistors of the drive that you swapped to the middle (B:).

Reverse the drive assignments in CMOS. When you first reapply power to the PC, you will probably receive an error message indicating that the equipment detected does not match the equipment specified in the CMOS Setup. This is because the physical drives are now reversed, but the CMOS still expects to find the floppy drives in their original positions. You'll need to start the CMOS Setup and reverse the floppy drive assignments. For example, if you had a 5.25-in 1.2-MB floppy as A: and a 3.5-in 1.44-MB floppy as B:, you'll need to assign a 3.5-in 1.44-MB floppy as A: and a 5.25-in 1.2-MB floppy as B: *after* you make the physical drive swap. Save your changes and reboot the computer so that your changes can take effect. Test both drives to verify that each is working.

Floppy Drive Troubleshooting

This section of the chapter is concerned with drive problems that cannot be corrected with routine cleaning or mechanical adjustments. To perform some of the following tests, you should have a known-good diskette that has been properly formatted. The diskette may contain files, but be certain that any such files are backed up properly on a hard drive or another floppy disk. *If you can't afford to lose the files on a floppy disk, don't use that disk.*

Floppy troubleshooting guidelines under Windows 95/98

Today, a great deal of everyday work takes place under Windows 95/98. As a result, floppy drive problems are often first noticed under Windows. When Windows reports trouble reading a floppy drive, try the steps below to identify and resolve the issue through Windows.

Check the floppy controller using the safe mode.   Start Windows in safe mode and try to access the floppy drive. To start Windows 95 in safe mode, restart the computer, then press the <F8> key when you see the message *Starting Windows 95*. Then choose *Safe Mode* from the Startup Menu. To start Windows 98 in safe mode, restart your computer, press and hold down the <Ctrl> key after your computer completes the power-on self-test (POST), and then choose *Safe Mode* from the Startup Menu. If you can access the floppy drive in safe mode, follow these steps:

■ Right-click the *My Computer* icon from your desktop, then click *Properties* on the menu that appears.

- Click the *Device Manager* tab, then double-click the *Floppy Disk Controllers* entry.

- Highlight the floppy disk controller for the drive you are having problems with, then click *Properties*.

- In Windows 95, click the *Original Configuration (Current)* check box to *clear* it. In Windows 98, click the *Disable In This Hardware Profile* check box to *select* it. This disables the Windows protected-mode driver for the floppy disk drive controller.

- Click *OK* and restart Windows normally.

If you can access the floppy disk drive successfully after following the procedure above, you may be faced with one or more of the following conditions:

1. The floppy disk drive controller may not be supported in protected mode.

2. There are drivers loading in the CONFIG.SYS or AUTOEXEC.BAT file that may be necessary for protected-mode access.

3. There are drivers loading in the CONFIG.SYS or AUTOEXEC.BAT file that may be causing conflicts in Windows and need to be disabled.

If you still cannot access the floppy disk drive, follow these steps to redetect the floppy drive controller:

- Right-click the *My Computer* icon from your desktop, then click *Properties* on the menu that appears.

- Click the *Device Manager* tab, then double-click the *Floppy Disk Controllers* entry.

- Highlight the floppy disk controller, click *Remove* to remove the controller, and then click *OK*.

- Open your *Control Panel*, then double-click the *Add New Hardware* icon.

- Click *Next*, and then click *Yes* to allow Windows to detect the hardware in your computer.

- When the *Add New Hardware* wizard is finished, restart the computer and try the floppy drive again.

Redetecting the floppy disk controller should correct addressing problems with the controller by detecting the correct address range. If the floppy disk controller is *not* detected correctly, there may be a problem with the floppy disk controller. If the floppy disk controller *is* redetected, but you still cannot access the floppy drive, there may be a problem with the diskette itself.

Suspect your diskette(s). One or more of your diskettes may be damaged. Use a disk utility (such as ScanDisk) to test the diskette for damage.

> **NOTE**: Never use a disk utility which is not compliant with Windows 95 or Windows 98. Noncompliant disk utilities can damage DMF disks. The Windows ScanDisk tool recognizes DMF disks and does not damage them.

You may also try the following command from a DOS command prompt:

```
C:\> copy a:\*.* nul        <Enter>
```

For example, if you are having problems with drive A:, insert a diskette you are having problems with in drive A: and type the command. This command copies the files on the diskette to a null device. If there is a problem copying the files, error messages appear on the screen, and that diskette is probably defective.

Suspect your tape backup. Floppy problems are known to occur when an Irwin tape backup unit is used under Windows 95. Windows 95 Setup removes the following statement from the [386Enh] section of the SYSTEM.INI file:

```
device=<path>\VIRWT.386
```

If you reinstall the Irwin tape backup software *after* you install Windows 95, this statement is placed in the SYSTEM.INI file again and can cause conflicts with floppy disk access in Windows. When this occurs, you must comment out that line in SYSTEM.INI.

Check the CMOS Setup.   Reboot your computer and verify that the floppy drive entries in your CMOS Setup are correct. If they are not, Windows will not be able to recognize your floppy drive hardware. If you must make changes to your CMOS Setup, remember to save your changes as you exit.

Check for device conflicts.   Device conflicts (reported by the Device Manager) can cause problems reading from and writing to floppy disks. You can generally resolve device conflict problems by changing or removing from *Device Manager* the resources that are causing the conflict. Typical conflicts occur with hard drive controller cards, video cards, or COM ports.

Symptoms

Symptom 2.1: The floppy drive is completely dead.   The system boots, but the diskette does not even initialize when inserted. This behavior can be caused by a number of important problems, so consider each possibility carefully before acting.

- *Check the diskette*. Make sure that the diskette is properly inserted into the floppy drive assembly. If the diskette does not enter and seat just right within the drive, disk access will be impossible. Try several different diskettes to ensure that the test diskette is not defective. It may be necessary to partially disassemble the computer to access the drive and allow you to see the overall assembly. Free or adjust any jammed assemblies or linkages to correct disk insertion. If you cannot get diskettes to insert properly, replace the floppy drive.

- *Check the drive power*. Loose connectors or faulty cable wiring can easily disable a floppy drive. Use your multimeter to measure dc voltages at the power connector. Place your meter's ground lead on pin 2; you should measure +12 V dc at pin 1. Ground your meter on pin 3; you should measure +5 V dc at pin 4. If either or both of these voltages is low or missing, troubleshoot your computer power supply or replace the supply outright.

- *Check the signal cable*. Verify that the drive's 34-pin ribbon cable is attached securely at the drive(s) and at the drive controller. Reattach the signal cable if it's loose, and try another signal cable if necessary.

- *Replace the floppy drive*. If the problem persists, chances are that the floppy drive is defective (perhaps the disk-in-place sensor has failed). Try replacing the floppy drive with a known-good drive from another system.

- *Replace the floppy drive controller*. If a new floppy drive still does not resolve the problem, you may have a defective floppy drive controller circuit. If so, you may also receive a floppy drive or controller error from the system BIOS at boot time. Try disabling the existing floppy controller and installing an expansion card controller (with only the floppy controller portion enabled).

Symptom 2.2: The floppy drive rotates a diskette, but will not seek to the desired track. This type of symptom generally suggests that the head positioning stepping motor is inhibited or defective, but all other floppy drive functions are working properly.

- *Check the drive for obstructions*. Carefully inspect the head positioning assembly to be certain that there are no broken parts or obstructions that could jam the read/write heads. You may wish to examine the mechanical system with a diskette inserted to be certain that the trouble is not a disk alignment problem which may be interfering with head movement. Gently remove any obstructions that you may find. Be careful not to accidentally misalign any linkages or mechanical components in the process of clearing an obstruction.

■ *Check the drive power.* Remove any diskette from the drive and reconnect the drive's signal and power cables. Apply power to the computer and measure drive voltages with your multimeter. Ground your multimeter on pin 2 of the power connector; you should measure +12 V dc at pin 1. Move the meter ground to pin 3; you should measure +5 V dc on pin 4. If either voltage is low or absent, troubleshoot your computer power supply or replace the supply outright.

■ *Check the signal cable.* Verify that the drive's 34-pin ribbon cable is attached securely at the drive(s) and at the drive controller. Reattach the signal cable if it's loose, and try another signal cable if necessary.

■ *Replace the floppy drive.* If the problem persists, chances are that the floppy drive is defective (perhaps the head positioning system has failed). Try replacing the floppy drive with a known-good drive from another system.

■ *Replace the floppy drive controller.* If a new floppy drive still does not resolve the problem, you may have a defective floppy drive controller circuit. If so, you may also receive a floppy drive or controller error from the system BIOS at boot time. Try disabling the existing floppy controller and installing an expansion card controller (with only the floppy controller portion enabled).

Symptom 2.3: The floppy drive heads seek properly, but the spindle does not turn.   This symptom suggests that the spindle motor is inhibited or defective, but all other floppy drive functions are working properly.

- *Check the drive for obstructions.* Power down the computer and remove the floppy drive. Carefully inspect the spindle motor, drive belt (if used), and spindle assembly. Make certain that there are no broken parts or obstructions that could jam the spindle. If there is a belt between the motor and the spindle, make sure it is reasonably tight—it should not slip. You should also examine the floppy drive with a diskette inserted to be certain that the diskette's insertion or alignment is not causing the problem. Double-check your observations using several different diskettes. Gently remove any obstruction(s) that you may find. Be careful not to cause any accidental damage in the process of clearing an obstruction. Do *not* add any lubricating agents to the assembly, but gently vacuum or wipe away any significant accumulations of dust or dirt.

- *Check the drive power.* Remove any diskette from the drive and reconnect the drive's signal and power cables. Apply power to the computer and measure drive voltages with your multimeter. Ground your multimeter on pin 2 of the power connector; you should measure +12 V dc at pin 1. Move the meter ground to pin 3; you should measure +5 V dc on pin 4. If either voltage is low or absent, troubleshoot your computer power supply or replace the supply outright.

- *Check the signal cable.* Verify that the drive's 34-pin ribbon cable is attached securely at the drive(s) and at the drive controller. Reattach the signal cable if it's loose, and try another signal cable if necessary.

- *Replace the floppy drive.* If the problem persists, chances are that the floppy drive is defective (perhaps the spindle motor control system has failed). Try replacing the floppy drive with a known-good drive from another system.

- *Replace the floppy drive controller.* If a new floppy drive still does not resolve the problem, you may have a defective floppy drive controller circuit. If so, you may also receive a floppy drive or controller error from the system BIOS at boot time. Try disabling the existing floppy controller and installing an expansion card controller (with only the floppy controller portion enabled).

Symptom 2.4: The floppy drive will not read from/write to the diskette. All other operations appear normal. This type of problem can manifest itself in several ways, but your computer's operating system will usually inform you when a diskette read or write error has occurred.

- *Check the diskette*. Begin by trying a known-good, properly formatted diskette in your suspect drive. A faulty diskette can generate some very perplexing read/write problems.

- *Clean the floppy drive*. If a known-good diskette does not resolve the problem, try cleaning the read/write heads thoroughly. Do *not* run the drive with a head cleaning disk inserted for more than 30 s at a time, or you risk damaging the heads with excessive friction.

- *Check the signal cable*. Verify that the drive's 34-pin ribbon cable is attached securely at the drive(s) and at the drive controller. Reattach the signal cable if it's loose, and try another signal cable if necessary.

- *Replace the floppy drive*. If the problem persists, chances are that the floppy drive is defective (perhaps the head read/write system has failed). Try replacing the floppy drive with a known-good drive from another system.

- *Replace the floppy drive controller*. If a new floppy drive still does not resolve the problem, you may have a defective floppy drive controller circuit. If so, you may also receive a floppy drive or controller error from the system BIOS at boot time. Try disabling the existing floppy controller and installing an expansion card controller (with only the floppy controller portion enabled).

Symptom 2.5: The drive is able to write to a write-protected diskette. When this kind of problem occurs, it is almost always the drive itself that is defective.

- *Check the diskette*. Remove and examine the diskette itself to verify that it is actually write-protected. If the disk is *not* write-protected, write-protect it appropriately, and try the diskette again. You might also like to try a different diskette.

- *Clean the floppy drive*. Try cleaning the drive by blowing clean compressed air into the drive (pay particular attention to cleaning off the write-protect sensor).

- *Replace the floppy drive*. If the problem persists, chances are that the floppy drive is defective (perhaps the write-protect sensor or on-board drive electronics has failed). Try replacing the floppy drive with a known-good drive from another system.

Symptom 2.6: The drive can recognize only either high- or double-density media, but not both. This type of problem usually appears in 3.5-in drives during the disk format process when the drive must check the media type.

- *Check the diskette*. Verify that you're using the correct disk type (this is actually a common oversight, since many generic diskettes are unmarked).

- *Clean the floppy drive*. Try cleaning the drive by blowing clean compressed air into the drive (pay particular attention to cleaning off the media type sensor).

- *Check the signal cable*. Verify that the drive's 34-pin ribbon cable is attached securely at the drive(s) and at the drive controller. Reattach the signal cable if it's loose, and try another signal cable if necessary.

- *Replace the floppy drive.* If the problem persists, chances are that the floppy drive is defective (perhaps the media type sensor or on-board drive electronics has failed). Try replacing the floppy drive with a known-good drive from another system.

Symptom 2.7: When a new diskette is inserted in the drive, a directory from a *previous* diskette appears. You may have to reset the system in order to get the new diskette to be recognized. This is the classic "phantom directory" problem; it is usually due to a drive or cable fault.

- *Check the signal cable.* Verify that the drive's 34-pin ribbon cable is attached securely at the drive(s) and at the drive controller. Reattach the signal cable if it's loose, and try another signal cable if necessary.

- *Check the drive's jumpers.* If this is a *new* drive installation, check the floppy drive's jumpers. Some floppy drives allow the DISK CHANGE signal to be enabled or disabled. Make sure that the DISK CHANGE signal is enabled.

- *Replace the floppy drive.* If the problem persists, chances are that the floppy drive is defective (perhaps the disk change logic in the drive's electronics has failed). Try replacing the floppy drive with a known-good drive from another system.

   NOTE: If you suspect a phantom directory, *do not* initiate any writing to the floppy disk—its FAT table and directories could be overwritten, rendering its contents inaccessible without careful data recovery procedures.

Symptom 2.8: Double-density (720-KB) 3.5-in diskettes are not working properly when formatted as high-density (1.44-MB) diskettes. This is a common problem when double-density diskettes are pressed into service as high-density diskettes. In actual practice, double-density diskettes use a lower-grade medium than high-density diskettes, and this makes double-density diskettes unreliable when used in high-density mode. Some good-quality diskettes will tolerate this misuse better than other, lower-quality diskettes. As a general rule, do *not* use double-density diskettes as high-density diskettes.

Symptom 2.9: Your 3.5-in high-density floppy drive cannot format high-density diskettes. You can read from and write to them just fine. This is a problem that plagues older computers (i286 and i386 systems) to which aftermarket high-density drives were added. The problem is a lack of BIOS support for high-density formatting— the system is just too old. In such a case, you have a choice. First, you can upgrade your motherboard BIOS to a version that directly supports 3.5-in high-density diskettes. You could also use the DRIVER.SYS utility, a DOS driver which allows an existing 3.5-in drive to be "redefined" as a new logical drive providing high-density support. A typical DRIVER.SYS command line would appear in CONFIG.SYS, such as

```
device = c:\dos\driver.sys /D:1
```

Symptom 2.10: There are no jumpers available on the floppy drive, so it is impossible to change settings. This is not a problem as much as it is an inconvenience. Typically, you can expect "unjumpered" floppy drives to be set to the following specifications;

- "Drive Select" *1* (B: drive)
- "Disk Change" (pin 34) *enabled*
- "Frame Ground" *enabled*

This configuration supports traditional single and dual (1.44-MB) floppy drive systems using twisted floppy cables.

Symptom 2.11: When using a combination floppy drive (called a combo drive), one of the drives does not work, while the other works fine. This problem is often caused by a drive fault. First, be sure to check the power connector—make sure that both +5 V and +12 V are adequately provided to the drive through the 4-pin "mate-n-lock" connector. If the drive is receiving the proper power, the drive itself has almost certainly failed—try a new drive.

Symptom 2.12: DOS reports an error such as *Cannot read from drive A:*. A diskette is fully inserted in the drive, and the drive LED indicates that access is being attempted.

■ *Check the diskette.* Begin by trying a known-good, properly formatted diskette in your suspect drive. A faulty diskette can generate some very perplexing read/write problems.

■ *Check the drive for obstructions.* Carefully inspect the spindle motor, drive belt (if used), and read/write head assembly. Make certain that there are no broken parts or obstructions that could jam the heads. You should also examine the floppy drive with a diskette inserted to be certain that the diskette's insertion or alignment is not causing the problem. Double-check your observations using several different diskettes. Gently remove any obstruction(s) that you may find. Be careful not to cause any accidental damage in the process of clearing an obstruction.

■ *Clean the floppy drive.* If a known-good diskette does not resolve the problem, try cleaning the read/write heads thoroughly. Do *not* run the drive with a head cleaning disk inserted for more than 30 s at a time, or you risk damaging the heads with excessive friction.

■ *Check the signal cable.* Verify that the drive's 34-pin ribbon cable is attached securely at the drive(s) and at the drive controller. Reattach the signal cable if it's loose, and try another signal cable if necessary.

- *Replace the floppy drive.* If the problem persists, chances are that the floppy drive is defective (perhaps the head read/write system has failed). Try replacing the floppy drive with a known-good drive from another system.

- *Replace the floppy drive controller.* If a new floppy drive still does not resolve the problem, you may have a defective floppy drive controller circuit. If so, you may also receive a floppy drive or controller error from the system BIOS at boot time. Try disabling the existing floppy controller and installing an expansion card controller (with only the floppy controller portion enabled).

Symptom 2.13: You cannot upgrade an XT-class PC with a 3.5-in floppy disk drive. XT systems support up to four double-density 5.25-in floppy disk drives. They will not support 3.5-in floppy disks at all. To install 3.5-in floppy disks, you should check your DOS version (you need to have DOS 3.3 or later installed). Next, you'll need to install an 8-bit floppy drive controller board (remember to disable any existing floppy controller in the system first). The floppy controller will have its own on-board BIOS to support floppy disk operations. Finally, take a look at the XT configuration switches and see that any entries for your floppy drives are set correctly. If you're using a stand-alone floppy controller, you may need to set the motherboard jumpers to *no floppy drives*.

Symptom 2.14: The floppy drive activity LED stays on as soon as the computer is powered up. This is a classic signaling problem which occurs after changing or upgrading a drive system. In virtually all cases, one end of the drive cable has been inserted backward. Make sure that pin 1 on the 34-pin cable is aligned properly with the connector on both the drive and the controller. If problems remain, the drive controller may have failed. This is rare, but try a new drive controller.

Symptom 2.15: You are unable to "swap" floppy drives so that A: becomes B: and B: becomes A:. This often happens on older systems when users want to make their 3.5-in aftermarket B: drive into their A: drive, and relegate their aging 5.25-in drive to B: instead.

- *Check the signal cable.* For floppy cables with a wire twist, the endmost connector is A: and the connector prior to the twist is B:. Reverse the connectors at each floppy drive to reverse their identities.

- *Check the drive jumpers.* If the cable has *no* twist (this is rare), reset the jumper ID on each drive so that your desired A: drive is set to DS0 (Drive Select 0) and your desired B: drive is jumpered to DS1. If you accomplish this exchange, but one drive is not recognized, try a new floppy signal cable.

- *Check the CMOS settings.* You'll need to reverse the floppy drive entries for your A: and B: drives, then reboot the system.

Symptom 2.16: The new drive does not work, or the system does not recognize the new drive. This is a classic problem in which the system does not recognize the newly installed drive; it is typically the result of incorrect or overlooked CMOS settings.

- *Check the CMOS settings.* Reboot the system and start the CMOS setup routine. Verify the floppy drive parameters against the actual physical drives in the system, then make sure that the correct data are entered in CMOS—you may have forgotten to save the data initially. Save the new data correctly and try the system again.

- *Check the signal cables.* Inspect the power and signal cables at the drive. Loose or incorrectly attached cables can effectively disable the drive. Install each cable carefully and try the system again.

- *Replace the floppy drive.* If the problem persists, chances are that the new floppy drive is defective.

Try replacing the floppy drive with a known-good drive from another system.

Symptom 2.17: You cannot boot the system from the new floppy drive. If the drive is recognized properly and operates as expected, the failure to boot actually may not be a failure—rather, the boot order established in your CMOS Setup may not be set to include the new drive. Often, the boot order is A: then C:, or C: then A:. If you installed a new floppy as B:, the system will not attempt to boot because it is not included in the boot order. Restart the CMOS Setup routine and adjust the boot order to address your new floppy drive first (e.g., B:/C: or A:/B:/C:).

Symptom 2.18: After the second floppy drive is installed, there are a lot of signal problems such as read or write errors. Chances are that you left the terminating resistors in place on the second (middle) floppy drive, resulting in signal errors. You should have a terminating resistor pack on the drive at the *end* of the daisy chain cable. Check that the terminating resistors are in place on drive A:, and remove the terminating resistors from the middle drive (B:). Also check that the signal cables are installed securely on both drives. Loose or damaged cables can cause signal problems.

Symptom 2.19: The floppy drive light comes on even when there is no diskette in the drive. This may happen at any time, particularly during shutdown or reboot of the system. One of the most common causes of excessive floppy drive activity is a Windows .PIF (Program Information File) shortcut pointing to the floppy drive. A .PIF shortcut is one that points to a DOS program, while a .LNK shortcut points to a Windows program. You should check for .PIF shortcuts to your floppy drive. Windows Explorer doesn't normally show the .PIF or .LNK extensions for shortcuts, but you can find them manually using the Windows 95/98 *Find* feature:

- Click *Start*, highlight *Find*, then click on *Files or Folders*.

- Enter *.PIF in the *Named* field.

- Use the *Browse* button to select your \Windows directory.

- Check *Include subdirectories*.

- Click the *Advanced* tab and enter either A: or B: in the *Containing text* field.

- Click the *Find Now* button.

If *Find* locates any shortcut in the \Windows\Desktop or any folder in the \Windows\Start Menu structure, that shortcut is probably causing the problem. The solution is to delete the reference or move the shortcut(s) to a directory other than the \Desktop or \Start Menu folder(s).

When floppy drive access seems to occur during shutdown or reboot, it may be that you have antivirus software (such as McAfee's VShield or Norton Anti-Virus Auto-Protect) set to check the floppy drive automatically. You'll need to disable autochecking of the floppy drive. For McAfee's VShield, right-click its icon from the taskbar and select *Properties*. Under the *Scan Floppies On* entry in the *Detection* tab, uncheck the *Shutdown* box. Remember to save your changes. For Norton AntiVirus Auto-Protect, right-click its icon from the taskbar and select *Options*. Click the *Advance* button, and under the *Check floppies* entry, uncheck the *Check floppies when reboot computer* box. Remember to save your changes.

Symptom 2.20: You cannot create a Windows 95/98 Startup Disk.   There are many possible problems which may prevent Windows from properly creating a Startup Disk, but the points below outline many of the most common issues.

- *Check the diskette*. The diskette itself may have 10 or more bad sectors, or the first sector may be damaged. Try a known-good diskette (preferably a high-quality or premium-grade diskette). Also, Windows 95/98 generally requires a high-density (1.44-MB) floppy disk in order to create a Startup Disk.

- *Check your antivirus software.* Many antivirus tools can interfere with floppy disk operations. Disable or uninstall your antivirus software according to the manufacturer's instructions.

- *Check the CMOS settings.* Reboot the system and start the CMOS Setup routine. Verify the floppy drive parameters against the actual physical drives in the system, then make sure that the correct data are entered in CMOS—you may have forgotten to save the data initially. Save the new data correctly and try the system again.

- *Disable/remove floppy tape devices.* Some older tape backup devices utilizing the floppy controller may prevent you from gaining access to the floppy drive. To work around this behavior, disconnect the tape backup device from the floppy controller *before* you attempt to create a Windows 95/98 Startup Disk, or disable the tape backup driver.

- *Replace the floppy drive.* If the problem persists, chances are that the new floppy drive is defective. Try replacing the floppy drive with a known-good drive from another system.

Web Contacts

Mitsumi: *http://www.mitsumi.com*

Teac: *http://www.teac.com*

Sony: *http://www.ita.sel.sony.com/products/ storage/*

3

LS-120 Drives

With multimegabyte text, image, multimedia, and CAD files now commonplace, the traditional 1.44-MB diskette is under a great deal of pressure—these diskettes are falling into disuse because it's hard to fit today's huge files on them. The LS-120 drive is intended to offer higher storage capacities (up to 120 MB) on magneto-optical diskettes, while still providing backward compatibility with existing floppy disks. The LS-120 also employs an ATAPI IDE interface (the same class of interface used by CD-ROMs and hard drives), so its performance is far better than the traditional 300 KB/s found with floppy drives. This chapter explains the capabilities of the LS-120, highlights a typical LS-120 installation, and covers many of the most persistent troubleshooting problems.

LS-120 Drive Layout and Characteristics

The LS-120 drive uses both magnetic *and* optical reading/writing techniques. This makes an LS-120 something of a cross between a floppy drive and a CD-ROM. Using this hybrid technology, the LS-120 can offer storage capacities of 120 MB (equivalent to about 83 floppy disks) on specially designed and formatted

"SuperDisks" (SuperDisk LS-120 diskettes by IMA-TION are usually recommended), but it is also *fully* backward-compatible with existing 1.44-MB diskettes (so *any* existing floppy disks are still fully usable). The LS-120 also provides much faster data transfers at up to 750 KB/s (five times the rate of a standard floppy). Unlike ordinary floppy drives, the LS-120 uses an ATAPI IDE interface, so the drive can be installed alongside existing hard drives and CD-ROM drives. The standard 3.5-in form factor means that the LS-120 can be installed in any existing drive bay as a floppy disk replacement. In fact, you might not even notice the difference between a floppy drive and an LS-120 drive at first glance.

Diskette compatibility and cleaning

Since the LS-120 is designed to work with 120- and 1.44-MB diskettes, there is often some confusion as to how diskettes may be interchanged. Here are the basic rules for diskettes:

- The LS-120 may read and write 120-MB, 1.44-MB, and 720-KB diskettes. You may even format 1.44-MB and 720-KB diskettes on the LS-120 (although you may need the latest LS-120 driver to ensure compatibility).

- 1.44-MB and 720-KB diskettes *cannot* be formatted to 120 MB in the LS-120 (only specially designed magneto-optical diskettes can work at 120 MB).

- LS-120 diskettes may *not* be read on 1.44-MB floppy drives—you *must* have an LS-120 drive in the system.

Imation (and other LS-120 clone makers) generally recommends that the drive heads be cleaned after 40 to 80 h of operation, depending on the cleanliness of the operating environment. As with floppy drive head cleaning, this regular maintenance offers an easy, practical, and thorough method for safely removing error-causing dust and debris from magnetic recording heads. As a rule, you should use a head cleaning kit designed specifically for an LS-120 drive. Ordinary floppy head cleaning disks can be too abrasive for an LS-120.

LS-120 Drive Installation and Replacement

The LS-120 drive offers higher storage capacities and faster performance, as well as bootable operation. However, you'll need to verify several important elements of your PC before installation can begin. As a minimum, you should check the following points.

Computer power. The LS-120 drive typically requires a minimum of a 486/66-MHz processor, 8 MB of RAM, and 5 MB of free hard drive space. While modern PCs easily meet these requirements, older systems should be evaluated carefully before planning an LS-120 installation.

Power connections. A power supply offers only a limited number of drive power connectors. In small systems, there may not be a free drive power connector for another floppy drive. When this occurs, you may use a "Y" splitter cable to add another power connector. However, place the Y cable in with the existing floppy drive (never split power from critical drives such as the hard drive). If you're using the LS-120 to replace an existing floppy, just reuse the existing power connector.

Drive bay space. The trend toward smaller, low-profile enclosures has put a lot of pressure on available drive space, so one of the first problems when planning for a new LS-120 drive is to locate an external drive bay. If you do not have an external drive bay available, you may be able to move a hard drive to an internal drive bay. This relocates the hard drive and frees an external drive bay for the LS-120 drive. If you're using the LS-120 as a replacement for your existing floppy drive, it's a matter of removing the existing floppy drive, then installing the LS-120 in that drive space.

> **NOTE**: If you're planning to replace a floppy drive with the LS-120, be sure to copy the LS-120 driver diskette to your hard drive *before* removing the floppy drive.

Drive controller space. Remember that the LS-120 drive uses your hard drive controller rather than the floppy drive controller. This means that you'll need an open connector on either your primary or your secondary drive controller channel. If you do not have an available signal connector (e.g., if your system has two HDDs, a CD-ROM, and a DVD-ROM drive), you may not be able to install the LS-120 drive without removing one of those existing drives first. Also, the LS-120 requires the LBA (Logical Block Addressing) mode for proper operation, so your drive controller should be an EIDE or Ultra-DMA type. Also keep in mind that the LS-120 will *not* operate from a tertiary IDE controller such as the IDE controller integrated onto a sound card.

BIOS compatibility. If you plan to use the LS-120 as a secondary storage device and *not* as a bootable drive, you'll probably continue to use your existing floppy drive, and so no BIOS adjustments are needed—the LS-120 will be enabled *solely* by device drivers. If you plan to use the LS-120 as a bootable drive, remember that you'll need to check the BIOS for compatibility. The boot order in your CMOS Setup should include the option for an LS-120 drive (your BIOS may use another designator, such as UHD floppy, Floptical, Removable Drive, and so on). If your BIOS does not provide such support, you may need to upgrade the BIOS before installing the LS-120 drive. Once the drive is installed and the old floppy drive is removed, remember to disable the floppy controller and change the boot order so that the system will boot from the LS-120.

NOTE: IBM MicroChannel PCs do not support bootable LS-120 drives.

Typical installation

Installing an LS-120 drive is often a three-step process: configure the drive jumper(s), mount and cable the drive, and configure the new drive in CMOS. While most LS-120 installations are quick and painless procedures—even for a novice—there are a few nuances that you should be aware of. When followed carefully, this process can typically be completed in under 30 min. If you're replacing an existing floppy drive, remove the floppy drive and its cable first, then follow the procedures below.

NOTE: It's normally a good idea to perform a complete system backup of your hard drives before attempting any kind of drive work. While LS-120 installation should not affect your hard drives in any way, backups will protect your data and system configuration from accidental data loss.

NOTE: Turn the system off and unplug it from the ac receptacle before proceeding—this protects both the new device and your personal safety.

Prepare the system. Remove the screws holding down the outer cover, and place those screws in a safe place. Gently remove the PC's outer cover and set it aside (out of the path of normal floor traffic). You should now be able to look into the PC and observe the open drive bay, the motherboard, and any expansion boards and drives that are installed.

NOTE: Remember to use an antistatic wrist strap whenever you work inside a PC. This will prevent damage to the computer's delicate electronics caused by accidental static discharge.

Prepare the drive bay. Now that the outer cover has been removed, you should open the desired drive bay. This may be as simple as removing the plastic bezel covering an empty bay (the bezel will usually pop right out). If you must relocate an existing drive, things get a bit more complicated. First, decide where the drive (almost always a hard drive) will be relocated to— often an internal bay in the rear of the PC. You can then remove the mounting screws, disconnect the power and signal cables from the hard drive, and slide the hard drive out of the bay. Remount the hard drive in the internal bay, and gently secure each screw into place (be careful not to overtighten the screws). Reattach the power and signal cables to the hard drive. Pay particular attention when connecting the signal cable. If the cable is installed backward, the hard drive will not function. The red or blue stripe along one side of the ribbon cable always marks pin 1.

The procedure is a bit easier when you are replacing an existing floppy drive. Unbolt the existing drive, then disconnect the power and signal cables. Slide the old drive out of the bay and set it aside carefully. If you have a good-quality antistatic bag available, seal the old drive in the antistatic bag. Also remove the floppy drive cable from the system. At this point, you should have an open drive bay. Take a quick inventory and make sure that you have an available IDE signal cable and power connector available.

> **NOTE**: When using a Y splitter to tap power from another drive, *never* split power from a hard drive. This can cause erratic drive (and system) operation.

Set the LS-120 jumpers. In virtually all cases, the LS-120 drive will be connected as the slave device to an existing master device (e.g., a CD-ROM drive) on the secondary drive controller channel. Check the LS-120 jumpers and verify that it is configured as a slave device. If there are currently no devices on the secondary channel (e.g., the system has only one HDD and one CD-ROM, both on the primary channel), you may need to use the LS-120 jumpers to reconfigure the drive as a master device. This allows the LS-120 to exist by itself on the secondary channel. Of course, you should refer to the documentation enclosed with your LS-120 drive for specific jumper arrangements and cautions.

Mount the LS-120 drive.   Now that the LS-120 drive is configured, slide it gently into the open drive bay. Line up the four mounting holes, and screw the drive in carefully. Be sure not to tighten the mounting screws excessively—this can warp the drive's frame and cause R/W problems or premature drive failure. Make it a point to use screws of the proper size and length to do the job. If you're placing the LS-120 into a larger 5.25-in drive bay, be sure to premount the drive in its extended frame before sliding the complete assembly into the drive bay.

Connect power and signal cables.   Once the drive is installed and mounted securely, connect the power and signal cables as required. The 4-pin power cable is relatively foolproof because of its keyed shape. Take care, however, to install the 40-pin signal cable connector in the correct orientation—if the signal cable is installed backward, the drive will not work (the system may not even boot). The red or blue stripe along one side of the ribbon cable always represents pin 1. As long as the drive is jumpered properly, you may place the LS-120 in either the middle or the endmost IDE connector. *Do not use the floppy drive signal cable.*

Update CMOS settings.   If you're using the LS-120 as a supplemental drive rather than a bootable drive (and the old floppy is still in place), skip this step. Otherwise, you must update the system CMOS entries to accommodate the new drive. Make sure that any tools or extra hardware are removed from the system, reattach the ac cord to the power supply, then reboot the computer. As the system boots, start the CMOS Setup routine and adjust the configuration as needed to disable the old floppy drive *and* floppy controller. Check to make sure that the LS-120 drive is identified properly along with your other IDE drive devices. Also configure the boot order to select the LS-120 as the first boot device. With the floppy drive removed and the LS-120 set as a boot device, the LS-120 should become the new A: drive. When the settings are correct, save the system CMOS and reboot the system so that your changes can take effect.

Test the drive. To test for bootability, insert a blank disk into the LS-120 and restart the PC. If you get a *non-system disk* error, the system has tried to boot from the LS-120. Now try booting the system from a known-good bootable disk—you should wind up at the A: command prompt. Try writing a few files to and reading them from the drive. You might also try for-matting a blank diskette in the new drive. If these tests are successful, you can be confident that the new drive is working properly. Be sure to remove any tools or hardware from the system, then reinstall the sys-tem's outer housings. Do not use excessive pressure to tighten the screws.

Driver installation

You do not need separate drivers when you are using the LS-120 under Windows 98, Windows 95 (OSR2), Windows NT 4.0, or Windows NT 3.51 with Service Pack 5 (SPS). These operating systems automatically detect your LS-120 drive. The drive shows up as the logical A: drive (3.5-in floppy) under *My Computer*. If you have other peripheral devices such as hard drives or CD-ROMs, they are automatically assigned the next available drive letter. If your operating system is Windows NT 4.0 or NT 3.51 (with SP5), you do not need to change your system settings. However, you *will* need drivers under DOS, Windows 3.1/3.11, Windows NT 3.51 (without SP5), and Windows 95/95A.

> **NOTE**: Since it's normal for LS-120 installation to shift your CD-ROM (and other drive) letter, you may have trouble running certain applications that expect to see the original drive letter. You may need to simply reinstall those applications.

DOS/Windows 3.1x installation

- For Windows 3.1x, select the *Run* option. Enter the path to the LS-120 drivers (i.e., `a:\install` or `c:\temp\install`) and press <Enter>.

- After the installer starts, select *Express Install* for the quickest installation process, then press <Enter>.

- Remove the driver diskette (if you used one) and reboot the PC.

- The system modifies your CONFIG.SYS file and saves a backup of the original file. Your system displays this message to verify the installation:

```
ID 2: LS-120 Ver 4 420 Direct Access Device (remov-
able)

ID 2 Drive Letter is D LS-120

LS-120 driver(s) connected

LS-120 driver installed
```

- If these messages do not appear, check your operating system type and version and then reinstall the device driver.

Windows 95/95A/NT 3.51 (without SP5) installation

- Click *Start* and select *Run*. Enter the path to the LS-120 drivers (i.e., `a:\setup` or `c:\temp\setup`) and press <Enter>.

- A menu-driven installation program guides you through the installation process. This process automatically updates the system's registry with the appropriate drivers.

- When the installation process is complete, remove the driver diskette (if you used one) and reboot the PC.

Windows NT 4.0/NT 3.51 (with SP5) installation

- From the *Control Panel*, double-click the *System* icon and then click *Device Manager*. A list of all the drivers used by the system appears.

- Select the ATAPI device driver and change its setting to *Started at boot*.

- Restart your computer. The LS-120 drive is now recognized as the logical A: or B: drive within *My Computer*.

  NOTE: For new NT installations, install the LS-120 drive *before* installing Windows NT. As you install Windows NT, your system automatically identifies the LS-120 drive and loads the appropriate drivers. After you restart your computer, the system recognizes the LS-120 drive as the logical A: or B: drive.

Uninstalling the device driver. When you remove the LS-120 drive, you'll also need to remove the drivers that accompany it. This is not a problem under Windows 98 and other newer operating systems, but you'll need to address the issue manually under Windows 95 and DOS.

- Under Windows 95, restart the SETUP.EXE installation program and check the *Uninstall SuperDisk Device Driver & Utility* button. Run the deinstallation process as you would an installation as described above.

- Under DOS or Windows 3.1x, search for the lines c:\atlas\atapimgr.sys **and** c:\atlas\

`mkels120.sys`) in the CONFIG.SYS file (and REMark out these lines everywhere they occur. Then reboot the system.

Changing the LS-120 drive letter. There may be times when it's necessary for you to change the LS-120 drive letter from its default setting. Follow the steps below to adjust the drive letter:

- Click *Start*, select *Settings*, then click *Control Panel*.
- In the *Control Panel*, double-click the *System* icon.
- Click on the *Device Manager* tab.
- Click on *Disk Drives*, and then double-click on the *LS-120* drive.
- Click on *Settings*, and set the desired drive letter.
- Restart your computer when prompted.

LS-120 Considerations and Issues

Ideally, you should be able to install and boot from an LS-120 drive with an absolute minimum of fuss. But the LS-120 is a relatively new class of bootable drive, and a system must meet several minimum requirements in order to support the drive. There are also several potential system compatibility problems that you should be aware of.

Booting and system BIOS

Perhaps the most interesting aspect of the LS-120 is that it's bootable in both 120- and 1.44-MB modes, so you can boot from either size of diskette. However, you'll need a motherboard or drive controller BIOS which is designed to accommodate the LS-120 (you'll see *LS-120* as a boot option in the CMOS Setup *Boot Order* entry). If your BIOS does not recognize the LS-120, you may need to upgrade the BIOS. The following three BIOS versions are known to support LS-120 technology:

- Award BIOS version 4.51PG or later
- AMI BIOS version 6.26.02 or later
- Phoenix BIOS version 6.0 or later

Booting and operating systems

While the LS-120 will work in DOS and in all versions of Windows and Windows 95, only Windows 95 release B (4.00.950B) and later will treat the LS-120 as bootable. All other versions of Windows 95 support the drive only as a removable and nonbootable disk which will not be assigned drive letter A: or B:. Make sure the LS-120 disk has been formatted to be bootable—this will be available as a check box item when formatting in Windows 95, or as a command line switch when formatting from a DOS prompt (adding the traditional /S switch to the Format command line. As an example, if you are formatting the A: drive (which is your LS-120) to be bootable, type

```
FORMAT A: /S
```

Also, although the LS-120 does work under Windows NT, there are several things you must pay particular attention to during installation. NT 4.0 and NT 3.51 (with Service Pack 5) have built-in support for the LS-120 and require no special drivers. Other versions of NT require running the SETUP.EXE utility from the WINDOWS directory on the LS-120 driver diskette. Remember to have the ATAPI service set to *enabled at boot*.

Compatibility with system manufacturers

You may encounter problems installing the retail version of an LS-120 drive on some systems built by major system houses such as Packard Bell or Compaq. Many major system houses use their own OEM version of the LS-120, which must be installed instead of the retail version. If you encounter such difficulties, check in with Technical Support for the system manufacturer and see if there are any known problems with retail LS-120 compatibility.

Compatibility with system utilities

The LS-120 is not fully compatible with all system utilities, most notably antivirus programs, some backup software, and drive utilities such as Norton Utilities. When the LS-120 is installed with such software, the drive (or the software) may fail to function normally. If you encounter read/write difficulties while using any such system utilities, try disabling or temporarily uninstalling them to determine if the problem goes away.

LS-120 device conflicts

Although the LS-120 is an IDE device, it is known to experience problems when installed in conjunction with certain other device configurations. In most cases, the LS-120 (or the other IDE device on the ribbon cable) may not be detected. This type of problem is usually fixed by reversing the drive positions on the ribbon cable or reversing the master/slave jumper relationship of the two devices.

For example, if your LS-120 is connected to the secondary IDE port and jumpered as the master device, an IDE CD-ROM is also connected to the secondary IDE port as a slave device, and now the CD-ROM is not functioning properly, change the jumpering on the two devices so that the LS-120 is the slave and the CD-ROM is the master.

In other cases, the LS-120 drive is not seen on the secondary IDE port regardless of the jumper settings. This is often because the motherboard chipset is not recognized properly by Windows 95, and so the secondary IDE port is left disabled. If the IDE port you are connecting to is listed in the Device Manager as a *Standard ESDI/IDE Port*, you'll need to contact your motherboard maker for the updated .INF file for Windows 95. If your motherboard uses an Intel chipset, you can go to Intel's Developer page, and search for the .INF file to update Windows 95. The URL for the Intel Developer site is *http://developer.intel.com/design/motherbd/ideinfup.htm*.

Finally, the LS-120 may be misidentified as a CD-ROM by the BIOS during system boot. If this occurs, you'll need to update your system BIOS from the system maker or motherboard manufacturer. Ideally, the drive should be identified as an *LS-120* or *UHD Floppy* (ultra-high density).

Drive overlay software

There are numerous types of drive overlay software in use today, such as Disk Manager, EZ-Drive, MaxBlast, and more. This overlay software is used to partition and prepare hard drives when the system BIOS will not support the drive's full size. In actual practice, overlay software can also affect other IDE drives (such as the LS-120) and result in performance problems.

If you're having trouble using the LS-120 and there is drive overlay software installed on the hard drive, you may need to remove the overlay software from the hard drive. If your system hardware will not support the full size of a given hard drive, you may need to upgrade the system BIOS or drive controller BIOS first in order to accommodate the drive. Then you can remove the overlay software.

> **NOTE**: Removing the overlay software will normally require you to change the drive geometry in the CMOS Setup, then repartition and reformat the drive completely, using FDISK and FORMAT. Be sure to perform a complete system backup before attempting to remove the overlay software.

**Driver support under Windows
95 A**

There have been reports of the A version of Windows
95 indicating that driver support for the LS-120 is
already available, when in fact it is not. This is almost
always because some utility program(s) installed *after*
Windows 95 has changed the dates of certain files from
your original Windows 95 installation or has changed
the generic IDE driver for Windows 95 to a newer one
in order to support another piece of hardware you have
installed. To fix this, you will need to use the REGED-
IT utility located in your Windows directory.

> **NOTE**: Improper editing of your Registry can make
> your system fail to boot, result in a loss of data, or force
> you to reinstall Windows 95. Changes should be made
> *only* under the direction of an experienced technician or
> someone experienced at editing the Registry. Be sure to
> make a backup copy of your Registry files before pro-
> ceeding.

Find the following section in your Registry:

```
HKey_Local_Machine\System\CurrentControlSet\
Services\Class\HDC
```

Find the entries under this section which refer to
ATAPI.MPD. Change all ATAPI.MPD entries to
ESDI_506.PDR. Exit your Registry editor and save
your changes. If you have problems restarting
Windows 95 after editing the Registry, you can always
reboot from a rescue diskette and reload your backup
copy of the Registry.

LS-120 Troubleshooting

**Symptom 3.1: After installing a parallel-port LS-120 drive,
you cannot access programs protected by a parallel-port
hardware key (a "dongle").** This is almost always a limitation of the dongle itself. Those hardware keys must

generally be connected to the parallel port *first*, then other parallel-port devices can be added. If the LS-120 drive is installed before the dongle, the dongle may not respond properly, and software that uses it may refuse to work. Try connecting the dongle first.

Symptom 3.2: You cannot boot from the LS-120 drive using a DOS 6.22, Windows 95, or Windows 95A (OSR1) boot diskette. In order to boot from an LS-120 device, both your operating system and your motherboard BIOS must support the LS-120.

- *Check your operating system.* Only Windows 98, Windows 95 (OSR2), and Windows NT 4.0 allow you to boot from either a 1.44-MB or 120-MB diskette. If your operating system is too old to support the LS-120 as a boot device, you'll need to upgrade your operating system.

- *Check the CMOS settings.* Examine the available options under your boot order. If you see an option such as SuperDisk, Floptical, LS-120, UHD Floppy, Removable Device, or Removable Drive, be sure to select that device as the first drive in your boot order. If no such entry is available, your BIOS may not fully support the LS-120 drive as a boot device, and a BIOS upgrade may be in order. If you cannot obtain a BIOS upgrade from the original system or motherboard maker, you can probably obtain a suitable upgrade from Unicore at *http://www.uni-core.com* or 800-800-BIOS.

Symptom 3.3: After you install an LS-120 drive, your CD-ROM (or other IDE-type device) does not work properly. There are a number of typical installation issues which may cause the new LS-120 drive to interfere with your existing drive(s).

- *Check your drive jumpers.* One drive must be set as the master device, and the other must be set as the slave device. Make sure that the drives are not both set the same way, or try reversing the master/slave relationship.

- *Check the signal cable*. Verify that the LS-120 is cabled properly. The signal cable should be secure and inserted in the proper orientation.

- *Try a different channel*. In a few cases, the LS-120 drive may not be compatible with the other drive on that same channel. You might try moving the drive to a different IDE channel or disconnecting the other drive from that channel to see if the LS-120 drive will operate normally by itself. If it will, you might want to replace that drive with one from another manufacturer.

Symptom 3.4: After installing the LS-120 device drivers, you can no longer play music CDs. This is a problem that sometimes occurs when the LS-120 drivers do not interact properly with the CD-ROM drivers. In many cases, this type of problem can be corrected by updating both the LS-120 and CD-ROM drives to their very latest protected-mode (Windows 95/98) drivers.

Symptom 3.5: The installation program aborts after stating that your system already has support for the LS-120. When running a SETUP.EXE program to install the LS-120 device drivers, you find an error message stating that your system already has support for the drive. The installation program then aborts without finishing the installation, but your LS-120 drive does not work. This can occur because the last step performed by the installation program is to look at the date stamp of the ESDI_506.PDR file. If the file is *newer* than July 1995, the installation program aborts. Edit the registry to change that entry from ESDI_506.PDR to ATAPI.MPD. Once you're renamed that entry, the setup program should operate normally and complete your installation.

Symptom 3.6: The CD-ROM drive letter shifts after the LS-120 drive is installed. For example, the CD-ROM was D:, but after installation of the LS-120, the LS-120 is now D: and the CD-ROM is E:. This is normal if the LS-120 drive is *not* made bootable (A:) in the CMOS Setup. When the LS-120 is not bootable, the LS-120 drivers are typically loaded first and take precedence over the CD-ROM when drive letters are assigned.

This is normal—do *not* try to reverse the CD-ROM and LS-120 drive letters (although you can do this through the drive's *Properties* dialogs under Windows). Doing so may cause one or both of the drives to be unreadable. If you have installed something from CD-ROM and it will not run now, try reinstalling the application on top of the older installation, so that it updates the drive letter for the new configuration.

Symptom 3.7: The LS-120 drive letter is greater than C:, but you cannot boot from the LS-120 because the floppy drive (which you removed from the system) still appears as A:. There are several important oversights that may account for this type of problem.

- *Check the CMOS settings*. Make sure that you have altered the boot order in your CMOS Setup so that the LS-120 drive is selected as the first boot device.

- *Upgrade the BIOS*. If you find that the LS-120 (or another similar entry such as UHD floppy or Floptical) drive is not listed among your available boot options, you may need to update your motherboard's BIOS and then adjust the boot order as outlined above.

- *Replace the floppy drive*. As an interim measure, you can replace the floppy drive A: so that you can boot from a diskette.

Symptom 3.8: After physical installation of the LS-120 drive, it is not detected as an ATAPI IDE device. This problem frequently occurs when trying to install the

LS-120 with an older drive controller. The LS-120 requires LBA (Logical Block Addressing)—the same mode used for newer hard drives. This requires an EIDE or newer Ultra-DMA drive controller. In some cases, you may be able to upgrade the system BIOS to enable the existing drive controller to support the LBA mode. If this is not possible, you may need to replace the existing drive controller with a newer drive controller card (incorporating its own on-board BIOS).

Symptom 3.9: After plugging in the USB LS-120 drive, you don't see an icon appear on the desktop. There are several possible reasons why the LS-120 drive might not appear after USB connection is made:

- Make sure that there is a properly formatted LS-120 diskette in the drive.

- Make sure you are using the cables that came with the drive, and see that all cables are securely connected.

- Make sure the computer and drive *both* have power (or that the USB hub controlling the drive is powered).

If problems persist, eject the diskette and power down the drive. Unplug and reseat the USB connection on the drive end. Plug the drive back into the power source (or hub), reconnect the USB cable at the computer end, and reinsert the diskette into the drive. If you still cannot get the USB LS-120 drive to work, try another drive.

Symptom 3.10: You disconnected the LS-120 drive while the PC was in suspend ("sleep") mode, and now it doesn't work right after connecting it to another PC. In virtually all cases, the LS-120 disk may be corrupted. You cannot disconnect the drive or eject the disk while there are still files opened on the LS-120 diskette. If there were files open when you disconnected the drive, the file (and perhaps the entire disk) may be corrupted. Try rebooting the PC and see if you can access any of the files on the disk.

Symptom 3.11: When copying files to/from a USB LS-120 drive, the computer froze when you disconnected the cable. Even though USB devices are physically "hot pluggable," they cannot be connected or disconnected while data transfer is taking place. The USB device must be idle before it's disconnected. In the future, be sure that the LS-120 drive's activity LED is out before disconnecting the USB cable.

Symptom 3.12: You cannot format a 1.44-MB diskette in an LS-120 drive. Virtually all LS-120 drives should be able to format older 720-KB and 1.44-MB diskettes. If you cannot get the diskette to format properly, chances are that you're using an older SuperDisk driver. For the Imation SuperDisk LS-120, you need driver version 1.2.5 or later. Check with the LS-120 drive maker to see if there's a driver patch or update available for download.

Symptom 3.13: You cannot format a 1.44-MB diskette in an LS-120 drive on a Windows NT platform. This is almost always caused by a problem with NT 4.0 using Service Pack 3. There are several possible solutions to this problem:

- Replace the ATAPI.SYS driver from Service Pack 2 (follow the procedure outlined in Microsoft's Knowledge Base article Q170572).

- Install Microsoft Post SP3 hot fixes (ATA-FIXI.EXE and IDE-FIXI.EXE), available from *ftp://ftp. microsoft.com/bussys/winnt/winnt-public/fixes/ usa/nt40/hotfixes-postSP3/*.

- Upgrade your version of Windows NT to Service Pack 4.

Symptom 3.14: You find one or more phantom drives with the LS-120. A "phantom drive" is a condition in which an extra drive designation appears, but neither the drive you are accessing nor the extra drive is readable.

- *Check your drivers.* You may be loading the driver for the LS-120 in DOS, as well as a DOS CD-ROM driver. If this is the case, REM out the line loading MSCDEX in your AUTOEXEC.BAT file. You may also need to manually set the drive letter for the CD-ROM in the *Device Manager*.

- *Check the CMOS settings.* If you removed your A: drive (intending to use your LS-120 as your boot drive), but now you have a "removable disk" *and* a floppy drive that doesn't display in *My Computer* (or the Device Manager), the problem is likely to be that your CMOS Setup still has a drive type set for drive A:. If the LS-120 is *replacing* your old A: drive, set the DRIVE TYPE for drive A: to *none* or *not installed*. If the phantom drive still appears, make sure you have enabled the option to boot from the LS-120 drive.

Symptom 3.15: You cannot read or format LS-120 media. This happens most frequently under Windows 3.1x and the initial release (the A version) of Windows 95. In this case, you probably need to have the DOS version of the LS-120 driver installed. Run the LS-120 setup disk from a DOS window and install the DOS driver support.

> **NOTE**: If you are using the B version of Windows 95, do *not* load the DOS driver support for the LS-120 (i.e., LS120.SYS). This DOS driver active in the background can cause data corruption.

This is also a known problem on some platforms which use the FMTLS120.EXE utility included with the Imation LS-120 SuperDisk drive. Do *not* use this utility—remove it from the system. Use the standard

DOS or Windows FORMAT function. Media formatted with the FMTLS120 utility may be corrupt and unrecoverable.

Symptom 3.16: You find that the LS-120 drive is running very slowly when using Windows 98. The LS-120 is supported natively under Windows 98, but you may need to make some changes to the disk setup. Right-click on *My Computer*, then select *Control Panel*, then *System*. The *System Properties* dialog will appear. Select the *Performance* tab, and click on the *File System* button. You should then see a *Removable Disk* tab. Select that tab, then enable *Write-Behind caching on all removable drives*. Restart the PC if necessary. Intermittent slowdowns may indicate a dirty drive. Use a disk cleaning kit certified for LS-120 drives to clean your LS-120 read/write heads.

Symptom 3.17: The LS-120 drive is running in the DOS compatibility mode. You'll need some new drivers to overcome this problem. Go to the Web site *http://support.microsoft.com/support/downloads* and download the files REMIDEUP.EXE and IOSUPD.EXE. After you install these new files, the LS-120 drive should be able to run in protected mode.

Symptom 3.18: The LS-120 drive's LED is constantly on after inserting a new diskette in the drive. This almost always means that the LS-120 diskette is damaged. Carefully eject the diskette and insert a new LS-120 diskette into the drive. If the new diskette works properly, the diskette that you removed should be reformatted or discarded.

Symptom 3.19: The LS-120's drive power indicator never flashes, or it remains lit continuously. This almost always means a problem with the drive's connections to your system. If the power LED *never* comes on at all, chances are that the drive is not receiving power.

Check the 4-pin power connector to the LS-120 drive. Reseat the power connector securely if necessary. If the power LED remains on *continuously*, it probably means that there's a problem with the signal cable— one end of the cable may be reversed or loose. Verify that the IDE cable is oriented properly, and see that it's secure. Reseat the signal cable (or try a new signal cable) if necessary.

Symptom 3.20: After installing the LS-120 drive, you find that the drive isn't responding and has no icon under Windows. There are several possible issues for you to consider:

- *Check the desktop*. The icon may simply be hidden— this is a common oversight. Auto-arranging the icons on your desktop should reveal any icons that may have been hidden under other icons.

- *Check the physical installation*. The drive may not be installed properly. Recheck the power and signal cables attached to the drive. See that they're secure and oriented properly. Also verify that the IDE port you've installed the LS-120 drive on is enabled (you can usually enable an IDE port through the CMOS Setup). If there was another device on the same IDE channel, you may wish to temporarily disconnect that device and try the LS-120 drive by itself, or to move the LS-120 drive to another IDE channel.

- *Update your bus mastering drivers*. Bus mastering can adversely affect the LS-120 drive. If you're using bus mastering, obtain and install the updated drivers for your system. If you cannot locate updated bus-mastering drivers, use Microsoft's default drivers. Get the READIMDE.EXE file from *ftp://ftp.microsoft.com/bussys/winnt/winnnt-public/fixes/usa/hotfixes-postSP3*.

Symptom 3.21: The system crashes with "blue screen" errors each time the LS-120 drive is accessed. This is a known problem when using antivirus software. If you're running McAfee's VirusScan software (or other antivirus software), disable the *Scan Floppies on Access* option, or any removable disk option which scans the LS-120 drive. This scanning process takes a great deal of time and can seriously bog down the drive's performance.

Symptom 3.22: When copying large files, the copy process is eventually interrupted with a "blue screen error." In virtually all cases, this indicates a defective diskette. The error occurs when the copy process encounters bad sectors on the 120-MB diskette. Try a new or known-good diskette to see if the problem goes away. If you find that the 120-MB diskette is bad, you may be able to run ScanDisk (in the media test mode) in an effort to map out the bad sectors—this may make the bad diskette usable again, although its reliability cannot be guaranteed.

This may also be an operating system problem. If you're using an older version of Windows 95 (the original release or OSR1 version), you'll need to install the latest device drivers for the LS-120 drive so that Windows 95 will support the LS-120 properly.

Symptom 3.23: A diskette is stuck in the LS-120 drive. This can happen on rare occasions when a poorly made diskette fails, or when foreign matter interferes with the disk eject mechanism. Carefully insert a pin or paper clip into the emergency eject hole, located on the Eject button. Press the pin or clip in the hole gently until the diskette ejects from the slot. You can then replace the diskette or clean the drive as necessary.

Symptom 3.24: You encounter *insufficient disk* space messages when using an LS-120 disk. You may also see this kind of problem with an error such as *cannot create file or folder*. An LS-120 disk will hold up to 120 MB of files, so disk space warnings often mean either that the disk is full or that there are too many files in the disk's directory.

- *Check the free space*. The first thing to do is to verify that there is adequate free space left on the LS-120 disk. If the disk has been used previously, it may already contain files that take up a considerable amount of space. If there are already files on the disk, use a fresh disk or delete unneeded files from the disk.

- *Check the file count*. Note the number of files listed in the root directory. FAT-based file systems impose a limit of 253 files in the root directory. If there are already 253+ files in the root directory, try creating subdirectories on the disk and storing additional files there, or use a fresh LS-120 disk.

Symptom 3.25: You find that you cannot "quick format" an LS-120 disk under Windows 95/98. This is a common problem when using an LS-120 drive under Windows. Windows 95 and Windows 98 do not natively support the LS-120's "quick format" option. Right-click on your LS-120 drive icon and select the *format* option to perform a full format. After the first diskette has been fully formatted, subsequent "quick formats" should work fine.

Symptom 3.26: You cannot use the DiskCopy command with an LS-120 drive. This is a known limitation of the DOS DiskCopy command—it will not support disks larger than 32 MB. If you need to copy 120-MB disks, use the utility suite that accompanied your LS-120 drive.

Symptom 3.27: Microsoft Backup does not eject the first LS-120 diskette when asking for the second diskette. This is a known issue with older versions of Microsoft Backup under Windows 95. You should upgrade to Windows 98 (or switch to a new third-party backup utility), which will properly support the LS-120 as a removable-medium drive.

Symptom 3.28: You cannot use Microsoft Backup to back up to an LS-120 drive. Although Microsoft Backup *will* work with an LS-120 drive, the software does not support diskettes larger than 32 MB. Microsoft will probably address the Backup issue in its next release of the utility. In the meantime, Imation has a software toolkit for the LS-120 drive. The SuperDisk Tools Kit is available from *http://store.imation.com* and includes the following utilities:

- CA Backup for fast and easy data protection

- CA InnocuLAN Anti-Virus to protect your files with virus detection

- Disk Consolidator, which combines multiple 3.5-in diskettes on a single 120-MB diskette

- Copy Disk to duplicate LS-120 diskettes

> **NOTE**: NovaStor offers a downloadable trial version of its NovaDisk backup program, which works flawlessly with LS-120-MB diskettes. You can obtain the program directly from NovaStar's Internet site at *http://www.novastor.com*.

Web Contacts

Imation: *http://www.imation.com*

Iomega Zip Drives

In order for removable media to be popular, they must have three basic characteristics: They must record quickly, they must hold a lot of data on a single cartridge (or other medium), and they must be portable between drives. Floppy disks are very portable, but they hold only a little data. Tapes hold a lot of data, but they are slow and are not very portable between drives. Hard drives are quite fast and hold a great deal of data, but they are simply not portable. CD-ROM drives are relatively fast, they hold a lot of data, and the CDs themselves are very portable, but you need specialized drives to "burn" a CD, and the disk can be used only once. The search for reusable, high-capacity media that are transportable between inexpensive, readily available drives has led Iomega to produce its Zip drive.

The Zip drive has become perhaps the single most popular nonstandard drive in production today—in fact, the Zip drive is so popular that some PC makers include it as standard equipment in new systems. Zip drives offer relatively fast seek times (29 ms) and can sustain data rates of 300 KB/s across the parallel port (or 1 MB/s via SCSI or IDE interfaces). Each cartridge can hold up to 100 MB (up to 250 MB in recent drive

versions), which is large enough to hold huge illustra-
tions, CAD layouts, and even small multimedia
presentations. When Zip drive is used with an SCSI
interface and a properly configured Adaptec SCSI controller, you may even boot your system from it. Zip
drives are available in both internal ATAPI and SCSI
versions, as well as external parallel-port and USB
versions. This chapter offers some installation guidelines for Zip drives, provides some tips for using them
most effectively, and covers a collection of troubleshooting procedures.

Zip Drive Installation and Replacement

Zip drives are generally not too difficult to install, but
there are some important guidelines that may help you
avoid possible problems. This part of the chapter highlights the installation sequence for parallel-port, USB-
port, and ATAPI IDE drives.

Parallel port

- Unpack the Zip drive and verify that all of the software and accessories are in the box.

- Turn off the computer and all of its peripherals.

- Connect the cable between the Zip drive and the
  computer's parallel port. Secure the cable but do not
  overtighten it. If there is a printer connected to the
  parallel port, disconnect it now.

- Connect the drive's power supply.

  NOTE: You can use a universal power supply—the supply included with your Zip drive can be used worldwide.
  It works at any voltage from 100 to 240 V. All you need
  is the appropriate plug adapter.

- Power up the Zip drive.

  NOTE: When you want to power down your Zip drive,
  first eject any disk from the drive, then push the power
  button to power down the drive.

- Boot the PC and allow Windows to fully load.

- After Windows starts, place the Zip software CD in the CD-ROM drive—the Setup program should start automatically. If you don't have a CD-ROM drive, you can download and install the software from the Iomega Web site.

- Follow the instructions to complete the software's installation. You'll need to restart the PC (and the Setup utility) to finish the installation.

  NOTE: You'll see a Guest window that allows you to choose the drive letters you want to use for your Zip drive (and other removable drives). If installing the Zip drive causes your CD-ROM drive letter to change, you should change it back; this prevents your having to reinstall applications or games.

- As an option, you may run the Iomega Parallel Port Accelerator utility, which can help to optimize the data transfer rate for your drive.

- If you have a printer, you can try connecting it to the Zip drive using a standard printer cable.

- This completes the general installation of a parallel-port Zip drive.

USB port

- Unpack the Zip drive and verify that all of the software and accessories are in the box.

- Boot the PC and allow Windows 98 to fully load. You *must* be using Windows 98 for proper USB support.

- After Windows 98 starts, place the Zip software CD in the CD-ROM drive—the Setup program should start automatically. If you don't have a CD-ROM drive, you may be able to download and install the software from the Iomega Web site.

- Follow the instructions to complete the software's installation. You'll need to restart the PC (and the Setup utility) to finish the installation.

NOTE: You'll be installing the drivers *before* connecting your USB Zip drive—this is typical of many USB devices.

- Connect the USB cable between the Zip drive and the computer's USB port. Do *not* use USB extension cables with the Zip drive—data loss may result.

- Connect the drive's power supply. Although USB is supposed to supply power to many devices, high-power devices such as drives require the use of a supplemental power supply. The drive's power LED will come on.

  NOTE: You can use a universal power supply—the supply included with your Zip drive can be used worldwide. It works at any voltage from 100 to 240 V. All you need is the appropriate plug adapter.

- Insert a new Zip disk into the drive. You will see the Zip drive icon in *My Computer* or Windows Explorer. Double-click on the Zip drive icon to access your Zip disk.

- This completes the general installation of a USB port Zip drive.

ATAPI IDE port

- Evaluate your system requirements. You'll need an empty 3.5- or 5.25-in drive bay and an open position on your primary or secondary hard-drive controller (preferably EIDE or later) in order to support an internal ATAPI IDE Zip drive.

  NOTE: A Zip drive meets the latest ATAPI specifications. However, some computers with early ATAPI support may not meet these specifications and may not work correctly with removable ATAPI drives like the Zip. If the computer locks up or fails to boot correctly after the Zip drive is installed, you may need to update your system BIOS and/or drive controller to a later model.

- Unpack the Zip drive and verify that all of the software and accessories are in the box.

- Turn off and unplug the computer, then remove the outer cover. On some computers (especially tower models), you may need to remove a plastic face plate as well in order to access an available drive bay.

- Identify your drive configuration. Examine the drive(s) currently connected to your primary and secondary hard-drive controller ports. Based on the current configuration, you can decide on the best way to install and configure the new Zip drive.

  - If your hard drive and CD-ROM are connected to different controller channels, try installing the Zip drive as the slave drive on the secondary drive controller port.

  - If your hard drive and CD-ROM are connected to the same controller channel, try installing the Zip drive as the master drive on the secondary drive controller port.

- Locate your secondary IDE connector. Find the wide, flat ribbon cable on the back of the CD-ROM and follow it. If the cable also connects to a hard drive, follow the cable back to the motherboard's connector (usually marked "pri IDE"), then locate the secondary drive controller (often marked "sec IDE"). If the cable does *not* also connect to the hard drive, follow the cable back to the motherboard's connector (which is often the secondary controller).

Installing the Zip as a slave device

- Check the jumpers. The Zip drive is configured as the slave device by default—this makes it the second device on the secondary drive controller channel. Double-check to verify that the drive is jumpered as slave. Also verify that the jumper on the first (master) device is in fact set to master.

- Locate an available drive bay. Select a 5.25- or 3.5-in drive bay to install the Zip drive. If you select a 3.5-in bay, you may need to remove the Zip drive's mounting rails. Since there is a limited amount of cable length between the first (master) drive and the Zip drive, try selecting a drive bay as close as possible to the master device (i.e., the CD-ROM drive).

- Insert the drive into a drive bay. Be sure that the drive is level and oriented properly.

- Remove the original IDE cable. Locate the wide ribbon cable attached between the first (master) device and the drive controller. Note the orientation of pin 1 (the red or blue stripe in the cable), then disconnect the cable from the drive and controller, and set the cable aside.

- Connect the new IDE cable. Use the new IDE cable, and connect the long end (the end furthest from the middle connector on the cable) to the secondary IDE port on the motherboard. Connect the middle connector to the first drive (i.e., the CD-ROM), and then connect the other end of the cable to the Zip drive. Be sure to verify the orientation of the cable.

- Connect power to the Zip drive. Locate an available drive power connector from the power supply and connect it securely to the Zip drive.

- Bolt down the Zip drive. Use the original mounting screws, and bolt the Zip drive into place. Do *not* overtighten the screws.

- Recheck the cables to be sure that nothing has been accidentally loosened, then reattach the computer's outer cover.

- Reconnect the ac power cord, turn the PC on, and allow Windows to load.

- After Windows starts, place the Zip software CD in the CD-ROM drive—the Setup program should start automatically. If you don't have a CD-ROM drive, you may be able to download and install the software from the Iomega Web site.

- Follow the instructions to complete the driver and utility software installation. You'll need to restart the PC (and the Setup utility) to finish the installation.

Installing the Zip as a master device

- Check the jumpers. The Zip drive is configured as the slave device by default—this normally makes it the second device on the secondary drive controller channel. Set the jumper so that the Zip drive is configured as the master device.

- Locate an available drive bay. Select a 5.25- or 3.5-in drive bay to install the Zip drive. If you select a 3.5-in bay, you may need to remove the Zip drive's mounting rails. Since there is a limited amount of cable length between the controller and the Zip drive, try selecting a drive bay as close as possible to the drive controller.

- Insert the drive into a drive bay. Be sure that the drive is level and oriented properly.

- Connect the new IDE cable. Use the new IDE cable, and connect the long end (the end furthest from the middle connector on the cable) to the secondary IDE port on the motherboard. Connect the other end of the connector to the Zip. Be sure to verify the orientation of the cable so that pin 1 (the blue or red stripe) is aligned with pin 1 on the drive and controller.

- Connect power to the Zip drive. Locate an available drive power connector from the power supply, and connect it securely to the Zip drive.

- Bolt down the Zip drive. Use the original mounting screws, and bolt the Zip drive into place. Do *not* overtighten the screws.

- Recheck the cables to be sure that nothing has been accidentally loosened, then reattach the computer's outer cover.

- Reconnect the ac power cord, turn the PC on, and allow Windows to load.

- After Windows starts, place the Zip software CD in the CD-ROM drive—the Setup program should start automatically. If you don't have a CD-ROM drive, you may be able to download and install the software from the Iomega Web site.

- Follow the instructions to complete the driver and utility software installation. You'll need to restart the PC (and the Setup utility) to finish the installation.

Getting the most from your Zip drive

The Zip drive is generally simple and straightforward to use, but if you're new to the Zip drive family, this part of the chapter covers some important nuances that you should be familiar with in order to achieve best operation from the drive.

Accessing a Zip drive.   To use the Zip drive, insert a Zip disk, then select the drive letter assigned to the Zip drive in *My Computer* (Windows 95/98 or Windows NT 4.0) or *File Manager* (Windows NT 3.51 or Windows 3.1). You can now read, write, or copy files to and from the Zip drive using the same techniques used with other drives on your system.

> **NOTE**: The green Power/Eject button will flash when the Zip drive is transferring data or when a Zip disk is inserted or ejected.

Inserting a Zip disk.   Push the disk gently into the drive slot, as you would insert a floppy disk. The green activity light will flash momentarily, then glow continuously. If the activity light continues to blink slowly, push the Eject button to eject the Zip disk, then reinsert it carefully. Remember that drive power should be connected before you insert a Zip disk.

Ejecting a Zip disk. There are two general means of ejecting a Zip disk: use the Eject button, or use the Iomega software *Eject* command. Remember that you should remove a Zip disk when the drive is not in use and remove a disk *before* disconnecting power or moving the Zip drive. If you need to remove a disk during a power failure, disconnect the power supply from the Zip drive and gently push a straightened paper clip into the emergency disk eject hole on the back of the drive. The disk mechanism should release the disk.

Powering the Zip drive and system. The Zip drive generally requires that power be available to it *before* your operating system starts to load—otherwise, Windows may not detect the drive at start time. Iomega usually suggests that you connect your PC, Zip drive, and printer (or other parallel-port device) to a power strip so that all three devices are powered simultaneously.

Powering down the Zip drive. The Power/Eject button on the 250-MB Zip drive allows you to power down the drive when it is not in use. In power-down mode, the drive uses a very small amount of power to support data pass-through (when a printer or scanner is connected to the Zip drive).

The Zip drive also has an automatic "sleep mode" that spins down a Zip disk after 15 min of inactivity—this feature minimizes power consumption when the Zip drive is not being accessed. During a "drive sleep," the green power light remains on, and the Zip disk automatically spins up again when it needs to be accessed. You can use the Iomega software to change the drive sleep setting.

Zip disk compatibility. The 250-MB Zip drive is fully backward-compatible, allowing you to read from and write to 100-MB Zip disks. However, because of the design of the 250-MB Zip drive, its performance when writing to a 100-MB Zip disk is significantly reduced— the time required to write information to a 100-MB Zip disk in a 250-MB parallel-port Zip drive may be more than *twice* that needed to write the same information to a 250-MB Zip disk. To get top performance from your 250-MB Zip drive, you should use 250-MB Zip disks whenever you want to store new information. Here are some important guidelines when using Zip disks:

- If you write data to a 100-MB Zip disk using a 250-MB Zip drive, and later find that the disk cannot be read by a 100-MB Zip drive, try reading the disk again in your 250-MB Zip drive.

- If the 250-MB Zip drive locks up when you're writing to a 100-MB Zip disk, you can verify that the drive is operating correctly by checking that the green activity light is blinking irregularly. A slow, steady blink may indicate a serious problem with the drive. If there is a slow, steady blink, try ejecting the disk and reinserting it.

- You can use only the Iomega Short Format option if you need to format a 100-MB Zip disk in a 250-MB Zip drive—the Long Format option is *not* supported for 100-MB Zip disks in a 250-MB Zip drive.

- A 250-MB Zip disk *cannot* be used in a 100-MB Zip drive—the 100-MB Zip drive will automatically reject a 250-MB disk.

Zip disk guidelines

Iomega Zip disks are rather delicate and sensitive, and must be treated with care in order to avoid damage to the disk or the drive, or loss of your important data. Here are some practical guidelines that can help you get a longer working life from your disks:

- Always make sure that the power supply is connected to the drive before inserting a Zip disk. Otherwise you might damage your drive.

- Never *force* a Zip disk into or out of the drive. If the Eject button doesn't work, power down the drive and try the emergency eject feature.

- Never use ordinary 3.5-in floppy diskettes or floppy head-cleaning disks in your Zip drive—such media are not compatible with the heads on a Zip drive, and thus may cause severe damage to the drive mechanism.

- Keep your Zip drive on a level surface. Avoid moving the drive when a Zip disk is inserted and in use.

- Always remove the Zip disk from the drive when you are transporting your Zip drive, even if it's just across the room.

- It is a good idea to return the Zip disk to its protective case when it's not in the drive.

- Avoid exposing the Zip drive or Zip disks to dust, direct sunlight, high temperature, moisture, and magnetic fields (such as from monitors and some speakers). Otherwise, you may eventually experience data loss or drive damage.

- If you have a printer connected through a Zip drive, make sure that the power supply is connected (even if you're not using the Zip drive). Power to the drive is required for correct data pass-through.

- Before connecting or disconnecting your Zip drive, always shut down the computer and disconnect power from the Zip drive.

Zip Drive Software Considerations and Testing

Getting the most from your Zip drive requires that you keep drivers and applications software up to date, installing and uninstalling those drivers manually if necessary. You'll also need to know how to adjust the Zip drive letter and how to format and write-protect your Zip media. This part of the chapter offers a series of essential Zip drive procedures.

Obtaining updated Zip software

New drivers and applications software are important to overcome performance problems and compatibility issues. The latest drivers for your Zip drive may be downloaded from Iomega's FTP site at *http://www.iomega.com/software/index.html*. Once you locate the proper page, choose the operating system you're using (Windows 95/98, Windows NT, Windows 3.1x/DOS, and so on). A listing describing each file available for download will guide you through the process. You may also order the latest Iomega software by calling 1-800-MY-STUFF (though there is a nominal charge when you order the software by phone).

Manually installing Zip parallel-port drivers

If you cannot install the Zip software automatically (i.e., there is no auto-run from the CD), you can use these steps to install the drivers manually under Windows 95/98. Start by uninstalling the existing Zip parallel-port driver:

- Click *Start*, highlight *Settings,* and click *Control Panel*.

- In the *Control Panel*, double-click the *System* icon.

- In the *System Properties* dialog, choose the *Device Manager* tab.

- Under *Device Manager*, click on the plus (+) symbol next to *SCSI Controllers*.

- If the *Iomega Parallel Port Interface* is listed, highlight the entry and click *Remove*.

NOTE: If there are no SCSI controllers listed in *Device Manager*, or if the *Iomega Parallel Port Interface* is not listed within SCSI controllers, the drive has not been installed yet.

Now manually install the Zip drivers for your parallel port:

- Insert the IomegaWare CD into your CD-ROM drive.

  NOTE: If the installation begins automatically, cancel the manual installation process.

- Click on *Start*, highlight *Settings*, then click *Control Panel*.

- In the *Control Panel*, double-click on *Add New Hardware*.

- Click on the *Next* button to begin the installation process.

- If you're prompted to have Windows search for new hardware, choose *No*.

- In the *Hardware Types* list, choose *SCSI controllers*, then click *Next*.

- In the next screen, choose *Have Disk*.

- At the *Install from disk* prompt, click the *Browse* button.

- From the *Drives* drop-down list, choose the drive letter of your CD-ROM drive.

- In the *Folders* list, double-click on the *w9xstuff* folder and select *OK* twice.

- In the *Models* list, choose the *Iomega Parallel Port Zip Interface*, select *Next*, and click *Finish*.

- Restart your computer—your driver is now installed.

Uninstalling Zip software

If you need to remove the Zip software (i.e., Iomega Tools) from your Windows 95/98 platform, use the *Add/Remove Programs* feature in your *Control Panel* to remove the *Iomega Tools for Windows 95* entry:

- Click *Start*, highlight *Settings*, and select *Control Panel*.

- In the *Control Panel*, double-click the *Add/Remove Programs* icon.

- Select *Iomega Tools for Windows 95* in the *Installed Program* list box, and click *Add/Remove*. Follow the program removal screens that appear.

- Click *OK* to close the *Add/Remove Programs* window.

- Restart Windows 98.

Changing the Zip drive letter

It may be necessary for you to change the drive letter assignment of your Zip drive in the event that there are drive problems or issues with other software-driven drives like CD-ROMs. Use the following steps to adjust the drive letter(s):

- Right-click the *My Computer* icon on your desktop, then choose *Properties*.

- Select the *Device Manager* tab.

- Click on the + next to the *CD-ROM* or *Disk drives* icon, and choose the *Settings* tab.

- Choose *Start Drive Letter* and assign the drive letter you need from the drop-down menu.

- Choose the same letter for *End Drive Letter*.

- Click *OK* and allow your system to reboot for changes to take effect.

- Repeat the steps above by clicking the "+" next to *Disk drives*, and assign a different drive letter to your Iomega drive.

Formatting Zip disks with Iomega software

The Iomega software that's installed with the Zip disk offers the facility for reformatting Zip disks if the need arises. Before you format a disk, remember that all of the information on it will become inaccessible, so use caution to avoid accidental data loss:

- Right-click the *Zip drive* icon on your Windows desktop.

- Select *Format* from the drive shortcut menu, and choose the format type:

   1. Use *Short Format* if you want to quickly erase all data on a disk so that you can reuse it.
   2. Use *Long Format with Surface Verify* if you are formatting a disk for which you have forgotten the password, or if you need to repair a disk that has developed read/write errors due to bad sectors.

- Click *Start* to begin formatting the Zip disk.

Formatting Zip disks with Windows 95/98 FORMAT

- Double-click the *My Computer* icon on your desktop.

- Right-click on the Iomega drive icon where you'd like to format your Zip disk.

- Select *format*, and specify the format type.

- Click *Start* to proceed with the format.

Formatting Zip disks with DOS

> **NOTE**: If you're in Windows, be sure to exit to DOS. Take note of your Iomega drive letter.

- Click *Start* and select *Shut Down*.

- Select *Restart your computer in MS-DOS mode*.

- Click *Yes*.

- Insert the disk that you would like to format into your Iomega drive.

- At the DOS prompt, type `format x:` (where `x:` is the letter of your Zip drive), then hit `<Enter>`.

- Type `Y` for yes to proceed with the format.

Protecting Zip disks

Iomega includes a special read/write-protect feature that allows you to write-protect a disk through software instead of with a mechanical write-protect switch. You can write-protect a disk (and assign a password that must be used to remove the write protection). You can also read/write-protect a disk so that it cannot be written to (or read from) without a password. Use the steps below to protect your disks:

- Insert the disk you want to protect into your Zip drive.

- Right-click the *Zip drive* icon on your Windows desktop.

- Select *Protect* from the drive shortcut menu.

- Choose the protection option you want to use.

  NOTE: Although Zip disk protection options are set using Iomega's software, the actual protection mechanism is part of the drive hardware—the disk protection cannot be bypassed using other software programs.

Zip Drive Troubleshooting

Symptom 4.1: Zip drive operation seems erratic, or you experience data transfer problems. In virtually all cases, this is a problem with the Zip drive's *cabling*. For external drives, check that the parallel-port cable or USB cable is attached securely. See that any screws or clips are holding the cables in place. For internal drives, verify that the 40-pin IDE cable or 50-pin SCSI signal cable is attached securely. (SCSI cable chains must also be terminated properly.)

If problems persist, there may be a problem with the controller operating your drive (i.e., the parallel port, USB port, IDE controller card, or SCSI adapter). Double-check the controller's configuration and see that each drive is jumpered (identified) properly.

Symptom 4.2: A Zip disk is automatically ejected after you insert it into the drive. The problem here is almost always the disk itself. You may be using a 250-MB Zip disk in a 100-MB Zip drive, or you may be using a non-Zip disk in the drive. Check the disk and verify that you're using the proper Zip disk for your drive. If the problem persists and the disk(s) operate in other Zip drives, the drive itself may be at fault.

Symptom 4.3: The Zip drive refuses to work with software "dongles" or other pass-through devices. This is a common problem because there is no single parallel-port specification—there are *some* parallel-port devices (multi-I/O adapters, scanners, printers, software dongles, and so on) that are not fully compatible with a Zip drive.

- *Remove the device.* The easiest way to check compatibility is to remove the dongle or other parallel-port device. If the Zip drive works, you know that the other device is at fault, and it may be necessary to update the dongle or other device.

- *Add a parallel port.* If you cannot replace, remove, or "tweak" your existing parallel-port devices, it may be necessary to add another parallel port to the system in order to support the Zip drive.

Symptom 4.4: There is no drive letter for the SCSI Zip drive under Windows 95/98. The drive does not appear to respond. In virtually all cases, the SCSI driver has not loaded properly.

- *Check the device driver(s).* Open the *Device Manager* and expand the *SCSI Controllers* entry, then check the *Iomega Adapter* line beneath it. If there is a yellow symbol with an exclamation mark on it, the Windows 95 driver did not load. Check the controller next by highlighting the *Iomega Adapter* line, then selecting *Properties*. Click on the *Resources* page, then verify that your I/O Range and IRQ options are set correctly—they *must* match the jumper settings on your adapter board. If you must update the resource settings manually, make sure the *Automatic Settings* box is *not* checked (and remember to save any changes). If you allocated new resources, you may have to shut off the PC and change jumper settings on the controller board itself to match the resources allocated in the *Device Manager*. Restart the computer—once the system reboots, the Windows 95 driver should load normally.

■ *Check the cables*. If problems persist, check the signal connector (especially for SCSI adapters). Make sure the SCSI cable is intact and connected to the drive properly. If problems continue, your SCSI adapter is probably installed correctly, but the bus may be terminated improperly. Make sure that you terminate both ends of the SCSI bus properly.

Symptom 4.5: There is no drive letter for the parallel-port Zip drive under Windows 95/98. Parallel-port drive problems can almost always be traced to faulty connections, port configuration issues, or driver problems.

■ *Check the cables*. Check the external power connector first. Parallel-port drives are powered externally. Make sure that the power pack is working, and see that the power cable is connected properly to the drive. If the drive does not appear to power up, try a different power pack or drive. Check the signal cable next, and make sure that you are using a good-quality, known-good parallel-port cable that is attached securely at the PC and at the drive. The Zip drive is very sensitive to devices such as copy protection modules (or dongles) and other pass-through devices. Try connecting the drive directly to the parallel port. Also disconnect any printers on the parallel port.

■ *Check the parallel port*. The parallel-port setup may be incorrect. Reboot the PC and enter CMOS Setup. Check to see that the parallel port is configured in EPP or bidirectional mode. If the problem continues in the EPP mode, try configuring the parallel port for compatibility mode.

■ *Check the host controller*. For SCSI installations, check the SCSI host controller. There is a known incompatibility between the Iomega Zip drive and the Adaptec 284x adapter—the Iomega PPA3 driver does not work with the Adaptec 284x controller. Check with Iomega for an updated driver.

■ *Check your driver(s)*. Open the *Device Manager* and find the *SCSI Controllers* entry (even though this is a parallel-port device). If there is no such entry, the driver is not installed. If you expand the *SCSI Controllers* section, there should be an entry for the *Iomega Parallel Port Zip Interface*. If there is not, the driver is not installed. Check for hardware conflicts. If the *Device Manager* entry for the *Iomega Parallel Port Zip Interface* has a yellow circle with an exclamation mark on it, the interface is configured improperly and is conflicting with other devices. Also check for device properties. Highlight the *Iomega Parallel Port Zip Interface* entry, click on *Properties*, then select the *Settings* page. Find the box marked *Adapter Settings*, then type

```
/mode:nibble /speed:1
```

Save your changes and reboot the system. If that fails, try reinstalling the drivers. Highlight the *Iomega Parallel Port Zip Interface* and select *Remove*. Then reinstall the drivers from scratch. Next, try running in DOS. Start the PC in DOS mode (command prompt only), then insert the Iomega installation disk and type

```
a:\guest      <Enter>
```

If the Zip drive still does not receive a drive letter, the parallel port may be faulty or incompatible with the drive. Try the drive on another system. If this tactic works on another system, the problem is definitely related to your original PC hardware. If the problem follows the drive, the fault is probably in the drive. Try another drive.

Symptom 4.6: An Iomega Zip drive displays a floppy disk icon under Windows 95/98.   However, the drive appears to operate properly. This is almost always due to the use of a real-mode DOS driver to support the Iomega drive and adapter. You will need to update the real-mode driver to an appropriate protected-mode driver for Windows 95. For SCSI adapters, you need to find the protected-mode SCSI driver for your particular SCSI adapter and install it through the *Add New Hardware* wizard in the *Control Panel*. After the protected-mode driver is installed, you can remove the obsolete real-mode driver from CONFIG.SYS. For native Iomega SCSI adapters, get the protected-mode drivers directly from Iomega. For parallel-port Zip drives, uninstall the old drive software and install the new Windows 95 driver software.

Symptom 4.7: The Zip drive takes over the CD-ROM drive letter in Windows 95/98.   You may simply need to switch drive letters between the Zip drive and the CD-ROM drive:

■ Open *Device Manager* and double-click on the *Disk Drives* entry.

- Highlight the *Iomega Zip drive* entry and click on *Properties*.

- Click on the *Settings* page.

- In the *Reserved Drive Letters* section, there is a *Start Drive Letter* and an *End Drive Letter* setting. Enter the desired drive letter for the Zip drive in both start and end drive entries (be sure to use the same drive letter for both start and end). Click on *OK*.

- Double-click on the *CD-ROM* entry.

- Highlight your *CD-ROM Drive* entry and click on *Properties*.

- Click on the *Settings* page.

- In the *Reserved Drive Letters* section, there is a *Start Drive Letter* and an *End Drive Letter* setting. Enter the desired drive letter for the CD-ROM drive in both start and end entries (be sure to use the same drive letter for both start and end). Click on *OK*.

- Click on *OK* to close *Device Manager*, then shut down and restart the computer.

Symptom 4.8: You encounter Zip drive letter problems under DOS. The drive letters following C: may change unexpectedly when Iomega drivers are installed to support a new device. This can interfere with applications that look at specific drives or with access to network resources. You will need to relocate the drives before you install Iomega software. Since the GUEST.EXE utility loads at the end of AUTOEXEC.BAT, the Iomega drive will be assigned the last drive letter. DOS assigns letters to network drives alphabetically after assigning letters to any internal or external drives connected to the computer. When a new drive is added, the network drive may be pushed down one letter (e.g., from E: to F:). Applications that reference specific drive letters may then fail to work correctly unless they are reinstalled or adjusted for the drive letter change. If you use a batch file to connect to a network, it will need to be updated to the new drive letter. A network log-in script may also need to be revised.

Use the DOS LASTDRIVE= command to relocate your first network drive letter further down the alphabet—this insulates your network drive letter assignment from future changes should you add other drives to your system. For example, you can make your network drive N: by adding the following line to the end of CONFIG.SYS. This would allow you to add ten drives (D: through M:) to a system without pushing down your network drive letter:

```
LASTDRIVE=M
```

> **NOTE**: Do not set your last drive to Z: or you will be unable to access any network drive. If you use multiple network drives, do not set your last drive to a letter late in the alphabet (such as X: or Y:), since that will limit the number of network drives you can use simultaneously.

Check your CD-ROM drive letters. CD-ROM drives have a specific drive letter determined by the /L option of MSCDEX in AUTOEXEC.BAT (for example, /L:E assigns the CD-ROM as drive E:). When a new drive is installed, DOS may assign the CD-ROM drive letter to the new drive, and the CD-ROM drive may seem to disappear. Change the drive letter for the CD-ROM to a letter not assigned to another drive. You may want to relocate your CD-ROM drive several letters down the alphabet so that you do not have to relocate it each time you add a new drive to your system. You must have a LASTDRIVE statement in CONFIG.SYS which sets the last drive equal to or later than the CD-ROM letter. Finally, check the overall system configuration. When DOS *does* reassign drive letters, be sure to check each of the points below:

- Edit the `PATH` statement in AUTOEXEC.BAT to correctly reference the new drive letter.

- Edit any batch files (including AUTOEXEC.BAT) to correctly reference new drive letters.

- Edit all Windows .INI files and Windows groups to correctly reference new drive letters.

- Check other application setup files and rerun the application's setup if drive letters cannot be edited.

- For networks, check your user log-in script for references to specific network drive letters.

- Reboot the computer and check major applications—those that do not work with the new drive letter may need to be reinstalled.

Symptom 4.9: You encounter duplicate ZIP drive letters.
You notice that the Zip drive (or another drive) has been assigned a duplicate drive letter. In most cases, the problem can be traced to a third-party SCSI adapter and drivers which conflict with Iomega SCSI drivers. *Do not use any drive before correcting this problem.* Open your CONFIG.SYS file and examine each driver that scans the SCSI bus to assign drive letters. Chances are very good that you have a third-party driver which is assigning a letter to the Zip drive, as well as an Iomega-specific driver that is assigning another letter to the Zip drive. Use a command-line switch with the third-party SCSI driver to limit the number of IDs that will be assigned.

Symptom 4.10: The GUEST utility cannot find an available drive letter.   If all drive letters are in use, GUEST will not be able to assign a drive letter to the Zip drive. Change the last drive designation. Use the DOS `LAST-DRIVE` command in the end of CONFIG.SYS to increase the number of available drive letters. Do not use a letter near the end of the alphabet.

Symptom 4.11: The system hangs when installing drivers for Windows 95/98. System hangups during installation are usually the result of hardware conflicts or problems. Check the signal cable first, and make sure that you are using a good-quality, known-good cable which is attached securely at the PC and the drive. Open the *Device Manager* and find the *SCSI Controllers*. If there is no such entry, the driver is not installed. If you expand the *SCSI Controllers* section, there should be an entry for the *Iomega Parallel Port Zip Interface*. If there is not, the driver is not installed.

Check for hardware conflicts. If the *Device Manager* entry for the *Iomega Parallel Port Zip Interface* has a yellow circle with an exclamation mark on it, the interface is configured improperly and is conflicting with other devices. Highlight the *Iomega Parallel Port Zip Interface* entry, click on *Properties*, then select the *Settings* page. Find the box marked *Adapter Settings*, then type

```
/mode:nibble  /speed:1
```

Save your changes and reboot the system. If problems continue, try running in DOS. Start the PC in DOS mode (command prompt only), then insert the Iomega installation disk and type

```
a:\guest      <Enter>
```

If the Zip drive still does not receive a drive letter, the parallel port may be faulty or incompatible with the drive. Try the drive on another system. If this tactic works on another system, the problem is definitely related to your original PC hardware. If the problem follows the drive, the fault is probably in the drive. Try another drive.

Symptom 4.12: After installing a Zip drive, you find that the other drives in the system are using the DOS compatibility mode. This is almost always the result of the

GUEST.EXE program. The real-mode GUEST.EXE program supplied by Iomega is designed to allow you to access the Zip drive in DOS and Windows 95, and this causes the other drives in your system to use the DOS compatibility mode (you may also notice a decline in drive or system performance). Try installing the protected-mode drivers for the Iomega drive:

- In the *Control Panel*, double-click the *Add New Hardware* icon.

- Click *Next*, click the *No* button, then click *Next*.

- Click *Other Devices*, and then click *Next*.

- In the *Manufacturers* box, click *Iomega*, and then click *Have Disk*.

- Install the files from the Windows 95 CD-ROM by inserting the CD-ROM in the drive, typing the following line in the *Copy Manufacturer's Files From* box, and then clicking *Next*:

```
<drive>:\drivers\storage\iomega
```

where `<drive>` is the drive letter of the CD-ROM drive.

- After the files are copied, click *Finish*.

- Restart the computer when prompted to do so.

Symptom 4.13: A Zip GUEST locks up or cannot locate the drive or adapter.   Chances are that an ASPI manager referenced in the GUEST.INI file is conflicting with hardware in the PC. This often happens in systems with two SCSI adapters (and parallel ports). Try editing the GUEST.INI file. Open the GUEST.INI file on your Iomega installation disk and specify *which* ASPI manager needs to load in order to access the Zip drive. Remember to make a backup copy of the GUEST.INI file before editing it. As an alternative, choose the Iomega SCSI adapter driver. If you are using a native

TABLE 4.1   A Listing of Native Iomega ASPI Drivers

Iomega adapter	ASPI manager
Zip Zoom SCSI Accelerator	ASPIPC16.SYS
Jaz Jet SCSI Accelerator	ASPI2930.SYS
Parallel Port Zip Drive	ASPIPPA3.SYS or ASPIPPM1.SYS
PPA-3 Adapter	ASPIPPA3.SYS
PC1616	ASPIPC16.SYS
PC800	ASPIPC8.SYS
PC2	ASPIPC2.SYS
PC4	ASPIPC4.SYS

Iomega SCSI adapter, choose the ASPI manager that applies to the adapter, as shown in Table 4.1. Once you have identified the proper ASPI manager for your adapter, REMark out all the ASPI lines in GUEST.INI except for the one that you need.

If you are using a non-Iomega SCSI adapter, you will need to add the complete path and filename for the driver to GUEST.INI and REMark out all the ASPI drivers. Once the GUEST.INI file is updated, save your changes and reboot the system, then run GUEST from the drive and directory containing the updated GUEST.INI file. If problems persist, try the drive on another system, or try a new drive on the suspect system.

Symptom 4.14: System recovery fails after the Zip Tools setup process is complete.   If the Zip Tools software for your Zip drive fails to install properly (or if the system hangs or was powered down), the Windows Startup group will have a Zip Setup icon that will attempt to run each time Windows is started. Delete the Zip icon in your Startup group, then reinstall the Zip software.

Symptom 4.15: The Zip drive setup could not find a Zip Tools disk for Zip parallel-port drives.   This is usually a problem with the GUEST.INI file, which needs to be edited for proper operation. Start the system from a clean floppy diskette, insert the Iomega installation disk, then try running the GUEST utility. If a drive letter is assigned, there may be a driver in CONFIG.SYS or AUTOEXEC.BAT that is conflicting with the Zip drive. If GUEST fails to assign a Zip drive letter from a clean boot, open the GUEST.INI file in a text editor, locate the `ASPI=ASPIPPA3.SYS` line, then add the switches `/MODE=1` `/SPEED=1`, which makes the complete command line appear as

```
ASPI=ASPIPPA3.SYS   SCAN   /INFO   SL360=NO   SMC=NO
/MODE=1 /SPEED=1
```

Reboot the PC and run the GUEST utility again. If GUEST does run, but you still cannot read the Zip Tools disk, make sure that the signal cables are secure between the drive and the system. If problems persist, try the Zip drive on another PC. If GUEST works on another PC, the original PC is using an incompatible parallel port. If the drive still refuses to work, try another Zip drive.

Symptom 4.16: You see error messages such as *Can't Find Zip Tools Disk* or *No Drive Letters Added* when using Zip parallel-port drives. In most cases, you will have to manually assign the proper ASPI driver by editing your GUEST.INI file. Open the GUEST.INI file on your Iomega installation disk. Highlight the ASPI driver line that reads `ASPIPPA3.SYS`, then add the following commands: `/MODE=1` `/SPEED=1`. Remember to make a backup copy of the GUEST.INI file before editing it. The final command line should appear as

```
ASPI=ASPIPPA3.SYS   SCAN   /INFO   SL360=NO   SMC=NO
/MODE=1 /SPEED=1
```

Save your changes to GUEST.INI, then run GUEST from the drive and directory that contains your edited GUEST.INI file. GUEST should now assign a drive letter to the Zip drive. Reboot the PC, start Windows, then run the Iomega Setup routine from the drive and directory which contains your edited GUEST.INI file. The Windows installation should now proceed normally.

Next, check the signal connector, and make sure that the parallel-port or SCSI cable is connected properly between the drive and the system. Try a known-good working signal cable. If problems persist, boot the system from a clean diskette and try running GUEST. If a drive letter is assigned properly, then there is a driver loading in CONFIG.SYS or AUTOEXEC.BAT which conflicts with the Zip drive. You will have to systematically locate the offending driver. Finally, try the Zip drive on another PC. If GUEST works on another PC, the original PC is using an incompatible parallel port. If the drive still refuses to work, try another Zip drive.

Symptom 4.17: Windows 3.11 allows the network drive letter to conflict with the Zip drive letter.   You may see this as a *No Zip Tools Disk Detected* message. The drive may also no longer be accessible from the File Manager or DOS prompt. The problem is that Windows for Workgroups allows GUEST to assign a drive letter that is already used by a network drive. Remap the shared volume—since GUEST is typically run first, you will need to alter the network drive letter under Windows for Workgroups.

Symptom 4.18: You cannot print while using a Zip drive. The Iomega parallel-port Zip drive works as a pass-through device, and the software allows the drive to share a parallel port with printers. However, some printers require two-way communication between the printer and the parallel port which conflicts with the Zip software, and this can cause data corruption and system lockups. In many cases, disabling the bidirectional communication features of the printer will clear the problem.

Canon printers. Several Canon printers use a driver that is incompatible with the Zip drive—the drivers need exclusive access to the parallel port for proper operation of the printer. To work around this problem temporarily, you can disable the drivers for that printer.

Canon BJ-610.   Insert two semicolons (; ;) in front of the following lines in the [386Enh] section of the SYSTEM.INI file:

```
DEVICE=WPSRCOM.386
DEVICE= WPSCREM.386
DEVICE=CANON BJ-610, WPSCR, LPT1
```

Canon BJC-610.   Insert two semicolons (; ;) in front of the following lines in the [386Enh] section of the SYSTEM.INI file:

```
DEVICE=WPSRCOM.386
DEVICE= WPSCREM.386
DEVICE=WPSRBND.386
```

In the WIN.INI file, insert two semicolons (; ;) in front of the following lines:

```
LOAD=WPSLOAD.EXE
DEVICE=CANON BJC-610, WPSCR, LPT1
```

Canon BJC-620.   Insert two semicolons (; ;) in front of the following lines in the [386Enh] section of the SYSTEM.INI file:

```
DEVICE=WPSRCOM.386
DEVICE= WPSCREM.386
DEVICE=WPSRBND.386
```

In the WIN.INI file, insert two semicolons (; ;) in front of the following lines:

```
LOAD=WPSLOAD.EXE

DEVICE=CANON BJC-620, WPSCR, LPT1
```

> **NOTE**: After these lines have been REMarked out, the Zip drive will function, but the printer will not. To restore printer capability, remove the semicolons from the WIN.INI and SYSTEM.INI files and restart Windows.

> **NOTE**: Rather than disabling the printers, you can install the drivers for the Canon BJC-600e (if you are using the Canon BJC-610 or BJ-610). If you are using the BJC-620 printer, install the Canon BJC-210 drivers. This allows access to both the Zip drive and the printer, although at a reduced resolution.

Canon Multi-Pass 1000. You cannot use this printer and the parallel-port Zip drive at the same time. The only way to make this printer and the Zip drive compatible is to change the output of the printer to *File* when you need to use the Zip drive, then back to *LPT1* when you want to use the printer. Use the following procedure to toggle the output from *File* to *LPT1* under Windows 95:

- Double-click on *My Computer*.
- Double-click on *Properties*.
- Right-click on *Canon Printer*.
- Click on *Details*.
- Click the down arrow button in the window labeled *Print to the following port*.
- Click on *FILE* (to switch back, choose *LPT1*).
- Click on *OK* at the bottom of your screen.

Okidata printers. The Okidata 600e also exhibits port problems when used with a Zip drive. To enable the Zip drive, insert two semicolons (; ;) in front of the following line in the [BOOT] section of the SYSTEM.INI file:

```
COMM.DRV=INSYTHCOMM.DRV
```

Just below that line, add the following line:

```
COMM.DRV=COMM.DRV
```

In the [386Enh] section of SYSTEM.INI, insert two semicolons (; ;) in front of the line

```
DEVICE=OKIPORT.386
```

In the WIN.INI file, insert two semicolons (; ;) in front of the lines

```
LOAD=C:\WINDOWS\SYSTEM\STATMON.EXE
DEVICE=OL600E, OKIGDI, LPT1
```

Lexmark printers. Most Lexmark printers can work with the Zip drive if bidirectional support is disabled. Under Windows 95/98, you can disable bidirectional support using the following steps:

- Right-click on the *My Computer* icon, then double-click on the *Printers* icon.

- Right-click on the *Lexmark* printer icon, then select *Properties*.

- Choose *Details* and select *Spool* settings, then choose *Disable Bidirectional support*.

- Save your changes and reboot the PC if necessary.

Hewlett-Packard printers. Hewlett-Packard printers are known for their extensive use of the parallel port, so it is quite common to encounter problems between recent HP printers and other parallel-port devices such as the Zip drive. Fortunately, there are some workarounds available for most HP models.

Hewlett Packard 4S, 4+, 4V, 4SI, 4L, 4P, and 5P. You need to disable the bidirectional communication between the printer and the system. This can be accomplished by executing the following command from the RUN command line:

```
c:\windows\dinstall -fdinstall.ins
```

You can also use the steps outlined below:

- Bring up the WIN.INI file through either SYSED-IT (in Windows) or EDIT (in DOS).

- In the first section of this file, you should see a line that reads `LOAD=HPSW.EXE`. You need to disable this line by inserting a semicolon (;) at the beginning of the line.

- Now scroll down to the section labeled [Spooler] and insert a semicolon (;) at the beginning of the line that reads `QP.LPT1=HPLJ4QP.DLL`.

- Save the WIN.INI file, exit Windows, and restart the system.

You can now use the HP printer and Zip drive together. These changes will not affect the printer—they just disable the status windows that may pop up telling the current status of the printer.

Hewlett Packard 5L.   If you installed your printer using the HOST option, you will need to uninstall the printer, then reinstall it using the PCL option:

- Disconnect the printer from the computer or the Zip drive.

- Select *Start, Settings*, then select the *Printers* icon.

- Click the HP 5L Printer icon and press `<Delete>`. When the system asks to delete files that were used only by this printer, choose *YES* (or *OK*).

- Reboot the computer with the printer still disconnected.

- When the computer reboots, use the 5L installation disks to reinstall the drivers. When prompted for a *Custom or Express Installation*, choose *Custom* and select *PCL Mode*.

If the problem persists, disable the WIN.INI line that reads `LOAD=HPLJ5W.EXE` by placing two semicolons (;;) at the beginning of the line. You will need to do the same with the line that reads `QP.LPT1=???` in the [Spooler] section of your WIN.INI file.

HP 5P, 5M, 6P, 6M, DeskJet 600c, and HP DeskJet printers. The Status Monitor utility (HPPROP-TY.EXE) loaded with these printers must be disabled. There are two ways to disable the HPPROP-TY.EXE utility which will disable the Status Monitor without disabling the printer. The quick fix is to hit `<Ctrl>` + `<Alt>` + `<Del>`, choose *HPPROP-TY*, then choose *End Task*. This closes the Status Monitor, but you need to remember to do this each time you boot the PC. For a more permanent fix, right-click on the *My Computer* icon. Open the *Windows* folder, then the SYSTEM folder. Right-click on the file *HPPROPTY.EXE* and rename this file to *HPPROPTY.BAK*. You may need to reboot the PC so that your changes will take effect.

Other HP printers. Another workaround for HP compatibility problems involves editing the HP printer's .INI file (located in the `\Windows` directory) in order to disable the status monitoring and bidirectional mode. This example uses the HP 855C, and the .INI file is called HPRDJC02.INI. The .INI file name will be different for the various models of printers (e.g., HPDJ850C.INI, HPDJ660C.INI, or HPLJ4.INI):

- Open the .INI file in Notepad.
- In the first section of the .INI file, find the line that reads

```
2DSMEnable=0200
```

and change this line to read:

```
2DSMEnable=0000
```

This will disable the status monitor.

- Now locate the [COMMON] section of the .INI file and find the line that reads

```
0Bidi=0100
```

Change this line to read

```
0Bidi=0000
```

This will disable the bidirectional mode of the printer.

- Save your changes and reboot the system.

Symptom 4.19: You encounter problems installing a Zip SCSI drive. In virtually all cases, SCSI problems can be traced to hardware problems or driver issues. Make sure that power is provided to the drive (see that the drive power light comes on). See that the SCSI signal cable is intact and connected securely between the drive and the SCSI adapter. Try a new signal cable. Both ends of the SCSI bus must be terminated properly. Make sure that terminators are installed in the correct places. Ensure that the Zip SCSI drive is assigned to an SCSI ID that is not in use by any other SCSI device. Finally, check the drivers—the drivers for your SCSI adapter and drive must be correct, use the right command-line switches, and must be the very latest versions. Also check for conflicts between SCSI drivers or other drivers in the system.

Symptom 4.20: The drive letter is lost each time the PC is turned off. In many cases, the GUEST utility does not load properly because it is at the end of AUTOEXEC.BAT. Relocate the GUEST command line—open the AUTOEXEC.BAT file and move the GUEST command line to a point earlier in the file. Ideally, the GUEST command line should be the entry immediately *following* the MSCDEX command line. Save your changes and reboot the computer. The GUEST utility should now load each time the system is rebooted.

Symptom 4.21: When installing IomegaWare software for your Zip drive, a virus checker reports a virus. The typical report may indicate a "Romeo & Juliet" virus. This is often an error made by the virus checker when its virus definitions mistake the IomegaWare for a virus. Disable the antivirus software *before* attempting to install the software. If the IomegaWare software installs without error, you may reenable the antivirus program after the installation is complete. If not, you may need to obtain an updated version of the antivirus software.

Symptom 4.22: You see an error message such as *Drive X does not exist.* There are several different causes for this kind of problem. Check the disk first. You must use a PC-formatted disk—a Mac-formatted disk will not work in a PC. Try several different disks. If the error message occurs on only *one* disk, try reformatting that disk (remember that formatting the disk will remove all data from the disk). If you're receiving the error using more than one disk (or if the disk will not format), the drive may be defective and should be replaced. Finally, there may be a driver or Terminate and Stay Resident (TSR) interfering with the Zip drive. Try a clean DOS boot to eliminate the use of real-mode drivers and TSRs, and try the drive again.

Symptom 4.23: Your Windows 98 system locks up when using a USB Zip drive. The most common problems occur when you connect or use the USB Zip drive in the wrong way. Verify that you're following the proper guidelines:

- Power up your USB Zip drive at the same time you turn on your computer (or immediately after).

- Wait at least 30 s before reconnecting your USB Zip drive to your computer (if you remove your USB Zip drive while your computer is on).

- Confirm that your computer meets the USB 1.1 specification. If it does not, do not combine your USB Zip drive with other low-speed devices (such as a USB keyboard or mouse).

- Use only USB hubs that have an independent power supply. If you connect the USB Zip drive to a non-powered hub, your computer may lock up—the USB Zip drive may not transfer data correctly or may not be recognized by your computer.

Symptom 4.24: When installing a USB Zip drive under Windows 95/98, you see an error such as *No Iomega drives found.* This error occurs when the Iomega Tools software fails to assign a drive letter to your Zip drive. The problem is your software—Iomega Tools is an older version of software that shipped with Zip and Jaz drives. IomegaWare is the latest version of the software. Iomega recommends that you obtain the most current version of the IomegaWare software from *www.iomega.com / software /.*

Download the IomegaWare package onto your system, then double-click on the icon to begin the installation process. Once you've downloaded and installed the software, you should no longer receive the error message. If you now have a drive letter, the updated software resolved your problem and you can now use your drive.

Symptom 4.25: You notice that USB Zip drive performance is poor. Other USB devices—digital cameras, page scanners, and other USB devices that process large amounts of data—running at the same time as the USB Zip drive can affect performance. Here are some tips to tweak performance:

- Disconnect all USB devices from your computer, then reconnect the USB Zip drive. Try the USB Zip alone and test performance again.

- Make sure that you are using the cable that came with your USB Zip drive.

- Close all open applications through the *Task Manager*.

Symptom 4.26: The system locks up when you connect other USB devices to your existing USB Zip drive. Computers that are not compliant with USB hub specification 1.10 may lock up when a device (such as a USB keyboard, mouse, or joystick) is plugged in while the USB Zip drive is connected. Contact your computer manufacturer to verify that your USB hub is version 1.10 compliant. If it is not, you will continue to experience lockups. To correct the problem, you may want to consider upgrading your USB hub. If the hub is compliant, you may need to update the USB drivers, update your Windows version, or stick with the USB Zip drive only.

Symptom 4.27: You see an error such as *Disk in drive X not formatted*. There are several different causes for this kind of error. Check the disk first. You must use a PC-formatted disk—a Mac-formatted disk will not work in a PC. Try several different disks. If the error message occurs on only *one* disk, try reformatting that disk (remember that formatting the disk will remove all data from the disk). If you're receiving the error using more than one disk (or if the disk will not format), the drive may be defective and should be replaced. Finally, there may be a driver or TSR interfering with the Zip drive. Try a clean DOS boot to eliminate the use of real-mode drivers and TSRs, and try the drive again.

Symptom 4.28: When formatting a Zip disk, the Iomega format software returns a fatal exception error. This type of formatting error is almost always a result of problems with outdated or corrupted Zip drivers. Such an error may appear as

```
"A fatal exception 0E has occurred at 0028:C3C64C51
in VXD IOMEGA (01) + 00000CB5. The current appli-
cation will be terminated. Pressing any key closes
the Explorer window."
```

You'll need to update the Zip driver(s). Check the Iomega Web site at *www.iomega.com* and obtain a new IOMEGA.VXD file. Click *Start*, highlight *Find*, and then click *Files or Folders*. Find the old IOMEGA.VXD file and replace it with the newer version.

Symptom 4.29: The Zip drive's green power light does not illuminate. The green light on a Zip drive indicates that the drive is plugged in and receiving power. If the light is *not* on, then either the drive is turned off or not plugged in or there is a physical problem with the drive.

- *Check the power button.* If there is *not* a disk in the drive, press the Eject button once—the Eject button doubles as a power button, so pressing it will turn the drive on and off. Inserting a disk will also turn the drive on automatically. If there is already a disk in the drive, the button functions as an Eject button, and the disk should be removed *before* turning off the power.

- *Unplug the drive.* Disconnect the drive from power and the computer. Take the drive to another outlet and plug the power cable in. If the light comes on, there may be a problem with the first power outlet. If the light does not come on, then the drive and/or the power supply needs to be replaced.

Symptom 4.30: You see an error such as *Cannot create or replace, make sure the disk is not full or write protected*. There are several different causes for this kind of error. Check the disk first. You must use a PC-formatted disk—a Mac-formatted disk will not work in a PC. Try several different disks. If the error message occurs on only *one* disk, try reformatting that disk (remember that formatting the disk will remove all data from the disk). If you're receiving the error using more than one disk (or if the disk will not format), the drive may be defective and should be replaced. Finally, there may be a driver or TSR interfering with the Zip drive. Try a clean DOS boot to eliminate the use of real-mode drivers and TSRs, and try the drive again.

Symptom 4.31: You encounter a fatal exception error when using the Iomega Copy Machine software. This kind of problem is typically due to an issue with the Zip drive's auto spin-down/eject feature, which is used when doing a multiple disk copy. It may be necessary for you to disable the auto spin-down/eject function. Start the Copy Machine software by choosing its icon within the Iomega *Tools folder*. Next, select *Options* and then *Runtime*. Deselect the *Auto Spin-Down/Eject* option by removing the check from the box. Finally, choose *OK* to accept the changes, and reboot the PC if necessary. When performing subsequent multiple disk copies, you'll be prompted to eject each disk by pressing the Eject button on the front of your Zip drive.

Symptom 4.32: You encounter an error such as *General failure reading drive X*. There are several different causes for this kind of error. Check the disk first. You must use a PC-formatted disk—a Mac-formatted disk will not work in a PC. There may be a driver or TSR interfering with the Zip drive. Try a clean DOS boot to eliminate the use of real-mode drivers and TSRs, and try the drive again. Finally, try several different disks. If the error message occurs on only *one* disk, try reformatting that disk (remember that formatting the disk will remove all data from the disk). If you're receiving the error using more than one disk (or if the disk will not format), the drive may be defective and should be replaced.

Symptom 4.33: You encounter an error such as *Insufficient disk space*. You may also see this error as *Disk is full* or *Destination is full*. This error message may be caused by several possible problems: The disk is full, it's exceeding the operating system's file limit, or the Zip disk is bad.

- *Check the disk space.* Use a tool like Windows Explorer to verify that there is actually enough free space on the Zip disk to contain the file(s) you need. If there is not, try copying fewer files, or use a fresh Zip disk.

- *Check the number of files.* Make sure that you have not exceeded the file limit of your operating system. Remember that DOS will not allow you to have more than 511 files in the root directory. Use Windows Explorer (or the DOS DIR command) to list the files on your Zip disk. The number of files in the root directory should be less than 511—if the number of files is 511, you'll have to move some files into other directories to reduce the number of files on the root directory.

- *Cycle power to the system.* If the error persists, try shutting down the computer and Zip drive, then repowering the system in the correct order.

- *Try several different disks.* If the error occurs on only one disk, try reformatting that disk (remember that formatting the disk will remove all data from the disk). If you're receiving the error using more than one disk (or if the disk will not format), the drive may be defective and should be replaced.

Symptom 4.34: When using Iomega Tools or other Zip drive software, you see an error such as *Program performed an illegal operation.* In virtually all cases, there is a conflict between the Zip software and another program running on your system. You'll need to reboot the system and isolate the offending software.

- *Reboot the system.* This will clear the error from memory and allow you to check other software. When you reboot the system, make sure to turn the power to the drive off and back on again.

- *Close all open programs.* Open the *Close Program* dialog box by pressing the <Ctrl> + <Alt> + <Del>

keys at the same time. Close open programs by highlighting a program and then choosing the *End Task* button (do *not* close Explorer). Close one application at a time, and try your Zip drive again after closing each. Once the problem is resolved, the last application that was closed is the one causing the conflict. Once you have determined which application is causing the conflict, either discontinue use of that application when using your Zip drive or obtain an updated version from the software maker (if possible).

- *Reinstall the Zip software*. If the problem persists, delete and then reinstall the Iomega Tools software.

Symptom 4.35: When using Microsoft Backup under Windows 95, you receive an error such as *The disk is full—disk linking is not supported*. This problem occurs because Microsoft Backup cannot back up over multiple disks (a.k.a. disk spanning). Instead of using Microsoft Backup, install the backup software intended for use with the Zip disk (such as 1-Step Backup).

To install Iomega Tools for Windows 95, put the Zip installation floppy in the A: drive. From the *Start* menu, select *Run*. In the *Open* dialog box, type A:\guest95 and then click *OK*. Guest95 should find a drive letter for your Zip drive. Now put your Zip Tools disk into the Zip drive. Double-click on the *My Computer* icon, then double-click on the Zip drive icon—you should see a folder called *W95stuff*. Double-click on the *W95stuff* folder, and double-click on *setup95.exe*. Follow the screen instructions to complete the installation.

Symptom 4.36: When using Iomega Tools software under Windows 95/98, you see an error message such as *No Iomega drives found*. This occurs when the Iomega Tools software fails to assign a drive letter to your Zip drive; it is often a fault of old software. Iomega Tools is an older version of software that shipped with Zip drives. IomegaWare is the latest version of the software and should be updated *before* troubleshooting in every possible case. You can download the various components of IomegaWare from the Iomega Web site at *www.iomega.com / software*. Start by downloading the Core IomegaWare Tools package onto your desktop, then double-click on the icon to begin the installation process. Once you have downloaded and installed the Core IomegaWare Tools software, you should no longer receive the error message.

Symptom 4.37: When installing IomegaWare software under Windows 98, you see an error such as *ISINST30 caused a general protection fault*. When you attempt to install the IomegaWare software, you may receive the following error message:

```
ISINST30 caused a general protection fault in mod-
ule _INS0433._MP at <address>
```

This error is caused by the Microsoft MSWHEEL.EXE wheel-mouse driver software. To resolve this error, you'll need to disable the wheel-mouse software, install the Zip software, then reenable the wheel-mouse software. Start by disabling the MSWHEEL.EXE program:

- Click on *Start*, point to *Programs, Accessories, System Tools*, and click *System Information*.

- Click the *System Configuration* utility on the *Tools* menu.

- Click the *Setup* tab.

- Click the check box next to MSWHEEL.EXE to clear the box.

- Click *File* and choose *Exit*.

- Restart your computer when prompted.

Install the IomegaWare software. Insert the IomegaWare CD into your CD-ROM drive, and installation should start automatically. If you need a later version of IomegaWare, you can download it from *www.iomega.com/software*. Now reenable the MSWHEEL.EXE program:

■ Click on *Start*, point to *Programs, Accessories, System Tools*, and click *System Information*.

■ Click the *System Configuration* utility on the *Tools* menu.

■ Click the *Setup* tab.

■ Click the check box next to MSWHEEL.EXE to add a check mark.

■ Click *File* and choose *Exit*.

■ Restart your computer when prompted.

Symptom 4.38: When using a Zip drive, you see an error such as *X:\ is not accessible. The device is not ready*. When the drive refuses to respond, there are several points to check.

■ *Check the Zip disk*. Verify that there is a Zip disk in the drive. If there is not a disk in the drive (or if the disk is ejected after you restart your computer), Windows will display the error message. Place a disk into your Zip drive, wait a few seconds, and click the *Retry* button.

■ *Check/disable read/write protection*. Read/write protection is a security feature that requires a password; it should be reserved for highly sensitive data. If your Zip disk is read/write-protected, you'll get the error message when you try to access a protected disk. The following steps should remove read/write protection:

1. Double-click on the *My Computer* icon.
2. Right-click on the icon that represents your Zip drive and choose the *Protect* option.
3. The *Present Disk Status* dialog will indicate whether your disk is read/write-protected.

4. If your disk is write-protected, you must remove the read/write-protection by selecting the *Remove Protection* button before accessing the disk.

NOTE: You'll need to enter the correct password in order to remove read/write protection. If you do not have the correct password, you'll be unable to remove that protection from the disk.

■ *Check the cables*. Shut down the drive and computer, disconnect the data cable from the Zip drive, and carefully examine both ends of the cable for bent or broken pins. If the cable is damaged, it should be replaced. If it is not, reconnect it securely. Restart your computer in Windows, place a Zip disk in the drive, and try accessing the disk again.

■ *Try the drive on another PC*. Install your Zip drive on a different computer and see if you can read the disk on that system. If so, there may be a problem with the original computer's interface. If the problem persists, the drive may be defective and require replacement.

Symptom 4.39: When using a Zip drive under Windows 95/98, you see an error such as *The disk in drive X: is not formatted*. This kind of behavior is almost always caused by incompatible formatting or software conflicts.

■ *Check the disk format*. You must use a PC-formatted Zip disk—a disk formatted for a Macintosh computer will not work. Zip disks come preformatted for either Macintosh or PC. A disk that is formatted for a Mac will have a small dot ($\cdot$) located on the lower left corner of the disk label. If you have a Mac-formatted disk and you wish to reformat it for use on your PC (remember that formatting will permanently remove all data from that disk):

1. Insert the Zip disk into the drive.

2. If you receive a message such as *The disk in drive X: is not formatted. Do you want to format it now?* choose *No*.

3. Double-click the *My Computer* icon, then right-click on the Zip drive's icon.

4. Select *Format*.

5. Select *Long Format with Surface Verify*.

6. Click *Start* and allow the process to complete.

- *Try the disk in a clean environment*. Boot to DOS and see if you can access the disk. If you can, there may be a software conflict; if you cannot, the trouble may be with the disk itself.

1. Restart your computer with a blank bootable diskette in drive A:.

2. When you get a *non-system disk* error message, eject the floppy disk from the A: drive and press the <F8> key twice.

3. From the Windows 95/98 Startup Menu, choose *Safe mode command prompt only*.

4. At the DOS prompt, type progra~1\iomega\ tools\guest to obtain a drive letter for your Zip drive.

5. Insert the Zip disk into the Zip drive.

6. At the DOS prompt, type dir X: (where X: is the drive letter assigned to your Zip drive) and read the directory of files on your Zip disk.

- *Try another Zip disk*. If the error occurs on only *one* disk, try reformatting that disk. If you're receiving the error message with more than one disk (or if the disk will not format), the drive is probably defective and should be replaced.

- *Try another parallel-port setting*. If problems persist, try setting another parallel-port mode such as bidirectional, standard, ECP, or EPP. In many cases, downgrading the parallel-port mode will correct hardware issues, but reduce drive performance.

Symptom 4.40: You see an error such as *Cannot create or replace—make sure the disk is not full or write-protected*. In most cases, this problem is caused by exceeding the file limit imposed by the operating system (i.e., 511 files under DOS).

■ *Check the disk space*. Use a tool like Windows Explorer to verify that there is actually enough free space on the Zip disk to contain the file(s) you need. If there is not, try copying fewer files, or use a fresh Zip disk.

■ *Check the number of files*. Make sure that you have not exceeded the file limit of your operating system. Remember that DOS will not allow you to have more than 511 files in the root directory. Use Windows Explorer (or the DOS DIR command) to list the files on your Zip disk. The number of files in the root directory should be less than 511—if the number of files is 511, you'll have to move some files into other directories to reduce the number of files on the root directory.

Symptom 4.41: You see an error message such as *No drives are supported by Iomega Tools*. The trouble is with your version of the Zip drive's software. Iomega Tools is an older version of IomegaWare software. To correct this error, you should download and install the latest version of IomegaWare software from Iomega's Web site at *www.iomega.com/software*. Install the IomegaWare software by double-clicking the file you have downloaded to your computer. This will begin the installation process.

Symptom 4.42: The Zip drive is clicking continuously. While a "click" is perfectly normal when you insert or remove a disk, a *continuous* clicking indicates a serious problem. This problem is often referred to as the "click of death" and is often related to a fault in the Zip drive (especially older versions of the Zip drive). Check the disk first. Try another Zip disk in the drive (make sure that the disk is blank in order to prevent damaging good disks). If the problem persists, the drive is almost certainly defective and should be replaced. Iomega recommends the following precautions for Zip disks:

- Eject disks prior to transporting any Zip drive—this forces the drive heads (which read and write to the disks) to park safely.

- Avoid dropping your drive—it will almost certainly damage internal structures.

- Make it a point to transport and store Zip disks in approved disk cases.

Iomega also offers a utility that tests the integrity of the drive heads and Zip media. If you're uncertain about the reliability of your Zip drive or disks, running the diagnostics could help isolate the problem (use a blank formatted disk while running these tests):

- Open *My Computer* or Windows Explorer.

- Right-click on the Zip drive icon in *My Computer* or Windows Explorer.

- Choose *Properties* from the menu.

- Click the *Diagnostics* tab.

- Click the *Diagnose Now* button to start the test.

The diagnostic will report *Passed* or *Failed*. If the diagnostic reports *Failed*, you should contact Iomega to repair or replace the drive.

Symptom 4.43: The Zip drive's LED flashes continuously. This almost always indicates a problem with the drive. When you insert or eject a disk (or copy files to or from your Zip drive), the light on the Zip drive will normally blink several times. If the light flashes continuously, there is a problem.

- *Check the disk*. Try ejecting and reinstalling the Zip disk (be sure to use a blank disk to avoid accidental data loss). You may also wish to try a different disk. If a new disk corrects the problem, the original disk is defective and should be replaced or discarded.

■ *Cycle the drive*. Power down the computer and Zip drive, then restart the system properly. After restarting the system, try the Zip disk(s) again. If the problem persists, the drive is probably defective and should be replaced. Otherwise, the drive simply needed to be cycled.

> **NOTE**: If the Zip drive is an external model, unplug the power cord from the drive, wait at least 5 s, and plug the power cord back into the drive.

Symptom 4.44: You cannot eject a Zip disk from a drive. This is a frequent problem reported with parallel-port Zip drives. If the Zip disk won't eject from the drive (either when pushing the Eject button or when using the software "eject" feature), there may be a hardware failure or an incorrect software setting.

■ *Close your open applications*. Press the <Ctrl> + <Alt> + <Del> keys simultaneously to open the *Close Program* dialog box. Close all open applications one at a time (except Explorer and Systray) by highlighting an application and choosing the *End Task* button. Once all applications are closed (except Explorer and Systray), try to eject the disk from the Zip drive using the Eject button on the front of the drive. If the disk ejects, there is a software application problem.

■ *Cycle the drive*. Power down the computer and Zip drive, then restart the system properly. After restarting the system, try ejecting the Zip disk(s) again. If the problem persists, the drive is probably defective and should be replaced. Otherwise, the drive simply needed to be cycled.

■ *Try another disk*. Insert a different blank formatted Zip disk into the drive (without connecting the data cable to the computer). If the disk ejects, the original disk is defective. If the disk still does not eject, the drive is probably defective and should be replaced.

- *Try the emergency eject button*. Remove the power cord from your Zip drive. Straighten out a paper clip and insert it into the emergency eject hole located on the back of the drive (above the right-hand cable connector). If the disk still refuses to eject, the drive is probably defective and should be replaced.

Symptom 4.45: You cannot format a 100-MB Zip disk in a 250-MB Zip drive. This is known to be a problem under Windows 3.1X. If you try to format a 100-MB disk in a 250-MB drive in Windows 3.1X, an error message indicates that the format has failed. This is an erroneous error—the format was successful, and files *can* be copied to and from the disk correctly. The disk and drive are working properly (no damage has occurred), but an incorrect message is being displayed.

Symptom 4.46: The Zip drive refuses to spin up. There are a variety of possible problems that might contribute to this symptom.

- *Try another disk*. Insert a different blank formatted Zip disk into the drive. If the new disk works properly, the original disk is defective. If the symptom persists, the trouble is with conflicting software or Zip drive problems.

- *Try a clean boot*. Real-mode drivers and TSRs can sometimes interfere with the Zip drive. Start the PC from a bootable DOS diskette. If the drive spins up, there is an issue with your startup files (CONFIG.SYS and AUTOEXEC.BAT). Try systematically REMarking out any files that might interfere with the Zip drive.

- *Check the parallel port*. If you're using a parallel-port Zip drive, change the mode of your parallel port to SPP, EPP, standard, or bidirectional.

- *Replace the drive*. If problems persist, the drive is probably defective and should be replaced.

Symptom 4.47: You notice poor performance with a parallel-port 250-MB Zip drive. Zip drive performance depends on the performance of your LPT port. Optimum performance requires a parallel port running in EPP mode—a parallel port in ECP or unidirectional mode may cause erratic performance. Access your system's CMOS Setup to reconfigure the parallel port. Once you have located the parallel port settings, choose either *EPP, bidirectional, SPP, standard, AT, PS/2, or fast mode*. Save your changes and reboot the system.

> **NOTE**: Your BIOS may not allow you to change the parallel-port mode (especially in older systems). In this case, you may be able to change the parallel-port mode through a jumper setting on the motherboard.

If you're using an SCSI Zip drive, check your cable length and optimize the chain. The combined SCSI chain length (the total of all cables in the SCSI chain) should not exceed 6 m (about 19.6 ft). This includes both internal and external SCSI devices. The fastest device should be the last (or farthest from the computer).

Symptom 4.48: There is no power light on the external Zip drive. The green light on an external Zip drive indicates that the drive is plugged in and receiving power. Check that all the connections are tight. If the problem persists and the light still does not come on, try another power supply to determine if the first one is defective. Also, plug the power supply into another outlet to determine whether the first outlet is the problem. If there is still no response, the drive is probably defective and should be replaced.

Symptom 4.49: The computer locks up after running the parallel-port accelerator utility. In some cases, a system lockup may occur after installing the parallel-port driver and then running the Parallel Port Accelerator. Sometimes running the Parallel Port Accelerator utility will cause the drive to stop running (or even cause the system to lock up during boot). Disconnect the Zip drive and reboot the computer. Remove the modifications made by the Parallel Port Accelerator:

- Right-click the *My Computer* icon and select *Properties*.

- Click on the *Device Manager* tab.

- Click the plus sign (+) next to *SCSI controllers*.

- Double-click on *Iomega Parallel Port Interface*.

- Click on the *Settings* tab.

- Remove all the information from the *Adapter settings* box.

- Click *OK*, then click *OK* again.

- Click *Yes* to restart your computer.

- Reconnect the Zip parallel-port drive and try it again.

Symptom 4.50: The computer locks up when running an open application if you try to eject a Zip disk. If a file or application that resides on your Zip disk is open or in use, and you try to eject that disk, the computer may lock up. Before you eject your Zip disk, make certain that you close any files or applications that may be open (or in use).

Symptom 4.51: There is a Zip disk read failure on the Zip drive under Windows 95/98. In virtually all cases, the problem is a defective Zip disk. Using an improperly formatted Zip disk in the drive may also cause a problem.

- *Check the disk*. Use a different Zip disk and see if that resolves the problem (or try the original disk on another Zip drive). Make sure to use a blank Zip disk so that you won't lose any critical data.

- *Try reformatting the disk.* If a different disk works, and the original disk seems to have a problem, try reformatting the original Zip disk:

  1. Double-click the *My Computer* icon on your desktop.
  2. Right-click on the Zip drive icon and select *Format*.
  3. Select *Long Format with Surface Verify*.
  4. Click *Start*, and click *Start* again.
  5. When the disk has finished formatting successfully, click *OK*.

  If you cannot format the Zip disk successfully, the disk is almost certainly defective and should be replaced.

- *Try the drive on another system.* If the disk can be read when the Zip drive is moved to another PC, there may be a problem with the PC or with the way in which the drive was connected to that system.

- *Suspect the drive.* If no disks can be read on the Zip drive, double-check the drive's installation and setup. If the problem persists, then the drive itself may be defective and should be replaced.

Symptom 4.52: You see a fatal exception error when using an ATAPI IDE Zip drive. This is a known issue under Windows 95 (and OEM2), but it was fixed under Windows 98. This problem occurs when you're using an Intel motherboard and AMI (or Intel) BIOS. The Zip drive may also be installed on the secondary IDE channel. The error may also occur when you start the computer without a disk in the drive, or when you eject the disk from the Zip drive. This is a problem with Windows 95, but it can be corrected by obtaining the latest update files for Windows:

- ESDI_506.PDR version 4.00.956 (dated 5/14/96) and later

- VOLTRACK.VXD version 4.00.954 (dated 3/6/96) and later

To install this update, download the REMIDEUP. EXE file from the Microsoft Software Library to an empty folder. In *My Computer* or Windows Explorer, double-click the REMIDEUP.EXE file, then follow the instructions on the screen. The following files are installed by REMIDEUP.EXE:

- ESDI_506.PDR 4.00.1116 8/25/97 11:16a 24,426 Windows\System\Iosubsys
- VOLTRACK.VXD 4.00.954 3/6/96 9:54a 18,518 Windows\System\Iosubsys

Symptom 4.53: You encounter Windows Protection errors at startup (the Windows logo screen) when using an HP printer and parallel-port Zip drive. This problem can occur if you have an HP 4000 or 8000 series printer attached to a Zip drive, and the Zip drive is attached to the parallel port. To work around this problem, disable bidirectional support in your computer's CMOS Setup (or in the properties of your printer). To disable bidirectional support:

- Click *Start*, highlight *Settings*, and click *Printers*.
- Right-click your *HP 4000* printer, and then click *Properties*.
- Click the *Details* tab, click *Spool Settings*, click *Disable bidirectional support for this printer*, click *OK*, and then click *OK* again.

Web Contacts

Iomega Web site: *www.iomega.com*

Imation for Zip media: *http://xenon.imationstudio.com/crossref/compsearch.nsf/comp+search*

Fuji for Zip media: *http://www.fujifilm.com/home/sbu/comprod/cp_magd.htm*

Hard Drives

The *hard disk drive* (or HDD) evolved to answer the incessant demands for permanent, high-volume, high-speed file and data storage in the PC. Early floppy disks provided simple and inexpensive storage, but they are slow, and programs quickly became far too large to store adequately on diskettes. Switching between multiple diskettes also proved to be a cumbersome proposition. By the early 1980s, hard drives had become an important part of PC architecture and helped to fuel further operating system and applications development; today, the hard drive is an indispensable element of the modern PC. The hard drive holds the operating system which boots the system, stores the multimegabyte applications and files we rely on, and even provides virtual memory for systems that are lean on RAM. Hard drive performance also has a profound effect on overall system performance. As you might imagine, hard drive problems can easily cripple a system. This chapter presents some essential principles of hard disk drives and provides you with some solutions for drive testing and troubleshooting.

IDE/EIDE Hard Drive Concepts

IDE (Integrated Device Electronics) hard drives have come a long way since their introduction in the late 1980s. In fact, IDE technology has come *so* far that it's difficult to keep all of the concepts straight. Let's start the chapter by examining the important concepts and attributes of IDE and its successors.

Binary megabytes vs. decimal megabytes

Most folks know that hard drive sizes are measured in "megabytes" (or MB) and "gigabytes" (or GB); however, beginners and experienced technicians alike are often confused by the difference between "binary megabytes" and "decimal megabytes" (or gigabytes). For example, you'll notice that when you install a new 4-GB hard drive, utilities like CMOS Setup, FDISK, and Windows Explorer will report only about 3.72 GB, but other utilities like CHKDSK report about 4 GB. This difference is often confusing, but it's due to the way in which manufacturers and software makers calculate drive capacity. *Technically*, hard drive capacity is calculated by multiplying the number of cylinders, sectors, and heads times 512:

$$\text{Capacity} = \text{cylinders} \times \text{heads} \times \text{sectors} \times 512 \text{ (bytes per sector)}$$

So if you're using an AC2850 drive with 1654 cylinders, 16 heads, and 63 sectors, you wind up with

$$1654 \times 16 \times 63 \times 512 = 853{,}622{,}784 \text{ bytes}$$

By comparison, an AC34000 drive with 7752 cylinders, 16 heads, and 63 sectors would yield

$$7752 \times 16 \times 63 \times 512 = 4{,}000{,}776{,}192 \text{ bytes}$$

The problem is that hard drive manufacturers use the notion of *decimal megabytes* (or decimal gigabytes) to determine the size of their hard drives. To calculate drive sizes in decimal megabytes, just divide the drive size by 1,000,000 (or 1,000,000,000 for gigabytes). For the AC2850, you'd get

$$853,622,784/1,000,000 = 853.6 \text{ MB}$$

For the AC34000, you'd get

$$4,000,776,192/1,000,000,000 = 4.0 \text{ GB}$$

Makes sense, right? The problem is that many software makers use *binary megabytes* (or binary gigabytes) to calculate drive sizes. A binary megabyte is 1,048,576 bytes, and a binary gigabyte is 1,073,741,824 bytes, so here's how a lot of software will report the AC2850:

$$853,622,784 \text{ bytes}/1,048,576 = 814 \text{ MB}$$

And here's the calculation for the AC34000:

$$4,000,776,192 \text{ bytes}/1,073,741,824 = 3.72 \text{ GB}$$

These are simply two slightly different ways of representing the same drives, so both methods are correct. The important issue here is that you recognize the difference, and do not mistake that difference for a problem with the drive.

IDE/ATA

IDE and ATA (AT Attachment) are basically one and the same thing: a disk drive scheme designed to integrate the controller onto the drive itself instead of relying on a stand-alone controller board as older MFM and RLL drives did. This approach reduces interface costs and makes drive firmware implementations easier. IDE proved to be a low-cost, easily configured system—so much so that it created a boom in the disk drive industry. Although the terms *IDE* and *ATA* are sometimes used interchangeably, ATA is the formal standard that defines the drive and how it operates, while IDE is really the "trade name" that refers to the 40-pin interface and drive controller architecture designed to implement the ATA standard.

ATAPI

One of the major disadvantages of ATA is that it was designed for hard drives only. With the introduction of CD-ROM drives in the late 1980s, designers needed a means of attaching CD-ROMs (and other devices such as tape drives) to the existing ATA (IDE) interface; rather than employing a stand-alone (proprietary) controller card. The *ATA Packet Interface* (or ATAPI) is an extension of the ATA (IDE) interface designed to allow devices other than hard drives to plug into an ordinary ATA (IDE) port. While hard drives enjoy ATA (IDE) support through BIOS, ATAPI devices require a device driver to support them. Booting from an ATAPI CD-ROM is possible only with an "El Torito" CD-ROM and the latest BIOS.

ATA-2, Fast-ATA, and EIDE

By the early 1990s, it became clear that ATA architecture would soon be overwhelmed by advances in hard drive technology. The hard drive industry responded by developing the ATA-2 standard as an extension of ATA. ATA-2 is largely regarded as a significant improvement to ATA—it defines faster PIO (Programmed I/O) and DMA (Direct Memory Access) data transfer modes, adds more powerful drive commands (such as the `Identify Drive` command to support autoidentification in CMOS), adds support for a second drive channel, handles block data transfers (block transfer mode), and defines new means of addressing sectors on the hard drive using *logical block addressing* (LBA). LBA has proven to be a very effective vehicle for overcoming the traditional 528-MB hard drive size limit. Yet ATA-2 continues to use the same 40-pin physical interface used by ATA and is backward-compatible with ATA (IDE) drives.

Along with ATA-2, you'll probably find two additional terms: EIDE (*Enhanced IDE*) and *Fast-ATA*. These are not standards—they are merely different implementations of the ATA-2 standard. EIDE represents the Western Digital implementation of ATA-2; it builds upon both the ATA-2 and ATAPI standards. This has been *so* effective that EIDE has become the generic term. Seagate and Quantum have thrown their support behind the Fast-ATA implementation of the ATA-2 standard. However, Fast-ATA builds on ATA-2 only. For all practical purposes, there is no significant difference between ATA-2, EIDE, and Fast-ATA, and you'll probably see these three terms used interchangeably (although this is not *technically* correct).

ATA-3

A more recent implementation of the ATA standard is ATA-3. It does not define any new data transfer modes, but it does improve the reliability of PIO Mode 4. It also offers a simple password-based security scheme, more sophisticated power management features, and Self-Monitoring Analysis and Reporting Technology (SMART). ATA-3 is also backward-compatible with ATA-2, ATAPI, and ATA devices. Since no new data transfer modes are defined by ATA-3, you may also see the generic term *EIDE* used interchangeably for this (although this is also not technically correct).

Ultra-ATA/33

The push for ever-faster data transfer rates is a never-ending one, and the Ultra-ATA standard represents an implementation of ATA/ATAPI-4 by providing a high-performance bus-mastering 33-MB/s DMA data transfer rate. The implementation of Ultra-ATA is usually called Ultra-DMA/33 (or UDMA/33). You'll need an Ultra-ATA drive, controller, and BIOS to support an

Ultra-ATA drive system, but it is fully backward-compatible with previous ATA standards. You can use ordinary 40-pin IDE-type cables for UDMA/33 unless any of the following issues occur:

- The standard cable is low-quality, damaged, or weakened by many installations.

- The system suffers from excessive signal noise—these systems may have multiple drives, dual power supplies, or an integrated CRT.

- The system is overclocked (or otherwise configured beyond the manufacturer's supported specifications).

Ultra-ATA/66

The Ultra-ATA standard for ATA/ATAPI-4 was upgraded to support an even faster high-performance bus-mastering 66-MB/s DMA data transfer rate. This more recent implementation of Ultra-ATA is usually called Ultra-DMA/66 (or UDMA/66). You'll need an Ultra-ATA/66 drive, controller, and BIOS to support an Ultra-ATA/66 drive system, but it is fully backward-compatible with previous ATA standards. Unlike in the Ultra-ATA/33 approach, you cannot use ordinary 40-pin IDE-type cables to connect drives and controllers. Instead, you'll need a specially designed 40-pin/80-conductor cable (typically provided with UDMA/66 drives). Also keep in mind that the operating system must be enabled for DMA transfers.

Common UDMA/66 issues

- Make sure that the signal cable is Ultra-ATA/66-capable. An Ultra-ATA/66-compliant cable is a 40-pin, 80-conductor cable with a black connector on one end, a blue connector on the other end, and a gray connector in the middle. In addition, pin 34 on the cable should be notched or cut (though this may be difficult to see with the human eye).

- Make sure the system board (motherboard) controller is capable of supporting Ultra-ATA/66. An Ultra-ATA/66-capable controller has a detect circuit which can detect that line 34 is missing on the cable. If there is no detect circuit, the system can wrongly detect the presence of an Ultra-ATA/66 cable and try to configure the device for a higher transfer rate.

- Some system board (motherboard) controllers may not successfully handle Ultra-ATA/66 on both the primary and secondary channels. If you have difficulty with a UDMA/66 device on the secondary controller channel, consider troubleshooting with the device in the primary master position.

- If you have trouble getting a UDMA/66 system configured properly, contact the system board (motherboard) or controller card manufacturer for the latest BIOS upgrade (and any Ultra-ATA/66 device drivers or patches).

- Make sure the operating system is DMA-capable, and verify that the DMA mode is activated. For Windows 95/98, check the drive's *Properties* dialog in the *Device Manager*.

- Make sure the Ultra-ATA/66-capable drive has been configured to run at Ultra-ATA/66 transfer rates. Some drives ship with the UDMA/66 mode disabled by default, and require a jumper change and/or software utility in order to activate the UDMA/66 mode.

Data transfer rates

Data transfer rates play a major role in drive performance. In practice, there two measures of data transfer: the rate at which data are taken from the platters, and the rate at which data are passed between the drive and the controller. The *internal* data transfer between the platters and the drive buffer is typically the slower rate. Older drives could run at around 5 MB/s, but newer Ultra-ATA drives like the Maxtor DiamondMax 2160 run at 14 MB/s. The *exter-*

nal data transfer between the drive and the controller (the *interface rate*) is often the *faster* rate. Older drives provided between 5 and 8 MB/s, but ATA-2 (EIDE) drives can operate at up to 16 MB/s. Ultra-DMA/33 drives can run at 33 MB/s, and Ultra-DMA/66 drives can handle burst data transfers of 66 MB/s. The modern standards of IDE/EIDE external data transfer are listed as PIO and DMA modes. The PIO mode specifies how fast data are transferred to and from the drive, as shown in Table 5.1.

You may notice that the EIDE-specific modes (PIO-3 and PIO-4) use the IORDY hardware flow control line. This means that the drive can use the IORDY line to slow down the interface when necessary. Interfaces without proper IORDY support may cause data corruption in the fast PIO modes (so you'd be stuck with the slower modes). When choosing an EIDE drive and controller, always be sure to check that the IORDY line is being used.

By comparison, DMA data transfers mean that the data are transferred *directly* between the drive and memory without using the CPU as an intermediary (as is the case with PIO). In true multitasking operating systems like OS/2, Windows NT, or Linux, DMA transfers leave the CPU free to do something useful during disk transfers. In a DOS or Windows environment, the CPU will have to wait for the transfer to finish any-

TABLE 5.1   Data Transfer Speeds vs. PIO Modes

PIO mode	Cycle time (ns)	Transfer rate (MB/s)	Notes
0	600	3.3	These are the old ATA (IDE) modes
1	383	5.2	
2	240	8.3	
3	180 IORDY	11.1	These are the newer ATA-2 (EIDE) modes
4	120 IORDY	16.6	

way, so in these cases DMA transfers don't offer that much of a multitasking advantage. There are two distinct types of direct memory access: ordinary DMA and bus-mastering DMA. Ordinary DMA uses the DMA controller on the system's motherboard to perform the complex task of arbitration, grabbing the system bus, and transferring the data. With bus-mastering DMA, all this is done by logic in the drive controller itself.

Unfortunately, the DMA controller on traditional ISA bus systems is slow—and out of the question for use with a modern hard disk. VL bus controller cards cannot be used as DMA targets at all, and can handle only bus-mastering DMA. Only EISA and PCI-based interfaces make non-bus-mastering DMA viable; EISA type B DMA will transfer 4 MB/s, and PCI type F DMA will transfer between 6 and 8 MB/s. Today, the proper software support for DMA is relatively rare (as are the interfaces supporting it). Still, the DMA data transfer modes are listed in Table 5.2.

Block mode transfers

Traditionally, an interrupt (IRQ) is generated each time a read or write command is passed to the drive. This causes a certain amount of overhead work for the host system and CPU. If it were possible to transfer *multiple* sectors of data between the drive and the host

TABLE 5.2   Data Transfer Speeds vs. DMA Modes

DMA Mode		Cycle time (ns)	Transfer rate (MB/s)	Notes
Single word	0	960	2.1	Also in ATA
	1	480	4.2	
	2	240	8.3	
Multiword	0	480	4.2	Also in ATA
	1	150	13.3	
	2	120	16.6	
	3	—	33.0	Ultra-DMA/33
	4	—	66.0	Ultra-DMA/66

without generating an IRQ, data transfer could be accomplished much more efficiently. Block mode transfers allow up to 128 sectors of data to be transferred at a single time, and can improve transfers as much as 30 percent. However, block mode transfers are not terribly effective on single-tasking operating systems like DOS—any improvement greater than a few percent usually indicates bad buffer cache management on the part of the drive. Finally, the block size that is optimal for drive throughput isn't always the best for system performance. For example, the DOS FAT (file allocation table) file system tends to favor a block size equal to the cluster size.

Ideas of bus mastering

Bus mastering is a high-performance enhancement to the drive controller interface on your system (you may see some motherboards or chipsets mention bus-mastering support as BM-IDE). When configured properly, bus mastering uses DMA data transfers to reduce the CPU's workload when it comes to saving or recalling data from the EIDE/IDE drive (such as a hard drive or ATAPI CD-ROM). By comparison, PIO data transfer modes are very CPU-intensive. Bus mastering is particularly useful if you have multiple disk-intensive applications running simultaneously. Many modern PCs support bus mastering, but to make the most of bus-mastering performance, your system must have *all* of the following elements:

- The motherboard (drive controller) must be bus-master IDE compliant.

- The motherboard BIOS must support bus mastering.

- You need a multitasking operating system (OS) such as Windows 95/98/2000.

- A bus-master device driver is needed for the operating system.

- And you need a bus-mastering-compatible EIDE/IDE device (disk drive, CD-ROM) that supports DMA multiword modes.

You *can* use bus-mastering IDE and non-bus-mastering IDE devices in the same system, but the non-bus-mastering IDE devices will reduce the overall performance of the bus-mastering devices. However, bus-mastering IDE is not a cure-all for system performance problems. In fact, bus mastering will probably not benefit the system significantly if you run DOS applications, work with only single applications at a time, or use multiple applications that are *not* disk-intensive.

Windows 95/98 IDE bus-master drivers. As you noticed above, you'll need a bus-master driver to support your operating system (namely Windows 95/98). The commercial release of Windows 95 offered only a generic solution (ESDI_506.PDR), and the version released with OSR2 is still quite basic. The bus-master drivers shipped with Windows 98 will generally offer better performance. For top performance, you should use the bus-master driver that accompanies your motherboard or other bus-master-compliant drive controller. You can check some of the following sources for current bus-master drivers:

- Drivers Headquarters: *http://www.drivershq.com/*
- Intel Bus Master Driver 3.0: *http://web2.iadfw.net/ksm/drivers/bmide_95.exe*
- Intel Bus Master Driver 2.85: *http://web2.iadfw.net/ksm/drivers/bmide285.exe*
- ASUS Bus Master Driver: *ftp://ftp1.asus.com.tw/pub/ASUS/Drivers/bmide_95.exe*
- Elitegroup (ECS) Bus Master Driver: *ftp://ftp.ecs.com.tw/pub/ide/triton/430v17.exe*
- Tyan Bus Master Driver 2.0: *ftp://204.156.147.247:21/pub/motherboard/tynbm20.zip*

Bus-master driver problems under Windows 95/98.   While bus mastering can clearly enhance the drive performance of a busy multitasking system, it is not without its problems. As it turns out, bus-master driver issues are the most prevalent problems. The two most common issues are as follows: (1) The CD-ROM or IDE-type HDD on the secondary drive channel disappears after the bus-master driver is installed, and (2) Windows 95/98 takes a long time to boot after bus-master drivers are installed.

In both cases, you'll notice that the secondary controller channel (IDE) no longer appears in the *Device Manager*. This is because bus-master drivers do not support ATA (IDE) controllers correctly. You'll need to install the bus-master driver for the primary (EIDE) drive channel and leave the PIO driver in place to support the secondary (IDE) drive channel. Install the bus-master driver, then alter the Registry to manually redirect the secondary IDE drive channel to use a standard IDE driver again:

> **NOTE**   *Altering the Windows 95/98 Registry can have a profound effect on your system, or even prevent the system from booting. Always make a backup copy of the original Registry files (SYSTEM.DAT and USER.DAT) before attempting to edit them.*

1. Start REGEDIT, load the Registry file, and find the entry

   ```
   HKEY_LOCAL_MACHINE/System/CurrentControlSet/con-
   trol/Services/Class/hdc
   ```

2. There should be four subdirectories, 0000–0003.

3. Find the one where *DriverDesc* reads something like *Primary Bus Master IDE controller* or *Secondary Bus Master IDE controller*, depending on the port you want to change (it should be 0002 or 0003). You'd most likely want to change the secondary entry.

4. In this subdirectory, change *PortDriver* from *ESDI_506.PDR* (or whatever bus master driver you're using) to *IDEATAPI.MPD*.

5. You can also change the *DriverDesc* to something like *Standard IDE/ESDI controller*—this will produce a more familiar entry when viewed in the *System Manager*.

6. Save your changes and reboot the computer.

Your secondary (IDE) drive controller channel should now be using a standard IDE driver, and the IDE devices on that channel (e.g., the CD-ROM) should now appear normally. Here's another trick that may shorten the startup time: Start Windows 95/98 in safe mode and delete all drives in *System Manager*. Then reboot the PC and allow Windows 95/98 to redetect all the drives automatically.

> **NOTE**: *Some technicians have suggested that configuring an ATAPI CD-ROM as the slave device when it's the only device on the secondary (IDE) drive channel might work when using bus-master drivers. Normally, the only IDE device would be jumpered as the master. Please note that this suggestion won't damage the CD-ROM or drive controller, but it has not been tested to verify that it actually works. Given the proliferation of bus-master hardware and software, there may be circumstances in which this suggestion may or may not work. Consider it as a last resort.*

Concepts of Drive Formatting

You can imagine a disk drive as being a big file cabinet. When the drive is first installed, the file cabinet is completely empty—there are no dividers or folders or labels of any kind to organize information. In order to make the drive useful, it must be formatted and partitioned. There are basically three steps to the format process: a low-level format, partitioning, and a high-level format. Each of these steps is critically important for the proper operation of a drive.

Low-level formatting

The *low-level format* is perhaps the most important step (and is responsible for most of a drive's long-term problems). Sector header and trailer information is written, along with dummy data. Intersector and intertrack gaps are also created. As you might imagine, the low-level format forms the foundation of a hard drive's organization. Since this information is written only once, age and wear can allow sector information to eventually fail. When this happens, the failed sector(s) are unreadable. Advanced drive features like translation, defect management, and zoned recording also complicate a proper low-level format.

This problem is further compounded by the fact that low-level formatting is hardware-specific, and most current drive makers low-level format their drives at the factory—those routines are rarely made available to technicians and end users. If you determine that an IDE or SCSI drive must be low-level formatted, make it a point to contact the drive manufacturer and obtain a proper low-level format utility written *expressly* for that particular drive model. Even leading professional utilities such as DrivePro strongly urge *against* low-level formats for IDE/EIDE drives except as a measure of last resort. If you attempt to invoke low-level IDE/EIDE formatting with a DOS DEBUG sequence or software utility, one of four things may happen:

- The drive will ignore the low-level formatter entirely.

- The drive will accept the formatter, but will erase only areas containing data (and fail to rewrite sector ID information).

- The drive will accept the formatter and erase vital servo information and other sector information (thus, the drive will be rendered completely unusable).

■ The drive will accept the formatter and perform a correct low-level format—this is highly unlikely.

> **NOTE**: *Any low-level format process will completely destroy all data on a drive. Back up as much of the drive as possible before attempting a low-level format. Do* not *attempt to low-level format a hard drive unless you have an appropriate utility from the drive maker—and then only as a procedure of last resort.*

There are three compelling reasons to try to low-level format a hard drive:

■ The drive has contracted a virus that cannot be removed without destroying the boot sector.

■ The drive is developing bad sectors at an increasing rate (usually due to age or failure).

■ You are changing from one operating system to another and wish to remove *everything* from the drive.

If you determine that low-level formatting is necessary, there are typically two courses that are open to you: You can use a low-level formatter tool included in the BIOS (such as an AMI BIOS), or you can use a software tool provided by your drive's manufacturer.

Low-level formatting through BIOS. Some BIOS versions have a built-in ATA-compatible "low-level format" utility (AMI is known for this, but there are other BIOS makers that may incorporate that type of feature). Before using the AMI BIOS formatting utility, make sure the AMI BIOS is dated after April 9, 1990. From the CMOS Setup, select *Hard Disk Utilities*, then select *Hard Disk Format*. The formatting utility will automatically take the hard drive parameters from the CMOS Setup so that you can verify them. The only major issue is the *Interleave*—the BIOS defaults to 3, but change it to 1. The other issue is *Mark Bad Tracks*—answer *no* to that question and proceed. This process may take anywhere from 15 min to an hour or more. When the process is complete, reboot the system with a DOS boot diskette. Run FDISK to partition the drive, then use FORMAT to format the drive.

> **NOTE**: *The AMI BIOS may offer two other options,* Auto Interleave *and* Media Analysis. *There is no need to run either of these utilities. If you do run the* Auto Interleave *utility, keep in mind that it may give inaccurate readings—remember that the* Interleave *should always be 1.*

Low-level formatting through software. A somewhat safer and more versatile approach is to use low-level formatting software provided by your hard drive's manufacturer. Such software would be ideally suited to your particular drive and reduces the possibility of accidental drive damage. For example, if you need to low-level format a Seagate drive, you could probably use the SGATFMT4.ZIP (Seagate Format) tool available from the Seagate Web site at *http://www.seagate.com/support/disc/drivers/discfile.shtml* (detailed instructions would be included in the self-extracting file).

Partitioning

Whereas low-level formatting is a hardware-specific process, *partitioning* is an operating system–specific process. After low-level formatting is complete, the drive must be partitioned before an operating system file system or boot information is written to the drive. Also, partitioning allows a large physical drive to be divided up into several smaller *logical* drives. There are several file systems in service today, but DOS, Windows 3.1x, and Windows 95 continue to use the file allocation table (FAT) system. The main criticism of the FAT is that sectors are grouped and assigned as clusters; this is a wasteful use of drive space (especially for large drives, where up to 64 sectors—32 KB—may be in a single cluster). One of the newly created partitions will be assigned as the boot partition, and a *master boot sector* (MBS) containing a special boot program and partition table will be written to the first sector. The MBS is often referred to as the *master boot record* (MBR). FDISK is the DOS utility used for drive partitioning. Different operating systems carry their own partitioning limitations:

- Versions of MS-DOS and PC-DOS after 3.30 (but before 4.0) have a 32 MB per partition limit.

- All versions of DOS have a 1024-cylinder limitation. To access more cylinders, you'll need a device driver or a controller card that offers a translate mode (e.g., LBA).

- DOS and Windows 95 are limited to 2.1 GB per partition.

- Versions of Windows NT 4.0 and earlier are limited to a 4.2-GB boot partition.

- Windows 95 OSR2 and Windows 98 use FAT32 partitions, which can support up to 2-TB partitions.

High-level (DOS) formatting

Even after partitioning, an operating system cannot store files on a drive. A series of data structures must be written to the drive. A *volume boot sector* (VBS), two copies of the *file allocation table*, and a *root directory* are written to each logical partition. High-level formatting also checks and locks out bad sectors so that they will not be used during normal operation. FORMAT is the DOS utility used for high-level formatting. It is interesting to note that the FORMAT utility will perform both low-level and high-level formatting for a floppy disk, but *not* for a hard drive.

File Systems and Tips

When you purchase an IDE/EIDE or SCSI hard drive today, it is already low-level formatted—that is, the cylinder, track, and sector information is already written onto the drive. This means you can partition the drive with FDISK and format the drive with FORMAT right out of the box. The process of FDISK and FORMAT prepares the drive for a particular file system. We won't talk much about the complexities of file systems in detail, but you should understand the basic FAT system and know some implications of FAT16 and FAT32.

FAT basics

Microsoft DOS, Windows 3.1x, and Windows 95/98 use a file allocation table to organize files on the drive. Sectors are organized into groups called *clusters*, and each cluster is assigned a number. Early drives (i.e., floppy drives) used a 12-bit number (known as FAT12), but hard drives typically used a 16-bit number (called FAT16). The newest releases of Windows 95 (OSR2) and Windows 98 assign a 32-bit number to each cluster (called FAT32). By assigning each cluster its own number, it is possible to store files in any available (unused) clusters throughout the drive without worrying about the file's size. As files are erased, those clusters become available for reuse. Overall, the FAT system has proven to be a versatile and reliable file management system.

The problem with the FAT system is that you have only as many clusters as can be specified by the number of bits available. For a 12-bit FAT, you can have only 4096 (2^{12}) clusters. For a 16-bit FAT, you can have 65,536 (2^{16}) clusters. If the drive is 120 MB, each cluster must then be about 120 MB/65,536 = 1.8 KB (2 KB in actual practice). If the drive is 500 MB, each cluster must be about 540 MB/65,536 = 7.6 KB (8 KB in actual practice). Since only *one* file can be assigned to any given cluster, the *entire* space for that cluster is assigned (even if the file is very small). So if you were to store a 2-KB file in an 8-KB cluster, you'd waste (8 KB − 2 KB = 6 KB! This wasted space is known as *slack space*. Of course, the FAT12 system was long since abandoned while hard drives were still about 32 MB, but you get the idea that very large drives can waste a serious amount of space when using a FAT system.

Another frequent complaint about the FAT file system is the phenomenon of *file fragmentation*. Since clusters are all independent, and clusters are assigned wherever space can be found, a file requiring more than one cluster can be scattered anywhere on the disk. For example, suppose you're editing a large image (it can take several megabytes). The file may use the 20 available clusters on track 345, 2 more available clusters on track 1012, 50 available clusters on track 2011, and so on. In theory, fragmentation is simply a harmless side effect of the FAT system. But in practice, badly fragmented files can force the hard drive to work unusually hard chasing down the various clusters associated with the file. Not only does this slow the drive's effective performance, but the extra work required of the drive may ultimately shorten its working life. The best way to correct this issue is to periodically "defragment" the disk with a utility like Defrag. Defragmenting the disk will rearrange all the clusters so that all of the clusters for any given file are contiguous.

FAT16

DOS (including DOS 7.0 of Windows 95) uses the FAT16 file system to store data. The FAT16 system uses 16-bit-cluster address numbers, which allow up to 65,536 clusters. Under FAT16, a cluster can be as big as 32 KB, which translates into a maximum partition size of $65,536 \times 32,768 = 2,147,483,648$ bytes (2.1 GB). While a 16-bit cluster number is much more efficient than a 12-bit cluster number, every file *must* take up at least one cluster, even if the file size is much smaller than the cluster. For the very large drives which we have today, the correspondingly large clusters can result in a significant amount of slack space. If the physical drive is larger than 2.1 GB, you must create subsequent logical partitions to utilize the additional space. For example, if you have a 3.1-GB drive, you can create one 2.1-GB partition, than create a second 1.0-GB partition. One way to reduce slack space is to create a larger number of smaller logical partitions; this results in smaller clusters.

Partitioning large hard drives

Chances are that you're already familiar with the DOS FDISK partitioning utility and have used it at one time or another to partition older hard drives. However, large hard drives (over 2 GB) present an unusual wrinkle for technicians: DOS and Windows 95 support only partitions up to 2 GB. When you install a hard drive that's larger than 2 GB, you need to create multiple partitions on the drive—if you don't, you won't be able to take advantage of the full drive capacity. The procedure below offers a step-by-step guide for partitioning large drives.

Partitioning a large hard drive with FAT16 FDISK

1. At the *FDISK Options* menu, select *4. Display partition information* and hit <Enter>. If the partition information display indicates that there are existing partition(s) on the drive, these partitions must be deleted *before* proceeding (select *3. Delete partition information* on the *FDISK Options* menu to remove any existing partitions).

2. At the *FDISK Options* menu, select *1. Create DOS partition or Logical DOS drive* and hit <Enter>. The *Create DOS partition or Logical DOS Drive* menu is displayed. Select *1. Create Primary DOS partition* and hit <Enter>.

3. The message *Do you wish to use the maximum available size for a Primary DOS Partition and make the Partition active (Y/N)* is displayed. Type N and press <Enter>.

   NOTE: *When this message is displayed, you* must *respond with* N. *If you reply* Y, *a primary partition of 2.048 GB will be created, and the system will not be able to access the remainder of the drive's capacity unless the partition is deleted.*

4. Type in the size of the primary partition (in megabytes). This value can be anywhere from 1 to 2048 MB (default). Then press the <Enter> key. The message *Primary DOS Partition created* is displayed. Press <Esc> to continue.

5. At the *FDISK Options* menu, select *1. Create DOS partition or Logical DOS drive* and press <Enter>. The *Create DOS partition or Logical DOS Drive* menu is displayed. Select *2. Create Extended DOS partition* and press <Enter>.

6. The *Create Extended DOS Partition* screen is displayed. Press <Enter> to place the remaining available space on the drive into the extended DOS partition.

   NOTE: *Unless all of the remaining drive space is placed into the extended DOS partition, the total capacity of the hard drive will not be available to the system.*

7. Press <Esc> to continue when the FDISK message *Extended DOS Partition created* appears on the monitor. FDISK will now prompt you to create logical drives for the extended DOS partition. The message *Enter logical drive size in megabytes or percent of disk space (%)...* is displayed.

8. Type the value desired for the capacity value of the logical drive size (up to 2048 MB) and press <Enter>. If you choose a value less than the displayed total size, you must continue entering drive

sizes until all of the available space has been assigned logical drive letters.

NOTE: *Remember that each logical DOS drive created represents a drive letter (e.g., C:, D:, E:, or F:).*

9. Press <Esc> to continue when the FDISK message *All available space in the Extended DOS Partition is assigned to logical drives* appears.

10. If the drive is going to be the primary boot drive, select *2. Set active partition* and press <Enter> at the *FDISK Options* menu. The *Set Active Partition* screen is displayed and the message *Enter the number of the partition you want to make active* is displayed. Press 1, then press <Enter>. The message *Partition 1 made active* is displayed. Press <Esc>.

11. Press <Esc> to exit FDISK. Exiting FDISK under DOS will cause the system to reboot. Under Windows 95, the system will return to the C:\WINDOWS\COMMAND> prompt, and the user will have to manually reboot the system.

12. After the system reboots, each drive letter assigned to the partitioned hard drive must be formatted with FORMAT. You should now be able to use the drive.

NOTE: *There have been a number of problems reported with the Windows 95 version of FDISK. As a rule, use the DOS 6.22 version of FDISK or the 16-bit version of FDISK included with OSR2.*

FAT32

Obviously, the limitations of FAT 16 are presenting a serious issue as hard drives passed 6 GB and beyond. Microsoft has responded by developing a 32-bit FAT system to implement in a service release of Windows 95 (called OSR2) and now in Windows 98. The upper 4 bits are reserved, so the system will actually access 2^{28}

268,435,456 clusters (over 256 million clusters). This allows single partitions of 8 GB with clusters only 4 KB in size. The maximum size of any given partition is 2 TB (yes, *terabytes*—thousands of gigabytes). FAT32 also eliminates the fixed size for a root directory, so you can have as many files and directories in the root as you want.

On the surface, this probably sounds like a great deal, but there are some major problems that you'll need to consider before you update to FAT32. First, DOS applications (without being rewritten) can access only files up to 2 GB, and Win32 applications can work with files up to 4 GB. By itself, that's not so bad, but FAT32 partitions are accessible *only* through the OSR2-enhanced Windows 95, Windows 98, and the corresponding DOS 7.X—no other operating system can read the partitions (including Windows NT). Also, any disk utilities written for FAT16 won't work for FAT32 (and can seriously damage your data).

Even though the OSR2 release ships with FAT32 versions of FDISK, FORMAT, SCANDISK, and DEFRAG, the version of DriveSpace 3 will *not* support FAT32. So if you're using drive compression, you're out of luck. Further, there are older APIs (application programming interfaces) in service that simply won't support FAT32, so some programs may refuse to work outright until the software is recompiled with FAT32-compliant APIs. DOS device drivers (such as those needed to support SCSI devices) will also have to be updated for FAT32. In other words, you'll lose your SCSI drives until suitable drivers become available. Finally, the OSR2 version of Windows 95 appears to *decrease* FAT32 drive performance (though that's not really an issue under Windows 98).

Partitioning and formatting for FAT32

Before you make the decision to use FAT32, you'll need to be familiar with the issues involved in partitioning and formatting. The basic steps in drive preparation are the same as those for FAT16, but FAT32 introduces a few wrinkles that you should understand. This part of the chapter describes the general process used to partition and format the drive under FAT32. First, a FAT32 partition can be created (with Windows 95 OSR2 or Windows 98) only under the following circumstances:

- The hard drive *must* be greater than 528 MB in *total* capacity.

- The partition size must be greater than 528 MB.

- You need an OSR2 Setup Disk or OSR2 Startup Disk made from another OSR2-configured PC (or a suitable Windows 98 Startup Disk).

- When the OSR2/98 FDISK prompts *Do you wish to enable large disk support? Y or N*, you'll need to answer Y. If you answer N, a FAT16 partition will be created.

Partitioning a large hard drive with FAT32 (OSR2/98) FDISK

1. Boot the PC with the Windows 95 OSR2 (or Windows 98) Startup Disk.

2. At the *Welcome to Setup* screen, press the <F3> key twice. This will terminate the execution of the Setup program and take you to the A: prompt.

   NOTE: *If you have an OSR2 Startup Disk from another PC, you can boot from that diskette instead and avoid the hassle of exiting the OSR2 Setup routine.*

3. Type FDISK and press <Enter>. You'll be prompted with *Do you wish to enable large disk support? Y or N*.

4. Type Y to create a FAT32 partition and press <Enter>. At this point, the *FDISK Options* menu

will appear on the screen. If there is more than one hard drive in the system, use option *5 (Change current fixed drive)* to select the desired drive to partition. Be careful: Partitioning the wrong drive will render any existing data on that drive inaccessible.

5. Select option *4* for *Display Partition Information* and press <Enter>. For a brand new hard drive, FDISK should respond *No Partitions Defined.* Any preexisting partitions (i.e., FAT16 partitions) must be *deleted* before you continue. Remember, this will delete *all* existing data on the hard drive.

6. Press the <Esc> key to return to the *FDISK Options* menu, then select option *1* for *Create DOS partition or Logical DOS drive* and press <Enter>. Next, select option *1* for *Create Primary DOS Partition* and press <Enter>.

7. After FDISK verifies the drive integrity, it will prompt you with *Do you wish to use the maximum available size for a Primary DOS Partition and make the Partition active (Y/N)?* Type Y and press <Enter>.

8. Exit FDISK by pressing the <Esc> key until you see the message *You must restart the system for changes to take effect.* Press the <Esc> key to exit FDISK, and remove the floppy diskette in drive A:. Reboot the computer using <Ctrl>+<Alt>+<Del>.

Formatting a large hard drive with FAT32 (OSR2/98) FORMAT

1. Boot the PC with the Windows 95 OSR2 (or Windows 98) Startup Disk.

2. At the *Welcome to Setup* screen, press the <F3> key twice. This will terminate the execution of the Setup program, and take you to the A: prompt.

> **NOTE**: *If you have an OSR2 Startup Disk from another PC, you can boot from that diskette instead and avoid the hassle of exiting the OSR2 Setup routine.*

3. Type FORMAT <insert your drive letter: here> and press <Enter> to start formatting (e.g., FORMAT D:). After **FORMAT** starts, you'll see the message; *WARNING all data on nonremovable disk drive <letter:> will be lost proceed with format? Y/N.*

4. Type Y and press <Enter>. The OSR2 FORMAT utility will then prepare the hard drive for use with FAT32.

Using the FAT32 "drive converter"

Windows 98 provides a drive converter which allows you to convert FAT16 partitions to FAT32 format. The simplest method is to just type cvt <drive>: /cvt32 and then press <Enter>. Remember that <drive> is the drive that you want to convert to the FAT32 file system. Another step-by-step approach is listed below:

- Click *Start*, select *Programs*, highlight *Accessories*, choose *System Tools*, click *Drive Converter* (FAT32), and then click *Next*.

- In the *Drives* box, click the drive that you want to convert to the FAT32 file system.

- Click *Next*, and then click *OK*.

- Click *Next*, click *Next*, and then click *Next* again.

- Allow the conversion process to complete.

- When the conversion is complete, click *Finish* and reboot the PC if necessary.

   IMPORTANT NOTE: *After you convert your hard disk to FAT32, you cannot convert back to the original FAT system. Before you convert to the FAT32 file system, uninstall any utilities or tools that protect or encrypt the master boot record or partition table (e.g., uninstall Bootlock included with Symantec Norton Your Eyes Only).*

NOTE: *The FAT32 converter may fail if your hard drive is less than 512 MB or has bad sectors (often resulting in data corruption).*

Creating a FAT32 Startup Disk for Windows 98

When booting from a floppy disk, it is often difficult for you to access FAT32 partitions because the operating system version on the floppy disk is not "FAT32-aware." The Windows 98 CD-ROM contains a program you can use to create a startup disk that *is* capable of creating and reading FAT32 partitions. Once you create the new diskette, you can simply leave the diskette in the drive and reboot the PC. Note that this boot disk does not contain all the programs included on the Windows 98 Startup Disk. To create a FAT32-aware Windows 98 Startup Disk from within Windows 98:

- Place the Windows 98 CD in your CD-ROM drive, and have a floppy disk handy.

- Click *Start*, highlight *Programs*, and then click *Windows Explorer*.

- Open the following folder on the Windows 98 CD:

  ```
  \Tools\Mtsutil\Fat32ebd
  ```

- Double-click the following file, and then follow the instructions to finish creating the disk:

  ```
  Fat32ebd.exe
  ```

- Write-protect the floppy disk.

If you want to create a FAT32-aware boot diskette from DOS:

- Place the Windows 98 CD-ROM in your CD-ROM drive, and have a floppy disk handy.

- Type each of the following lines (where `<drive>` is the drive letter of your CD-ROM drive):

```
windows\smartdrv.exe <drive>:          <Enter>

cd\tools\mtsutil\fat32ebd              <Enter>

fat32ebd.exe                           <Enter>
```

- Now follow the instructions to create the disk.
- Write-protect the floppy disk.

> **NOTE**: *The SMARTDRV.EXE utility is not required in order to create a Windows 98 Startup Disk—it simply helps speed up the creation process.*

Understanding the master boot record

The master boot record (or MBR) is information which is normally stored in the first sector of the hard drive. This information is simply a small data structure that identifies where an operating system (OS) is located on the drive, so that the OS can be loaded into the system's memory (RAM) at boot time. The MBR contains two elements: executable code (a.k.a. a "program") and a *partition table* that identifies each partition residing on the hard drive.

The executable code (or MBR program) begins the boot process by looking up the partition table to determine what partition holds the operating system. It then loads the boot sector of the partition containing the OS into RAM, and transfers execution of the program to the partition boot sector. The partition boot sector then finishes loading the operating system files into RAM.

Creating/restoring the MBR. The MBR is created during the partition process (using FDISK). If the MBR is corrupted or damaged, you can often restore it using FDISK with the /MBR switch, such as

```
C:\ FDISK /MBR                    <Enter>
```

Remember to back up as much of the drive as possible *before* attempting this command. It should not corrupt the drive partitions or its data, but it *could*.

The MBR and drive overlay software. When a system BIOS or drive controller will not support the full size of a drive, you typically have the option of upgrading the BIOS (and/or drive controller) or using "drive overlay" software such as EZ-Drive or MaxBlast or other products. The use of overlay software will affect the way an MBR is configured. When drive overlay software (e.g., EZ-Drive) controls a hard drive, the MBR is stored on the *second* sector of the hard drive—the first sector contains EZ-Drive code (also known as EZ-BIOS). Sectors 3 through 17 also contain EZ-Drive code which is referred to as the INT13 Handler (INT13 deals with hard disk services). When the system is powered on, it looks at the first sector of the hard drive for boot instructions. In this case, the boot sequence is as follows:

- EZ-Drive code loads from sector 1 on the drive.

- EZ-Drive loads the INT13 Handler located in sectors 3 through 17 and uses this information to set up the hard drive for proper access at its full capacity.

- EZ-Drive loads the regular Master Boot Record found in sector 2, which in turn loads the operating system.

Viruses and the MBR. A common type of virus is one that replaces the MBR with its own code. Each time a computer is started, the code in the MBR is loaded into memory. If the MBR contains a virus, the virus code is loaded every time a system starts up, making this type of virus *very* dangerous. Some MBR viruses do little more than display a message on your screen, while others can destroy your data. An MBR virus usually enters a system through a floppy disk that the system accessed either at startup or while the system was on. If your BIOS supports an MBR protection feature, this prevents new information from being written to the MBR, so make sure that this feature is *enabled* in the CMOS Setup.

Understanding Drive Capacity Limits

Capacity limitations are encountered whenever a computer system BIOS (and operating system) is unable to identify (or *address*) physical locations on a hard drive. This is *not* a problem with the design or structure of the hard drive itself, but rather a limitation of the system's BIOS or operating system. If the problem is in the BIOS, it is not capable of translating the addresses of the sectors beyond a certain number of cylinders—thus limiting the capacity of the hard drive to less than its full amount. If the problem is in the operating system, the file structure (FAT) is limited in the number of physical locations (or addresses) that can be entered in the FAT. Drive manufacturers first encountered BIOS limitations in 1994 with the release of 540-MB (ATA-2/EIDE) hard drives. Operating system limitations were discovered with the release of hard drives larger than 2.1 GB. Your exact limitations vary depending on your BIOS version and the operating system. Today, you'll probably encounter BIOS with limitations at 2.1-, 4.2-, and 8.4-GB levels. Operating systems like DOS and Windows 95 have a 2.1-GB partition size limitation and Windows NT has a 4.2-GB partition size limit, but Windows 95 OSR2 and Windows 98 can access much larger drives using the FAT32 file system. This part of the chapter is intended to help you understand and correct these drive size limitations.

Cylinder limits in BIOS

BIOS is the key to hard drive addressing through the use of Int. 13 services. Today, you'll find that there are three major BIOS limitations:

- BIOS versions dated *prior* to July 1994 will typically experience a 528-MB drive size limit. BIOS cannot support more than 1024 cylinders. Logical block addressing (LBA) mode capability did not become widely accepted until after this point.

- BIOS versions dated *after* July 1994 will typically experience a 2.1-GB drive size limit. BIOS cannot support more than 4093 to 4096 cylinders. Even though LBA is being used correctly, the BIOS makers simply imposed an artificial limit on the number of addressable cylinders.

- BIOS versions dated *after* 1996 can support drives over 528 MB and support drives over 2.1 GB, but they may experience a 4.2- or 8.4-GB drive size limit. Once again, the BIOS cannot support the number of cylinders (around 8190) needed to handle these larger drives—even though LBA is being used correctly.

Partition limits in the operating system

File systems used by various operating systems are also subject to drive size limits. FAT16-type operating systems (DOS, the commercial release of Windows 95, Windows NT with FAT16, and OS/2 with FAT16) are typically limited to 2.1-GB drive sizes. Windows NT using NTFS has a 4-GB drive size limit. When you use a physical hard drive which is larger than these limits, you'll need to create multiple partitions on the drive in order to access all of the available space. With the introduction of FAT32 with Windows 95 OSR2 and

Windows 98, drives up to 2 TB (terabytes) can be accessed as a single partition.

Overcoming capacity limits

Since 1994, the PC industry has been working hard to overcome the drive size limits imposed by BIOS and operating systems. Unfortunately, drive size limits still plague older systems. This is particularly prevalent because many systems that are a few years old are now being upgraded with the huge hard drives that are on the market. As a result, drive size support problems are the most frequent issues encountered during drive upgrades. Still, there are several tactics that have become available for technicians.

The 528-MB limit. Supporting large (EIDE) hard drives over 528 MB will clearly require a system upgrade. There are three possible solutions to the problem: Upgrade the motherboard BIOS to support LBA, upgrade the drive controller with one using an on-board BIOS which supports LBA, or partition the drive with a drive overlay utility like Disk Manager or EZ-Drive. If the system is older than 1994, a new drive controller and on-board BIOS will probably yield a noticeable drive system performance improvement. If price is the primary concern, drive overlay software is free (included with most new hard drives) and requires no invasive hardware upgrade.

2.1-, 4.2-, and 8.4-GB limits. The difficulty with these limits is that there are several possible symptoms that can crop up:

- *Truncation of cylinders.* Cylinder truncation occurs when the BIOS limits the number of cylinders reported to the operating system to 4095. The BIOS may display the drive as having more than 4095 cylinders, but it still reports only a total of 4095.

- *System hangs up at POST.*   A system hang-up
  occurs when the BIOS has a problem truncating the
  cylinders and locks the system up during power-on
  self-test (POST). This is most frequently caused by
  the auto-detect feature some BIOS versions have
  implemented.

- *Cylinder wrap.*   With cylinder wrapping, the BIOS
  takes the remaining number of cylinders from the
  maximum allowed (4095) and reports it to the operating system. For example, if the drive listed 4096
  cylinders, the BIOS would report only 1 cylinder to
  the operating system.

- *System hangs at boot time.*   This usually occurs for
  drives larger than 4.2 GB. A system hang occurs
  when the operating system hangs up during initial
  loading (either from a floppy diskette or from existing hard drives). This can be caused by the BIOS
  reporting the number of heads to the operating system as 256 (100h). The register size DOS/Windows
  95 uses for the head count has a capacity of two hex
  digits (equivalent to decimal value 255).

In virtually all cases, these symptoms represent a
BIOS compatibility problem and can be corrected by a
BIOS upgrade. You should contact the system or motherboard maker to inquire if a BIOS update is available.
If you cannot upgrade the motherboard BIOS directly,
you can install a new drive controller with an LBA-
compatible BIOS that *will* support additional cylinders.
You may also be able to adjust the drive's "translation" to overcome BIOS cylinder limits. You may find
that these huge hard drives seem to auto-detect correctly in BIOS, and that the problem crops up when
you try to partition the drive. The partition may seem
to be created properly through FDISK, but the system
hangs when rebooting. Although this is an operating
system limitation, it appears that the appropriate way
to deal with the problem is to account for it in the system BIOS. Fortunately, there is a temporary

workaround to the problem (until you get the BIOS upgraded).

> **NOTE**: *You should first verify that you have a new enough BIOS to handle drives over 2 GB correctly.*

To set up a drive over 4 GB (under an older BIOS):

1. "Auto-detect" the drive in CMOS Setup.
2. Manually adjust the number of heads from 16 to 15.
3. Multiply the number of cylinders by 16/15 (rounded down to a whole number). Since 16/15 is 1.06667, the simplest way to multiply by 16/15 would be to multiply by 1.06667 (and then round down to a whole number).
4. Adjust the number of cylinders to this larger amount.
5. Write down these adjusted values for cylinders, heads, and sectors.
6. Save changes to CMOS, then partition and format the drive.

As an example, Table 5.3 illustrates some workaround parameters that can be used with popular models of hard drives over 4 GB. While this can be considered a *temporary* workaround, there should be no problem with continuing to use a hard drive that is set up this way. If an updated BIOS version becomes available at a later date, it should not be necessary to repartition and reformat the drive.

> **NOTE**: *The important thing to keep in mind in using the above workaround is that you must keep a record of the translation values used so that they can be reentered if the contents of CMOS RAM are lost or if the drive is moved to another system. Write the values on masking tape, and stick the tape on the drive itself.*

Operating system limits. You basically have two solutions for overcoming drive size limits through an oper-

TABLE 5.3 Possible CMOS Work-arounds for Huge
Hard Drives

Model	Factory CHS Values	Work-around CHS Values
Maxtor 85120A	9924 × 16 × 63	10,585 × 15 × 63
Micropolis 4550A	9692 × 16 × 63	10,338 × 15 × 63

ating system. If you continue to use FAT 16, you'll need to create partitions equal to or smaller than 2 GB. If the drive is larger than 2 GB, you can make multiple partitions on the drive. This makes more than one logical drive for the system to deal with, but it will allow you to use the entire drive capacity. As an alternative, you can upgrade to a FAT 32 system such as the OSR2 version of Windows 95, which should easily handle partitions over 32 GB.

Hard Drive Installation/Replacement Guidelines

Hard drives must be installed when building new PCs, adding supplemental drives to an existing system, or replacing outdated or failed drives. The installation process is not terribly complicated, but it can be confusing to the novice. This part of the chapter offers some basic guidelines for IDE-type drive installation.

Select jumper configurations

An IDE-type drive may be installed as a master or slave device on any hard drive controller channel. These master/slave settings are handled through one or two jumpers located on the rear of the drive (right next to the 40-pin signal cable connector). One of your first decisions when planning an installation should be to decide the drive's configuration:

- If you're installing only one hard drive in the system, it must be jumpered as the master device. Note that the master drive on the primary drive controller channel will be the boot drive (e.g., drive C:).

■ If you're installing a second hard drive alongside the first, that second drive must be jumpered as the slave device.

■ If you're installing a second hard drive on the second drive controller channel, it should be jumpered as the master device (any other device should be reconfigured as a slave device).

> NOTE: *Refer to the documentation that accompanies your particular hard drive in order to determine the exact master/slave jumper settings. If you do not have the drive documentation handy, check the drive manufacturer's Web site for online information.*

Attach cables and mount the drive

■ Turn off and unplug the PC, then remove the outer cover to expose the computer's drive bays.

■ Attach one end of the 40-pin drive interface cable to the drive controller connector on your motherboard (or drive controller card). Remember to align pin 1 on the cable (the side of the cable with the blue or red stripe) with pin 1 on the drive controller connector.

> NOTE: *A 40-pin/80-conductor cable is required in order to run in Ultra-DMA/66 mode. Attach the blue end of the connector to the drive controller end, the black connector to the master (or single) drive, and the gray connector (if there is one) to the slave drive.*

■ Locate an available drive bay for the hard drive. Remove the plastic housing covering the drive bay, then slide the drive inside. Locate the four screw holes needed to mount the drive. In some cases, you may need to attach mounting rails to the drive so that the drive will be wide enough to fit in the drive bay. You may mount the drive horizontally (usually with the circuit board down) or vertically.

- Attach the 40-pin signal cable and the 4-pin power connector to the new drive, then bolt the drive securely into place. Do not overtighten the screws, since this may damage the drive. If you do not have an available 4-pin power connector, you may use an appropriate Y splitter if necessary to split power from another drive (preferably the floppy drive).

Configure the CMOS Setup

Before you attempt to partition or format your new drive, you must configure your computer's BIOS to accept the drive (through the CMOS Setup).

- Turn the computer on. As your computer starts up, watch for a message that describes how to run the CMOS Setup (e.g., *Press F1 for Setup*). Press the appropriate key to start the CMOS Setup program.

- Select the *hard drive settings* menu. To set the drive parameters, choose the *primary master* or *primary slave* (or *secondary master / slave*, depending on how you've physically installed the drive).

- Select *automatic drive detection* if available. This option automatically configures the computer for your new drive. If your BIOS does not provide automatic drive detection, select user-defined drive settings and enter the appropriate geometry values from the drive documentation. As a rule, *Write Precomp* and *Landing Zone* parameters are set to zero.

- Verify that the LBA mode is enabled for your drive. Many BIOS versions use the LBA mode to access drives with capacities greater than 528 MB. Most BIOS will automatically set this mode during the auto-detection process.

- Enable the Ultra-DMA mode if it is available (and both the drive and controller support it).

- Save the settings and exit the CMOS Setup program. Your computer will automatically reboot.

Finish the drive preparation

Boot the system with a Windows 95/98 Startup Disk containing FDISK and FORMAT. You will use these utilities to partition and format the drive, respectively. Partition the disk with FDISK. If you use a FAT16 version of FDISK, you cannot create partitions greater than 2.1 GB. If you use the FAT32 version of FDISK, you can create extremely large partitions. Now use FORMAT to prepare the drive for your operating system. Again, use the proper version of the FORMAT utility for the FAT system you plan on using. You can find detailed instructions in the "File Systems and Tips" section above.

Reassemble the computer

Double-check all of your signal and power cables to verify that they are secure, then tuck the cables gently into the computer's chassis. Check that there are no loose tools, screws, or cables inside the chassis. Now reattach the computer's outer housing(s).

Drive Testing and Troubleshooting

Fortunately, not all hard drive problems are necessarily fatal. True, you may lose some programs and data (back up your hard drive frequently), but recovery from many drive problems is possible without resorting to drive replacement. Instead of focusing on repairing a hard drive's electronics or mechanics, today's repair tactics focus on repairing a drive's *data*. By reconstructing or relocating faulty drive information, it is often possible to recover from a wide variety of drive problems. If that fails, the drive (and/or its controller) must be replaced. Before you begin any sort of drive troubleshooting, you should take the following steps:

- Gather a DOS boot disk or Windows 95/98 Startup Disk. If you don't have a boot disk on hand, you should make one now, *before* continuing.

- Gather your DOS installation disk(s) or Windows 95/98 installation CD-ROM. If you need to reinstall the operating system or any of its components at some point, these will be invaluable.

- Gather any hard drive/controller diagnostics that you'll need.

- Back up as much as you can from your hard drive(s) before attempting any sort of drive service.

General troubleshooting guidelines

Although most drive installations and replacements will proceed flawlessly, many times problems will crop up. If you've installed a hard drive and it does not function properly, perform the following basic checks before examining specific symptoms:

- *Be careful about power and static.* Always turn off the computer before changing jumpers or unplugging cables and cards. Wear an antistatic wrist strap (or use other antistatic precautions) while working on your computer or handling a drive.

- *Verify compatibility.* Verify that the drive controller and drive are appropriately matched to each other (and to your computer). For example, an Ultra-DMA/66 drive will not run at top speed on an Ultra-DMA/33 controller.

- *Check all cards.* Verify that all expansion cards (including the drive controller card) are seated in their slots on the motherboard and are secured with mounting screws. Often one or more cards may be displaced when a PC is opened for service.

- *Check all connectors and cables.* Make sure that all ribbon and power cables are securely connected. Ribbon cables are easily damaged (especially at the connectors). Try a new cable that you know is good. Make sure no connector pins are bent. Verify that pin 1 on the interface cable is aligned with pin 1 on the drive and the controller.

■ *Verify drive jumper settings.* Review the instructions in your drive's manual (and in your host adapter installation guide), and see that all appropriate jumpers are installed—or removed—as necessary. Incorrect or duplicated jumper settings (e.g., two master drives on the same channel) can easily interfere with drive operation.

■ *Check your power supply capacity.* Each time you add a new device to your computer, make sure your computer's power supply can support the total power demand. Install a larger (higher-wattage) power supply if necessary.

■ *Verify the drive settings in your CMOS Setup.* The drive settings in the CMOS Setup must not exceed the physical specifications of your drive. Also, the settings must not exceed the limitations set by the operating system and BIOS. Try the CMOS Setup's auto-detect feature to identify the drive, or consider upgrading the BIOS and/or drive controller.

■ *Check for viruses.* Before you use an unknown diskette in your system for the first time, scan the diskette for viruses. Also scan the system for viruses periodically.

Potential problems with Y splitters

On rare instances, you may find that a drive will not function—or is damaged outright—when you use a Y power adapter (or Y splitter). This can happen because a number of Y splitters on the market are incorrectly wired. Y splitters consist of a clear plastic plug with 4 metal prongs on one end (which attaches to an existing power connector from the power supply) and 2 sets of wires leading to 2 plugs with female connections on the other ends (which are attached to internal devices such as hard drives, CD-ROM drives, and so on). The problem with some of these newer connectors is that the wires are attached incorrectly on one of the female connectors.

Examine both female connectors—make certain that both of the female connectors are lined up with the two rounded corners facing up and both of the squared corners facing down. The four wires attached to the female connectors should now be in the following order (from left to right):

Yellow (+12 V dc), black (ground), black (ground), and red (+5 V dc)

If this order is reversed on one of the connectors, then your Y splitter is faulty and should not be used. As a rule, you should never split power from the hard drive under any circumstances.

Potential problems with bus speeds beyond 66 MHz

Many Pentium, PentiumPro, and Pentium MMX motherboards offer an adjustable system bus clock that may be set either by the system BIOS or with jumpers. This bus speed setting allows you to increase the system bus clock above 66 MHz—usually to 75 or 83 MHz. Most drives have no problem with the higher bus clock speeds, but some problems may result because of the way some motherboards handle the interaction between the higher bus speeds (above 66 MHz) and the IDE-type interface.

On some motherboards, when the system clock is increased above 66 MHz, the PCI bus (ideally 33 MHz) is also increased; this higher speed reduces the PCI bus I/O cycle time. This change in the I/O cycle time violates the IDE specification and may cause disruptions in the communications between the hard drive and the PCI bus. This is *not* a faulty hard drive or drive design. When the PCI bus speed is forced over 33

MHz because of higher bus speed settings, you may see problems such as data loss, data corruption, and failure of the system to recognize the hard drive on bootup. Higher bus speeds will not cause any kind of permanent hard drive failure, and returning the system bus speed to 66 MHz will usually eliminate the problem(s). The best solution to this problem is to either return the motherboard to a 66-MHz bus speed or upgrade the motherboard with a model in which the PCI bus speed is asynchronous of the bus speed. This allows you to increase the bus speed, but the PCI clock will remain fixed at 33 MHz.

> **NOTE**: *Because of the differences between drive designs, it is possible that some drives may not have any problems responding at higher bus speeds, while other models may have serious problems. It's virtually impossible to determine which drives will or won't be affected.*

> **NOTE**: *Current Pentium II and Pentium III motherboards designed to operate up to 100 MHz or higher are almost all asynchronous, and should not pose a problem. But this issue may crop up when working with slightly older motherboards or systems.*

Troubleshooting DOS compatibility-mode problems

One of the great advantages enjoyed by Windows 95/98 is that it operates in the protected mode—drivers and software can be executed beyond the traditional real-mode RAM limit of 1 MB. By comparison, DOS is a real-mode environment. DOS programs and drivers can be executed only within the first 640 KB of RAM (the conventional memory area). If Windows 95/98 cannot establish protected-mode operation for a drive, it will fall back to real-mode driver support. This is known as *DOS compatibility mode*. Unfortunately, real-mode support often impairs system performance. If you notice that one or more of the hard drives in a system is using DOS compatibility mode (there may be an error message such as *Compatibility Mode Paging reduces overall system performance*), you'll need to track down and correct the cause. In general, Windows 95/98 may invoke the DOS compatibility mode for any of the following reasons:

- A questionable device driver, TSR, or computer virus has hooked the INT 21h or INT 13h chain before Windows 95/98 loaded.

- The hard disk controller in your computer was not detected by Windows 95/98.

- The hard disk controller was removed from the current configuration in *Device Manager*.

- There is a resource conflict between the hard disk controller and another hardware device.

- The Windows 95/98 protected-mode driver is missing or damaged.

- The Windows 95/98 protected-mode driver detected incompatible or unsupportable hardware.

You can use the following procedure to isolate and correct the cause of DOS compatibility-mode problems:

1. Open the *Control Panel*, double-click the *System* icon, then choose the *Performance* tab in the *System Properties* dialog. You can identify which drive is using DOS compatibility mode and why.

2. If the driver name listed as causing the DOS compatibility mode is MBRINT13.SYS, your computer may be infected with a boot-sector virus, or you are running real-mode disk overlay software (for an IDE hard disk with more than 1024 cylinders) that is *not* compatible with Windows 95/98 protected-mode disk drivers.
   - Run a current antivirus program to detect and remove boot-sector viruses (such as Norton Anti-

Virus, or NAV). You may need to rewrite your boot sector using a DOS command such as FDISK /MBR.

- If you cannot detect any virus activity, check any drive overlay software. For example, if you're using Disk Manager, make sure that you're using Disk Manager 7.0 or later (use Disk Manager 7.04 if you're running DriveSpace 3, included with the Microsoft Plus! pack). You may need to make similar updates if you're running other drive overlay software.

3. If the driver name that is listed in step 2 is *also* in the CONFIG.SYS file, contact the driver's manufacturer to determine whether there is a more recent version of the driver that allows protected-mode operation in Windows 95/98. You may be able to download and install the latest driver version from the driver manufacturer's Web site.

4. If no driver is listed on the *Performance* tab, check to make sure that the hard disk controller is listed in the *Device Manager*. If it is not, install it through the *Add New Hardware* wizard. If the wizard cannot detect the controller automatically, run the wizard again, but do not let it attempt to detect the hardware in your computer; instead, select the controller specifically from the hardware list. If your particular controller is not listed, contact the manufacturer of the disk controller to obtain a Windows 95/98 protected-mode disk driver (or a Windows 3.1x 32-bit disk access "FastDisk" driver if available).

NOTE: *If the hard disk controller is listed in* Device Manager, *but has a red "X" over it, it has been removed from the current hardware profile. Click* Properties *for the controller in* Device Manager, *and then click the check box corresponding to the current hardware profile under* Device Usage.

5. If the hard disk controller *is* listed in the *Device Manager* but has a yellow "!" over it, there is a

resource conflict (IRQ, I/O, DMA, or BIOS address range) with another device, the protected-mode driver is missing or damaged, or the *Disable all 32-bit protected-mode disk drivers* check box has been selected in *File System* properties.

- Double-click the *System* icon in the *Control Panel*, click the *Performance* tab, and then click *File System*. Select the *Troubleshooting* tab and see that the *Disable all 32-bit protected-mode disk drivers* check box has *not* been selected.

- Resolve any resource conflicts with other devices in the system.

- Check to make sure that the protected-mode driver is in the \Windows\SYSTEM\IOSUBSYS directory and is loading properly. To find which driver is providing 32-bit disk access, click *Properties* for the disk controller in *Device Manager* and click the *Driver* tab to see which driver files are associated with the controller. For most IDE, EIDE, and ESDI disk controllers, 32-bit disk access is provided by the ESDI_506.PDR driver. For SCSI controllers, Windows 95 often uses SCSIPORT.PDR and a "mini port" (or .MPD) driver. Restart Windows 95/98, press <F8> when the *Starting Windows 95/98* message appears, then select a *Logged* (BOOTLOG.TXT) start. If the 32-bit driver is listed as loading properly, you're all set. Otherwise, the driver may be missing or damaged—try reinstalling the respective 32-bit drivers.

6. Load SYSTEM.INI into a text editor and check to see if the Mh32bit.386 driver is being loaded (check for a line that reads device=mh32 bit.386). This driver is installed by MicroHouse EZ-Drive software and is *not* compatible with the Windows 95/98 protected-mode disk drivers. Unfortunately, this driver is not removed by Windows 95/98 Setup, so you'll need to disable the line manually, save your changes, and reboot the PC.

7. If all else fails, you may be able to achieve protect-ed-mode support from the disk controller by dis-abling any of the controller's advanced features (i.e. caching, fast or "turbo" modes) or by reducing data transfer rates. You might also try systematically dis-abling advanced IDE controller features in the CMOS Setup.

8. If problems persist, you may have to replace the drive controller with a model that better supports protected-mode operation.

Detecting a DDO

A dynamic drive overlay (or DDO) is used to support access to a large hard drive when the system BIOS or drive controller is unable to. Since the DDO can some-times cause problems with drive access and system performance, it must be detected before removal. You can use the telltale signs below to identify the presence of a DDO on a Windows 95/98 system:

- *DDO startup message.* When you boot your com-puter, a message may be displayed on the screen that shows the DDO manufacturer's name (or prompts you to press a key to boot to a floppy disk). Current versions of drive overlay software may not display this message by default.

- *BIOS revision date.* Computers made before 1994 generally do not support LBA. If your BIOS shows an early revision date, it will probably need a DDO in order to support hard drives over 528 MB.

- *FDISK* /status *switch.* Boot your computer with a Windows 95/98 Startup Disk and type fdisk /status from the command prompt. Verify that the sum of the existing partitions is larger than the total hard disk space. If it is, a DDO is at work.

- *Windows 95/98 Startup Disk.* Reboot your com-puter with the Windows 95/98 Startup Disk (this will prevent the DDO program from loading), and then boot to a command prompt. Check to see if files on the C: drive are accessible. If not, the drive is inaccessible because a DDO has not been loaded for the hard drive.

- *Verify file names.* Some drive overlay files use an .OVL or a .BIN extension. At the command prompt, type `dir /a *.bin` or `dir /a *.ovl` to check for the existence of files other than DRVSPACE.BIN and DBLSPACE.BIN. If there are other such files, a DDO is probably installed.

- *Check CONFIG.SYS.* Drive overlay software may be loaded from the CONFIG.SYS file in order to access drives *other* than the active boot partition of the master drive on the primary IDE controller. If there is DDO software called in CONFIG.SYS, disable it there if necessary.

Removing a DDO

When you install a drive overlay utility like EZ-Drive or MaxBlast (or other similar software), there may be a point where it's necessary to remove it. You may need to do this when you upgrade the BIOS and/or drive controller, and so the dynamic drive overlay (or DDO) software is no longer required. In most cases, you can remove your DDO without losing any data, as long as you have an alternative means of accessing the drive (i.e., an updated BIOS or drive controller). The example below illustrates the use of Disk Manager, but other utilities will follow a similar process.

> **IMPORTANT NOTE**: *Before you remove a DDO from a drive, make a complete backup copy of all the data on your hard drive. Also run CHKDSK or ScanDisk (or a third-party equivalent) to detect and repair any damaged files. If the DDO removal program encounters a serious file problem (or is interrupted by a power loss or hardware failure), the removal will fail and your data can be lost.*

1. Boot the computer to drive C:, then insert your DiscWizard diskette (or CD).

2. Type DM to start Disk Manager, and choose the *Select Installation Options Menu*.

3. Select the *Maintenance Menu*.

4. Select *Migrate Dynamic Drive*. This option moves the data on your drive so that they can be accessed *without* the DDO. Remember that this conversion may take up to an hour to complete (depending on the size of your drive).

5. When the conversion has finished, exit Disk Manager, remove the diskette, and reboot the computer.

6. Enter your CMOS Setup program, and configure the hard drive with the appropriate number of cylinders, heads, and sectors as specified for your drive model.

7. Save your changes in the CMOS Setup and reboot again.

8. When your computer has rebooted, insert the DiscWizard diskette into drive A:.

9. Type A:\DM to start Disk Manager, and choose the *Maintenance Menu*.

10. Select *Uninstall Disk Manager*.

11. Select the correct drive to uninstall from, and allow the process to complete.

12. When the uninstall is complete, exit Disk Manager and reboot the system.

NOTE: *Disk Manager can also remove a drive overlay placed by the EZ-Drive program. Simply select* Convert Drive Format *from the* Maintenance Menu.

Hardware symptoms

Now it's time to review some problems and solutions. The important concept here is that a hard drive *prob-*

lem does not necessarily mean a hard drive *failure*. The failure of a sector or track does not automatically indicate physical head or platter damage—that is why software tools have been so successful at restoring operation (and even recovering data).

> **IMPORTANT NOTE**: *Drive troubleshooting has the potential to destroy any data on the drive(s). Before attempting to troubleshoot hard disk drive problems, be sure to back up as much of the drive as possible. If there is no backup available, do not repartition or reformat the drive unless absolutely necessary, and all other possible alternatives have been exhausted.*

> **NOTE**: *The term* IDE-type *drive is taken to mean any drive using a 40-pin IDE-style interface: IDE, EIDE, ATAPI IDE, Ultra-DMA/33, and Ultra-DMA/66 (using the 40-pin/80-conductor cable). Specific drive types or exceptions will be denoted.*

Symptom 5.1: The hard drive is completely dead. The drive does not spin up, the drive light doesn't illuminate during power-up, or you see an error message indicating that the drive is not found or not ready.

- *Check the drive power*. Make sure the 4-pin power connector is inserted properly and completely. If the drive is being powered by a Y connector, make sure any interim connections are secure. Use a voltmeter to measure the +5-V (pin 4) and +12-V (pin 1) levels. If either voltage (especially the +12-V supply) is unusually low or absent, replace the power supply.

- *Check the signal cable*. Also check your signal cable. See that the drive's signal interface cable is connected securely at both the drive and controller ends. For IDE-type drives, this is the 40-pin ribbon cable. If the cable is visibly worn or damaged, try a new cable.

- *Check the CMOS Setup*. The PC cannot use a hard drive that it can't recognize, so enter the CMOS Setup routine and verify that all the parameters entered for the drive are correct. Heads, cylinders, sectors per track, landing zone, and write precompensation must all be correct—otherwise, POST will not recognize the drive. If you have an auto-detect option available, try that also. Remember to save your changes in CMOS and reboot the system.

- *Replace the drive or controller*. If problems continue, the hard drive itself may be defective. Try a known-good hard drive. If a known-good drive works as expected, your original drive is probably defective and should be replaced. If a known-good hard drive fails to operate, replace the drive controller board.

Symptom 5.2: You see drive activity, but the computer will not boot from the hard drive.   In most cases, there is a drive failure, boot-sector failure, or DOS/Windows file corruption.

- *Check the signal cable*. Make sure that the drive's signal cable is connected securely at both the drive and the controller. If the cable is visibly worn or damaged, try a new one.

- *Check the CMOS Setup*. Verify that all of the parameters entered for the drive are correct. Heads, cylinders, sectors per track, landing zone, and write precompensation must all be correct—otherwise, POST will not recognize the drive. If the BIOS provides an option to auto-detect the drive, try that as well.

- *Check the boot sector*. Boot from a floppy disk and try accessing the hard drive. If the hard drive is accessible, chances are that the boot files are missing or corrupt. Try a utility such as DrivePro's Drive Boot Fixer. You might also try running FDISK /MBR, which will rebuild the drive's master boot record. *Be careful:* The FDISK /MBR command may render the files on your drive inaccessible.

- *Check the drive and controller*. You may have a problem with your drive system hardware. If you cannot access the hard drive, run a diagnostic such as Windsor Technologies' PC Technician. Test the drive and drive controller. If the controller responds but the drive does not, try repartitioning and reformatting the hard drive. If the drive still doesn't respond, replace the hard drive outright. If the controller doesn't respond, replace the hard drive controller.

Symptom 5.3: There are errors during drive reads or writes. Magnetic information does not last forever, and sector ID information can gradually degrade to a point where you encounter file errors.

- *Check for file problems*. Start by checking for any file structure problems on the drive. Use a utility such as ScanDisk to examine the drive and search for bad sectors. If a failed sector involves part of an .EXE or .COM file, that file is now corrupt and should be restored from a backup.

- *Try a low-level format*. If you cannot isolate file problems, you may need to consider a low-level (LL) format. Low-level formatting rewrites sector ID information, but the sophistication of today's drives makes LL formatting almost impossible. If the drive manufacturer provides a drive preparation utility, you should back up the drive, run the utility, FDISK, FORMAT, and restore the drive from its backup.

Symptom 5.4: Hard drive performance appears to be slowing down over time. In virtually all cases, diminishing drive performance can be caused by file fragmentation. Far less often, you may be faced with a computer virus.

- *Boot the system "clean"*. Start the PC with a clean boot disk and make sure that there are no TSRs or drivers being loaded.

- *Check for viruses*. After a clean boot, run your antivirus checker and make sure that there are no memory-resident or file-based viruses.

- *Check for file fragmentation.* If the system checks clean for computer viruses, you should check for file fragmentation next. Start your defragmentation utility (such as Defrag) and check to see the percentage of file fragmentation. If there is more than 10 percent fragmentation, you should consider running the defragmentation utility after preparing Windows. Before defragmenting a drive, reboot the system normally, start Windows, access the Virtual Memory controls for your version of Windows, and shut down virtual memory. Leave Windows and boot the system clean again. Restart your defragmentation utility and proceed to defragment the disk. This process may take several minutes, depending on the size of your drive. Once defragmentation is complete, reboot the system normally, start Windows, access the Virtual Memory controls for your version of Windows, and recreate a permanent swap file to support virtual memory. You should now notice a performance improvement.

Symptom 5.5: You can access the hard drive correctly, but the drive light stays on continuously. A continuous LED indication is not *necessarily* a problem as long as the drive seems to be operating properly. Check the drive and drive controller for drive "light jumpers"—examine the drive itself for any jumper that might select latched mode vs. activity mode. If there are no such jumpers on the drive, check the drive controller or motherboard. Set the jumper to activity mode to see the drive light during access only. Next, consider the possibility of drive light *error messages.* Some drive types (especially SCSI drives) use the drive activity light to signal drive and controller errors. Check the drive and controller documents to determine if there is any error indicated by the light remaining on.

Symptom 5.6: You cannot access the hard drive, and the drive light stays on continuously. This usually indicates a reversed signal cable and is most common when you are upgrading or replacing a drive system.

- *Check the signal cable*. In virtually all cases, one end of the signal cable is reversed. Make sure that both ends of the cable are installed properly (remember that the red or blue stripe on one side of the cable represents pin 1).

- *Replace the drive controller*. If problems persist, replace the drive controller. It is rare for a fault in the drive controller to cause this type of problem, but if trouble persists, try a known-good drive controller board.

Symptom 5.7: You see a *No Fixed Disk Present* error message on the monitor.   This kind of problem can occur during installation or at any point in the PC's working life.

- *Check the power connector*. Make sure the 4-pin power connector is inserted properly and completely. If the drive is being powered by a Y-connector, make sure any interim connections are secure. Use a voltmeter to measure the +5-V (pin 4) and +12-V (pin 1) levels. If either voltage (especially the +12-V supply) is unusually low or absent, replace the power supply.

- *Check the signal connector*. Make sure the drive's signal cable is connected securely at both the drive and the controller. If the cable is visibly worn or damaged, try a new one.

- *Check the CMOS Setup*. Enter the CMOS Setup routine and verify that all the parameters entered for the drive are correct. Heads, cylinders, sectors per track, landing zone, and write precompensation must all be correct—otherwise, POST will not recognize the drive. You might also try auto-detecting the drive.

- *Check for hardware conflicts.* Make sure that there is no other expansion device in the system using the same IRQs or I/O addresses used by your drive controller. If there is, change the resources used by the conflicting device. If your drive system uses a SCSI interface, make sure that the SCSI cable is terminated properly.

- *Replace the hard drive or controller.* If problems continue, try a known-good hard drive. If a known-good drive works as expected, your original drive is probably defective. If problems persist with a known-good hard drive, replace the drive controller board.

Symptom 5.8: Your drive spins up, but the system fails to recognize the drive.   Your computer may flag this as a Hard-disk error or Hard-disk controller failure during system initialization.

- *Check the signal connector.* Make sure that the interface signal cable is inserted properly and completely at the drive and controller. Try a new signal cable.

- *Check the drive jumpers.* See that a primary (master) drive is configured as primary, and a secondary (slave) drive is configured as secondary. For SCSI drives, see that each drive has a unique ID setting, and check that the SCSI bus is terminated properly.

- *Check the CMOS Setup.* Enter the CMOS Setup routine and verify that all the parameters entered for the drive are correct. Heads, cylinders, sectors per track, landing zone, and write precompensation must all be correct—otherwise, POST will not recognize the drive. Try using the auto-detect feature if it is available.

- *Check the partition.* If the CMOS is configured properly, you should suspect a problem with the partition. Boot from a floppy disk and run FDISK to check the partitions on your hard drive. Make sure that there is at least one DOS partition. If the drive is to be your boot drive, the primary partition must be active and bootable. Repartition and reformat the drive if necessary.

■ *Try another hard drive or controller*. If a known-good drive works as expected, your original drive is probably defective. If a known-good hard drive fails to work as expected, replace the drive controller.

Symptom 5.9: Your IDE drive spins up when power is applied, then rapidly spins down again.   The drive is defective, or it is not communicating properly with its host system.

■ *Check the power connector*. Make sure the 4-pin power connector is inserted properly and completely into the drive.

■ *Check the signal connector next*. See that the interface signal cable is inserted properly and completely at the drive and controller. Try a new signal cable.

■ *Check the drive jumpers*. The primary (master) drive should be configured as primary, and a secondary (slave) drive should be configured as secondary. For SCSI drives, see that each drive has a unique ID setting, and check that the SCSI bus is terminated properly.

■ *Replace the drive*. If problems persist, try a known-good hard drive. If a known-good drive works as expected, your original drive is probably defective.

Symptom 5.10: You see a *Sector not found* error message. This problem usually occurs after the drive has been in operation for quite some time and is typically the result of a media failure. Fortunately, a bad sector will affect only one file.

■ *Try recovering the file*. Use a utility such as SpinRite from Gibson Research (or another data recovery utility) and attempt to recover the damaged file. Note that you may be unsuccessful and have to restore the file from a backup later.

- *Check the disk media.* Use a disk utility (such as ScanDisk) to evaluate the drive, then locate and map out any bad sectors that are located on the drive.

- *Try a low-level format.* If problems persist, perform a low-level format (if possible). Lost sectors often occur as drives age and sector ID information degrades. Low-level formatting restores the sector IDs, but LL formatting is performed at the factory for IDE/EIDE and SCSI drives. If there is a LL formatting utility for your particular drive (available from the drive manufacturer), and ScanDisk reveals a large number of bad sectors, you might consider backing up the drive completely, running the LL utility, repartitioning, reformatting, then restoring the drive. If ScanDisk maps out bad sectors, you may need to restore those files from a backup.

Symptom 5.11: You see a *1780 or 1781 ERROR* on the system. The classical 1780 error code indicates a Hard Disk 0 Failure, while the 1781 error code marks a Hard Disk 1 Failure.

- *Boot the system clean.* Start the PC with a clean boot disk and make sure that there are no TSRs or drivers being loaded.

- *Check for viruses.* If you haven't done so already, run your antivirus checker and make sure that there are no memory-resident or file-based viruses.

- *Check the boot files.* If you can access the hard drive once your system is booted, chances are that the boot files are missing or corrupt. Try a utility such as DrivePro's Drive Boot Fixer to recover the boot files, or recopy the boot files with SYS, and recreate the master boot record with FDISK/MBR. Otherwise, you will need to repartition and reformat the disk, then restore disk files from a backup.

- *Replace the hard drive or controller.* If you cannot access the hard drive, run a diagnostic such as Windsor Technologies' PC Technician. Test the drive and drive controller. If the controller responds but the drive does not, try repartitioning and reformatting the hard drive. If the drive still doesn't respond, replace the hard drive outright. If the controller doesn't respond, replace the hard drive controller.

Symptom 5.12: You see a *1790 or 1791 ERROR* on the system. The classical 1790 error code indicates a *Hard Disk 0 Error*, while the 1791 error code marks a *Hard Disk 1 Error*.

- *Check the signal connector.* Make sure that the interface signal cable is inserted properly and completely at the drive and controller. Try a new signal cable.

- *Check the partition.* Boot from a floppy disk and run FDISK to check the partitions on your hard drive. Make sure that there is at least one DOS partition. If the drive is to be your boot drive, the primary partition must be active and bootable. Repartition and reformat the drive if necessary.

- *Replace the hard drive or controller.* If a known-good drive works as expected, your original drive is probably defective. If problems persist with a known-good hard drive, replace the drive controller board.

Symptom 5.13: You see a *1701 ERROR* on the system. The 1701 error code indicates a hard drive POST error—the drive did not pass its POST test.

- *Check the power connector.* Make sure the 4-pin power connector is inserted properly and completely. If the drive is being powered by a Y connector, make sure any interim connections are secure. Use a voltmeter to measure the +5-V (pin 4) and +12-V (pin 1) levels. If either voltage (especially the +12-V supply) is unusually low or absent, replace the power supply.

- *Check the CMOS Setup*. Enter the CMOS Setup routine and verify that all of the parameters entered for the drive are correct. Heads, cylinders, sectors per track, landing zone, and write precompensation must all be correct—otherwise, POST will not recognize the drive. Try auto-detecting the drive.

- *Try a low-level format*. If problems persist, perform a low-level format (if possible). If there is a LL formatting utility for your particular drive (available from the drive manufacturer), you may consider backing up the drive completely, running the LL utility, repartitioning, reformatting, then restoring the drive.

Symptom 5.14: The system reports random data, seek, or format errors.   Random errors rarely indicate a permanent problem, but identifying the problem source can be a time-consuming task.

- *Check the power connector*. Make sure the 4-pin power connector is inserted properly and completely. If the drive is being powered by a Y connector, make sure any interim connections are secure. Use a voltmeter to measure the +5-V (pin 4) and +12-V (pin 1) levels. If either voltage (especially the +12-V supply) is unusually low, replace the power supply.

- *Check the signal connector*. Make sure that the interface signal cable is inserted properly and completely at the drive and controller. Try a new signal cable. Also try rerouting the signal cable away from the power supply or "noisy" expansion devices.

- *Check the drive orientation*. If problems occur after remounting the drive in a different orientation, you may need to repartition and reformat the drive or return it to its original orientation. Try relocating the drive controller away from cables and "noisy" expansion devices.

- *Check the turbo mode.* If your system has a turbo mode, your ISA drive controller may have trouble operating while the system is in turbo mode. Take the system out of turbo mode.

- *Replace the drive controller.* If the problem disappears, try a new drive controller.

- *Check the media.* The disk media may also be defective. Use a utility such as ScanDisk to check for and map out any bad sectors. Once bad sectors are mapped out, you may need to restore some files from your backup.

- *Try the hard drive and controller in another system.* If the drive and controller work in another system, there is probably excessive noise or grounding problems in the original system. Reinstall the drive and controller in the original system and remove all extra expansion boards. If the problem goes away, replace one board at a time and retest the system until the problem returns. The last board you inserted when the problem returned is probably the culprit. If the problem persists, there may be a ground problem on the motherboard. Try replacing the motherboard as an absolute last effort.

Symptom 5.15: You see an *Error reading drive C:* error message.   Read errors in a hard drive typically indicate problems with the disk media, but may also indicate viruses or signaling problems.

- *Check the signal connector.* Make sure that the interface signal cable is inserted properly and completely at the drive and controller. Try a new signal cable.

- *Boot the PC clean.* Start the PC with a clean boot disk and make sure that there are no TSRs or drivers being loaded.

- *Check for viruses.* If you haven't done so already, run your antivirus checker and make sure that there are no memory-resident or file-based viruses.

- *Consider the drive's orientation.* If problems occur after remounting the drive in a different orientation, you may need to repartition and reformat the drive or return it to its original orientation.

- *Check the disk media.* Use a utility such as ScanDisk to check for and map out any bad sectors. Once bad sectors are mapped out, you may need to restore some files from your backup.

- *Try another hard drive.* If a known-good drive works as expected, your original drive is probably defective and should be replaced.

Symptom 5.16: You see a *Track 0 not found* error message. A fault on track 00 can disable the entire drive, since track 00 contains the drive's FAT. This can be a serious error that may require you to replace the drive.

- *Check the signal connector.* Examine the drive signal connector, and verify that the interface signal cable is inserted properly and completely at the drive and the controller. Try a new signal cable.

- *Check your partitions.* Boot from a floppy disk and run FDISK to check the partitions on your hard drive. Make sure that there is at least one DOS partition. If the drive is to be your boot drive, the primary partition must be "active" and bootable. Repartition and reformat the drive if necessary.

- *Replace the hard drive.* Try a known-good hard drive. If a known-good drive works as expected, your original drive is probably defective.

Symptom 5.17: You see a *Hard Disk Controller Failure*, or a large number of defects in the last logical partition. This is typically a CMOS Setup or drive controller problem. Enter the CMOS Setup routine and verify that all the parameters entered for the drive are correct. If the geometry specifies a larger drive, the system will attempt to format areas of the drive that don't exist, resulting in a large number of errors. If CMOS is configured correctly, there may be a problem with the hard drive controller. Try a new hard drive controller. If a new drive controller does not correct the problem, the drive itself is probably defective and should be replaced.

Symptom 5.18: The IDE drive (<528 MB) does not partition or format to full capacity. When relatively small hard drives do not realize their full capacity, the CMOS Setup is usually at fault. The drive parameters entered into CMOS must specify the *full* capacity of the drive, using a geometry setup that is acceptable. If you use parameters that specify a smaller drive, any extra capacity will be ignored. If there are more than 1024 cylinders, you must use an alternative "translation geometry" to realize the drive's full potential. The drive maker can provide you with the right translation geometry. Also check your DOS version—older versions of DOS use a partition limit of 32 MB. Upgrade your older version of DOS to 6.22 (or MS-DOS 7.0 with Windows 95).

Symptom 5.19: The EIDE drive (>528 MB) does not partition or format to full capacity. This type of problem may also be due to a CMOS Setup error, but it is almost always due to poor system configuration.

- *Check the CMOS Setup*. The drive parameters entered into CMOS must specify the *full* capacity of the drive. If you use parameters that specify a smaller drive, any extra capacity will be ignored. If there are more than 1024 cylinders, you must use an alternative translation geometry to realize the drive's full potential. The drive maker can provide you with the right translation geometry. Also check the CMOS Setup for LBA. EIDE drives need logical block addressing to access over 528 MB. Make sure that there is an entry such as LBA Mode in CMOS.

Otherwise, you may need to upgrade your mother-board BIOS to have full drive capacity.

■ *Check the drive controller.* If you cannot upgrade an older motherboard BIOS, install an EIDE drive controller with its own controller BIOS—this will supplement the motherboard BIOS.

■ *Check the drive overlay software.* If neither your motherboard nor your controller BIOS will support LBA mode, you will need to install drive overlay software (such as EZ-Drive or Drive Manager).

Symptom 5.20: You see *Disk Boot Failure, nonsystem disk*, or *No ROM Basic—SYSTEM HALTED* error messages. There are several possible reasons for these errors.

■ *Check the signal connector.* Make sure that the interface signal cables are inserted properly and completely at the drive and controller. Try some new signal cables.

■ *Boot the PC clean.* Start the PC with a clean boot disk and make sure that there are no TSRs or drivers being loaded that might interfere with drive operation. If you haven't done so already, run your antivirus checker and make sure that there are no memory-resident or file-based viruses.

■ *Check the CMOS Setup.* Enter the CMOS Setup routine and verify that all the parameters entered for the drive are correct. Heads, cylinders, sectors per track, landing zone, and write precompensation must all be entered accurately.

■ *Check your partitions.* Boot from a floppy disk and run FDISK to check the partitions on your hard drive. Make sure that there is at least one DOS partition. If the drive is to be your boot drive, the primary partition must be active and bootable.

■ *Replace the drive or controller.* It is also possible that the hard drive itself is defective. Try a known-good hard drive. If a known-good drive works as expected, your original drive is probably defective. If problems persist with a known-good hard drive, replace the drive controller.

Symptom 5.21: The hard drive in a PC is suffering frequent breakdowns (i.e., between 6 and 12 months). When drives tend to fail within a few months, there are some factors to consider.

- *Check the PC power.* If the ac power supplying your PC is "dirty" (i.e., has lots of spikes and surges), power anomalies can often make it through the power supply and damage other components. Remove any high-load devices such as air conditioners, motors, or coffee makers from the same ac circuit used by the PC, or try the PC on a known-good ac circuit. You might also consider a good UPS to power your PC.

- *Consider drive utilization.* Excessive drive use may be another factor. If the drive is being worked hard by applications and swap files, consider upgrading RAM, adding cache, or disabling virtual memory to reduce dependence on the drive.

- *Defragment the drive.* Periodically run a utility like Defrag to reorganize the files. This reduces the amount of "drive thrashing" that occurs when loading and saving files.

- *Consider the environment.* Constant low-level vibrations, such as those in an industrial environment, can kill a hard drive. Smoke (even cigarette smoke), high humidity, very low humidity, and caustic vapors can ruin drives. Make sure the system is used in a stable office-type environment.

Symptom 5.22: A hard drive controller is replaced, but during initialization, the system displays error messages such as *Hard Disk Failure* or *Not a recognized drive type.* The

PC may also lock up. Some drive controllers may be incompatible with some systems. Check with the controller manufacturer to see if there have been any reports of incompatibilities with your PC. If so, try a different drive controller board.

Symptom 5.23: A new hard drive is installed, but it will not boot, or a message appears such as *HDD controller failure*. The new drive has probably not been installed or prepared properly.

- *Check the power connector*. Make sure the 4-pin power connector is inserted properly and completely. If the drive is being powered by a Y connector, make sure any interim connections are secure. Use a voltmeter to measure the +5-V (pin 4) and +12-V (pin 1) levels. If either voltage (especially the +12-V supply) is unusually low or absent, replace the power supply.

- *Check the signal cable*. Make sure the drive's signal interface cable is connected securely at both the drive and the controller. If the cable is visibly worn or damaged, try a new one.

- *Check the CMOS Setup*. Enter the CMOS Setup routine and verify that all the parameters entered for the drive are correct. Heads, cylinders, sectors per track, landing zone, and write precompensation must all be correct—otherwise, POST will not recognize the drive.

- *Check the drive's preparation*. The drive may not be prepared properly. Run FDISK from a bootable diskette to partition the drive, then run FORMAT to initialize the drive. Then run SYS C: to make the drive bootable.

Symptom 5.24: The drive will work as a primary drive, but not as a secondary (or vice versa). In most cases, the drive is simply jumpered incorrectly, but there may also be timing problems. Check the drive jumpers first.

Make sure that the drive is jumpered properly as a primary (single drive), primary (dual drive), or secondary drive. The drive signal timing may also be off. Some IDE/EIDE drives do not work as primary or secondary drives with certain other drives in the system. Reverse the primary/secondary relationship. If the problem persists, try the drives separately. If the drives work individually, there is probably a timing problem, so try a different drive as the primary or secondary.

Symptom 5.25: You install a Y adapter which fails to work. Some Y adapters are incorrectly wired and can cause severe damage to any device attached to them. Examine the power connector first. Make certain that both of the female connectors are lined up with the two chamfered (rounded) corners facing up and both of the squared corners facing down. The four wires attached to the female connectors should now be in the following order from left to right: yellow (+12 V dc), black (ground), black (ground), red (+5 V dc). If this order is reversed on one of the connectors, then your Y power adapter is faulty and should not be used.

Symptom 5.26: During the POST, you hear a drive begin to spin up and produce a sharp noise. This problem can be encountered with some combinations of drives, motherboards, and motherboard BIOS. This type of problem can easily result in data loss (and media damage). Check the motherboard BIOS version first, then contact the PC system manufacturer and see if a BIOS upgrade is necessary. Try a BIOS upgrade. Otherwise, replace the drive controller. Often a new drive controller may resolve the problem if the motherboard BIOS cannot be replaced.

Symptom 5.27: You're using an Ultra-DMA hard drive, but there is no *DMA* check box available in the drive's *Properties* dialog. If the *DMA* check box is unavailable, this may suggest that Windows does not view the drive as Ultra-DMA-capable. This could be a driver issue, or your hard drive (or motherboard drive controller) may not support Ultra-DMA. Assuming that the drive and motherboard both support Ultra-DMA operation, make sure that you are running the latest bus-master drivers (these are installed by default if your motherboard supports them)—you may need to download the latest bus-master drivers from the drive controller maker or the motherboard manufacturer. Once the proper drivers are installed, Windows 98 will automatically handle all transfer rates that the drive and motherboard support.

Symptom 5.28: After installing a large HDD (unpartitioned), you cannot access the floppy drive. This will effectively hang the system and prevent you from completing the hard drive's installation. In most cases, this is due to an issue with the drive size. Some BIOS versions cannot perform the proper translation on an 8.4-GB (or larger) drive, and will hang the system as a result. Try setting the drive up using the following parameters:

- Cylinders: 1023
- Heads: 16
- Sectors: 63

Of course, this represents a small IDE drive, and the system will tell you that this is a 504- or 528-MB drive. If you are then able to boot to a floppy disk, you may either upgrade the BIOS or drive controller to support the large hard drive natively, or install drive overlay software such as Disk Manager or MaxBlast.

Symptom 5.29: After you configure a drive with the correct parameters (e.g., 16,383 × 16 × 63), the system still indicates that the drive is only 504 or 528 MB. Keep in mind that 528 MB (or 504 MB) is the limitation of the original cylinder/head/sector translation method used on IDE drives. This problem was resolved with LBA translation technique. Make sure that the CMOS Setup is configured to use LBA if it is available. If it is not, you may need to upgrade the BIOS (or drive controller) or install drive overlay software such as Disk Manager or MaxBlast.

Symptom 5.30: When replacing or repartitioning certain Compaq systems, you can no longer access the system's setup. This occurs because you removed the diagnostic partition. Some Compaq computers store the system BIOS information in a non-DOS or diagnostic partition on the hard drive, instead of storing it on a chip on the motherboard as most other systems do. If you have such a Compaq model and you install the new drive as a master, you will need to copy or reinstall the diagnostic partition onto the new drive. If you don't, you will not be able to access your CMOS Setup upon bootup. If you install the new drive as a slave or nonboot drive, you do not need to reinstall this partition. In addition, if you're planning to install the drive with an older version of Western Digital's EZ-Drive, you must use version 9.06w or later.

If you install the new drive as a master, you can use drive overlay software to copy the diagnostic partition and your data from the old drive to the new one. If you're only concerned about the diagnostic partition, you can use the drive overlay software to transfer the data, then reformat the drive. As long as you do this under the DDO's control (i.e., assuming that EZ-BIOS installed itself), it will not affect the diagnostic partition. Just boot to C:, insert the startup disk, then start formatting. If you have more than one partition, make sure you format the *correct* drive letters corresponding to the other partitions.

> **NOTE**: *When trying to access the diagnostic partition, you may encounter an error message that refers to a memory conflict. This is a known issue, and you will need to contact Compaq directly for detailed instructions should this occur.*

Symptom 5.31: You detect hard drive errors caused by damaged data or physical damage. You may receive one of the following error messages when you are starting or using your computer:

- *Serious Disk Error Writing Drive <X>*
- *Data Error Reading Drive <X>*
- *Error Reading Drive <X>*
- *I/O Error*
- *Seek Error—Sector not found*

These error messages indicate either damaged data or physical damage on the hard disk. Run ScanDisk to examine the hard drive. Running ScanDisk with the *Thorough* option selected examines the drive for physical damage—if damaged data are detected, ScanDisk allows you to save the damaged data to a file (or discard the data). Keep in mind that ScanDisk's surface scan may take a considerable amount of time on large hard disks. If ScanDisk is unable to repair damaged data (or indicates that the drive suffers from physical damage), you'll need to replace the drive.

Symptom 5.32: You find that a PC using an Ultra-DMA controller/drive may lock up when running Windows 95 (OSR2). The lockup occurs when the drive is being accessed. This problem occurs when there's a hardware error while data are being read from the hard drive. When the error happens during an Ultra-DMA data transfer, the Windows device driver does not successfully recover from the error and retry the operation, and so the system halts. This is a known issue with Windows 95 OSR2, and an update file (REMIDE-UP.EXE) is available for download from the Microsoft Web site. The updated file Esdi_506.pdr version 4.00.1116 (dated 8/25/97 or later) should fix the problem under Windows 95 OSR2.

Symptom 5.33: You encounter errors accessing a hard drive with its spin-down feature enabled. This frequently occurs under Windows 95 (and OSR2), and you may find that incorrect data are read or written to the drive, or you may encounter general protection faults (GPFs). This type of problem is known to occur under Windows 95 (and OSR2) if the drive requires more than 7.5 s to spin-up—an error is then generated in the Windows 95 driver, resulting in incorrect data being read from the drive (which can result in GPFs). You can work around this problem by disabling hard disk spin-down on the *Disk Drives* tab using the *Power* tool in *Control Panel*. An update file (REMIDE-UP.EXE) is available for download from the Microsoft Web site. The updated file ESDI_506.PDR version 4.00.1113 (dated 12/6/96 or later) should fix the problem under Windows 95 (and OSR2). For Windows 95, the VOLTRACK.VXD version 4.00.954 (dated 3/6/96 or later) file is also installed.

File system symptoms

Symptom 5.34: One or more subdirectories appear lost or damaged. Both the root directory of a drive and its FAT contain references to sub directories. If data in either the root directory or the file allocation table are corrupt, one or more subdirectories may be inaccessible by the drive. Try repairing the drive's directory structure. Use ScanDisk (with DOS 6.2 or later) to check the disk's directory structure for problems, then correct any problems that are reported.

Symptom 5.35: The hard drive was formatted accidentally. A high-level format (using the FORMAT utility) does not actually "destroy" data; rather, it clears the file names and locations kept in the root directory and FAT—this prevents DOS from finding those files. You will need to recover those files. Use a utility such as UNFORMAT (or another file recovery utility) which can reconstruct root directory and FAT data. This is not always a perfect process, and you may not be able to recover all files. If that's the case, you can restore the missing files from a backup.

Symptom 5.36: A file has been deleted accidentally. Mistyping a file name (or forgetting to add the proper drive specification) can accidentally erase files from places you did not intend to erase. You can often recover those files if you act quickly. Use a utility such as UNDELETE (or another file recovery utility) to restore the deleted file(s). This is not always a perfect process, and you may not be able to recover every file.

Symptom 5.37: The hard drive's root directory is damaged. A faulty root directory can cripple the entire disk, rendering *all* subdirectories inaccessible. You may be able to recover the root directory structure. Use a utility like DISKFIX (with PC Tools) to reconstruct the damaged FATs and directories. If you have been running MIRROR, DISKFIX should be able to perform a very reliable recovery. You may also try other recovery/corrective utilities such as DrivePro or ScanDisk. However, if you cannot recover the root directory reliably, you'll need to reformat the drive, then restore its contents from a backup.

Symptom 5.38: You see a *Bad* or *Missing Command Interpreter* error message.   This is a typical error that appears when a drive is formatted in one DOS version but loaded with another. Compatibility problems occur when you mix DOS versions. Start by booting the PC with a clean boot disk, and make sure that there are no TSRs or drivers being loaded. If you haven't done so already, run your antivirus checker and make sure that there are no memory-resident or file-based viruses. Finally, make sure that the drive is partitioned and formatted with the version of DOS you intend to use. Also be sure to use FORMAT with the /S switch, or SYS C: in order to transfer system files to the drive.

Symptom 5.39: You see an *Incorrect DOS version* error.
You attempted to execute an external DOS command
(e.g., FORMAT) using a version of the utility which is *not*
from the same DOS version as the COMMAND.COM
file which is currently running. Reboot with a corresponding version of COMMAND.COM, or get a version
of the utility which matches the current version of
COMMAND.COM.

**Symptom 5.40: The hard drive is infected by a bootblock
virus.** You may detect the presence of a bootblock
virus (a virus which infects the MBR) by running an
antivirus utility or by receiving an warning from the
BIOS bootblock protection feature. In every case, you
should attempt to use the antivirus utility to eradicate
the virus. You may also remove a bootblock virus by
using FDISK /MBR (though that could render the contents of your disk inaccessible). If you're using drive
overlay software such as Disk Manager, you can usually rewrite the code through the *Maintenance Menu*
within the Disk Manager utility itself.

Symptom 5.41: You see a *File Allocation Table Bad* error.
The operating system has encountered a problem with
the FAT. Normally, there are two copies of the FAT on
a drive—chances are that one of the copies has become
damaged. It may also be possible that there is no partition on the drive to begin with. Run ScanDisk; this
may be able to correct the problem by allowing you to
select which copy of the FAT you wish to use. If the
problem continues, you'll need to back up as many files
as possible and reformat the drive.

**Symptom 5.42: DOS requires you to *Enter Volume Label,*
but the label is corrupt.** Some versions of DOS (e.g.,
DOS 3.x) require you to enter the volume label when
formatting a hard drive or deleting a logical drive partition using the FDISK command. However, if the volume label is corrupted (or was changed by a third-party

utility to contain lowercase letters), this is impossible. To correct this problem, use the LABEL command to delete the volume label, then use FORMAT or FDISK. When you are prompted for the volume label, press <Enter> (which indicates *no* volume label). If LABEL doesn't successfully delete the volume label, you can use the following debug script to erase the first sector of the drive and make it appear unformatted, then repartition and reformat the drive. Start DEBUG, then type the following:

```
- F 100 L 200 0      ;Create a sector of zeros at
                       address 100

- W 100 2 0 1        ;Write information at address
                       100 to sector 0 of drive 2

- Q                  ;Quit DEBUG
```

For DOS versions 5.x and later, you can use the following command to handle the problem:

```
format /q /v:VOLUME x:
```

where VOLUME is the new volume name you want to assign to the hard disk drive, and x: is the drive letter you want to format.

Symptom 5.43: You cannot empty the Recycle Bin under Windows 95/98. There are several possible issues. When you right-click the *Recycle Bin*, the *Empty Recycle Bin* command may be unavailable (or the *Properties* command may be unavailable). You may also find that files you delete may be permanently deleted, rather than simply "moved" to the *Recycle Bin*. In virtually all cases this problem is caused when your fixed hard disk is marked as a removable drive. You'll have to unmark the hard drive:

- Click *Start*, select *Settings*, and then double-click *Control Panel*.

- Double-click the *System* icon.

- Click the *Device Manager* tab.

- Double-click the *Disk Drives* branch to expand it.

- Click your hard disk, and then click *Properties*.

- On the *Settings* tab, click the *Removable* check box to clear it.

- Click *OK*, then click *OK* again.

- Restart your computer.

> **NOTE**: *You cannot use this procedure on a true removable drive. If the drive is removable, the* Removable *option is reset when you restart the computer.*

Software-oriented symptoms

Symptom 5.44: Software diagnostics indicate an average access time that is longer than that specified for the drive. The average access time is the average amount of time needed for a drive to reach the track and sector where a needed file begins.

- *Check your timing*. Review your drive specifications and verify the timing specifications for your particular drive—its timing may be correct.

- *Defragment the drive*. Start your defragmentation utility (such as Defrag), and check to see the percentage of file fragmentation. If there is more than 10 percent fragmentation, you should consider running the defragmentation utility.

- *Check your software*. Also keep in mind that different software packages measure access time differently. Make sure that the diagnostic subtracts system overhead processing from the access time calculation. Try one or two other diagnostics to confirm the measurement.

- *Check similar drives*. Before you panic and replace a drive, try testing several similar drives for comparison. If only the suspect drive measures incorrectly, you may not *need* to replace the drive itself just yet, but you should at least maintain frequent backups in case the drive is near failure.

Symptom 5.45: Software diagnostics indicate a slower data transfer rate than specified. This is often due to less-than-ideal data transfer rates rather than to an actual hardware failure.

- *Check your timing*. Review your drive specifications and verify the timing specifications for your particular drive—its timing may be correct.

- *Check your data transfer modes*. Enter the CMOS Setup routine and verify that any enhanced data transfer modes are enabled (such as PIO Mode 4). This can increase the data transfer rate substantially.

- *Defragment the drive*. Start your defragmentation utility (such as Defrag), and check to see the percentage of file fragmentation. If there is more than 10 percent fragmentation, you should consider running the defragmentation utility.

- *Check your software*. Also keep in mind that different software packages measure access time differently. Make sure that the diagnostic subtracts system overhead processing from the access time calculation. Try one or two other diagnostics to confirm the measurement.

- *Check for low-level formatting*. If the drive is an IDE/EIDE type, make sure that no one has performed a low-level format—this may remove head and cylinder skewing optimization and result in a degradation of data transfer. This error generally cannot be corrected by end-user software.

- *Check termination*. If the drive is a SCSI type, make sure the SCSI bus is terminated properly—poor termination can cause data errors and result in retransmissions that degrade overall data transfer rates.

Symptom 5.46: The FDISK procedure hangs up or fails to create or save partition records for the drive(s). You may also see an error message such as *Runtime error*. This type of problem often indicates a problem with track 00 on the drive.

- *Check the signal connector*. Make sure that the interface signal cables are inserted properly and completely at the drive and controller. Try some new signal cables.

- *Check the drive setup*. Enter the CMOS Setup routine and verify that all the parameters entered for the drive are correct. Heads, cylinders, sectors per track, landing zone, and write precompensation must all be appropriate. Check with the drive maker and see if there is an alternative translation geometry that you can enter instead. If the BIOS supports autodetection, try autodetecting the drive.

- *Check your version of FDISK*. The version of FDISK you are using must be the same as the DOS version on your boot diskette—older versions may not work.

- *Check your partition(s)*. Run FDISK and see if there are any partitions already on the drive. If so, you may need to erase any existing partitions, then create your new partition from scratch. *Remember that erasing a partition will destroy any data already on the drive.*

- *Check for media defects*. Use a utility such as ScanDisk to check the media for physical defects, especially at track 00. If there is physical damage in the boot sector, you should replace the drive.

- *Check for emergency drive utilities*. Some drive makers provide low-level preparation utilities that can rewrite track 00. For example, Western Digital provides the WD_CLEAR.EXE utility.

- *Replace the hard drive*. If problems still persist, replace the defective hard drive.

Symptom 5.47: After using FDISK to partition a large hard drive, the system hangs when booting from a floppy disk. This is almost always an issue with the system BIOS (or drive controller), which cannot properly support a large (8.4 GB+) drive. Some BIOS versions are confused when they encounter an 8.4-GB or larger hard drive, and they assign it 0 heads by mistake. Under these conditions, you'll be able to partition the drive with FDISK, but the partition table that it creates will contain invalid information. When you boot to a floppy disk, the operating system on that floppy disk attempts to access the partition table on the hard drive. The invalid information created by FDISK causes the operating system to hang. The solution is to upgrade the system BIOS (or the drive controller) to support the large drive natively or install drive overlay software such as Disk Manager or MaxBlast.

Symptom 5.48: FDISK reports an error such as *no space to create partition* or *disk is write protected*. There are several possible causes for this type of behavior.

- *Check the CMOS Setup*. Chances are that your BIOS has enabled virus protection for the master boot record (also referred to as Boot Sector Write Protect). You must go into the system's CMOS Setup and disable that feature before partitioning a drive (or installing/upgrading an operating system).

- *Check the drive jumpers*. Some hard drives require the use of two jumpers rather than just one. Verify that your drive is jumpered properly for its place in your particular drive configuration (i.e., single master, master with slave, or slave).

- *Upgrade the BIOS or drive controller*. If the problem persists, the BIOS may not be able to support your drive properly. Check for a BIOS upgrade (or upgrade the drive controller), or install drive overlay software such as Disk Manager or MaxBlast.

Symptom 5.49: FDISK refuses to partition the drive and hangs the system or returns a runtime error. In many cases, track 00 on the drive has been corrupted. If you can perform a low-level format of the drive, try using the disk manufacturer's LL formatting (or drive preparation) utility to reconstruct track 00. For example, Western Digital's Data Lifeguard Tools utility *http://www.wdc.com/service/ftp/drives.html#dlgtools* can be used to perform a "pseudo" LL format on Western Digital drives. From the main menu, choose *Diagnostics*, select the correct drive, and choose *Write Zeros*. After the operation completes, run FDISK again. Your particular drive manufacturer may offer other similar utilities. If this does not resolve the problem, the drive itself may need to be replaced.

Symptom 5.50: The high-level (DOS) format process takes too long. In almost all cases, long formats are the result of older DOS versions. Check your DOS version. MS-DOS version 4.x tries to recover hard errors— which can consume quite a bit of extra time. You will probably see a number of *Attempting to recover allocation units* messages. Your best course is to upgrade the MS-DOS version to 6.22 (or MS-DOS 7.x with Windows 95/98). Later versions of DOS abandon hard error retries.

Symptom 5.51: You install Disk Manager to a hard drive, then install DOS, but DOS formats the drive back to 528 MB. After Disk Manager is installed, you must create a "rescue disk" to use in conjunction with your DOS installation. There are two means of accomplishing this. First:

- Create a clean DOS bootable disk.
- Copy two files from the original Disk Manager disk to your bootable disk: XBIOS.OVL and DMDRVR.BIN.

- Create a CONFIG.SYS file on this bootable disk with these three lines:

```
DEVICE=DMDRVR.BIN
FILES=35
BUFFERS=35
```

- Remove the bootable diskette and reboot the system.

- When you see *Press space bar to boot from diskette*, do so—the system will halt.

- Insert the rescue disk in drive A:, and press any key to resume the boot process.

- At the A: prompt, remove your rescue disk, insert the DOS installation disk, then type SETUP.

- You will now install DOS files without overwriting the Disk Manager files.

or use an alternative approach:

- Create a clean DOS bootable disk.

- Insert the original Disk Manager diskette in the A: drive and type

```
DMCFIG/D=A:
```

- You will prompted to insert a bootable floppy in drive A:.

- You will need to remove and insert the bootable disk a few times as Drive Manager files are copied.

- Remove the floppy and reboot the system.

- When you see *Press space bar to boot from diskette*, do so—the system will halt.

- Insert the rescue disk in drive A:, and press any key to resume the boot process.

- At the A: prompt, remove your rescue disk, insert the DOS installation disk, then type SETUP.

- You will now install DOS files without overwriting the Disk Manager files.

Symptom 5.52: ScanDisk reports some bad sectors, but cannot map them out during a surface analysis. You may need a surface analysis utility for your particular drive that is provided by the drive maker. For example, Western Digital provides the WDATIDE.EXE utility for its Caviar series of drives. It will mark all "grown" defects and compensate for lost capacity by utilizing spare tracks.

> **NOTE**: *These types of surface analysis utilities are typically destructive. Make sure to have a complete backup of the drive before proceeding. Also, the utility may take a very long time to run, depending on your drive's capacity.*

Symptom 5.53: ScanDisk reports an *Out of Memory* error after copying data from a smaller drive to a larger one. The data seem to copy successfully, but when you run ScanDisk, you get an *Out of Memory* error (or you have a problem using Defrag). Chances are that you've copied data from a smaller drive to a larger drive that uses FAT32 (you're running Windows 95 OSR2 or Windows 98) using some utility that can copy the contents of one hard drive to another. The utility may have created an image of the drive which was copied to the other, or it may have copied data sector by sector from one drive to the other.

If you used an older utility (or version of EZ-Drive) to copy the data, the clusters were probably not correctly resized for the new FAT32 partition. When a partition is formatted, it is divided into clusters, or small blocks. These clusters are used to store data, and the size of a cluster is determined by the size of the partition. Older copy utilities often do not support FAT32 properly and will incorrectly size the cluster on the new FAT32 partition when they transfer data from the old drive to the new one. You can verify if this has occurred by running CHKDSK from a DOS prompt.

The correct cluster sizes for FAT32 partitions are listed here:

- 512 MB to 8.2 GB = 4-KB cluster size
- 8.2 to 16.4 GB = 8-KB cluster size
- 16.4 to 32.8GB = 16-KB cluster size
- 32.8 GB and higher = 32-KB cluster size

If CHKDSK reports an incorrect cluster size for your partition, you need to erase the data and copy them using an updated utility.

Symptom 5.54: You cannot get 32-bit access to work under Windows 3.1x. You are probably not using the correct hard drive driver. Check your EIDE BIOS. If your motherboard (or drive controller) BIOS supports LBA, obtaining a driver should be easy. Either the drive maker provides a 32-bit driver on a diskette accompanying the drive, or a driver can be downloaded from the drive maker's BBS or Internet Web site. If the motherboard (or drive controller) does not support LBA directly, you can install drive overlay software such as Ontrack's Disk Manager (7.0 or later), and run DMCFIG to install the 32-bit driver software.

Symptom 5.55: Drive diagnostics reveal a great deal of wasted space on the drive. You probably have a large drive partitioned as one or more FAT16 logical volumes. If you deal with large numbers of small files, it may be more efficient to create multiple smaller partitions utilizing smaller clusters. As an alternative, you may choose to repartition the drive using FAT32, which supports much larger partitions (while allowing for smaller clusters).

Symptom 5.56: After installation of a new hard drive, Windows 98 detects the drive only if it's noted as "removable" in the Device Manager. Chances are that you missed one or two steps and neglected to partition and

format the drive. All hard disk drives must be partitioned before they can be formatted—even if the drive
is going to have only a single partition. Windows 98
incorrectly allows you to format an unpartitioned drive
if you designate the drive as removable. Using a drive
this way will almost certainly result in data loss. The
solution is to back up any data on the drive, then
remove the checkmark from the *removable* box in the
Windows 98 Device Manager. Next, use FDISK to create at least one primary and active partition. Reboot
the system, then format the partition(s) with FOR-
MAT. This process will destroy any data on the drive,
but should correct the recognition issue.

**Symptom 5.57: When upgrading Windows 95 OSR2 to
Windows 98, you see an *SU0013 error*.** When drive C: is
configured as a "removable media" device and you are
using the FAT32 file system, you may see an error such
as *SU0013—Setup cannot create files on your startup
drive and cannot set up Windows 98*. To circumvent
this issue, you'll need to run Setup from DOS:

- Boot your computer with a Windows 98 Startup
  Disk.

- On the *Startup* menu, choose *Start Computer with
  CD-ROM Support*, and then press <Enter>.

- At the A: prompt, type <drive>:\>win98\setup,
  where <drive> is the drive letter assigned to your
  CD-ROM drive, and then press <Enter>.

- Follow the instructions shown to complete the Setup
  process and complete the upgrade.

**Symptom 5.58: You find that the System Configuration
Utility will not work under Windows 98.** When you run
the System Configuration Utility, the following items
may not work:

- Diagnostic Startup—Interactive Load
- Enable Startup Menu

- Disable Scandisk After bad shutdown
- Disable SCSI Double-Buffering

This problem occurs if you use any version of the DriveSpace disk compression software to compress your hard disk in place (i.e. you compress the entire hard disk). When you compress a hard disk in place, DriveSpace swaps hard disk letters after the initialization of the compressed volume file (CVF). Because the System Configuration Utility is not aware of the drive letter swap, it edits the MSDOS.SYS file on the CVF instead of the MSDOS.SYS file on the host drive. This is a problem with Windows 98.

To correct this problem, edit the MSDOS.SYS file on the host drive (usually drive H:) after DriveSpace is loaded. Note that DriveSpace hides the host drive by default. To make the host drive visible, follow these steps:

- Click *Start*, highlight *Programs*, select *Accessories*, select *System Tools*, and then click *DriveSpace*.

- Click the compressed drive (where the hidden drive is a host drive), and then click *Properties* on the *Drive* menu.

- Click the *Hide Host Drive* check box to clear it.

- Click *OK*.

Now start a word processor such as EDIT and load the MSDOS.SYS file for the host drive, then adjust the MSDOS.SYS file as follows (if the appropriate line does not exist, create it in the [Options] section):

- To enable diagnostic startup, edit or add the line `orig_diag_BootMenu=1`. To disable the option, remove the line or change the value from 1 to 0.

- To enable the *Startup Menu*, edit or add the line `BootMenu=1`. To disable the option, change the value from 1 to 0.

- To disable *automatic ScanDisk after an incorrect shutdown*, edit or add the line `AutoScan=0`. To enable the option, change the value from 0 to 1.

- To enable *SCSI double-buffering*, edit or add the line `DoubleBuffer=1`. To disable *SCSI double-buffering*, change the value from 1 to 0.

Symptom 5.59: You encounter an invalid command line error when using NAI Nuts & Bolts DiskMinder. This problem occurs when recovering after an improper shutdown under Windows 98. It occurs if you're using the NAI Nuts & Bolts DiskMinder program instead of ScanDisk as your disk repair program. NAI Nuts & Bolts DiskMinder is unable to correctly interpret the `/simpleui` switch used with ScanDisk in the WIN.COM file. To work around this problem, simply ignore the error message; DiskMinder can continue normally. Check with the program maker to see if a patch or update is available.

Symptom 5.60: Norton DiskDoctor refuses to run after an improper shutdown under Windows 95/98. After you upgrade Windows 95 to Windows 98 (or reinstall Windows 95/98), the Norton DiskDoctor utility (included with Symantec Norton Utilities 2.0s or 3.0x) doesn't run automatically after an improper shutdown of Windows—ScanDisk for DOS is used instead. Norton Utilities updates the Win.com file to run the Norton DiskDoctor utility (NDD.EXE) when Windows 95/98 is shut down incorrectly. When you upgrade Windows 95 to Windows 98 (or reinstall Windows 95/98), the WIN.COM file is replaced, and ScanDisk is then used as the default disk utility. You can correct this problem simply by reinstalling Norton Utilities. You could also create an alternative utility file for DiskDoctor. At a command prompt (from within Windows 95/98), enter the following commands:

```
cd\windows\command

copy ndd.exe scandisk.alt
```

This creates a copy of the Norton DiskDoctor utility named Scandisk.alt. When Windows 95/98 is shut down improperly, the Scandisk.alt file (now the Norton DiskDoctor utility) is run automatically.

Symptom 5.61: ScanDisk incorrectly reports hard drive problems under Windows 98. When you upgrade from Windows 3.x to Windows 98, Setup may quit and recommend that you run ScanDisk to repair your hard disk—but no errors are found after you run ScanDisk. This is a known problem with Windows 98; it occurs when your Windows 3.x-based computer is configured to use a network server for virtual memory. To work around this issue, run Windows 98 Setup with the /is parameter (Setup runs normally, but skips ScanDisk), such as

```
setup /is
```

Symptom 5.62: When running CHKDSK.EXE from a command prompt, you receive an *F parameter not specified* error. This issue may occur under Windows 95/98, and the entire error message usually appears, such as

```
Errors found, F parameter not specified. Correc-
tions will not be written to disk. CHKDSK cannot
check the validity of this drive because the
following path is too long:

<Path>
```

This problem typically occurs when the command line you type contains more than 67 characters. To get around this issue, use ScanDisk instead of CHKDSK to check your hard disk for errors.

Symptom 5.63: While using APC PowerChute, Defrag locks up the system after selecting a disk to defragment. This problem occurs when you're using APC

PowerChute Plus 5.0 or 5.0.1 under Windows 98—these versions of PowerChute Plus are designed for Windows 95 only. To work around this problem, quit PowerChute Plus before using Defrag:

- Press <Ctrl> + <Alt> + <Del> to open the *Close Program* dialog box.

- Click *PowerChute Plus*, and then click *End Task*.

- Do the same thing for *Iconclnt*.

- Now run Defrag normally.

To restart PowerChute Plus after Defrag is completed, simply reboot the computer. For a more permanent fix to this problem, obtain updated software from APC.

Symptom 5.64: Defrag causes a GPF in USER.EXE under Windows 95/98. When you try to run Defrag from System Agent or Task Scheduler, you may receive a general protection fault (or GPF) in USER.EXE. This may occur if the task information for DEFRAG has become damaged. Delete the Defrag task from System Agent or Task Scheduler, and then create a new task.

FAT32 symptoms

Symptom 5.65: You cannot place a FAT32 partition on a drive. The trick to establishing a FAT32 partition on a drive is to partition the drive correctly. Try the following steps to partition a drive:

- In the Windows 95/98 *Device Manager*, select the drive, and then click on *Properties*.

- Click *Settings*, and then click the *Int13 Unit* check box to select it.

- Quit the *Device Manager* and restart Windows 95/98.

- Once Windows 95/98 is restarted, open an MS-DOS session and use the FDISK command to partition the drive (be careful not to partition an existing drive accidentally).

- Restart Windows 95/98 again. You should be able to format the drive and use the FAT32 file system.

Symptom 5.66: After moving a FAT32 SCSI hard drive from one controller to another, you cannot read or write reliably to the SCSI drive. This is because SCSI drives are highly controller-dependent to begin with, and you should be prepared to repartition and reformat SCSI drives *whenever* you change the SCSI host controller. This behavior is particularly evident when you partition and format a hard disk using a SCSI controller that fully supports Int 13 extensions, and you then move the hard disk to a controller that does *not* fully support Int 13 extensions. To move a drive using the FAT32 file system to a different controller, you must verify that *both* controllers fully support Int 13 extensions in the same manner—if they do not, data loss will most likely occur.

Symptom 5.67: When you try to compress a drive with DriveSpace or DriveSpace 3, you receive the following error message: *Drive C cannot be compressed because it is a FAT32 drive.* This is because DriveSpace was designed to work with the FAT12 and FAT16 file systems, and cannot be used on drives with the FAT32 file system. Unfortunately, there is no correction for this problem, and Microsoft is considering an update for a future release. In the meantime, your only options are to avoid using drive compression or to use a third-party drive compression tool which *is* FAT32 compatible. Check out the Stacker site (*www.stac.com*).

Symptom 5.68: When booting from diskette, you cannot access your FAT32 hard drive partition(s). The system boots fine from the hard drive. This is an issue with the boot diskette. Boot diskettes made with older versions of DOS or Windows are not FAT32-aware and

cannot support access to your FAT32 hard drive parti-
tion(s). For example, you cannot access your Windows
98 FAT32 drive when booting from a Windows 95a
Startup Disk. Create a Windows 98 Startup Disk in
order to boot your FAT32 system.

Symptom 5.69: You encounter an error message such as
Setup found a compressed volume or a disk cache utility.
This can occur if you try to install a retail version of
Windows 95 over an OSR2 version of Windows 95.
There are actually a number of problems that can crop
up when installing an older version of Windows 95.
The initial error usually appears like

```
Setup found a compressed volume or a disk-cache
utility on your computer. Quit setup and check your
compressed volume with your disk-compression soft-
ware or remove the disk-cache utility. Then run
Setup again.
```

If you continue trying to install Windows 95 on a hard
disk using the FAT32 file system, you may receive the
following error message:

```
SU-0013
```

If you are installing the retail version of Windows 95
over OSR2 on a hard disk using the FAT16 file system,
Setup continues, but it experiences numerous file version conflicts that generate the following message:

```
A file being copied is older than the file cur-
rently on your computer. It is recommended that you
keep your existing file.
```

If you click *Yes* to keep the newer files, Setup finishes,
but when you restart the computer, you may experience either of the following symptoms:

- The computer stops responding (hangs) at the logo
  screen.

- You receive the error message *Fatal Exception 0D has occurred at 0117:00007E1F*.

Starting Windows 95 in safe mode may generate the following error message:

```
Fatal Exception 0D has occurred at 0117:00007E1F
```

To verify the version you are installing, type `ver` at a command prompt. Version 4.00.950 (files dated 7-11-95) is the retail version and OEM (non-OSR2) version. Version 4.00.1111 (files dated 8-24-96) indicates the Windows 95 OEM Service Release 2 (OSR2). Do *not* install the retail or OEM (non-OSR2) version of Windows 95 into an existing Windows 95 OSR2 folder. If you are installing to a hard disk using the FAT16 file system, install to a *different* folder.

> **NOTE**: *Do* not *install the retail or OEM version of Windows 95 on a hard disk using the FAT32 file system.*

You should reinstall OSR2 using the OSR2 CD provided by your OEM. If an OSR2 CD-ROM was not provided to you by your OEM, the OSR2 files may have been provided in a folder on your hard disk. To locate this folder, type the following command at a command prompt:

```
dir *.cab /s
```

To reinstall OSR2, run SETUP.EXE from the folder containing the OSR2 cabinet (.cab) files. If you cannot reinstall ORS2, contact your OEM (the company that sold the system) for assistance.

Symptom 5.70: You cannot use SHARE.EXE in Windows 95. The SHARE.EXE utility is not supported in the OSR2 release of Windows 95. In order to support the FAT32 file system, SHARE.EXE support has been disabled in the real-mode MS-DOS kernel regardless of whether or not you have any drives using the FAT32 file system. Instead, file sharing and locking capabilities are provided by VSHARE.VXD in OSR2 and are not supported in MS-DOS mode.

> **NOTE**: *You may not be able to install or run some MS–DOS based programs or 16-bit Windows-based programs that require SHARE.EXE.*

> **NOTE**: *Some programs (such as Microsoft Word version 6.0 for Windows and Quattro Pro version 6.0 for Windows) do not require SHARE.EXE to be loaded in order to start. Instead, some programs simply look for a file named SHARE.EXE in either the root folder or the DOS folder. This file can be a zero-byte file created with a text editor like EDIT or Notepad. Other programs may simply look for the string* share *in the AUTOEXEC.BAT file.*

Symptom 5.71: The system may hang up when certain drive software is used under FAT32.   After installing the drive software (e.g., PC Tools Pro 9.0), the computer will probably hang up during startup after you see the following message:

```
Analyzing drive C:
Reading system areas
```

In virtually all cases, this occurs because your drive software is *not* compatible with the FAT32 file system in Windows 95 OSR2 (or Windows 98). You can contact the software maker (such as Symantec for PC Tools Pro 9.0 at *www.symantec.com*) for a FAT32-aware version of the software. As a work-around, you can use a text editor (e.g., EDIT or Notepad) to edit the AUTOEXEC.BAT file and disable the command line that starts the software. For PC Tools Pro 9.0, you'd REMmark out its line as

```
REM call pctools.bat
```

Symptom 5.72: You encounter errors using IBM antivirus utilities on a FAT32 file system.   In actual practice, you'll probably encounter either of the following symptoms:

- When you are installing IBM Anti-Virus, the Setup program offers to scan for viruses. If you choose to scan, you may receive an error message stating that the master boot record could not be read.

- When you are scanning for viruses on a drive using the FAT32 file system, IBM Anti-Virus may report that errors occurred while it was checking for viruses. The error log may contain the following information: *Errors during virus checking: unexpected error code 18.*

Older versions of IBM Anti-Virus are *not* written to work with the new FAT32 file system included with OSR2 and Windows 98. There is no work-around for this: you'll need to obtain an updated version of IBM software or use a different antivirus tool which is FAT32-aware.

Symptom 5.73: When using Defrag on a FAT32 system, you encounter an error message such as *DEFRAG0026 Make sure disk is formatted.* You may also see an error such as

```
Windows cannot defragment this drive. Make sure the
disk is formatted and free of errors. Then try
defragmenting the drive again.
```

This error can be caused when running an earlier version of DEFRAG.EXE than the version included with Windows 95 OSR2 (or Windows 98). To resolve this problem, extract a new copy of the DEFRAG.EXE file from your original Windows 95 OSR2 (or Windows 98) CD:

- Open an MS-DOS prompt in Windows 95/98.

- Change to the Windows folder, and then type the following line:

```
ren defrag.exe defrag.xxx
```

- Insert the OSR2 CD, OSR2 disk 6, or Windows 98
  CD in the appropriate drive. If you are using the
  CD-ROM, type the following line:

```
extract   <x\:win95\win95_05.cab   defrag.exe   /l
<z>:\windows
```

where <x> is the CD-ROM drive letter and <z> is the
drive containing the Windows folder. If you are using
disk 6, type the following line:

```
extract  <x>:\win95_06.cab defrag.exe /l <z>:\win-
dows
```

where <x> is the drive containing disk 6 and <z> is the
drive containing the Windows folder.

**Symptom 5.74: You see an _Invalid Media_ error message
when formatting a FAT32 partition.**   When you try to format a FAT32 file system partition larger than 8025
MB (8 GB) from within Windows 95/98, you may
receive the following error message:

```
Verifying <xxx.xx>M

Invalid media or track 0 bad-disk unusable

Format terminated
```

where <xxx.xx> is the size of the partition. This
error occurs if there is a non-DOS partition preceding
the extended DOS partition _and_ the primary DOS
partition has been formatted using the real-mode
FORMAT.EXE command. To correct this problem,
you'll need to reformat the volume using the following
steps:

- Click the _Start_ button, click _Shut Down_, click
  Restart The Computer In MS-DOS Mode, and then
  click _Yes_.

- Type the following command and then press
  `<Enter>`:

  `format <drive>:`

where `<drive>` is the drive letter for the partition you
want to format.

- When the partition is formatted, type `exit` to
  restart Windows 95/98.

**Symptom 5.75: Opening a folder seems to take a very long
time.** When you open a folder in Microsoft Explorer on
a drive using the FAT32 file system, one or both of the
following problems may occur:

- It may seem to take an unusually long time before
  the window is accessible.

- The Working in Background pointer may appear for
  a long time.

This problem occurs because the total space used by all
directory entries in the folder exceeds 32 KB. To
resolve this issue, move some files to a different folder.

**Symptom 5.76: You find that your FAT32 system works in
compatibility mode when using Ontrack Disk Manager.**
After you install FAT32 on a drive that uses Ontrack
Disk Manager (version 6.03 or 7.04), one or both of the
following problems may occur:

- All drives use MS-DOS compatibility mode.

- The computer seems to take an unusually long time
  to boot.

This happens because the dynamic drive overlay (or
DDO) is unable to find files in the root folder that it
needs in order to start correctly. A dynamic drive overlay makes calculations for the starting root folder clus-

ter based on FAT12 and FAT16 volumes, and returns a
value of zero for FAT32 volumes (this is due to changes
made in the root directory structure). The overlay software searches all possible clusters in the root folder for
its overlay files. You'll need to configure Disk Manager
to avoid searching the root folder for overlay files.

> **NOTE**: *Configuring Disk Manager software to avoid
> searching the root folder causes Disk Manager not to
> hook the DOS arena chain, forcing Disk Manager to load
> low in conventional memory.*

**Symptom 5.77: The OSR2 version of Windows 95 will now
allow dual booting with Windows 3.1x.**   If you try to dual-
boot Windows version 3.x on a computer running
Windows 95 OSR2, you'll receive one of the following
error messages:

- *This version of Windows does not run on MS-DOS
  6.x or earlier.*

- *You started your computer with a version of MS-
  DOS incompatible with this version of Windows.
  Insert a Startup diskette matching this version of
  Windows and then restart.*

- *The system has been halted. Press CTRL+ALT+
  DELETE to restart your computer.*

- *This version of Windows cannot be run on this version of DOS.*

Beginning with OSR2, dual-booting with Windows 3.x
is not supported in Windows 95. To dual-boot between
Windows 3.x and Windows 95, you'll need to install the
retail version of Windows 95. If you have FAT32 drives,
you need to remove the FAT32 partitions and create
FAT16 partitions with the Windows 95 or MS-DOS 6.x
version of FDISK.EXE.

> **NOTE**: *Neither MS-DOS 6.x nor the early retail ver-
> sion of Windows 95 will recognize a FAT32 volume.*

> **NOTE**: *Windows 3.x was designed to use the FAT12 and FAT16 file system, and could potentially damage a FAT32 volume.*

Symptom 5.78: After you install Windows 98 (or convert a partition to FAT32), Windows 98 reports *DOS Compatibility Mode.* This can occur when the drive controller has not been detected properly under Windows 98. Try rebooting the PC and see if Windows 98 will redetect the drive controller (you may need to *Remove* the drive controller entry from the *Device Manager* before rebooting the system). For specific details about resolving compatibility-mode problems, refer to the compatibility-mode troubleshooting guide at the start of this section.

Symptom 5.79: After converting a drive to FAT32, you notice that tools like ScanDisk and Defrag take much longer to run. This is an undesired side effect of the FAT32 file system. It takes Defrag and ScanDisk a fixed amount of time to examine a single cluster, regardless of that cluster's size. Since FAT32 uses smaller clusters, there are many times more clusters, and so such utilities take considerably longer than they used to. Microsoft compensates for this by including the Tune Up Wizard, which allows you to schedule such tasks to take place when you're away from the computer.

Symptom 5.80: The FAT32 conversion utility crashed after reporting that it found bad sectors. This is a side effect of ScanDisk. If ScanDisk has marked any sectors bad, the FAT32 converter will refuse to run, even if they are fixed by third-party disk utilities (e.g., Data Lifeguard Tools). ScanDisk uses the FAT to keep track of bad sectors. But even if third-party utilities remap bad sectors at the hardware level, ScanDisk is not aware of those changes. One solution is to wipe the hard drive clean and start over (in which case you'd just partition the drive using FAT32 to begin with). Here's an easier workaround when there are only a few bad sectors:

- Before using the FAT32 conversion utility, perform a complete backup of your hard drive.

- Run your third-party disk utility software (e.g., Data Lifeguard Tools) to make sure that any bad sectors have been remapped.

Open a DOS window and type:

```
cvt x: /cvt32
```

where x is the drive letter you wish to convert.

- The converter will then run, disregarding any sectors that have previously been marked bad by ScanDisk.

Symptom 5.81: The FAT32 converter under Windows 98 cannot locate the drive partition to be converted.   When using the Windows 98 drive converter tool to convert a drive from FAT16 to FAT32, you may receive an error message such as *Drive converter unable to find the drive partition*. This problem can occur if you try to convert a FAT16 logical drive that begins above the 8.0-GB mark. For example, if you have a 10-GB hard disk with five 2.0-GB FAT16 partitions, you may have trouble converting the fifth drive (e.g., drive G:) to FAT32. To work around this problem, delete all of your partitions above the 8.0-GB mark, and then recreate your partitions.

> **IMPORTANT NOTE**: *All data on the specific partition or drive will be deleted, so back up your data before you perform the following steps.*

- Click *Start*, select *Programs*, then click *MS-DOS Prompt*.

- At the command prompt, type FDISK, press Y when you're prompted to *enable large disk support*, and then press <Enter>.

- Press 4, and then press <Enter>.

- Press Y, and then press <Enter>. Observe the partition information for all of the drives listed on this screen, and then press <Esc>.

- Press 3, press <Enter>, press 3, and then press <Enter> again.

- Press the letter that corresponds with the last drive listed in the extended partition, and then press <Enter>. For a 10.0-GB drive with five 2.0-GB partitions, the fifth "drive" would be G: (the only one remaining in FAT16 format).

- Type the volume label displayed to the left of the drive letter exactly as it is displayed, and then press <Enter>.

- Press Y, press <Enter>, press <Esc>, and then press <Esc> again.

- Press 1, press <Enter>, press 3, and then press <Enter> again.

- You're prompted to use all of the remaining available drive space—press Y, and then press <Enter>.

- Press <Esc> to exit FDISK, type EXIT, and then press <Enter>.

- Restart your computer so that your changes will take effect.

- Double-click *My Computer*, right-click *drive G:*, and then click *Format*.

- Click *Full*, click *Start*, and then click *OK*.

Web Contacts

MicroHouse: *http://www.microhouse.com*

Symantec: *http://www.symantec.com*

Maxtor: *http://www.maxtor.com*

Quantum: *http://www.quantum.com*

Seagate: *http://www.seagate.com*

Western Digital: *http://www.wdc.com*

Windows 95 Emergency Recover Utility: *http://www.microsoft.com/windows/download/eruzip.exe*

CD-ROM Drives

The *compact disk* (or CD) first appeared in the commercial marketplace in early 1982. Sony and Philips developed the CD as a joint venture and envisioned it as a reliable, high-quality replacement for aging phonograph technology. With the introduction of the audio CD, designers demonstrated that huge amounts of information can be stored simply and very inexpensively on common, nonmagnetic media. Unlike earlier "analog" media (e.g., cassette tapes or albums), the CD recorded data in *digital* form through the use of physical "pits" and "lands" in the disk. The digital approach allowed excellent stereo sound quality which does not degrade each time the disk is played, but also attracted the attention of PC designers, who saw CDs as a natural solution for all types of computer information (text, graphics, programs, video clips, audio files, and so on). The CD-ROM drive is now standard equipment on both desktop and mobile PC systems. This chapter introduces some essential concepts of CD-ROM technology and presents a comprehensive suite of troubleshooting techniques.

Understanding CD Media

Commercial CDs are mass-produced by stamping the pattern of pits and lands onto a molded polycarbonate disk (known as a *substrate*). It is this stamping process (much like the stamping used to produce vinyl records) that places the data on the disk. But the disk is not yet readable—there are additional steps that must be performed in order to transform a clear plastic disk into a viable, data-carrying medium. The clear polycarbonate disk is given a silvered (reflective) coating so that it will reflect laser light. Silvering coats all parts of the disk side (pits and lands) equally. After silvering, the disk is coated with a tough, scratch-resistant lacquer that seals the disk from the elements (especially oxygen, which will oxidize and ruin the reflective coating). Finally, a label can be silk-screened onto the finished disk before it is tested and packaged.

CD data

CDs are not segregated into concentric tracks and sectors, as magnetic media are. Instead, CDs are recorded as a single, continuous *spiral* track that runs from the spindle to the lead-out area. The spiral track is formed by physical pits and lands that represent the digitally encoded data. Each pit is about 0.12 m (micrometer) deep and 0.6 m wide. Pits and lands may range from 0.9 to 3.3 μm in length. There are approximately 1.6 m between each iteration of the spiral. Given these microscopic dimensions, a CD-ROM disk offers a data storage capacity equivalent to about 16,000 tracks per inch (tpi).

During playback, CDs use a highly focused laser beam and laser detector to sense the presence or absence of pits. Figure 6.1 illustrates the reading behavior. The laser/detector pair is mounted on a carriage which follows the spiral track across the CD. A laser is directed at the underside of the CD, where it

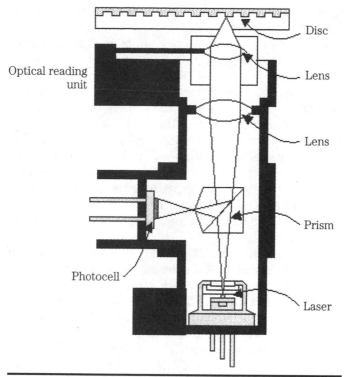

Figure 6.1 Reading a typical compact disk.

penetrates more than 1 mm of clear plastic before shin-
ing on the reflective surface. When laser light strikes a
land, the light is reflected toward the detector, which,
in turn, produces a very strong output signal. When
laser light strikes a pit, the light is slightly out of
focus. As a result, most of the incoming laser energy is
scattered away in all directions, and so very little output signal is generated by the detector. As with floppy
and hard drives, it is the *transition* from pit to land
(and back again) that corresponds to binary levels, *not*
the presence or absence of a pit or land. The analog
light signal returned by the detector must be converted to logic levels and decoded. A process known as

eight-to-fourteen modulation (EFM) is very common with CD-ROMs.

A CD-ROM *data frame* is composed of 24 synchronization bits, 14 control bits, 24 of the 14-bit data symbols you saw previously, and 8 complete 14-bit error correction (EC) symbols. Each symbol is separated from the next by an additional 3 merge bits, bringing the total number of bits in the frame to 588. Thus, 24 bytes of data are represented by 588 bits on a CD-ROM, expressed as a number of pits and lands. There are 98 frames in a data *block*, so each block carries 98 $\times$ 24 = 2048 bytes (2352 with error correction, synchronization, and address bytes). The basic CD-ROM can deliver 153.6 KB of data (75 blocks) per second to its host controller.

Remember that the CD-ROM disk is recorded as one continuous spiral track running around the disk, so the ordinary sector and track ID information that we associate with magnetic disks does not apply very well. Instead, information is divided in terms of 0 to 59 *min*, and 0 to 59 *s* recorded at the beginning of each block. A CD-ROM (like an audio CD) can hold up to 79 *min* of data. However, many CD-ROMs tend to limit this to 60 min, since the last 14 min of data are encoded in the outer 5 mm of disk space, which is the most difficult to manufacture and keep clean in everyday use. There are 270,000 blocks of data in 60 min. At 2048 data bytes per block, the disk's capacity is 552,950,000 bytes (553 MB). If all 79 min are used, 681,984,000 bytes (681 MB) will be available in 333,000 blocks. Most CD-ROMs run between 553 and 650 MB in normal production.

Caring for compact disks

A compact disk is a remarkably reliable long-term storage medium (conservative estimates place the life expectancy of a high-quality commercial CD at about 100 years). However, the longevity of a CD is affected by its storage and handling—a faulty CD can cause file and data errors that you might otherwise interpret as a defect in the drive itself. Below are some tips to help you protect and maintain the disk media:

- *Don't bend the disk.* Polycarbonate is a forgiving material, but you risk cracking or snapping (and thus ruining) the disk.

- *Don't heat the disk.* Remember, the disk is plastic. Leaving it by a heater or on the dashboard of your car will cause melting.

- *Don't scratch the disk.* Laser wavelengths have a tendency to look past minor scratches, but a major scratch can cause problems. Be especially careful of circular scratches (those that follow the spiral track). A circular scratch can easily wipe out entire segments of data, and these would be unrecoverable.

- *Don't use chemicals on the disk.* Chemicals containing solvents such as ammonia, benzene, acetone, carbon tetrachloride, or chlorinated cleaning solvents can easily damage the disk's plastic surface.

   NOTE: *A buildup of excessive dust or fingerprints can interfere with the laser beam enough to cause disk errors. When this happens, the disk can be cleaned easily using a dry, soft, lint-free cloth. Hold the disk by its edges and wipe radially (from hub to edge).* Do not wipe in a circular motion. *For stubborn stains, moisten the cloth with a bit of fresh isopropyl alcohol (*do not use water*). Place the cleaned disk in a caddy or jewel case for transport and storage.*

CD-ROM/CD-R Standards and Characteristics

Like so many other PC peripheral devices, the early CD-ROM faced a serious problem of industry standardization. Just recording the data on a CD is not enough—the data must be recorded in a way that *any*

CD-ROM drive can read. Standards for CD-ROM data and formats were developed by consortiums of influential PC manufacturers and interested CD-ROM publishers. This kind of industrywide cooperation has made the CD-ROM one of the most uniform and standardized peripherals in the PC market. With the broad introduction of CD recorders into the marketplace, it is also important for you to understand the major concepts and operations of CD recorders. This part of the chapter explains many of the key ideas needed to master CD-ROM and CD-R drives.

High Sierra

In 1984 (before the general release of CD-ROMs), the PC industry realized that there must be a standard method of reading a disk's VTOC (volume table of contents)—if there were not, the CD-ROM market would become extremely fragmented as various (incompatible) standards vied for acceptance. PC manufacturers, prospective CD publishers, and software developers met at the High Sierra Hotel in Lake Tahoe, California, to begin developing just such a uniform standard. By 1986, the CD-ROM standard file format (dubbed the *High Sierra* format) was accepted and approved. High Sierra remained the standard for several years, but it has since been replaced by ISO 9660.

ISO 9660

High Sierra was certainly a workable format, but it was primarily a domestic U.S. development. When it was placed before the International Standards Organization (ISO), High Sierra was tweaked and refined to meet international needs. After international review, High Sierra was absorbed (with only a few changes) into the *ISO 9660* standard. Although many technicians refer to High Sierra and ISO 9660 interchangeably, you should understand that the two standards are *not* the same. For the purposes of this book,

ISO 9660 is the current CD-ROM/CD-R file format, and all CD recorders are capable of recording a disk in the ISO 9660 format.

By adhering to ISO 9660, CD-ROM drive makers can write software drivers (and use MSCDEX under MS-DOS) to enable a PC to read the CD's VTOC. ISO 9660 also allows a CD-ROM disk to be accessed by any computer system and CD-ROM drive that follows the standard. Of course, just because a disk is recognized does not mean that it can be used. For example, an ISO 9660-compliant Mac can access a ISO 9660 MPC disk, but the files on the disk cannot be used by the Mac.

CD-ROM/CD-R standards ("books")

When Philips and Sony defined the proprietary standards that became CD audio and CD-ROM, the documents were bound in different colored covers. By tradition, each color now represents a different level of standardization. The *Red Book* (a.k.a. the *Compact Disk Digital Audio Standard* or CEI IEC 908) defines the media, the recording and mastering process, and the player design for CD audio. When you listen to your favorite audio CD, you are enjoying the benefits of the Red Book standard. CDs conforming to Red Book standards will usually have the words "Digital Audio" printed below the disk logo. Today, Red Book audio may be combined with programs and other PC data on the same disk.

The *Yellow Book* standard (or *ISO 10149:1989*) makes the CD-ROM suitable for PC use by defining the additional error correction data needed on the disk and the detection hardware and firmware needed in the drive. When a disk conforms to Yellow Book standards, it will usually be marked "Data Storage" beneath the disk logo. "Mode 1" Yellow Book is the typical operating mode which supports computer data. "Mode 2" Yellow Book (also known as the *XA format*) supports compressed audio data and video/picture data. The Yellow Book standards build on the Red Book, so virtually all CD-ROM drives are capable of playing back CD audio.

The *Orange Book* (a.k.a. the *Recordable Compact Disk Standard*) is the key to CD recorders and serves to extend the basic Red and Yellow Book standards by providing specifications for recordable products such as (Part 1) *magneto-optical* (or MO) drives and (Part 2) *write-once CD-R* drives. Virtually all of the CD-recorder and CD-rewriter products on the market today adhere stringently to the Orange Book standard.

The *Green Book* standard defines an array of supplemental standards for data recording and provides an outline for a specific computer system that supports CD-I (compact disk interactive). Most interactive kiosks and information systems using CD-I disks are based on Green Book standards. The *Blue Book* is the standard for laser video disks and their players (now heading toward obsolescence with the emergence of DVD video). Finally, the *White Book* standards define CD-ROM video.

The multispin drive

The Red Book standard defines CD audio as a stream of data that flows from the player mechanism to the amplifier (or other audio manipulation circuit) at a rate of 150 KB/s. This data rate was chosen for truest reproduction of music taken off the disk. When the Yellow Book was developed to address CD-ROMs, this basic data rate was carried over. Designers soon learned that computer data can be transferred much faster than Red Book audio information, so the *multi-spin* (or *multispeed*) drive was developed to work with Red Book audio at the normal 150-KB/s rate, but run faster for Yellow Book data in order to multiply the data throughput.

The first common multispin drives available were "2X" drives. With the drive running at two times the normal data transfer speed, data throughput can be doubled from 150 KB/s to 300 KB/s. If Red Book audio is encountered, the drive speed drops back to 150 KB/s. Increased data transfer rates make a real difference in CD-ROM performance, especially for data-intensive applications such as audio/video clips. CD-ROM drives with 4X transfer speed (600 KB/s) can transfer data four times faster than a Red Book drive. Table 6.1 lists the average data rates for CD-ROM drives up to 24X.

The MPC

One of the most fundamental problems in writing software for PCs is the tremendous variability in the possible hardware and software configurations of individual machines. The selection of CPUs, motherboard chipsets, DOS versions, available memory, graphics resolutions, drive space, and other peripherals makes the idea of a "standard" PC almost meaningless. Most software developers in the PC market use a base (or minimal) PC configuration to ensure that a product will run properly in a "minimal" machine. CD-ROM multimedia products have intensified these performance issues because of the unusually heavy demands posed by real-time audio and graphics. Microsoft assembled some of the largest PC manufacturers to create the *Multimedia Personal Computer* (or MPC) standard. By adhering to the MPC specification, software developers and consumers can anticipate the minimal capacity needed to run multimedia products. For the CD-ROM, 8X or faster drives will provide acceptable performance for almost every multimedia application.

Effects of CD-ROM caching

The limiting factor of a CD-ROM is its data transfer rate. Even a fast multispin CD-ROM takes a fairly substantial amount of time to load programs and files into memory, and this causes system delays during CD-ROM access. If the PC could *predict* the data need-

TABLE 6.1 Data Transfer Rates for CD-ROM Drives

Speed	Data transfer rate		
	CD-ROM (Mode 1) 2048 bytes/block	CD-ROM (Mode 2) 2336 bytes/block	CD-I XA (Form 2) 2324 bytes/block
1×	153.6 KB/s (0.15 MB/s)	175.2 KB/s (0.17 MB/s)	174.3 KB/s (0.17 MB/s)
2×	307.2 KB/s (0.3 MB/s)	350.4 KB/s (0.35 MB/s)	348.6 KB/s (0.34 MB/s)
4×	614.4 KB/s (0.61 MB/s)	700.8 KB/s (0.70 MB/s)	697.2 KB/s (0.69 MB/s)
6×	921.6 KB/s (0.92 MB/s)	1051.2 KB/s (1.05 MB/s)	1045.8 KB/s (1.04 MB/s)
8×	1200 KB/s (1.2 MB/s)	1401.6 KB/s (1.40 MB/s)	1394.4 KB/s (1.39 MB/s)
10×	1500 KB/s (1.5 MB/s)	1752.0 KB/s (1.75 MB/s)	1743.0 KB/s (1.74 MB/s)
12×	1800 KB/s (1.8 MB/s)	2102.4 KB/s (2.10 MB/s)	2091.6 KB/s (2.09 MB/s)
14×	2100 KB/s (2.1 MB/s)	2452.8 KB/s (2.45 MB/s)	2440.2 KB/s (2.44 MB/s)
16×	2400 KB/s (2.4 MB/s)	2803.2 KB/s (2.80 MB/s)	2788.8 KB/s (2.78 MB/s)
18×	2700 KB/s (2.7 MB/s)	3153.6 KB/s (3.15 MB/s)	3137.4 KB/s (3.13 MB/s)
20×	3000 KB/s (3.0 MB/s)	3504.0 KB/s (3.50 MB/s)	3486.0 KB/s (3.48 MB/s)
22×	3300 KB/s (3.3 MB/s)	3854.4 KB/s (3.85 MB/s)	3834.6 KB/s (3.83 MB/s)
24×	3600 KB/s (3.6 MB/s)	4204.8 KB/s (4.20 MB/s)	4183.2 KB/s (4.18 MB/s)

ed from a CD and load those data into RAM or virtual memory (i.e., the hard drive) during background operations, the *effective* performance of a CD-ROM drive could be enhanced dramatically. CD-ROM caching utilities provide a "look-ahead" ability that enables CD-ROMs to continue transferring information in anticipation of use.

However, CD-ROM caching is a mixed blessing. The utilities required for caching (e.g., SmartDrive) must reside in conventional memory (or be loaded into upper memory). In systems that are already strained by the CD-ROM drivers and other device drivers that have become so commonplace on PC platforms, adding a cache may prevent some large DOS programs from running. Keep this in mind when evaluating CD-ROM caches for yourself or your customers.

> **NOTE:** *Windows 95 and 98 have discontinued the use of SmartDrive in favor of their own internal caching features. If you are using Windows 95/98, you may optimize the CD-ROM cache through the* File System Properties *dialog. Click on* Start, Settings, Control Panel, *then double-click on the* System *icon. Select the* Performance *tab, and click the* File System button, *then select the* CD-ROM *tab. You can then optimize the CD-ROM cache size and access pattern.*

Bootable CD-ROM (El Torito)

Traditionally, CD-ROM drives have not been bootable devices. Since the CD-ROM drive needs software drivers, the PC always had to boot *first* in order to load the drivers. This invariably required a bootable hard drive or floppy drive. When building a new system, this required you to boot from a floppy disk, install DOS and the CD-ROM drivers, and *then* pop in your Windows 95/98 CD for setup. In early 1995, the "El Torito" standard, which provides the hardware and software specifications needed to implement a bootable CD-ROM, was finalized. You need three elements to implement a bootable CD-ROM:

- A bootable CD-ROM drive mechanism (almost always fitted with an EIDE/IDE interface)

- A BIOS that supports the bootable CD-ROM (now common on most new motherboards)

- A CD with boot code and an operating system on it (e.g., Windows NT 4.0)

CD-ROM Installation and Replacement

CD-ROM drives are generally easy devices to install or replace. Most are installed as master devices located on the secondary IDE drive controller channel, although a few will coexist as slave devices alongside a hard drive or other drive device. The most important issue to remember is that the BIOS will not support the CD-ROM directly (even if the BIOS identifies the CD-ROM at boot time)—you'll need real-mode drivers for the CD-ROM under DOS or protected-mode drivers for the CD-ROM under Windows. This part of the chapter covers the guidelines needed to install a basic internal IDE-type CD-ROM.

Select jumper configurations

An IDE-type CD-ROM drive may be installed as a master or slave device on any hard drive controller channel. These master/slave settings are handled through one or two jumpers located on the rear of the drive (right next to the 40-pin signal cable connector). One of your first decisions when planning an installation should be to decide the drive's configuration:

- If you're installing the CD-ROM as the first drive on the secondary drive controller channel, it must be jumpered as the master device.

- If you're installing the CD-ROM drive alongside another drive (on either the primary or the secondary drive controller channel), the CD-ROM must be jumpered as the slave device.

NOTE: *Refer to the documentation that accompanies your particular CD-ROM drive to determine the exact master/slave jumper settings. If you do not have the drive documentation handy, check the drive manufacturer's Web site for online information.*

Attach cables and mount the drive

- Turn off and unplug the PC, then remove the outer cover to expose the computer's drive bays.

- Attach one end of the 40-pin drive interface cable to the drive controller connector on your motherboard (or drive controller card). Remember to align pin 1 on the cable (the side of the cable with the blue or red stripe) with pin 1 on the drive controller connector.

- Locate an available drive bay for the CD-ROM drive. Remove the plastic housing covering the drive bay, then slide the drive inside. Locate the four screw holes needed to mount the drive. In some cases, you may need to attach mounting rails to the drive so that the drive will be wide enough to fit in the drive bay. In virtually all cases, you should mount a tray-driven CD-ROM drive horizontally (although caddy-loaded CD-ROM drives may be mounted vertically).

- Attach the 40-pin signal cable and the 4-pin power connector to the new drive, then bolt the drive securely into place. Do not overtighten the screws, since this may damage the drive. If you do not have an available 4-pin power connector, you may use an appropriate Y splitter if necessary to split power from another drive (preferably the floppy drive).

- Attach the small 4-pin CD-audio signal cable from the CD-ROM to the CD-audio input connector on your sound card. This connection allows you to play music CDs directly through your sound card. Verify that the CD-audio cable is compatible with your sound card (otherwise you may need a specialized cable from the sound card's manufacturer).

Configuring the CMOS Setup

Although the CD-ROM does require driver support, recent motherboard designs can identify the ATAPI IDE CD-ROM drive in BIOS, so you should configure your computer's BIOS to accept the drive if possible (through the CMOS Setup).

■ Turn the computer on. As your computer starts up, watch for a message that describes how to run the CMOS Setup (e.g., *Press F1 for Setup*). Press the appropriate key to start the CMOS setup program.

■ Select the *hard drive settings* menu, and choose the drive location occupied by the CD-ROM drive (i.e., primary slave, secondary slave, or secondary master, depending on how you've physically jumpered and installed the drive).

■ Select *automatic drive detection* if available—this option will automatically identify the new drive. If your BIOS does *not* provide automatic drive detection, select *none* or *not installed* for the CD-ROM and rely on drivers *only*.

■ Save the settings and exit the CMOS Setup program. Your computer will automatically reboot.

Reassemble the computer

Double-check all of your signal and power cables to verify that they are secure, then tuck the cables gently into the computer's chassis. Check that there are no loose tools, screws, or cables inside the chassis. Now reattach the computer's outer housing(s).

Install the software

In order to complete your CD-ROM installation, you'll need to install the software drivers that accompanied the drive on diskette or CD. Windows 95/98 systems will generally detect the presence of the new CD-ROM and prompt you for the protected-mode drivers automatically. Under DOS, you may need to run an "installer" routine to add the real-mode drivers to your system and update your CONFIG.SYS and AUTOEXEC.BAT files to load those drivers. If there's no real-mode installer, you'll need to update your startup files manually (see "Understanding the Software" below). After you install the drivers and reboot the system, the CD-ROM should be ready for use.

Understanding the Software

Hardware alone is not enough to implement a CD-ROM drive. In an ideal world, BIOS and MS-DOS would provide the software support to handle the drive, but in practice, the variations among CD-ROM designs and interfaces make it impractical to provide low-level BIOS services. Manufacturers provide a hardware-specific device driver used to communicate with the CD-ROM and interface, and a DOS extension (MSCDEX) provides file handling and logical drive letter support. This part of the chapter explains the operations and features of real-mode CD-ROM device drivers and MSCDEX.

> **NOTE:** *If you're using a Windows 95/98 platform and do not require use of the CD-ROM under DOS, you can omit the installation of real-mode drivers and skip this section of the chapter.*

Device drivers

A low-level device driver allows programs to access the CD-ROM drive properly at the register (or hardware) level. Since CD-ROM drives are designed in different ways, they require different device drivers. If you change or upgrade the drive at any point, the device driver must be upgraded as well. A typical device driver uses a .SYS extension and is initiated by adding its command line to the PC's CONFIG.SYS file, such as

```
DEVICE=HITACHIA.SYS /D:MSCD000 /N:1 /P:300
```

> **NOTE:** *The* DEVICE *command may be replaced by the* DEVICEHIGH *command if you have available space in the upper memory area (UMA).*

A CD-ROM device driver will typically have three command-line switches associated with it. These parameters are needed to ensure that the driver installs properly. For the example command line shown above, the /D switch is the *name* used by the driver when it is installed in the system's device table. This name must be unique and matched by the /D switch in the MSCDEX.EXE command line (covered later). The /N switch is the number of CD-ROM drives attached to the interface card. The default is 1 (which is typical for most general-purpose systems). Finally, the /P switch is the I/O port address the drive's adapter card resides at. As you might expect, the port address should match the port address on the physical interface. If there is no /P switch, the default is 0300h.

There's an additional wrinkle when using SCSI-based CD-ROM drives: The PC must be fitted with a SCSI adapter and configured with an ASPI driver in order to allow the SCSI adapter to interface to the drive (this is also true if you're using other SCSI drives). A typical ASPI driver entry would appear in CONFIG.SYS, such as

```
DEVICE=C:\SCSI\ASPIPPA3.SYS /L=001
```

> **NOTE:** *If there are no SCSI hard drives in the system, the SCSI adapter's on-board BIOS ROM can usually be disabled.*

MSCDEX.EXE

DOS was developed at a time when no one anticipated that large files would be accessible to a PC, and it is severely limited in the file sizes that it can handle. With the development of CD-ROMs, Microsoft created an extension to MS-DOS that allows software publishers to access 650-MB CDs in a standard fashion: the Microsoft CD-ROM Extensions (MSCDEX). Like most software, MSCDEX offers some vital features and has a few limitations, but it is required by a vast majority of CD-ROM products. Obtaining MSCDEX is not a problem; it is generally provided on the same disk as the CD-ROM's low-level device driver. Newer versions of MSCDEX can be obtained by searching the Microsoft Web site (*www.microsoft.com*).

In actual operation, MSCDEX is loaded in the AUTOEXEC.BAT file. It should be loaded *after* any mouse driver and loaded *before* any MENU, SHELL, DOSSHELL, or WIN line. It should also be loaded *before* any .BAT file is started. Keep in mind that if a .BAT file loads a network, MSCDEX must be included in the batch file *after* the network driver. Further, MSCDEX must be loaded after that network driver with the /S (share) switch in order to hook into the network driver chain. If you want to use the MS-DOS drive caching software (SmartDrive) to buffer the CD-ROM drive(s), load MSCDEX *before* SmartDrive. The MSCDEX /M (number of buffers) switch can be set to 0 when using SmartDrive. If you find that SmartDrive is interfering with MPC applications like Video for Windows, you can load SmartDrive *before* MSCDEX and set the /M switch for at least 2. When loading MSCDEX, remember that the MSCDEX /D switch *must* match the /D label used in the low-level driver. If it does not, MSCDEX will not load. If SETVER is loaded in the CONFIG.SYS file, be sure to use the latest version of MSCDEX.

Although the vast majority of CD-ROM bundles include installation routines that automate the installation process for the low-level driver and MSCDEX, you should understand the various command-line switches (shown in Table 6.2) that make MSCDEX operate. Understanding these switches may help you to overcome setup problems.

Troubleshooting CD-ROM Drives

Though the vast majority of CD-ROM problems are due to software or setup problems, the drives themselves are delicate and unforgiving devices. Con-

TABLE 6.2   MSCDEX Command-Line Switches

/D:x	Device name	The label used by the low-level device driver when it loads. MSCDEX must match this label for the device driver and MSCDEX to work together. A typical label is MSCD000.
/M:x	Buffers allocated	The number of 2-KB buffers allocated to the CD-ROM drives. There are typically 8 buffers (16 KB) for a single drive and 4 buffers for each additional drive. This number can be set to 1 or 2 if conventional memory space is at a premium.
/L:x	Drive letter	This is the optional drive letter for the CD-ROM. If this is not specified, the drive will be automatically assigned to the first available letter (usually D:). There must be a LASTDRIVE= entry in CONFIG.SYS to use a letter higher than the default letter. When choosing a letter for the LASTDRIVE entry, do not use Z; if you do, network drives may not install after MSCDEX.
/N	Verbose option	This switch forces MSCDEX to show memory usage statistics on the display each time the system boots.
/S	Share option	This switch is used with CD-ROM installations in network systems.
/K	Kanji option	This instructs MSCDEX to use Kanji (Japanese) file types on the CD if they are present.
/E	Expanded memory	This allows MSCDEX to use expanded memory for buffers. There must be an expanded memory driver running (e.g., EMM386.EXE) with enough available space to use it.

sidering that their prices have plummeted over the last few years (and are still continuing to drop), there is little economic sense in attempting a lengthy repair. When a fault occurs in the drive or in its adapter board, your best course is typically to replace the defective drive outright.

General symptoms

Symptom 6.1: The drive has trouble accepting or rejecting a CD. This problem is typical of motorized CD-ROM drives, where the disk is accepted into a slot or placed in a motorized tray, so you don't see this issue in caddy-type CD-ROM drives.

- *Check for obstructions.* Before performing any disassembly, check the assembly through the CD tray for any obvious obstructions. If there is nothing obvious, expose the assembly and check each linkage and motor drive gear very carefully. Carefully remove or free any obstruction. Be gentle when working around the load/unload assembly. Notice how it is shock mounted in four places.

- *Replace the CD-ROM drive.* If the problem persists, there is most likely a problem in the tray motor or mechanism. Your best course is to replace the CD-ROM drive outright.

Symptom 6.2: The optical read head does not seek (a.k.a. drive seek error). An optical head is used to identify pits and lands along a CD-ROM and to track the spiral data pattern as the head moves across the disk. The optical head must move very slowly and smoothly to ensure accurate tracking. Head movement is accomplished by using a linear stepping motor (or *linear actuator*) to shift the optical assembly in microscopic increments—head travel appears perfectly smooth to the unaided eye. Check the drive for any damaged parts or obstructions. When the optical head fails to seek, the easiest and fastest fix is simply to replace the CD-ROM mechanism outright.

Symptom 6.3: The disk cannot be read. This type of problem may result in a DOS-level *sector not found* or *drive not ready* error.

- *Clean the CD and drive optics.* Check the CD itself to ensure that it is the right format, inserted properly, and physically clean. Cleanliness is very important to a CD. While the laser will often look past any surface defects in a disk, the presence of dust or debris on a disk surface can produce serious tracking (and read) errors. Try a different disk to confirm the problem. If a new or different disk reads properly, the trouble may indeed be in (or *on*) the original disk itself. Not only must the disk be clean, but the head optics must also be clean. Gently dust or clean the head optics as suggested by your drive's particular manufacturer.

- *Check the cables.* Examine the power connector and signal cable between the drive and its controller board. Be sure that the cable is connected correctly and completely.

- *Replace the CD-ROM drive.* Either the drive's optical head or its electronics are defective. Your best course here is to try replacing the drive. If problems persist on a drive with a proprietary interface, replace the adapter board.

Symptom 6.4: The disk does not turn. You may not hear the disk spin up for access. The disk must turn at a *constant linear velocity* (CLV) which is directed and regulated by the spindle motor.

- *Check for obstructions.* If the disk is not spinning during access, check to be sure that the disk is seated properly and is not jammed or obstructed.

- *Recheck the drive's installation.* Before beginning a repair, review your drive installation and setup

carefully to ensure that the drive is properly configured for operation on your system. If the computer
does not recognize the CD drive (i.e., *invalid drive
specification*), there may be a setup or configuration
problem (either the low-level device driver or
MSCDEX may not have loaded properly).

- *Clean the drive optics.* If your particular drive provides you with instructions for cleaning the optical
head aperture, perform that cleaning operation and
try the drive again. A fouled optical head can sometimes upset spindle operation.

- *Replace the CD-ROM drive.* If the drive's activity
LED comes on when drive access is attempted, but
the disk still doesn't turn (you may also see a corresponding DOS error message), the drive spindle system is probably defective.

**Symptom 6.5: The optical head cannot focus its laser
beam.** To compensate for the minute fluctuations in
disk flatness, the optical head mounts its objective lens
into a small focusing mechanism which is little more
than a miniature voice coil actuator—the lens does not
have to move very much at all to maintain precise
focus. If the focus is out or not well maintained, the
laser detector may produce erroneous signals. This
may result in DOS drive error messages.

If random but consistent DOS errors appear, check
the disk to be sure that it is *optically* clean—dust and
fingerprints can result in serious access problems. Try
another disk. If a new disk continues to perform badly,
try cleaning the optical aperture with clean (photography-grade) air. If problems persist, the optical system
is probably damaged or defective. Try replacing the
CD-ROM drive mechanism outright.

Symptom 6.6: Audio is not being played by the sound card.
In most cases, there is a problem with the CD-audio
connection or system mixer setting.

- *Check the CD*. Double-check to verify that the CD you're trying to play actually contains Red Book audio (don't try to "play" data CDs).

- *Check the headphone output*. Try playing the music CD with a set of headphones attached to the CD-ROM drive. If there is no audio from the headphone jack, adjust the volume control. If there is still no music, the drive is probably defective and should be replaced.

- *Check the sound card and mixer*. Try playing .WAV or MIDI files through the sound card and verify that the card's volume setting is adequate. If you cannot play any sounds at all, there may be a problem with the sound card or its drivers rather than with the CD-ROM drive. Open the sound card's mixer applet and verify that the CD-audio channel volume is enabled and turned up to an appropriate level.

- *Check the CD-audio cable*. Verify that the CD-audio cable is appropriate for your sound card and CD-ROM drive, and see that it's attached securely at both ends. Try another CD-audio cable.

Symptom 6.7: There is no audio being generated by the drive. Normally you can listen to CD audio using the drive's headphone jack. Check your headphones on another stereo to verify that the headphones are working. Also adjust the headphone volume using the small dial located on the front of the CD-ROM drive. If the problem persists and *no* audio is being generated, the headphone amplifier circuit in the CD-ROM is probably defective and should be replaced.

Symptom 6.8: You see a *Wrong DOS version error message* when you attempt to load MSCDEX. You are running MS-DOS 4, 5, or 6 with a version of MSCDEX which does not support it. The solution is to change to the correct version of MSCDEX. The version compatibility for MSCDEX is shown below:

- v1.01 14,913 bytes (no ISO 9660 support—High Sierra support only)

- v2.00 18,307 bytes (High Sierra and ISO 9660 support for DOS 3.1–3.3)

- v2.10 19,943 bytes (DOS 3.1–3.3 and 4.0—5.x support provided with SETVER)

- v2.20 25,413 bytes (same as above with Win 3.x support—changes in audio support)

- v2.21 25,431 bytes (DOS 3.1–5.0 support with enhanced control under Win 3.1)

- v2.22 25,377 bytes (DOS 3.1–6.0 and higher with Win 3.1 support)

- v2.23 25,361 bytes (DOS 3.1–6.2 and Win 3.1 support—supplied with MSDOS 6.2)

When using MS-DOS 5.x to 6.1, you will need to add the SETVER utility to CONFIG.SYS in order to use MSCDEX v2.10 or v2.20 properly (i.e., DEVICE = C:\DOS\SETVER.EXE). SETVER is used to tell programs that they are running under a version of DOS other than DOS 5.0. This is important, since MSCDEX (v2.10 and v2.20) refuses to work with DOS versions higher than 4.0. SETVER is used to fool MSCDEX into working with higher versions of DOS. In some versions of DOS 5.0 (such as Compaq DOS 5.0), you will need to add an entry to SETVER for MSCDEX (i.e., SETVER MSCDEX.EXE 4.00). This entry modifies SETVER without changing the file size or date.

Symptom 6.9: You cannot access the CD-ROM drive letter under DOS. The drive is probably available under Windows 95/98. You may see an error message such as *Invalid drive specification*. This is typically a problem with the CD-ROM drivers. The MS-DOS extension MSCDEX has probably not loaded. Switch to the DOS subdirectory and use the MEM /C function to check the loaded drivers and terminate and stay resident programs (TSRs). If you see the low-level driver and MSCDEX displayed in the driver list, check the CD-ROM hardware. Make sure that the signal cable between the drive and the drive controller is inserted properly and completely. If problems persist, try replacing the drive controller.

If you do *not* see the low-level driver and MSCDEX shown in the driver list, inspect your CONFIG.SYS and AUTOEXEC.BAT files. Check that the drivers are included in the startup files to begin with. Make sure that the label used in the /D switch is the same for both the low-level driver and MSCDEX. If the label is not the same, MSCDEX will not load. If you are using MS-DOS 5.0, be sure the SETVER utility is loaded. You could also try updating MSCEDX to version 2.30 or later.

Symptom 6.10: You see an error when you try to load the low-level CD-ROM driver.   Check that you are using the proper low-level device driver for your CD-ROM drive. If you are swapping the drive or drive controller board, you probably need to load a new driver. If the driver fails to load with original hardware, the drive controller board may have failed, or its jumper settings may not match those in the driver's command-line switches. Check the signal cable running between the drive and the adapter board. If the cable is crimped or scuffed, try replacing the cable. Next, try replacing the adapter board. If problems persist, try replacing the CD-ROM drive mechanism itself.

Symptom 6.11: You see an error such as *Not ready reading from drive D:.*   Check that a suitable disk is inserted in the drive and that the drive is closed properly. Make sure that the low-level device driver and MSCDEX are loaded correctly. If the drivers do not load, there may be a problem with the drive controller board (or with the drive mechanism itself). Also check that the data cable between the drive and the adapter is connected properly and completely. If problems persist, suspect a weakness in the PC power supply (especially if the system is heavily loaded or upgraded, or if there is a Y splitter cable feeding the CD-ROM). Try a larger supply in the system. If problems persist, replace the CD-ROM drive. If a new drive does not correct the problem, try a different drive controller.

Symptom 6.12: SmartDrive is not caching the CD-ROM properly in DOS. The version of SmartDrive supplied with DOS 6.2x provides three forms of caching, although older forms of SmartDrive (such as the ones distributed with Windows 3.1 and DOS 6.0 and 6.1) will *not* adequately cache CD-ROM drives. The BUFFERS statement also does *not* help caching. So if you are looking to SmartDrive for CD-ROM cache, you should be using the version distributed with DOS 6.2x. You should also set BUFFERS=10,0 in the CONFIG.SYS file, and the SmartDrive command line should come *after* MSCDEX. When using SmartDrive, you can change the buffers setting in the MSCDEX command line (/M) to 0—this allows you to save 2 KB per buffer.

> **NOTE:** *SmartDrive is* not *used by Windows 95/98, which employs its own CD caching scheme. Try disabling SmartDrive when running under Windows 95/98.*

Symptom 6.13: After installation of the CD-ROM drivers, the system reports significantly less available RAM. This is usually a caching issue with CD-ROM driver software, and you may need to adjust the CD-ROM driver software accordingly. This type of problem has been documented with Teac CD-ROM drives and CORELCDX.COM software. If the software offers a command-line switch to change the amount of XMS allocated, reduce the number to 512 or 256. Check with tech support for your particular drive for the exact command-line switch settings.

Symptom 6.14: The CD-ROM drivers will not install proper- ly on a drive using compression software. This is usu- ally because you booted from a floppy disk and attempted to install drivers *without* loading the com- pression software *first*. Before doing anything else, check the loading order—allow your system to boot from the hard drive *before* you install the CD-ROM drivers. This allows the compression software to assign all drive letters. As an alternative, boot from a compression-aware floppy disk. If you *must* boot the system from a floppy disk, make sure the diskette is configured to be fully compatible with the compression software being used.

Symptom 6.15: You see an error indicating that the CD- ROM drive is not found. This type of problem may also appear as loading problems with the low-level driver. There are several possible reasons why the drive hard- ware cannot be found.

- *Check the power connector*. Make sure that the 4-pin power connector is inserted properly and complete- ly. If the drive is being powered by a Y connector, make sure that any interim connections are secure. Use a voltmeter and measure the +5-V (pin 4) and +12-V (pin 1) levels. If either voltage (especially the +12-V supply) is unusually low or absent, replace the power supply.

- *Check the signal connector*. See that the drive's sig- nal interface cable is connected securely at both the drive and the controller. If the cable is visibly worn or damaged, try a new one.

- *Check for hardware conflicts*. Inspect the drive con- troller card (especially if it's a proprietary con- troller) and make sure that the adapter's IRQ, DMA, and I/O address settings are correct. They must also match the command-line switches used with the low-level driver. If the controller is for a

CD-ROM alone, you may also try installing the controller in a different bus slot.

- *Check the SCSI bus.* If your CD-ROM uses a SCSI interface, make sure that the SCSI bus cable is properly terminated at both ends.

- *Replace the drive/controller.* If problems persist, replace the drive controller first, then replace the CD-ROM drive if necessary.

Symptom 6.16: In a new installation, the driver fails to load successfully for the proprietary interface card. In almost all cases, the proprietary interface card (or drive controller) has been configured improperly. Check the drive controller card first: Verify that the interface card is configured with the correct IRQ, DMA, and I/O address settings, and check for hardware conflicts with other devices in the system. In some cases, you may simply enter the drive maker (e.g., Teac) as the interface type during driver installation. Make sure that the interface is set properly for the system and your particular drive. Check the driver's command line next—the driver's command-line switches should correctly reflect the drive adapter's configuration.

Symptom 6.17: The CD-ROM driver loads, but you see an error such as *CDR101 (drive not ready)* or *CDR103* (CDROM disk not High Sierra or ISO). You are using a very old version of the low-level driver or MSCDEX. Check your driver version (it may be outdated). Contact the drive manufacturer's tech support (or Web site) and see that you have the very latest version of the low-level driver. For very old drives, there may also be a later generic driver available. Check your version of MSCDEX next. Since low-level drivers are often bundled with MSCDEX, you may also be stuck with an old version of MSCDEX. You can usually download a current version of MSCDEX from the same place you get an updated low-level driver, or download it from Microsoft at *www.microsoft.com*.

Symptom 6.18: You are having trouble setting up more than one CD-ROM drive. You must consider both hardware and software issues. Check the drive controller first—make sure that the drive controller will support more than one CD-ROM on the same channel (most standard or nonproprietary controllers should). If it will not, you will have to install another drive controller to support the new CD-ROM drive. Low-level drivers present another problem, since you will need to have *another* copy of a low-level driver loaded in CONFIG.SYS—one for each drive. Make sure that the command-line switches for each driver match the hardware settings of the corresponding drive adapter. Finally, check your copy of MSCDEX. You need only one copy of MSCDEX in AUTOEXEC.BAT, but the /D: switch must appear twice, once for *each* drive ID.

Symptom 6.19: Your CD-ROM drive refuses to work with an IDE port. It may very well be that the drive uses a nonstandard or proprietary port (other than IDE). You must connect the CD-ROM drive to a compatible drive adapter, so try replacing the drive adapter board with the correct type. If the drive is proprietary, it will *not* interface to a regular IDE port. It may be necessary to purchase a drive adapter specifically for the CD-ROM drive. As an alternative, you might choose to upgrade the CD-ROM drive to a model which *will* use a standard IDE-type controller.

Symptom 6.20: You cannot get the CD-ROM drive to run properly when mounted vertically. CD-ROM drives with motorized drive trays generally cannot be mounted vertically—disk tracking simply will not work correctly. The only CD-ROM drives that can be mounted vertically are those with caddies, but you should check with the manufacturers of those drives before proceeding with vertical mounting.

Symptom 6.21: The SCSI CD-ROM drive refuses to work when connected to an Adaptec SCSI interface. Other SCSI drives are working fine. This is a common type of problem with SCSI adapters, and is particularly recognized with Adaptec boards because of their great popularity. In most cases, either the Adaptec drivers are the wrong version for your adapter or they are corrupted. Try turning off *Sync Negotiations* on the Adaptec SCSI interface and rebooting the system. Your SCSI drivers may also be buggy or outdated. Check with Adaptec technical support (*www.adaptec.com*) to determine if there are later drivers that you should use instead.

Symptom 6.22: You see a *No drives found* error when the CD-ROM driver line is executed in CONFIG.SYS. In most cases, the driver command-line switches do not match the hardware configuration of the drive controller, or your low-level driver may be missing or corrupt.

- *Check the CD-ROM driver.* Open CONFIG.SYS into a word processor and verify that the low-level driver has a complete and accurate command line. Make sure that any command-line switches are set correctly. Also verify that the driver referenced in the command line is actually present on the hard drive.

- *Check the MSCDEX driver.* Open AUTOEXEC.BAT into a word processor and verify that the MSCDEX command line is accurate and complete. Also confirm that any MSCDEX command-line switches are set correctly. You might try updating your version of MSCDEX.

- *Check your CD-ROM cache.* If you are using SmartDrive with DOS 6.0 or later, try adding the /U switch to the end of your SmartDrive command line in AUTOEXEC.BAT.

- *Check for hardware conflicts.* Make sure that there are no other hardware devices in the system that may be conflicting with the CD-ROM drive controller. If problems persist, replace the drive controller, or replace the CD-ROM drive if necessary.

Symptom 6.23: The LCD on your CD-ROM displays an error code. Even without knowing the particular meaning of *every* possible error message, you can be assured that most CD-based error messages can be traced to the following causes (in order of ease):

- *Bad caddy.* The CD caddy is damaged or inserted incorrectly. The CD may also be inserted into the caddy improperly. With a motorized tray, the CD may be inserted improperly.

- *Bad mounting.* The drive is mounted improperly, or mounting screws are shorting out the drive's electronics.

- *Bad power.* Check the +12 and +5 V powering the CD-ROM drive. If there is low power, you may need a new or larger supply. Remove any Y splitter that may be tapping the drive's power.

- *Bad drive.* Internal diagnostics have detected a fault in the CD-ROM drive. Try replacing the drive.

- *Bad drive controller.* Drive diagnostics have detected a fault in the drive controller. Try replacing the drive controller or SCSI adapter (whichever interface you're using).

Symptom 6.24: When a SCSI CD-ROM drive is connected to a SCSI adapter, the system hangs when the SCSI BIOS loads. In most cases, the CD-ROM drive supports plug-and-play, but the SCSI controller's BIOS does not. Disable the SCSI BIOS through a jumper on the controller (or remove the SCSI BIOS IC entirely) and use a SCSI driver in CONFIG.SYS instead. You may need to download a low-level SCSI driver from the adapter manufacturer.

NOTE: *If there are other SCSI drives on the adapter which rely on the SCSI BIOS (e.g., SCSI hard drives), it* *may not be possible to disable the SCSI BIOS. In that case, a separate SCSI controller may be needed.*

Symptom 6.25: You see an error such as *Unable to detect ATAPI IDE CD-ROM drive, device driver not loaded.* You have a problem with the configuration of your IDE/EIDE controller hardware. Check the signal cable first, and make sure that the 40-pin signal cable is attached properly between the drive and controller. IDE CD-ROM drives are typically installed on a secondary 40-pin IDE port. Make sure that there is no device in the system using the same interrupt request (IRQ) or I/O address as your secondary IDE port. Finally, make sure that any command-line switches for the low-level driver in CONFIG.SYS correspond to the controller's hardware settings.

Symptom 6.26: The CD-ROM drive door will not open once the 40-pin IDE signal cable is connected. You should only need power to operate the drive door. If the door stops when the signal cable is attached, there are some possible problems to check.

■ *Check the power connector*. Make sure that both +5 and +12 V are available at the power connector. Verify that the power connector is attached securely to the back of the CD-ROM drive.

■ *Check the IDE signal cable*. The 40-pin signal cable is probably reversed at either the drive or the controller. Try a different signal cable. Also make sure that the 40-pin IDE drive is plugged into a true IDE port, not a proprietary (non-IDE 40-pin) port.

■ *Replace the CD-ROM drive*. If problems persist, try a known-good CD-ROM drive.

Symptom 6.27: You are using an old CD-ROM, and you can play CD audio, but you cannot access directories or other computer data from a CD. Older proprietary CD-ROM drives often used *two* low-level drivers, one for audio and one for data; you probably have only one of the drivers installed. Check your low-level drivers first, and verify that any necessary low-level drivers are loaded in the CONFIG.SYS file. Also confirm that any command-line switches are set properly. Some older sound boards with integrated proprietary CD-ROM drive controllers may not work properly with the drivers required for your older CD-ROM drive. You may have to alter the proprietary controller's IRQ, DMA, or I/O settings (and update the driver's command-line switches) until you find a combination where the driver and controller will work together.

Symptom 6.28: An IDE CD-ROM is not detected on a 486 PCI motherboard. This is a known problem when using Aztech CD-ROM drives and 486 PCI motherboards with SIS 82C497 chipsets. The motherboard bus noise is far too high, and this results in misinterpretation of the IDE interface handshaking signals [namely, drive detection signal (DASP) and PDIAG]. As a consequence, the CD-ROM drive sometimes (or always) is not detected. You may be able to resolve this problem by connecting the IDE CD-ROM drive as a slave device to the hard disk, although you may need to slow the hard drive's data transfer mode to accommodate the slower CD-ROM drive.

Symptom 6.29: You notice that Matsushita CD-ROM drives are misdetected as Matshita. This occurs under Windows 95, Windows 95 OSR2, and Windows 98. This is a problem with the CD-ROM drive itself—these drives return Matshita (instead of Matsushita) as the device description when they are enumerated by Windows. You'll need to check with Matsushita for a firmware upgrade, driver fix, or other corrective options. You may also choose to replace the CD-ROM drive outright.

Symptom 6.30: An IDE CD-ROM is not detected when it is "slaved" to an IBM hard drive. This is a known problem with Aztech IDE CD-ROM drives and IBM Data 3450 hard drives. The pulse width for the drive detection signal (DASP) is not long enough for the CD-ROM to identify itself properly. This results in the improper detection of an Aztech IDE CD-ROM. You should make the CD-ROM drive a master device on its own IDE channel or (if possible) upgrade the CD-ROM drive's firmware to utilize more reliable timing. If the CD-ROM manufacturer has no firmware upgrades available, and you cannot reconfigure the CD-ROM on another IDE channel, you'll need to replace the CD-ROM *or* the hard drive.

Symptom 6.31: The CD-ROM drive will not read or run CD Plus or Enhanced CD titles. This is a known problem with Acer CD-ROM models 625A, 645A, 655A, 665A, 525E, 743E, 747E, and 767E. The CD Plus (or Enhanced CD) titles use a nonstandard data format released and supported by Sony. The new format is for interactive CD titles that incorporate video clips and music, and the data structures on these CDs cannot be recognized by these CD-ROM drive models. In this case, you'll need to upgrade the CD-ROM drive outright to a newer model which *can* accommodate newer file types.

Symptom 6.32: You notice that the LED indicator on the CD-ROM is always on. The drive seems to be working properly. This is not necessarily a problem. Some CD-ROM drive models (such as the Acer 600 series) use the LED indicator as a Ready light instead of as a Busy light. Whenever a CD is loaded in the drive, the LED will be lit, and it will remain lit whether the drive is being accessed or not. This feature lets the user determine whether or not a CD-ROM disk is currently loaded in the drive by simply checking the LED. There may be a jumper on the CD-ROM drive that allows you to switch the indicator light from Ready mode to Busy mode.

Symptom 6.33: The drive vibrates or makes a great deal of noise with certain CD and CD-R disks. This is almost always due to an unbalanced disk in high-speed (i.e., 12X and faster) CD-ROM drives. A disk may become unbalanced from improper silk screening or the application of a label. When the unbalanced disk is rotated at high speeds, the entire drive tends to vibrate (often this vibration resonates inside the case, making the sound seem even louder). Make sure that each disk used in the drive is evenly marked or labeled. If the problem seems to occur on all disks, verify that the drive itself is mounted securely to the chassis.

Symptom 6.34: The system locks up when you use a Panasonic "Big 5" CD-ROM drive under Windows 95. This trouble is known to occur if you're using IDE bus-master drivers with the Panasonic "Big 5" 5-disk CD-ROM changer (model SQ-TC510N). The Panasonic drive will require new firmware to overcome this problem, so contact Panasonic to update the device with the latest firmware revision. To avoid this problem in the meantime, remove the CD-ROM changer from your system.

Windows-related symptoms

Symptom 6.35: The front panel controls of your SCSI CD-ROM drive do not appear to work under Windows 95/98. Those same controls appear to work fine in DOS. Windows 95/98 uses SCSI commands to poll removable media devices every 2 s in order to see if there has been a change in status. Since SCSI commands to the CD-ROM generally have higher priority than front panel controls, the front panel controls may appear to be disabled under Windows 95/98. Try pressing the front panel controls repeatedly. You may be able to correct this issue by disabling the CD-ROM polling under Windows 95/98.

Symptom 6.36: You cannot change the CD-ROM drive letter under Windows 95/98. You need to change the drive's settings under the *Device Manager:*

- Open the *Control Panel* and select the *System* icon.

- Once the *System Properties* dialog opens, click on the *Device Manager* page.

- Locate the entry for the CD-ROM. Click on the "+" sign to expand the list of CD-ROM devices.

- Double-click on the desired CD-ROM.

- Once the CD-ROM drive's *Properties* dialog appears, choose the *Settings* page.

- Locate the current drive letter assignment box and enter the new drive designation. Multiple letters are needed only when a SCSI device is implementing LUN addressing (i.e., multidisk changers).

- Click on the *OK* button to save your changes.

- Click on the *OK* button to close the *Device Manager*.

- A *System Settings Change* window should appear. Click on the *Yes* button to reboot the system so that the changes can take effect, or click on the *No* button so that you can make more changes to other CD-ROMs before rebooting the system. Changes will not become effective until the system is rebooted.

Symptom 6.37: You installed Windows 95/98 from a CD-ROM disk using DOS drivers, but when you remove the real-mode CD-ROM drivers from CONFIG.SYS, the CD-ROM no longer works. You need to enable protected-mode drivers by running the *Add New Hardware* wizard from the *Control Panel:*

- Boot Windows 95/98 using the real-mode drivers for your CD-ROM and its interface.

- Open the *Control Panel* and select the *Add New Hardware* icon.

- Proceed to add new hardware, but do *not* let Windows 95/98 attempt to autodetect the new hardware. Use the diskette with protected-mode drivers for the new installation.

- When the new software is installed, Windows 95/98 will tell you that it must reboot before the hardware will be available—*do not reboot yet*.

- Open a word processor such as Notepad and edit the CONFIG.SYS and AUTOEXEC.BAT files to REMark out the real-mode drivers for your CD and the reference to MSCDEX.

- Shut down Windows 95/98, then power down the system.

- Check to be sure that the CD-ROM interface is set to use the resources assigned by Windows 95/98 (this is not necessary if the interface is PnP or a standard IDE-type controller).

- Reboot the system—your protected-mode drivers should now load normally.

Symptom 6.38: Your CD-ROM drive's "parallel-port–to–SCSI" interface worked with Windows 3.1x, but does not work under Windows 95/98. This problem is typical of the NEC CD-EPPSCSI01 interface and is usually due to a problem with the driver's assessment of your parallel-port type (i.e., bidirectional, unidirectional, or enhanced parallel port).

- *Cold boot the computer*. Since typical parallel-port–to–SCSI interfaces get their power from the SCSI device, the external drive must be powered up *first*.

- *Check the CMOS Setup*. Start your CMOS Setup routine first and see what mode your parallel port is set to operate in. Make sure it is set to a mode which is compatible with your parallel-port drive.

- *Check the MSCDEX driver*. Update your version of MSCDEX if necessary. Change the MSCDEX command line in AUTOEXEC.BAT to load from the C:\WINDOWS\CONTROL\ directory, and remove the /L:x parameter from the end of the MSCDEX command line (if present).

- *Check the device drivers.* If you're using real-mode drivers for the interface, place a switch at the end of the interface's command line that tells the driver what mode your parallel port is operating in. For example, the Trantor T358 driver (MA358.SYS) uses the following switches (yours will probably be different):

  /m02 for unidirectional mode (also known as "standard" or "output only")

  /m04 for bidirectional mode (also known as PS/2 mode)

  /m08 for enhanced mode

- *Disable the real-mode drivers.* Remove or REMark out any references to the interface's real-mode drivers in CONFIG.SYS, then remove or disable the MSCDEX command line in AUTOEXEC.BAT. Start Windows 95/98, open the *Control Panel*, select the *System* icon, then choose the *Device Manager* page. Find the SCSI adapter settings and expand the *SCSI Controllers* branch of the device tree. Select the device identification line for your parallel-port–to–SCSI interface, then click on the *Properties* button. Click on the *Settings* page. In the *Adapter Settings* dialog box, type in the same parameter that would have been used if you were using real-mode drivers. Click on the *OK* buttons to save your changes, then select *Yes* to reboot the system.

- *Check/replace the adapter itself.* If problems persist, check the technical support for your parallel-port–to–SCSI adapter and see if there are any known problems with your particular setup or any updated drivers available for download.

Symptom 6.39: You see a message such as *CD-ROM can run, but results may not be as expected.* This simply means that Windows 95/98 is using real-mode drivers. If protected-mode drivers are available for the CD-ROM drive, you should use those instead. You may download and install protected-mode drivers from the CD-ROM manufacturer's Web site.

Symptom 6.40: The CD-ROM works fine in DOS or Windows 3.1x, but sound or video appears choppy under Windows 95/98. There are several factors that can affect CD-ROM performance under Windows 95.

- *Install the latest protected-mode drivers.* Windows 95 performance (and stability) is severely degraded by real-mode drivers, so start by removing or disabling any real-mode drivers. Try installing the protected-mode drivers for your CD-ROM drive instead. If protected-mode drivers are not available for your drive, you may consider upgrading the CD-ROM hardware.

- *Avoid real-mode applications under Windows 95/98.* Real-mode applications that are run under Windows 95/98 can cripple a system's performance. Try exiting any DOS or Windows 3.1x applications that may be running on the Windows 95/98 desktop. Also exit unneeded Windows 95/98 applications, since additional applications take a toll on processing power. Try exiting any Windows 95 applications that may be running in the background.

- *Free "wasted" resources.* Try rebooting the system to ensure that Windows 95/98 has the maximum amount of resources available before running your CD-ROM application.

Symptom 6.41: You can't read a video CD-I disk in Windows 95 using any ATAPI/IDE CD-ROM drive. The built-in ATAPI driver in Windows 95 cannot read raw data in 32-bit disk access mode. Note that such symptoms can also happen to any ATAPI/IDE-compatible CD-ROM as long as it is using the built-in ATAPI driver in Windows 95. You should update the CD-ROM's ATAPI driver to a current manufacturer-specific version. As another alternative, you can use the following procedure:

- Disable the 32-bit disk access feature of Windows 95.

- Under the Windows 95 desktop, click *Start* and choose *Settings* and *Control Panel*.

- Click on the *System* icon and select the *Performance* option.

- Choose *File System* and select the *Troubleshooting* option.

- At the *Troubleshooting* dialog, click on *Disable all 32-bit disk access*.

- Edit AUTOEXEC.BAT and append the following line (where <path> is the path name of your Windows 95 software):

```
C:\<path>\COMMAND\MSCDEX.EXE  /D:MSCD000
```

Symptom 6.42: You cannot play CD audio on a particular CD-ROM under Windows 95. Replacing the CD-ROM resolves the problem. This is a known incompatibility issue with Acer 525E CD-ROM drives and Windows 95 (this does not affect the integrity of programs and data). Windows 95 will mute the CD audio on this and many other brands of double-speed IDE CD-ROMs. If you cannot obtain a patch directly from Microsoft or from the CD-ROM manufacturer, your only real alternative is to replace the CD-ROM drive.

Symptom 6.43: After upgrading to Windows 98, you notice multiple CD-ROM letters. You may see up to four CD-ROM drives displayed in *My Computer* and/or *Windows Explorer*, even though you have only *one* CD-ROM drive in the computer. This problem is known to occur with NEC 4×4, 4×6, 4×8, or 4×16 CD-ROM drives if you've installed the NEC Single CD tool in your previous version of Windows. To correct the problem, simply reinstall the NEC Single CD tool under Windows 98 using the disk included with your NEC 4×CD-ROM drive. You may also wish to download and install the latest versions of that software (and the CD-ROM drivers).

Symptom 6.44: After upgrading to Windows 98, you encounter problems with the CD-ROM and hard drive. Once the upgrade to Windows 98 is complete, the following symptoms may occur:

- You cannot access your CD-ROM drive.

- Hard disks connected to the IDE-type controller are forced to use DOS compatibility mode.

- Another drive that is about 13 MB in size appears in *My Computer* and/or *Windows Explorer*.

This is a known problem when Helix Hurricane for Windows 95 (by Helix Software) is installed on your computer. To correct this issue, you'll need to remove Hurricane using its uninstall tool (you may be able to patch or update Hurricane, but you'll need to contact the program manufacturer). Restart your computer, and use the *Startup Menu* to boot to the Windows 98 *Safe Mode Command Prompt Only*. Run the uninstall tool in the folder where Hurricane is installed. If the uninstall tool is not available, you can disable Hurricane manually:

- Use a text editor (such as Notepad) to open the AUTOEXEC.BAT file.

- Disable the line containing QWATCH.COM in the AUTOEXEC.BAT file by REMarking out that command line.

- Save and close the AUTOEXEC.BAT file.

- Use a text editor to open the SYSTEM.INI file.

- Disable the following lines in the [386Enh] section of SYSTEM.INI by placing a semicolon (;) at the beginning of each line:

```
device=<path>\arpl.386

device=<path>\Winsa.386

device=<path>\Winguard.386

device=<path>\vxmsems.386

device=<path>\windrv.386

device=<path>\vcache16.386

device=<path>\vsectd.386

device=<path>\heapx.386
```

- Now change the following lines in the [Boot] section of SYSTEM.INI from `system.drv=<path>\sys-drv.drv` to `system.drv=System.drv` and from `display.drv=<path>\winsa256.drv` to `display.drv=Pnpdrvr.drv`.

    NOTE: *If your original display driver was not PNPDRVR.DRV, start Windows in the safe mode and change the display driver to the appropriate version.*

- Save and close the SYSTEM.INI file, then reboot the computer.

Symptom 6.45: Your CD-ROM changer doesn't work after you upgrade to Windows 98. This is a known problem with the AST Advantage 828 computer with a CD-ROM changer—after an upgrade to Windows 98, a single CD-ROM drive may be displayed in *Device Manager* (and the CD-ROM changer may be displayed as *Unknown Hardware* under the *Other Devices* entry). This problem will occur if the SmartCD Manager software is installed on an AST system with a Torisan (Sanyo) CDR-C36 6× 3-disk CD-ROM changer. The SCDMGRT3.VXD file located in the

\Windows\System\Iosubsys folder will typically prevent Windows 98 from detecting the CD-ROM changer. To correct this problem, you'll need to move the SCDMGRT3.VXD file into a different folder. You may also check for an updated version of SCDM-GRT3.VXD from AST or Sanyo.

Symptom 6.46: Your SmartCD Manager software does not work under Windows 98.   After upgrading to Windows 98, you may find that your Torisan (Sanyo) 3-disk CD-ROM drive now has three separate drive letters assigned to it. This problem may occur even though the SmartCD Manager program has assigned only one drive letter to this device. The problem occurs because Windows 98 replaces the CDVSD.VXD and TORISAN3.VXD files included with the SmartCD Manager program, and the updated versions of these files are *not* compatible with your SmartCD Manager software. To correct this problem, simply reinstall the SmartCD Manager program.

Symptom 6.47: The auto insert notification feature prevents a system's automatic suspend modes from working. Many current computers include power management features that place the computer in a suspended power state (a.k.a. a power-down mode) after a given period of inactivity. If the auto insert notification option is enabled for IDE-type CD-ROM drives when power management is also enabled, the computer may not suspend automatically. This typically occurs because some IDE-type CD-ROM drives use the ATA GET MEDIA STATUS command method for polling. However, a power management system will detect the action as drive activity. Since a drive then appears to be in use, the power management system will not power down the system (this is a known issue with Windows 95 OSR2). You can work around this issue by disabling the auto insert notification option for affected drives.

As a more permanent fix, you may also download and install the REMIDEUP.EXE file from Microsoft's Web site. This update will install the following file update: ESDI_506.PDR version 4.00.956 (dated 5/14/96). Of course, later versions of the file should also work.

Symptom 6.48: The computer locks up while browsing a CD-ROM. This often occurs in some Compaq Deskpro computers under Windows 95/98 after a Hewlett-Packard CD-RW drive is installed. Your computer may halt when you try to use *My Computer* or *Windows Explorer* to view the CD-RW drive. In most circumstances, this type of problem is driver-related. When dealing with Compaq systems, Compaq uses a custom device driver file named CPQDFVS.VXD. This file is located in the \Windows\System\Iosubsys folder and can lock up the computer when you try to read from the CD-RW drive. To work around this problem for the Compaq, delete or rename the CPQDFVS.VXD file. To correct this issue on a more permanent basis, contact Compaq for a patch or update to the CPQD-FVS.VXD file.

Symptom 6.49: You cannot read Rock Ridge CD-ROM extensions under Windows. This occurs because Windows 95 and 98 are simply not designed to support the Rock Ridge CD-ROM extensions. Rock Ridge is a means of storing POSIX file system extensions on a CD-ROM, but Windows 95/98 uses the Joliet file system (which allows for deep subdirectories and long filenames) instead of the Rock Ridge CD-ROM format. If you need to read Rock Ridge–formatted CD-ROMs in Windows 95/98, configure real-mode driver support for the CD-ROM using the Windows 95/98 version of MSCDEX.EXE in AUTOEXEC.BAT and the DOS device drivers (provided by the CD-ROM drive manufacturer) in CONFIG.SYS.

Symptom 6.50: Under Windows 98, an Alps DC544 CD-ROM changer appears as four individual CD-ROM drives in *My Computer or Windows Explorer.* This problem occurs because the ALPSTRAY.EXE program does not work correctly in Windows 98. To work around this issue, use the Alps DC544 CD-ROM changer as if it were four different CD-ROM drives. As a more permanent fix, check with Alps for an updated ALPSTRAY.EXE file.

Symptom 6.51: The Pioneer DR-UA124X CD-ROM drive disables your IDE channel under Windows 95/98. You may see a yellow exclamation point next to an IDE port in your *Device Manager*. This problem frequently occurs when you have a Pioneer CD-ROM drive (e.g., the DR-UA124X) installed on your computer, and you cannot access the CD-ROM drive connected to that IDE port. The Pioneer DR-UA124X CD-ROM drive's *firmware* causes this problem. You'll need to reenable real-mode support for the drive. Use any text editor (e.g., Notepad) to open the AUTOEXEC.BAT file. Find the MSCDEX command line and remove the REM statement at the beginning of that line. Save your changes and restart the computer. As an alternative, you may contact Pioneer for a firmware update or exchange.

Symptom 6.52: Your Toshiba Tecra 750 locks up when Windows 98 starts. This is a known issue with Toshiba Tecra PCs with CD-ROM drives, and it can occur if all of the following conditions exist:

- The computer uses an IDE-type CD-ROM drive.

- The IDE controller which is operating the CD-ROM drive is using the driver shipped with Windows 98.

- You enable direct memory access (DMA) support for the CD-ROM drive.

This problem is caused by the IDE chipset used in Toshiba Tecra 750 computers. You may be able to correct this trouble by installing the Toshiba drivers rather than using the native Windows drivers:

■ Turn off the computer.

■ Physically remove the CD-ROM drive from the computer.

■ Restart the computer.

■ Install the Toshiba drivers for the IDE controller. (If you don't have the drivers on a floppy disk already, download them from Toshiba's Web site.)

■ Shut down the computer.

■ Put the CD-ROM drive back into the computer.

■ Restart your computer.

■ Windows should start normally and redetect the CD-ROM drive.

Symptom 6.53: When loading an audio CD in the drive, you receive a *no disk loaded* error. This problem can occur under Windows 95 or 98, and is typically caused when the MCI CD audio driver is not installed. You'll need to verify that the CD audio device driver is enabled:

■ Open the *Control Panel* and double-click on the *Multimedia* icon.

■ On the *Advanced* or *Devices* tab, double-click *Media Control Devices*.

■ Double-click *CD Audio Device (Media Control)*.

■ Verify that the *Use This Media Control Device* entry is selected.

If the driver is enabled, but you still receive the error message, try removing and reinstalling the device. To accomplish this, click *Remove* on the *General* tab in your *CD Audio Device (Media Control)* properties, and then follow these steps:

■ Open the *Control Panel* and double-click the *Add New Hardware* icon.

- Click *Next*, click *No*, and then click *Next*.

- In the *Hardware Types* box, click *Sound, Video, and Game Controllers*, and then click *Next*.

- In the *Manufacturers* box, click *Microsoft MCI*.

- In the *Models* box, click *CD Audio Device (Media Control)*.

- Click *Next*, click *Finish*, and then restart your computer.

.Symptom 6.54: You get poor performance from a CD-based program under Windows 95/98. When running a program that accesses a CD-ROM, you may notice that the program is not performing very well. You may notice slow data transfer in a business or reference program, or "skipping" (choppy audio or video) in a multimedia program. In many cases, this problem crops up when the *Supplemental Cache Size* and/or *Optimize Access Pattern For* settings are not configured correctly for your particular CD-ROM drive. Optimize your CD-ROM settings as follows:

- Click *Start*, highlight *Settings*, click *Control Panel*, and double-click the *System* icon.

- On the *Performance* tab, click *File System*, then click the *CD-ROM* tab.

- Move the *Supplemental Cache Size* slider to the right to allocate *more* memory (RAM) for caching data from the CD-ROM drive, or to the left to allocate *less* RAM for caching data (many multimedia programs perform better with a *smaller* cache because these program tend not to reuse data).

- For reading continuous data (such as .AVI files), use a higher setting in the *Optimize Access Pattern For* box. For reading random data, increase the *Supplemental Cache Size* setting and decrease the *Optimize Access Pattern For* setting.

■ Click *OK*, then click *Close*. Restart the PC when prompted to do so.

Symptom 6.55: You cannot access a CD-ROM on an Acer 91 Pentium-based PC under Windows 95/98. After you upgrade an Acer computer from an earlier version of Windows to Windows 95/98, you may find that the CD-ROM drive is not detected, or that 32-bit disk and file access are not available. These problems may also occur when you upgrade an Acer computer to Windows 95/98. This issue occurs when the CD-ROM drive is connected to a CMD CSA-6400E PCI IDE controller— the CMD640X.SYS real-mode driver used with Acer computers is designed to work in Windows 3.1 and does *not* work in Windows 95/98. To correct this problem, install the Windows 95/98 version of the CMD CSA-6400E PCI IDE driver or download the self-extracting file CMDWIN95.EXE from Acer's Web site (*www.acer.com / aac / win95 / upgrades / ftp.htm*).

> **NOTE:** *If you use the CMD 6400 PCI controller's protected-mode driver, 32-bit disk and file access is functional, but the CD-ROM drive is not detected. If you use the CMD 6400 PCI controller's real-mode driver CMD640X.SYS, the CD-ROM drive is detected, but 32-bit disk and file access is not available.*

> **NOTE:** *All Acer computer systems with a part number starting with 91.AA043 or 91.AA260 (using the CMD CSA-6400E PCI IDE controller and a Maxtor 7546AT hard disk) running Windows 95/98 will exhibit this problem.*

Symptom 6.56: You cannot access a CD-ROM drive under Windows 95/98. When you try to access your CD-ROM drive in Windows, you may encounter one of the following symptoms:

■ You cannot run executable (.EXE) files.

■ You cannot view complete directory listings.

■ You get a *Device not found* error message.

These problems will develop if you're using an older version of the MSCDEX.EXE file which is not compatible with Windows 95/98. This commonly occurs when you install certain real-mode CD-ROM drivers—an older version of the MSCDEX.EXE file is copied to the hard disk, and the AUTOEXEC.BAT file is updated to utilize this older file. Modify the AUTOEXEC.BAT file manually to address the correct version of MSCDEX.EXE:

■ Use any text editor (such as Notepad) to open the AUTOEXEC.BAT file.

■ Locate the MSCDEX command line, then modify the line to read

```
<drive>:\<windows>\command\mscdex.exe <parameters>
```

where `<drive>` is the drive letter where the Windows folder is located, `<windows>` is the name of the folder in which Windows is installed, and `<parameters>` are the parameters from the original command line. Make sure to use all the parameters exactly as they are used in the original line.

■ Save and then close the AUTOEXEC.BAT file.

■ Restart your computer.

Symptom 6.57: A Sony CD-ROM drive is not detected during Windows 95/98 Setup. This problem can occur when the Sony CD-ROM drive is attached to a Media Vision sound card. Setup searches for Sony CD-ROM drives at several base I/O addresses, but a Sony CD-ROM drive attached to a Media Vision sound card is not in the range of addresses that Setup checks. As a result, Setup retains the existing real-mode drivers for the CD-ROM drive, and this often reduces system performance. You can get around this problem by setting up the Sony CD-ROM drive in Windows manually:

- Click the *Start* button, highlight *Settings*, and click *Control Panel*.

- Double-click the *Add New Hardware* icon, and then click the *Next* button.

- Click the *No* option button, and then click *Next*.

- Click *CD-ROM Controllers*, and then click *Next*.

- In the *Manufacturers* box, click *Sony*. In the *Models* box, click *Sony Proprietary CD-ROM Controller*, and then click *Next*.

- Click *Next*, and then click *Finish*.

- When you are prompted to restart your computer, click *No*.

- Click the *Start* button, highlight *Settings*, and then click *Control Panel*.

- Double-click the *System* icon.

- On the *Device Manager* tab, double-click the *CD-ROM Controllers* entry, and then double-click *Sony Proprietary CD-ROM Controller*.

- Click the *Resources* tab.

- In the *Settings Based On* box, click *Basic Configuration 0*.

- Click the *Use Automatic Settings* check box to clear it.

- Use the *Change Settings* button to modify the resources to match the CD-ROM drive's settings.

- Click *OK*.

- Restart your computer when you're prompted to do so.

> **NOTE:** *To verify that the CD-ROM drive is set up correctly, check it in* Device Manager *to see that no prob-*

lems are reported in the Device Status *box. Also, make sure that you can read a CD-ROM in the CD-ROM drive.*

Symptom 6.58: The system locks up while copying data from the CD-ROM under Windows 95/98. When you are copying a large directory structure from a CD-ROM drive to a local hard disk, your computer may lock up (forcing you to reboot). This problem is typically caused by the CD-ROM "read ahead" feature—the feature can cause the CD-ROM drive controller to be driven faster than it was designed to be. To prevent this problem, reduce the read-ahead caching level for your CD-ROM:

- Click the *Start* button, highlight *Settings*, then click *Control Panel*.

- Double-click the *System* icon.

- On the *Performance* tab, click *File System*, then click the *CD-ROM* tab.

- In the *Optimize Access Pattern For* box, click the setting that matches the CD-ROM drive that you're using. Click *OK*, then restart the computer when you are prompted to.

- If the problem persists, repeat this process, selecting a *lower* read-ahead value (or select *No Read-Ahead*).

Symptom 6.59: Two CD-ROM drive letters appear in *My Computer* under Windows 95/98. When you use *My Computer or Windows Explorer*, two CD-ROM drives may be displayed (even though you have only one CD-ROM drive in your computer). When you try to access either CD-ROM drive, your computer may lock up. This problem can occur if you have both the real-mode CD-ROM device drivers *and* the Windows 95/98 CD-ROM device drivers installed. To resolve this problem, use the *System Configuration Editor* (SYSEDIT.EXE) to disable the real-mode CD-ROM device drivers:

- Click *Start*, click *Run*, type `sysedit` in the *Open* box, and then click *OK*.

- Select the AUTOEXEC.BAT file, locate the line that loads the real-mode CD-ROM device drivers, and then type `rem` followed by a space at the beginning of the line. For example:

```
rem c:\windows\command\mscdex.exe /d:mscd001
```

- Select the CONFIG.SYS file, locate the line that loads the real-mode CD-ROM device drivers, and then type `rem` followed by a space at the beginning of the line. For example:

```
rem device=c:\cdrom\cdrom.sys /d:mscd001
```

- On the *File* menu, click *Exit*.

- Click *Yes* when you're prompted to save the CONFIG.SYS and AUTOEXEC.BAT files.

- Restart your computer.

Symptom 6.60: The CD-ROM refuses to run automatically under Windows 95/98 when a disk is inserted. This may occur even when the auto insert notification feature is enabled. In most cases, the trouble is caused by an incorrect value in the registry. To resolve this problem, use Registry Editor to locate the following key:

```
HKEY_CURRENT_USER\Software\Microsoft\Windows\Cur-
rentVersion\Policies\Explorer\NoDriveTypeAutoRun
```

Then modify the value for the `NoDriveTypeAutoRun` key to `0000 95 00 00 00` (or `0x95` in REGEDT32. EXE). After you make this change, quit the Registry Editor and restart your computer.

Symptom 6.61: A CD-ROM icon appears for a hard drive under Windows 95 OSR2 or Windows 98. When you attempt to review your drives through *My Computer*, your hard disk icon may appear as a CD-ROM icon. If you double-click the CD-ROM icon in *My Computer*, you may receive an error message such as *Cannot find autorun.exe*. This problem can occur if the AUTORUN.INF file has been located in the root folder of your hard disk. To correct the problem, rename the AUTORUN.INF file to AUTORUN.OLD:

- Click *Start*, point to *Find*, and then click *Files Or Folders*.

- In the *Named* box, type `autorun.inf` and then click *Find Now*.

- Right-click on *AUTORUN.INF* in the list of found files, and then click *Properties*.

- Click the *Read-Only* check box to clear it, and then click *OK*.

- Right-click on *AUTORUN.INF* in the list of found files, and then click *Rename*.

- Type `autorun.old` and then press <Enter>.

- Restart your computer.

Symptom 6.62: You receive an error such as *CD-ROM cache acceleration file is invalid* under Windows 98. This kind of problem is typically encountered when using Quarterdeck SpeedyROM version 1.0 under Windows 98. Also, even though SpeedyROM may offer to reconstruct this file, you may continue to receive the same error message whenever you restart your computer. This trouble is generally caused when your computer's BIOS is configured to use a Fast Reboot feature. To correct it, disable the Fast Reboot feature in your computer's CMOS Setup.

> **NOTE** *Your BIOS may use a term other than Fast Reboot to identify the feature, so refer to your system's documentation for more CMOS Setup details.*

Web Contacts

Hewlett-Packard: *http://www.hp.com*

Plextor: *http://www.plextor.com/*

Pinnacle Micro: *http://www.pinnaclemicro.com/*

Smart and Friendly: *http://www.smartandfriend-ly.com*

Teac: *http://www.teac.com/dsp/p_dsp.html*

CD-R Drives

While CD-ROM drives bring a great deal of reliable storage potential to the PC, until recently it has not been possible to record CDs on the desktop—the technology required to create audio and computer CDs has traditionally been terribly complex and expensive, and limited by the PC computing power of the day. Since the early 1990s, however, CD recorder (or CD-R) technology has steadily become more reliable and economical. Today, virtually any Pentium-based PC with a SCSI bus and 1 GB or more of hard drive space can support a high-speed CD-R drive for under $400 (U.S.). This chapter explains the technologies and troubleshooting techniques that are unique to CD-R drives.

Understanding CD-R Concepts

CD recorders are very similar to CD-ROM drives; the two primary differences are in the *laser* and the *media*. In a CD-R drive, the laser wavelength and power levels can be modified to actually "write" pits and lands to blank CD-R media. This is often called "burning" a disk because that's actually what the laser is doing to the disk. Recordable media appear very similar to "pressed" CD media, but with two important variations. First, the polycarbonate CD-R substrate is preformed with a track spiral, into which data will be written during recording. The substrate is then coated with a greenish translucent layer and backed with a reflective layer of gold, and then protective lacquer is applied over the gold. These translucent and gold layers allow the recorded pits and lands to be read back after recording. This part of the chapter highlights some important CD-R concepts that you'll need to master.

"Orange Book certified" media

The Orange Book (Part II) is the primary specification for CD-R media, and all CD-R media should meet the Orange Book criteria for recordability and playback. Philips and Sony (the originators of the Orange Book specification) provide Orange Book certification of CD-R media. CD-R media which are *not* "Orange Book certified" should generally be avoided.

Multisession CDs

One of the problems with early recordable CDs was that once the CD was written, it could not be appended. This means that if 123 MB of data are written to a CD, the remaining 527 MB of storage potential on the disk is lost. CD developers sought a means of adding new data to a CD which had been previously recorded. This *multisession* capability means that a CD can be written in terms of "sessions" and subsequent sessions can be linked to previous sessions, allowing the CD to be systematically filled (although it still cannot be erased).

A CD-R recorder that supports multisession recording can write a disk that will have multiple sessions linked together, with each session containing its own lead-in, program, and lead-out areas. In effect, each session is treated as a different CD. Any multisession-capable CD-ROM can access the data in any session.

By comparison, a "pressed" CD-ROM or a CD-R written in "Disk at Once" mode contains only one lead-in area, program area, and lead-out area.

NOTE: *Some older CD-ROM drives which are not multisession-capable can read only the first session of a multisession disk.*

Fixation vs. finalization

Each session written to a disk (whether the disk is multisession or single-session) must be "fixed" before the session can be read. *Fixation* is the process of writing the session's lead-in and lead-out information to the disk. This process finishes a writing session and creates a table of contents. Fixation is *required* before a CD-ROM or CD-Audio player can play the disk. Disks which are "fixated for append" can have additional sessions recorded later (each with its own session lead-in and lead-out), creating a multisession disk. When a disk is *finalized*, the absolute lead-in and lead-out for the entire disk are written, along with information which tells the reader not to look for subsequent sessions. This final table of contents (TOC) conforms to the ISO 9660 file standard.

Disk-at-Once

Disk-at-Once is a CD writing mode that requires data to be written continuously, without any interruptions, until the entire data set is transferred to the CD-R. The complete lead-in, program, and lead-out are written in a single writing process. All of the information to be recorded needs to be staged on the computer's hard disk prior to recording in the Disk-at-Once mode. Recording in the Disk-at-Once mode eliminates the linking and run-in and run-out blocks associated with multisession and packet recording modes (which often are interpreted as uncorrectable errors during the glass mastering process).

NOTE   *This mode is usually preferred for disks that are sent to a CD-ROM replication facility when CD-R is the source medium.*

Track-at-Once

The Track-at-Once writing mode is the key to multi-session capability. It allows a session to be written in a number of discrete write events, called *tracks* because the written sessions contain complete "tracks" of information. The disk may be removed from the writer and read in another writer (given proper software) before the session is fixated.

Incremental and packet writing

Track-at-Once writing is a form of incremental (a.k.a. multisession) writing which mandates a minimum track length of 300 blocks and a maximum of 99 tracks per disk. A track written "at once" has 150 blocks of overhead for run-in, run-out, pre-gap, and linking purposes. In contrast, *packet write* is a method in which several write events are allowed *within* a track, thus reducing the demands of overhead data. Each writing "packet" is bounded by 7 blocks of data: 4 for run-in, 2 for run-out, and 1 for linking.

Caring for recordable CDs

As a rule, recordable CDs are as rugged and reliable as ordinary pressed CDs. Still, you should observe some rules for the careful handling and storage of recordable media:

- *Maintain a comfortable environment.* Don't expose recordable disks to sunlight or other strong light for long periods of time. Also avoid high heat and humidity, which can damage the physical disk. Always keep blank or recorded media in clean "jewel" cases for best protection.

- *Don't write on the disk*. Don't use alcohol-based pens to write on disks—the ink may eventually eat through the top (lacquer) surface and damage your data. Also, don't use ballpoint or other sharp-tipped pens because you may scratch right through the lacquer surface and damage the reflective gold layer (and ruin your data).

- *Don't use labels on the disk*. Don't put labels on disks unless the labels are *expressly* designed for recordable CDs. The glue may eat through the lacquer surface just as some inks do, and/or the label may unbalance the disk and cause problems in reading it back or recording subsequent sessions. Never try to remove a label—you might tear off the lacquer and some of the reflecting surface.

- *Watch your media quality*. Many different brands of recordable CD media are now available in the marketplace. Quality varies from brand to brand (and even from batch to batch within a given brand). If you have repeated problems that can be traced to the blank media you are using, try using a different brand or even a different batch of the same brand.

- *Don't use Kodak Photo CDs*. Avoid the use of Kodak Photo CDs on everyday CD recorders. Kodak Photo CDs are designed to be used only with Kodak Photo CD professional workstations. Although the disks are inexpensive, they have a protection bit which prevents them from being written on many CD recorders. When you attempt to write these disks on recorders which recognize the protection bit, you will receive an error message.

CD-R Installation and Replacement

CD-R drives are generally easy devices to install or replace. Most are installed as master devices located on the secondary IDE drive controller channel, although a few will coexist as slave devices alongside a hard drive or some other drive device. The most important issue to remember is that the BIOS will not support the CD-R directly (even if the BIOS identifies the CD-R at boot time)—you'll need real-mode drivers for the CD-R under DOS or protected-mode drivers for the CD-R under Windows. This part of the chapter covers the guidelines needed to install a basic internal IDE-type CD-R.

Select jumper configurations

An IDE-type CD-R drive may be installed as a master or a slave device on any hard drive controller channel. These master/slave settings are handled through one or two jumpers located on the rear of the drive (right next to the 40-pin signal cable connector). One of your first decisions when planning an installation should be to decide the drive's configuration:

- If you're installing the CD-R as the first drive on the secondary drive controller channel, it must be jumpered as the master device.

- If you're installing the CD-R drive alongside another drive (on either the primary or the secondary drive controller channel), the CD-R must be jumpered as the slave device.

  NOTE *Refer to the documentation that accompanies your particular CD-R drive to determine the exact master/slave jumper settings. If you do not have the drive documentation handy, check the drive manufacturer's Web site for online information.*

Attach cables and mount the drive

- Turn off and unplug the PC, then remove the outer cover to expose the computer's drive bays.

- Attach one end of the 40-pin drive interface cable to the drive controller connector on your motherboard (or drive controller card). Remember to align pin 1 on the cable (the side of the cable with the blue or red stripe) with pin 1 on the drive controller connector.

- Locate an available drive bay for the CD-R drive. Remove the plastic housing covering the drive bay, then slide the drive inside. Locate the four screw holes needed to mount the drive. In some cases, you may need to attach mounting rails to the drive so that the drive will be wide enough to fit in the drive bay. In virtually all cases, you should mount a tray-driven CD-R drive horizontally (although caddy-loaded CD-R drives may be mounted vertically).

- Attach the 40-pin signal cable and the 4-pin power connector to the new drive, then bolt the drive securely into place. Do not overtighten the screws, since this may damage the drive. If you do not have an available 4-pin power connector, you may use an appropriate Y splitter if necessary to split power from another drive (preferably the floppy drive).

- Attach the small 4-pin CD-audio signal cable from the CD-R to the CD-audio input connector on your sound card. This connection allows you to play music CDs directly through your sound card. Verify that the CD-audio cable is compatible with your sound card (if it is not, you may need a specialized cable from the sound card's manufacturer).

    NOTE *If you already have a CD-ROM drive in the system that is providing CD audio to the sound card, you may choose to use the CD-R instead or to leave the CD-ROM's audio cable alone. If your sound card has a second CD audio connector, you may be able to wire the CD-R's audio to your sound card also.*

Configuring the CMOS Setup

Although the CD-R does require driver support, recent motherboard designs can identify the ATAPI IDE CD-R drive in BIOS, so you should configure your computer's BIOS to accept the drive if possible (through the CMOS Setup).

- Turn the computer on. As your computer starts up, watch for a message that describes how to run the CMOS Setup (e.g., *Press F1 for Setup*). Press the appropriate key to start the CMOS Setup program.

- Select the *hard drive settings* menu, and choose the drive location occupied by the CD-R drive (i.e., *primary slave*, *secondary slave*, or *secondary master*, depending on how you've physically jumpered and installed the drive).

- Select *automatic drive detection* if available—this option will automatically identify the new drive. If your BIOS does *not* provide automatic drive detection, select *none* or *not installed* for the CD-R, and rely on drivers *only*.

- Save the settings and exit the CMOS Setup program. Your computer will automatically reboot.

Reassemble the computer

Double-check all of your signal and power cables to verify that they are secure, then tuck the cables gently into the computer's chassis. Check that there are no loose tools, screws, or cables inside the chassis. Now reattach the computer's outer housing(s).

Install the software

In order to complete your CD-R installation, you'll need to install the software drivers that accompanied the drive on diskette or CD. Windows 95/98 systems will generally detect the presence of the new CD-R and prompt you for the protected-mode drivers automatically. Under DOS, you may need to run an installer routine to add the real-mode drivers to your system, and to update your CONFIG.SYS and AUTOEXEC.BAT files to load those drivers. If there's no real-mode installer, you'll need to update your start-up files manually (see "Understanding the SOFTware" below). After you install the drivers and reboot the system, the CD-R should be ready for use. Before you can burn your own CDs, you'll also need to install the CD authoring software (e.g., Adaptec Easy CD Pro) and other utilities from the drive's installation disk.

Understanding the Software

Hardware alone is not enough to implement a CD-R drive. In an ideal world, BIOS and MS-DOS would provide the software support to handle the drive, but in practice, the variations among CD-R designs and interfaces make it impractical to provide low-level BIOS services. Manufacturers provide a hardware-specific device driver used to communicate with the CD-R and interface, and a DOS extension (MSCDEX) provides file handling and logical drive letter support. This part of the chapter explains the operations and features of real-mode CD-R device drivers and MSCDEX.

> **NOTE** *If you're using a Windows 95/98 platform and do* not *require use of the CD-R under DOS, you can omit the installation of real-mode drivers and skip this section of the chapter.*

Device drivers

A low-level device driver allows programs to access the CD-R drive properly at the register (or "hardware") level to serve as a CD-ROM drive. Since CD-R drives are designed in different ways, they require different device drivers. If you change or upgrade the drive at any point, the device driver must be upgraded as well. A typical device driver uses a .SYS extension and is initiated by adding its command line to the PC's CONFIG.SYS file, such as

```
DEVICE=HITACHIA.SYS /D:MSCD000 /N:1 /P:300
```

> **NOTE** *The* DEVICE *command may be replaced by the* DEVICEHIGH *command if you have available space in the upper memory area (UMA).*

A CD-R device driver will typically have three command-line switches associated with it. These parameters are needed to ensure that the driver installs properly. For the example command line shown above, the /D switch is the *name* used by the driver when it is installed in the system's device table. This name must be unique and matched by the /D switch in the MSCDEX.EXE command line (covered later). The /N switch is the number of CD-R drives attached to the interface card. The default is 1 (which is typical for most general-purpose systems). Finally, the /P switch is the I/O port address at which the drive's adapter card resides. As you might expect, the port address should match the port address on the physical interface. If there is no /P switch, the default is 0300h.

There's an additional wrinkle when using SCSI-based CD-R drives: The PC must be fitted with a SCSI adapter and configured with an ASPI driver in order to allow the SCSI adapter to interface to the drive (this is also true if you're using other SCSI drives). A typical ASPI driver entry would appear in CONFIG.SYS as

```
DEVICE=C:\SCSI\ASPIPPA3.SYS /L=001
```

> **NOTE** *If there are no SCSI hard drives in the system, the SCSI adapter's on-board BIOS ROM can usually be disabled.*

MSCDEX.EXE

DOS was developed at a time when no one anticipated that large files would be accessible to a PC, and it is severely limited in the file sizes that it can handle. With the development of CD-ROMs (and later CD-R and CD-RW drives), Microsoft created an extension to MS-DOS that allows software publishers to access 650-

MB CDs in a standard fashion: the Microsoft CD-ROM Extensions (MSCDEX). Like most software, MSCDEX offers some vital features and has a few limitations, but it is required by a vast majority of CD-ROM-type products. Obtaining MSCDEX is not a problem; it is generally provided on the same disk containing the CD-R's low-level DOS device driver. Newer versions of MSCDEX can be obtained by searching the Microsoft Web site (*www.microsoft.com*).

In actual operation, MSCDEX is loaded in the AUTOEXEC.BAT file. It should be loaded *after* any mouse driver and *before* any MENU, SHELL, DOSSHELL, or WIN line. It should also be loaded *before* any .BAT file is started. Keep in mind that if a .BAT file loads a network, MSCDEX must be included in the batch file *after* the network driver. Further, MSCDEX must be loaded after that network driver with the /S (share) switch in order to hook into the network driver chain. If you want to use the MS-DOS drive caching software (SmartDrive) to buffer the CD-R drive(s), load MSCDEX *before* SmartDrive. The MSCDEX /M (number of buffers) switch can be set to 0 when using SmartDrive. If you find that SmartDrive is interfering with MPC applications like Video for Windows, you can load SmartDrive *before* MSCDEX, and set the /M switch for at least 2. When loading MSCDEX, remember that the MSCDEX /D switch *must* match the /D label used in the low-level driver. If it does not, MSCDEX will not load. If SETVER is loaded in the CONFIG.SYS file, be sure to use the latest version of MSCDEX.

Although the vast majority of CD-R bundles include installation routines that automate the installation process for the low-level driver and MSCDEX, you should understand the various command-line switches (refer to Table 6.2) that make MSCDEX operate. Understanding these switches may help you to overcome setup problems.

Upgrading CD-R firmware

You may be able to update the firmware used in your CD-R drive. This may be necessary in order to correct bugs or fix drive compatibility problems with the system. The steps below offer a guideline that you can refer to when upgrading CD-R firmware.

> **NOTE:** *The steps below are based on an internal Plextor SCSI CD-R drive. You should always refer to the Web page or README file that accompanies the new firmware download. Be sure to download the correct firmware version for your drive—installing the wrong firmware can permanently disable the drive.*

- Power off your system completely.

- Locate the CD-R drive and place its "flash" jumper in the flash upgrade position.

- Make sure that the power cable and the signal cable (i.e., SCSI or IDE) are still connected.

- Power on your system and boot "clean" to a command-line prompt.

- Make sure that the CD-R appears in program mode. For an internal Plextor SCSI CD-R, you'll see that all four LEDs on the front panel of the drive are blinking.

- When the system comes up, execute the new firmware program (e.g., FIRM412.EXE), which you may receive or download from the manufacturer, and use the new firmware (*.BIN) file.

- When the .EXE application starts, specify the location of the .BIN file.

- Click the *Update* button to begin the flash process.

- When the *Update* button becomes highlighted again, the flash process is complete.

- Power off the system and reset the CD-R drive's "flash" jumper to its original position.

- Power on the system normally.

Troubleshooting CD-R Drives

CD recorders present some special problems for the typical PC. Many high-performance CD-R units use the SCSI interface in order to provide more consistent data transfer from the system to the drive. Installing a CD-R may require the addition (and expense) of a SCSI adapter and driver software. CD recording demands a substantial commitment of hard drive space—perhaps as much as 1 GB—in order to create an *image file* for recording (an image file basically converts the data to be recorded into the pits and lands that must be encoded to the blank disk). So if you're tight on drive space, you may also need another hard drive to support the CD-R. Finally, CD-Rs require a constant and uninterrupted flow of data during the recording process. If the CD-R data buffer empties, the recording process will halt, and your blank CD will be ruined. This means you'll need fast hard drives and a high-performance interface (i.e., PIO Mode 4). This part of the chapter explains some of the problems associated with installing and using a CD-R, and illustrates a series of troubleshooting symptoms and solutions.

CD recording issues

Writing data to a recordable CD is a complex process that demands a great deal from your PC's hardware and software. Most of this complexity is hidden by the power of the CD authoring program, but there are a number of important factors that you should be aware of which can influence the success of CD recording. This part of the chapter covers the principal issues involved in CD recording.

File sizes. The sheer *amount* of data being written to the CD is less important than the individual file sizes—the recorder may have trouble locating and opening small files quickly enough to send them smoothly to the CD recorder, whereas fewer large files are typically problem-free.

System interruptions.   Any interruption in the flow of data is fatal to CD recording, so make sure that your CONFIG.SYS and AUTOEXEC.BAT files do not load any TSR utilities which may periodically interrupt the computer's drive operations. Utilities like screen savers, calendar alarms or reminders, and incoming faxes are just a few features which will interrupt disk writing. If the PC is part of a network, you should temporarily disable network sharing so that no one tries to access the files you're trying to write to the CD.

The hard disk.   The hard drive is a critical component of the CD-R system because you must transfer data from the HDD to the CD-R at a rate that is adequate to keep the recorder's buffer filled. There are three major issues when considering your hard drive: speed, file fragmentation, and thermal calibration.

- *Speed*. In order for you to write a virtual image file to a compact disk, the hard disk from which you are writing must have a transfer rate fast enough to keep the CD-R drive buffer full. This usually means an average hard disk access time of 19 ms or less. It would also help to use a high-performance drive interface such as Ultra-DMA/33 or SCSI-3.

- *Fragmentation*. This issue is also related to speed. Searching all over a very fragmented hard disk for image file data can cause drive operations to slow down. In many cases, a badly fragmented hard drive cannot support CD-R operations. Be sure to defragment your hard drive before creating an image file.

- *Thermal calibration*. All hard disks periodically perform an automatic thermal calibration to ensure proper performance. Calibration interrupts hard disk operations for as much as 1.5 s. Some hard disks force a calibration at fixed intervals even if the disk is in use, causing interruptions which are fatal to CD writing. This problem is worse when the image file is large and the writing process takes longer. If you can select a new hard drive to support CD-R operations, choose a drive with "intelligent" thermal calibration (it postpones recalibration until the drive is idle).

CD recorder speed. Typical CD recorders are capable of writing at 2× or 4× the standard writing/playback speed of 150 KB/s (75 sectors/s). Recording speed is simply a matter of how fast the bits are inscribed on the disk surface by the laser. It has nothing to do with how fast you can read them back or how much data you can fit on the disk. However, higher recording speeds can accomplish a writing process in a shorter period of time. Faster recording speeds are certainly a time saver, but they also require larger recording buffers (and those buffers empty faster). As a consequence, faster recorders will demand a faster hard drive and interface to support data transfer. In most cases, "buffer underrun" problems can be corrected by slowing down the recording process rather than upgrading the drive system.

When you write a real ISO image file from hard disk to CD, speed is rarely a problem because the image is already one gigantic file. The files and structures are already in order and divided into CD-ROM sectors, so it is only necessary to stream data off the hard drive to the CD recorder. When you write from a virtual image, things get trickier because a virtual image is little more than a list. The CD authoring program must consult the virtual image database to find out where each file should go in the image and where each file is actually stored on the hard disk. The authoring software must then open the file and divide it into CD-ROM sectors—all while sending data to the CD recorder in a smooth, continuous stream. Locating and opening each file is often the more time-consuming part of the recording process (which is why "on-the-fly" writing is more difficult when you have many small files).

CD recorder buffer. All CD recorders have a small amount of on-board buffer memory. The CD recorder's buffer helps to ensure that there are always data ready to be written because extra data are stored as they arrive from the computer. The size of the buffer is critical to trouble-free writing—a slowdown or interruption in the transfer of data from the computer will not interrupt writing so long as the buffer is not completely emptied. The larger the buffer, the more safety margin you have in case of interruptions. If your CD recorder has a very small buffer and your hard disk is slow, you may find it difficult (or impossible) to write virtual images to CD on the fly. When this occurs, you can make a real ISO image file on the hard disk and record to CD from that, use a faster hard disk subsystem, or upgrade your CD recorder's buffer (if possible).

> **NOTE:** *If you want to write a virtual image to CD on the fly and you have a slow hard disk, it is generally safest to write at 1× speed. Alternatively, create a real ISO image file first and record from that. In most situations where your hardware configuration is adequate (a fast, defragmented hard disk, few small files, and a good-sized CD recorder buffer), you can successfully write virtual images straight to CD. However, it's always best to test first, and create a real ISO image file only if necessary.*

Typical compatibility problems

Even when CDs record perfectly, it is not always possible to read them correctly in other drives. The following notes highlight three common compatibility issues.

Problems reading recordable CDs. Recordable CDs frequently cannot be read in older CD-ROM drives. If the CD can be read on the CD-R but *not* on a standard CD-

ROM drive, check the disk recording utility to make sure that the session containing the data you just wrote is *closed*—CD-ROM drives cannot read data from a session which is not closed.

If your recorded disk is ejected, you receive an error message, or you have any random problems accessing files from the recorded disk, the problem may be that your CD-ROM drive is not well calibrated to read recorded CDs. Try the disk on another CD-ROM drive, or upgrade the CD-ROM.

If you recorded the disk using DOS filenames, but there are difficulties in reading back the recorded CD with DOS or Windows, it may be that you have an older version of MSCDEX (before version 2.23) on your system. Check your MSCDEX version, and update it if necessary.

Problems reading multisession CDs.   If you can see only data recorded in the first session on the CD (and not those recorded in subsequent sessions), it may be that the disk was recorded in CD-ROM (Mode 1) format, but your multisession CD-ROM drive recognizes only CD-ROM XA (Mode 2) multisession CDs. If this happens, you may need to re-record the disk in the correct mode. Of course, your CD-ROM drive must support multisession operation in the first place. If you can see only data recorded in the last session, you may have forgotten to link your new data with data previously recorded on the CD. Refer to the instructions for your CD recorder and review the steps required to create a multisession CD.

CD-ROM drive incompatibility with recordable CDs.   It may seem that you can write a CD without trouble, and you can read it properly on your CD-R—but when you put the disk in a standard CD-ROM drive, the disk is ejected. You may also see error messages such as *No CD-ROM* or *Drive not ready*, or you have random problems accessing some files or directories. You may also find that the problems disappear when you read the CD on a different CD-ROM drive.

At first, you may suspect a problem with the original CD-ROM drive, but the difficulty may be due to compatibility problems with some CD-ROM drives (especially older ones) and recorded CDs. Some CD-ROM drive lasers are not calibrated to read recordable CDs (often the surface is different from that of factory-pressed CDs). If your CD-ROM drive reads mass-produced (silver) CDs but not recordable CDs, check with the CD-ROM drive manufacturer to determine whether this is the problem. In some cases, a drive upgrade which will resolve the problem may be available.

> **NOTE:** *The combination of blank disk brand and CD recorder can also make a difference. Use blank CD media that have been recommended by the CD-R manufacturer.*

Typical multisession CD issues

You may encounter older CD-ROM drives that have trouble reading multisession CDs. Multisession disks are recorded according to the Orange Book (Part II) standard, which states that sessions can be written in *either* the CD-ROM or the CD-ROM XA format. A fully compliant multisession CD-ROM drive should always be able to access at *last* session on a disk *regardless* of its format.

Unfortunately, there have been misunderstandings and misinterpretations of the Orange Book standard, but to understand the problem, you need to know a bit of history. Multisession recording was first used by Kodak for its Photo CD initiative. Now, one roll of film does *not* fill up a Photo CD disk, so when you take your disk and a new roll of film for new Photo CD processing, the new photos are added in a "new session." This new session is linked to previous sessions so that you can see *all* the photos on the disk, no matter how many sessions they are recorded in.

Kodak chose the CD-ROM XA for its Photo CD disk format for reasons which had *nothing* to do with the Orange Book standard. But since Photo CD was the first reason that CD-ROM drive manufacturers had to create multisession drives, many assumed that the Kodak approach to multisession (i.e., CD-ROM XA) was the *only* way. Accordingly, they wrote software drivers which assume that a multisession disk must be XA. When one of these drivers sees a disk which is not XA, it assumes that the disk is also *not* multisession, and it tells the CD-ROM drive to read only the first session on the disk. The result is that a multisession disk is read as if it were a single-session disk, and you see only the data in the first session.

CD-ROM drive manufacturers have generally resolved this glitch in newer drives and drivers (i.e., 8× CD-ROM and later drives), but if you record a multisession disk in CD-ROM format, you may find that some older drives (even those specified as "multisession" drives) may not read beyond the first session on the disk. If you need to share multisession disks with others, you should test to see which format their CD-ROM drives can handle. To be on the safe side, write your disk in the CD-ROM XA format. A more permanent fix is to upgrade the older CD-ROM to a model which is fully multisession-compliant.

> **NOTE:** *You cannot mix formats on the same disk—a multisession disk containing both CD-ROM and CD-ROM XA sessions would be unreadable on most drives.*

Buffer underruns

CD writing is a real-time process that must run constantly at the selected recording speed *without interruptions*. Most of the time, your computer will pass data to the CD-R faster than they are needed. This keeps the CD-R's buffer constantly filled with a reserve of data waiting to be written, so that small slowdowns or interruptions in the flow of data from the computer will not interrupt the writing process. The CD-R's internal buffer stores these extra data as they arrive to help maintain a steady flow of data to the writing laser.

The size of the buffer is critical to trouble-free writing. Remember that a slowdown or interruption in the transfer of data from the computer will not stop a writing cycle so long as the buffer is not *completely* emptied. The larger the buffer, the more safety margin you have in case of interruptions. A *buffer underrun* error means that for some reason the flow of data from hard disk to CD-R was interrupted long enough for the CD recorder's buffer to be emptied, and writing was halted. If this occurs during an actual write operation (rather than a prewriting test), your recordable disk may be ruined. The checklist below covers many of the typical issues that may trigger a buffer underrun.

Hard disk issues

- *"Dumb" thermal recalibration.* Disable thermal recalibration on the drive before writing, or allow 1 h or so for the system temperature to stabilize before writing.

- *Excessive file fragmentation.* Defragment the drive with Defrag before burning a CD.

- *Insufficient free space.* The CD-R will almost certainly require some amount of temporary workspace on the hard drive. If there is insufficient free space on the hard drive, you may need to free additional space by offloading unneeded files or upgrading the drive itself.

- *Too many small files.* When you are recording on the fly, many small files may present too much of a load on your data transfer system, so try making an ISO image file first.

- *Damaged files.* Files which are damaged or corrupted will often cause errors which will interrupt the flow of data. Run ScanDisk and Defrag to locate any possible file system problems before recording.

■ *Recording files in use*. Make sure that no files to be recorded are currently in use by any application.

Hardware issues

■ *Slow hard drives*. Older hard drives may not support data transfer speeds high enough to keep the CD-R buffer filled. If you use slow hard drives, make an ISO image file first rather than writing on the fly.

■ *Burst data transfers*. Source devices that operate in "burst" data transfer modes may have difficulty keeping the CD-R buffer filled. Try disabling the burst mode—this may slow the overall data transfer, but it may even out the flow of data, making it easier to keep the buffer filled.

■ *CD-R controller configuration*. Verify that the IDE or SCSI controller operating the CD-R is configured for optimum performance (i.e., use bus-master drivers for IDE controllers).

■ *Sync problems*. Certain combinations of drives and controllers may not synchronize data properly. Check that you're using the recommended hardware devices for proper CD-R operation.

■ *Outdated device drivers*. Verify that you're using the latest device drivers for the CD-R, controller, and other related devices in the system.

■ *Slow computer speed*. Systems older than 486 platforms may simply be too old to support the data transfer needs of a CD-R. Verify that your system meets the minimum system requirements for your particular CD-R model.

■ *CD-R quality*. Be sure to use good-quality CD-R disks that are recommended by the CD-R manufacturer. Dirty, old, or scratched disks may not function.

Memory-resident software issues. CD-R systems may encounter buffer underrun problems when the following types of software are at work on your system. You may wish to systematically disable the following software types:

- Antivirus software

- Screen saver software

- System agent software

- Scheduler software

- TSR (terminate and stay resident) software

- Network software

- System sounds

- Animated icons or utilities

- Any program that may activate on its own

Windows 95 issues

- *Insufficient virtual memory*. Adjust your Virtual Memory settings to use at least 32 MB of RAM for virtual memory.

- *Disable auto insert notification*. If you have more than 16 MB of RAM, disable auto insert notification for the CD-ROM.

- *Change the system's role*. If you have more than 16 MB of RAM, change the hard drive's "typical role" to network server.

Tips to avoid buffer underruns

- Always set audio disks to write at 1×.

- Change the DMA transfer rate for the drive controller card being used.

- Defragment your hard drive at least once a week to prevent files from being scattered across the hard drive.

- Disable or remove all software in the computer *except* the operating system, the recording software, and the drivers for your source devices and CD-R.

- Disk-to-disk copying generally requires a SCSI 2, fully ASPI-compliant CD-ROM drive (at least 4×). Copying audio requires a source CD-ROM drive which supports digital audio extraction.

- Do not record across a network—copy the desired files to your local hard drive first.

- Do not try to copy empty directories, zero-byte files, or files that may be in use by the system at the time.

- For best results, use SCSI 2 (or faster) source devices.

- In any operating system, always use the newest drivers from your SCSI controller card manufacturer.

- Log out of any networks, if possible (including Windows for Workgroups and/or Microsoft Network).

- Make sure your hard drive does smart thermal recalibration, so that it won't recalibrate if the CPU is being used.

- Make sure your SCSI controller card is *fully* ASPI-compliant.

- Write more than 10,000 very small files to an .ISO image first or record at 1× if possible in order to ease data transfer demands.

- Record at a slower speed (e.g., 2× rather than 4×).

- Make sure that the temporary directory always has free space at least twice the size of the largest file you are recording.

- Try a different hard disk and/or gold recordable disk.

- With DOS 6.22 or below and a source hard disk 1 GB or larger, partitions should be kept smaller than

1 GB so that hard disk cluster size is 16 KB instead of 32 KB.

- Write an .ISO image to the hard disk first (if you have enough hard drive space).

General CD-R symptoms

CD recorders are subject to a large number of potential errors during operation. Many typical recording errors are listed below. In most cases, the error is not terribly complex, and can be corrected in just a few minutes once the nature of the problem is understood. Keep in mind that the actual error message is dependent on the CD recorder software in use, so your actual error messages may vary just a bit.

> **NOTE** *For basic CD-related issues, refer to Chapter 6 for CD-ROM troubleshooting information.*

Symptom 7.1: Absorption control error <xxx>. This error most often means that there is a slight problem writing to a recordable disk—perhaps caused by a smear or a speck of dust. It does not *necessarily* mean that your data have not been correctly recorded. A sector address is usually given so that you can (if you wish) verify the data in and around that sector. When writing is completed, try cleaning the disk (on the nonlabel side) gently with a lint-free cloth. If the error occurs again, try a new disk.

Symptom 7.2: Application code error. This error typically occurs when you try to write Kodak recordable CDs (Photo CDs) on non-Kodak CD recorders. These disks have a protection bit which is recognized only by the Kodak CD-R—other recorders will not record these disks. In this case, you'll need to use standard blank CDs.

Symptom 7.3: Bad ASPI open. The CD-R ASPI driver is bad or missing, and the SCSI CD-R cannot be found.

Check the installation of your CD-R drive and SCSI adapter, then check the driver installation. Try reinstalling the SCSI driver(s).

Symptom 7.4: Buffer underrun at sector <xxx>. Once an image file is generated, CD writing is a real-time process which must run constantly at the selected recording speed, *without interruptions*. The CD recorder's buffer is constantly filled with data from the hard drive waiting to be written. This buffering action ensures that small slowdowns or interruptions in the flow of data from the computer do not interrupt the writing process. A *buffer underrun* message indicates that the flow of data from hard disk to CD recorder was interrupted long enough for the CD recorder's buffer to be emptied, and writing was halted. If this occurs during an actual write operation rather than a test, your CD may be damaged.

To avoid buffer underruns, you should remove as much processing load as possible from the system. For example, make sure that no screen savers or other terminate and stay resident (TSR) programs are active (they can momentarily interrupt operations). Close as many open windows as possible. See that your working hard disk cannot be accessed via a network.

For SCSI CD-R drives, the CD recorder's position in the SCSI chain—or the cable length between the computer and the CD recorder—may cause data slowdowns. Try connecting the CD recorder as the first peripheral in the SCSI chain (if you have not done so already), and use a shorter SCSI cable (if possible) between the CD recorder and the SCSI host adapter.

Symptom 7.5: The current disk already contains a closed audio session. Under the Red Book standard for audio CDs, all audio tracks must be written in a *single* session. If you add audio tracks in more than one session, playback results will be unpredictable. Most CD-ROM drives will play back all audio tracks on a CD, even if they are recorded in several different sessions, but most home and car CD players can play back only the tracks in the *first* session. If you continue to record audio in a different session, you may have problems reading subsequent audio sessions.

Symptom 7.6: The current disk contains a session that is not closed. In actual practice, CD-ROM drives can read back only one data track per session, so avoid recording another data track in an open session. Be sure to close the session *before* writing additional data to the disk.

Symptom 7.7: The currently selected source CD-ROM drive or CD recorder cannot read audio in digital format. This is more of a warning than a fault. Reading audio tracks in "digital format" is *not* the same as playing the music, and few CD-ROM drives are able to read audio tracks in digital format (only Red Book format). You may need to copy the music data from the CD to the hard drive first, then postprocess the digital audio data through the application used to make the new CD.

Symptom 7.8: Data overrun/underrun. The SCSI host adapter has reported an error which is almost always caused by improper termination or a bad SCSI cable. Recheck the installation of your SCSI adapter, cabling, and termination. You may also need to reduce the processing overhead needed by unused applications.

Symptom 7.9: The destination disk is smaller than the source disk. This error commonly occurs when you're trying to duplicate an existing CD to the CD-R. There is not enough room on the recordable CD to copy the source CD. Try recording to a blank CD-R disk. Use 74-min media instead of 60-min media. Some CDs cannot be copied because of the TOC (table of contents) overhead in CD recorders, and also because of the calibration zone overhead. You may need to break up the source CD between two or more different CD-R disks.

Symptom 7.10: The disk already contains tracks and/or sessions that are incompatible with the requested operation. This error appears if you are trying to add data in a format which is different from the data format already on the disk. For example, you'll see this type of error if you try to add a CD-ROM XA session to a disk that already contains a standard CD-ROM session. A disk containing multiple formats is *unreadable*, so you are not allowed to record the different session type.

Symptom 7.11: The disk is write-protected. You are attempting to write to a CD-R disk which has already been closed. Do *not* try writing to disks which are closed—instead, use a fresh blank disk for writing.

Symptom 7.12: Error 175-xx-xx-xx. This error code often indicates a buffer underrun. See the information about buffer underruns contained at the start of this section.

Symptom 7.13: Error 220-01-xx-xx. This error code often indicates that some of your software cannot communicate with a SCSI device, possibly because your SCSI bus was reset. In many cases, this is caused by conflicts between real-mode and protected-mode SCSI drivers working in a Windows 95/98 system. Try REMarking out any real-mode SCSI drivers in your CONFIG.SYS file (the protected-mode drivers provided for Windows 95/98 should be sufficient on their own). You may need to download and install updated protected-mode drivers for the SCSI host adapter and CD-R drive (as well as other SCSI devices which may be installed).

Symptom 7.14: Error 220-06-xx-xx. This error code often indicates a SCSI selection time-out error, which suggests a SCSI setup problem—usually with the SCSI host adapter. Contact your SCSI host adapter manufacturer for detailed installation and testing instructions. You may need to adjust the SCSI BIOS Setup or update the SCSI drivers in your system.

Symptom 7.15: Error reading the table of contents (TOC) or program memory area (PMA) from the disk. This recordable disk is defective or has been damaged (probably during a previous write operation). Do *not* try and write to this disk. Unfortunately, there is very little you can do here except to discard the defective disk.

Symptom 7.16: General protection fault. This type of problem has been identified with the Adaptec AHAr-152x family of SCSI host adapters and is caused by outdated driver software. You can solve this problem by upgrading to version 3.1 (or later) of Adaptec's EZ-SCSI software. If you're not using Adaptec software, check for current drivers for whatever SCSI adapter you're using.

Symptom 7.17: Invalid logical block address. This error message usually means that the CD mastering software has requested a data block from the hard disk which either does not exist or is illegal. This may suggest a corrupted hard disk or damaged ISO file. Exit the CD-mastering software and run ScanDisk and Defrag to check and reorganize your hard drive. You may need to rebuild an ISO file or reload damaged files from a backup.

Symptom 7.18: Last two blocks stripped. This message appears when you are copying a track to hard disk if the track you are reading was created as multisession-compliant (following the Orange Book standard). This is because a multisession track is always followed by two run-out blocks. These are included in the count of the total size (in blocks) of the track, but they do not contain data and cannot be read back. This message appears to alert you just in case you notice that you got two blocks fewer than were reported for the read length. Don't panic—you haven't lost any data.

Symptom 7.19: MSCDEX errors are being encountered. Early versions of MSCDEX (prior to version 2.23) had problems with filenames containing "illegal" ASCII characters such as a hyphen. If a directory contains a filename with an illegal ASCII character, you can still see all the files by doing a directory (DIR) from DOS, or you can open the illegally named file. However, one or more files listed *after* the illegal one may not be accessible or may give errors. You should update MSCDEX to the latest available version. As an alternative, you may REMark out the real-mode driver and MSCDEX command lines in your startup files and allow Windows 95/98 to rely exclusively on protected-mode drivers.

Symptom 7.20: DOS or Windows cannot find the CD-R drive.   There are several possible reasons why the CD-R drive cannot be found by software. First, turn the computer off and wait at least 15 s. Make sure the IDE or SCSI adapter card is firmly seated and secured to the computer case. The IDE or SCSI adapter must also be properly configured. Check the IDE or SCSI cable and see that it is properly attached to the adapter and drive. Turn the computer on. If problems persist, make sure that the correct IDE or SCSI drivers are installed, and that any command-line switches are set correctly.

Symptom 7.21: No write data (buffer empty).   The flow of data to the CD-R drive must be extremely reliable so that the CD-R's working buffer is never empty when the CD-R prepares to write a block of information to disk. This message indicates that the flow of data from the hard disk to the CD recorder has been interrupted (similar to the buffer underrun error).

- *Check for processing overhead.* Ensure that no screen savers, other TSR utilities, or unneeded open windows which might momentarily interrupt operations are active. Your working hard disk should not be accessible over a network.

- *Check the SCSI setup.* The SCSI CD recorder's position in the SCSI chain or the length of cabling between the SCSI adapter and the CD recorder may also cause data slowdowns. Try connecting the CD recorder as the first device in the SCSI chain (you may need to reterminate the SCSI chain), and keep the SCSI cable as short as possible.

- *Check the file caching.* Windows 3.1x requires the use of a RAM cache to manage the flow of data. *SmartDrive* (the caching utility supplied with Windows 3.1x) is necessary for writing virtual images to CD on the fly. However, when writing a real ISO image from hard disk to CD, it may cause a buffer underrun. If a buffer underrun occurs during testing or writing of a real ISO 9660 image under Windows 3.1x, exit to the DOS shell and type the following:

```
smartdrv x-
```

where x is the letter of the hard drive from which you will write the ISO image. This disables SmartDrive for the specified drive so that CD writing can proceed smoothly.

Symptom 7.22: Read file error. A file referenced by the virtual image database cannot be located or accessed. Make sure that the suspect file is not being used by you or by someone else on a network. The file may also be damaged or corrupt, so exit the CD-R application and run ScanDisk and Defrag to check the file system for problems. You may need to reload damaged files from a backup.

Symptom 7.23: Selected disk image file was not prepared for the current disk. This type of error message occurs if you prepared the disk image file for a *blank* CD, but you are now trying to record it to a CD *already* containing data (or vice versa). In either case, you would wind up writing a CD that couldn't be read at all because the CD addresses calculated for the disk image are wrong for that actual CD. If you are given the option of writing anyway, select *No* to abort because it is very unlikely that the writing operation would yield a readable CD. Retry the operation with a known-blank CD-R disk.

Symptom 7.24: Selected disk track is longer than the image file. The disk verify process fails immediately because the source ISO 9660 image file and the actual ISO 9660 track on the CD are not the same size—the disk track is actually longer than the image file, which could indicate a defective CD-R drive. Retry the operation with a good-quality CD-R disk. If the problem persists, you might try replacing the CD-R drive.

Symptom 7.25: Selected disk track is shorter than the image file. The disk verify process fails immediately because the source ISO 9660 image file and the actual ISO 9660 track on CD are not the same size—the disk track is actually shorter than the image file, which could indicate a defective CD-R drive. Retry the operation with a good-quality CD-R disk. If the problem persists, you might try replacing the CD-R drive.

Symptom 7.26: The "disk in" light on the drive does not blink after you turn on the computer. In virtually all cases, there is no power reaching the CD-R drive. For internal CD-R drives, make sure the computer's 4-pin power cable is properly connected to the CD-R drive unit. For external CD-R drives, make sure the power cord is properly connected to the back of the CD-R drive unit and is plugged into a grounded power outlet.

Make sure the power switch on the back of the drive is on. Refer to your CD-R drive's installation guide for more detailed information.

Symptom 7.27: Write emergency. This error occurs if the drive is interrupted during a write action. It is commonly seen when writing Red Book audio, but it can also occur with data recordings. For example, one typical reason for a write emergency is dust particles that cause the laser to jump off the track. In most cases, the CD-R disk is ruined, and you'll need to retry the write process with a good-quality disk.

Symptom 7.28: The CD-R is recognized by Windows 95/98, but it will not function as a normal CD-ROM drive. The drive appears normally in the Windows 95/98 *Device Manager*. However, the driver which is operating the CD-R drive may not allow the drive to function as a normal CD-ROM reader. For example, this is a known problem with the Philips CDD2000 CD-R. Check to see if there is an updated Windows 95/98 CD-R driver which can overcome this limitation. If there is not, you may need to replace the CD-R drive with an upgraded model whose drivers *do* support CD-ROM-type functionality on the CD-R drive.

Symptom 7.29: You cannot read CD-R (gold) disks in some ordinary CD-ROM drives. This is actually a very complex issue because there are a number of important factors which affect the way in which a CD is read.

- *Check the laser calibration.* Some older CD-ROM drive lasers are not calibrated to read recordable disks (whose recorded surface is slightly different from that of pressed disks). If your CD-ROM drive reads mass-produced (silver) CDs but not recordable CDs, check with the CD-ROM drive manufacturer to determine whether laser calibration is the problem. You may be able to return the CD-ROM drive for factory recalibration, or you can replace the CD-ROM drive with a newer model that is better calibrated for reading both CD-ROM and CD-R disks.

- *Check the CD-ROM compatibility*. Fast CD-ROM drive operations may be another problem. In order to work as fast as they do, some CD-ROM models must perform unconventional operations such as a laser calibration in the lead-out area to determine the approximate position of several tracks. With some CD recorders, the session lead-out is not recorded correctly, and this can cause problems with gold disk compatibility.

- *Check the CD-R software*. The CD-R authoring software can be a problem. Any authoring software can sometimes produce incorrect tracks as a result of bugs or recording glitches. A good way to check whether incompatibility problems lie with the originating software is to test the same gold disk on several CD-ROM drives. If one drive is capable of reading the gold disk back correctly, chances are that the problem was *not* in the recording process. If no drives can read the CD-R disk, then the disk may have been damaged in the recording process.

- *Update or disable MSCDEX*. Consider your version of MSCDEX. Although MSCDEX (the Microsoft extension for reading CD-ROMs) will allow non-ISO legal characters in filenames, versions of MSCDEX *prior* to 2.23 have a problem dealing with filenames which contain the hyphen. If a directory contains a filename with a hyphen in it, you will be able to see all the files by doing a DIR from DOS. But any files listed *after* the file with the illegal name are not accessible—when trying to open them, you would get a *file not found* message. MSCDEX 2.23 appears to have fixed this bug. You may also REMark the real-mode drivers and MSCDEX command lines in your startup files and rely on protected-mode drivers under Windows 95/98.

Symptom 7.30: You encounter *buffer miscompare* errors when using a SCSI host adapter diagnostic utility. In many cases, you probably have a DMA channel conflict with another card (or device) in the system. Check the settings of every card or device that uses an IRQ, DMA channel, or I/O port address, and compare these settings to the ones used for the SCSI host adapter. If there is a DMA conflict, change the DMA channel on the SCSI card to an unused channel.

Another possibility is that you're dealing with a motherboard that doesn't support bus mastering (not all PCs support bus mastering). For example, a Gateway 2000 P5-133 has only one bus-mastering slot, which is normally occupied by the video adapter. If the SCSI adapter (e.g., an Adaptec AHA-1535 card) is installed in a non-bus-mastering slot in this machine, the system may freeze when trying to access a CD from the CD-R drive. It may be necessary to upgrade the motherboard to access additional bus-mastering slots.

Symptom 7.31: You encounter a *servo tracking error* when writing a CD. A servo tracking error message is reported by the CD-R drive when it is unable to record to the medium (the blank disk)—this is similar to when a needle "skips" on a phonograph. There is a microscopic groove imprinted on the surface of each CD-R disk which guides the laser during writing. There are a number of reasons why a servo tracking error might occur.

- *Check for defective media*. Defective media can include a bad disk, a bad lot of disks, or an unsupported brand of media (not all CD-R disk media work the same on all CD-R drives). For example, the Pinnacle Micro RCD-1000/5020/5040 series drives support the following disk brands: DOT, Taiyo Yuden, Mitsubishi, Sony, 3M, TDK, Verbatim, and Kodak Infoguard. Make sure that you're using a blank disk that's certified to work with your particular drive, and try another disk (or disk brand) if necessary.

- *Check the data you're recording.* Verify that the amount of data you are trying to record does not exceed the capacity of the disk. Your recording software will usually prevent you from making that mistake, but it has no way of adjusting for previously failed sessions or bad blocks on the media. Either of these can cause the software to calculate the remaining free space incorrectly, so that it differs from what is *actually* free.

- *Clean the drive and disk.* There may be a dirty lens within the drive which prevents the laser from focusing on the surface of the media. Use a can of compressed air to blow out the inside of the drive through the front access door or tray.

- *Check for excessive temperature.* A servo tracking error may also occur if the ambient temperature inside the drive itself is too high. If your drive is external, remove the filter from the back of the drive and use compressed air to clean it out. Confirm that the cooling fan works when the unit is powered on— if it does not, the drive may need to be replaced. If your drive is internal, verify that it receives enough air circulation by removing the computer's case, letting the drive cool off for a while, and then rerunning the recording session. If the problem persists, replace the drive.

Symptom 7.32: You notice frequent "pops" or "clicks" between CD audio tracks. This is almost always a result of your particular CD recording software. The "pops" or "clicks" heard between tracks on CD digital audio (CD-DA) disks are caused when recording without using the Disk-at-Once option. When you select the Disk-at-Once option in the authoring software, the laser will remain powered on between tracks (and run-in/run-out blocks are written without interruption).

Keep in mind that the Disk-at-Once feature is not currently available on some software packages, so check the manual of your CD authoring software to see if there is a Disk-at-Once feature—if there is not, you may have an outdated or "lite" version which will require an upgrade. For example, the Disk-at-Once feature is available with Easy-CD Pro version 1.1.409 and later (but not in Easy-CD 95). By comparison, Corel CD Creator does not support true Disk-at-Once, even as late as version 2.01.079.

Another possible cause for pops between tracks occurs when a .WAV file is created improperly (or it is corrupt). Some early shareware audio editing software had problems saving .WAV files properly, and bugs caused pops to occur between tracks (and at other various points throughout a song). These .WAV files were corrupted by the editing software.

The most recent problem with .WAV files is the use of "extended information." Some .WAV editing software packages allow the user to save the .WAV file in an extended .WAV format, as well as in the standard .WAV format. If extended information is included in the .WAV file (author name, date, and so on), this will cause a pop to occur when the CD is played back through a standard audio CD player. Make sure you can save a .WAV file *without* this extra information to avoid the problem.

Symptom 7.33: On your home stereo, the disk will not repeat play after the last track.   When you set your home stereo CD player to "repeat playback" after the last track, the CD playback simply stops—it will not repeat. Some audio CD players cannot play back a burned audio disk properly if there are B0h and C0h pointers in the disk's table of contents. B0h and C0h pointers are used to point to the next session, and are created on disks written using the Track-at-Once (or multisession) option. CDs written using Disk-at-Once do not contain these pointers because there are no subsequent sessions. If you would like to have a disk which is fully compatible with audio CD, use the Disk-at-Once option during recording.

Symptom 7.34: You cannot access a CD-R after upgrading to Windows 98. You may find this happens most frequently with Philips CDD200 or HO 4020I CD-R drives. It is almost always due to problems with Corel CD Creator 2.0 being present on your system. There are two means of correcting this problem. First, uninstall Corel CD Creator and install other CD authoring software (e.g., Adaptec Easy CD Creator Pro), which should be better able to support the CD-R drive. If you cannot replace the CD authoring software, check with the CD-R maker to see if there is a firmware upgrade available for the CD-R drive.

Symptom 7.35: When upgrading to Windows 95/98, you receive a *fatal exception 0E* error. While you are installing Windows, when Setup restarts your computer for the last time, you may see a "blue screen" error such as

```
A fatal exception 0E has occurred at 0028:C02A0201
in VXD IOS(04)+00001FC9
```

This problem can typically occur if Corel CD Creator 2.0 is installed on your computer. Windows 95/98 is known to be incompatible with the CDRASPI.VXD file installed by Corel CD Creator 2.0. You can work around this problem by renaming the CDRASPI.VXD file:

- Start Windows 95/98 in the safe mode.

- Click *Start*, highlight *Find*, and then click *Files or Folders*.

- In the *Named* box, type cdraspi.vxd and then click *Find Now*.

- In the list of found files, right-click the cdraspi.vxd file, and then click *Rename*.

- Type a new name for the `cdraspi.vxd` file (such as `cdraspi.old`), and then press `<Enter>`.

- Restart your computer normally.

Symptom 7.36: You receive a *Windows protection* error with EZ-SCSI 4.0 and Easy CD Pro 95. After you install the Adaptec EZ-SCSI 4.0 and the Adaptec Easy-CD Pro 95 programs under Windows 98, you may receive the following error message:

```
Windows Protection Error: You need to restart your
computer.
```

You may be able to use Windows, but you may not be able to use the EZ-SCSI 4.0 and Easy CD Pro 95 programs. You'll need to restart Windows 98 in the safe mode and remove (uninstall) both EZ-SCSI 4.0 and Easy CD Pro 95. Check with Adaptec for updated versions of both programs.

Symptom 7.37: You receive an error when recording an audio track under 4 s. If you try to record an audio track or .WAV file that is less than 4 s long, you will get a message indicating that a certain track cannot be written because it is less than 4 s long. Do not use .WAV files of less than 4 s. The audio standard for compact disk (red book) does not allow for audio files of less than 4 s. Make the audio file longer and try recording it again.

Symptom 7.38: You get poor audio quality from the CD-R. Changes in recording speed (from 4× to 2× to 1×) have little or no effect on the quality of the recording. Most current CD authoring software allows the use of IDE-style CD-ROM devices as source drives for copying audio CDs (Red Book or CD-DA). The Digital Audio Extraction (or DAE) test will pass, yet the copy process results in poor audio quality. Program and data CDs usually copy without problems. In virtually all cases, the problem is the source CD-ROM drive.

Use the source CD-ROM drive to extract a troublesome audio CD track to the hard disk as a .WAV file (name it CDTEST.WAV). Now use the CD-R to extract the same audio track to the hard disk as a .WAV file (name it WTEST.WAV). Play the two .WAV files from the hard drive and compare them. If the CDTEST.WAV file contains the same clicks/pops that you encountered during recording, yet the CD-R is producing clean .WAV files, then your source drive is *not* producing high-quality digital audio extraction. There are three ways around this problem:

- Use the CD-R as the source *and* destination (check the CD-R manual and CD authoring software for detailed instructions on how to do this).

- Purchase a new CD-ROM drive guaranteed to support high-speed DAE.

- Use the CD authoring software settings to slow down the DAE rate. For example, in Easy CD Creator, the DAE rate is found under *Tools*, *Options*, and *Advanced* tab. You can experiment by extracting tracks as .WAV files after making those changes and testing their quality by playing them from the hard drive.

Web Contacts

AcerOpen: *http://www.acercomponents.com/POL_CD-Drives.htm*

Adaptec: *http://www.adaptec.com/cdrec/* (CD Creator 2.x and Adaptec's Easy CD Creator Deluxe 3.0)

Aztech: *http://www.aztech.com.sg/c&t/spec_cd.htm*

CDR Publisher: *http://www.cdr1.com*

CeQuadrat: *http://www.cequadrat.com/* (WinOnCD 3.0 software)

Philips: *http://www.pps.philips.com*

Smart and Friendly: *http://www.smartandfriendly.com*

Teac: *http://www.teac.com/*

CD-RW Drives

Ever since the introduction of CD-ROM drives, recording your own CDs has been an elusive goal. Recordable CDs went a long way toward filling that gap, but CD-R disks can be written only once—they are not erasable. With the development of rewritable CD (CD-RW) technology, it finally became possible to write files to CD with the same ease as to a floppy disk or hard drive. Today, virtually any Pentium-based PC with a SCSI/IDE bus and 1 GB or more of hard drive space can support a high-speed CD-RW drive for under $400 (U.S.). At first, the choice between CD-R and CD-RW drives may seem confusing because of the similarity between the two technologies, but there are very real reasons to select either the CD-R or the CD-RW technologies. CD-Rs are best suited for permanently saving (archiving) large project files or sharing (distributing) noneditable files or presentations. CD-RW drives are best suited for saving files which change quickly, such as email records or Microsoft Money files. This chapter explains the technologies and troubleshooting techniques that are unique to CD-RW drives.

Understanding CD-RW Concepts

The ISO 9660 file system has long been the established standard in CD-ROM and CD recording (by comparison, Mac systems use the HFS approach). In fact, ISO 9660 is one of the key elements that propelled CD-ROM drives to the status of standard equipment on the PC by the early 1990s. With the broad introduction of CD-RW drives, however, ISO 9660 has been replaced by the *Universal Data Format* (or simply UDF) file system. This part of the chapter offers some essential background on UDF and explains how the use of UDF affects the compatibility of CD-RW disks with existing CD-ROM and CD-R drives.

Let's start with some perspective on ISO 9660. The ISO 9660 file system grew out of the original High Sierra file system of the late 1980s. All the files recorded on your CD-ROM use the ISO 9660 format. Both Windows and Mac operating systems can read ISO 9660 disks because they provide built-in ISO 9660 readers—the reader is totally transparent to the end user.

While ISO 9660 is just fine for existing CD-ROM and CD-R drives, it is really not sufficient to support the new generation of CD-RW drives *and* the emerging DVD drives. CD-RW drives require that files be added incrementally (one file at a time) *without* a waste of overhead space, and that individual files be able to be erased at will to make room on a disk. In addition, DVD drives require a file system that can support drives at least 4 GB in size. These demands are well beyond the scope of ISO 9660.

UDF addresses all of these concerns by providing a format that can add and erase individual files as needed, and also support the large disk space promised by DVD. Another advantage of UDF is its cross-platform compatibility—a UDF disk can be read by both Mac and Windows platforms. For example, a file could be written using a Mac, then read back on a Windows PC.

The UDF file format is also able to maintain Mac file attributes (i.e., icons, resource forks, and file types), whereas ISO 9660 cannot do this.

Working with UDF

The DirectCD technology used with CD-RW drives reads and writes to the CD-RW disk using the UDF format. If you're working on a PC with a CD-RW drive (or plan on installing one yourself), chances are that you'll be using a DirectCD applet to invoke UDF on that disk. There are currently two versions of UDF. UDF 1.02 is the version used on current DVD-ROM and DVD-Video disks. UDF 1.5 is a superset of 1.02 that adds support for CD-R and CD-RW drives. If you're using DirectCD under Windows 95/98, chances are that you're using UDF 1.5.

Disk capacity under UDF

An important issue to keep in mind when using DirectCD is that you never get the same data capacity from a CD-RW disk that you do from a CD-R disk under ISO 9660. Traditional CD-Rs under ISO 9660 can provide a full 650 MB from a blank 74-min disk. By comparison, UDF demands a certain amount of recording overhead, which reduces the overall amount of data which can be recorded on a CD-R or CD-RW disk. In normal operation, you can fit up to 493 MB on a CD-RW disk under DirectCD. On a CD-R disk under DirectCD, you can fit up to 618 MB.

UDF and disk compatibility

There's only one little problem with UDF: Windows 95 does not support it natively. The DirectCD drivers installed with a CD-RW drive will allow Windows 95 to read UDF disks in a CD-RW drive, but using DirectCD (UDF) disks in other drives is a little trickier. When DirectCD begins writing data to a disk, it opens a session. Before any CD-ROM drive can read a disk, the session must be closed. When you eject a disk from a CD-RW drive using the DirectCD applet, you can choose to close the disk to ISO 9660. If you do *not* close the disk to ISO 9660 when you eject it, you cannot read it on a CD-ROM drive—you must read it on a CD-R or CD-RW drive fitted with DirectCD. This is a limitation of CD-ROM drives, not of the DirectCD software. Table 8.1 outlines the compatibility of UDF disks.

If you close the disk to UDF, you can still read the UDF format, but you'll need a Multi-Read CD-ROM drive and a UDF reader utility. For example, when you install Adaptec's UDF Reader in your system, you should be able to read your closed-session CD-R and CD-RW disks on CD-ROM drives, regardless of whether they are ISO 9660 or UDF.

Multi-Read CD-ROM drives

UDF reader utilities are designed to support the new generation of Multi-Read CD-ROM drives. Multi-Read is a specification developed and endorsed by the Optical Storage Technology Association (OSTA) and accepted by the industry at large. Most new CD-ROM drives on the market today (manufactured after mid-1997) are Multi-Read-compatible. To be Multi-Read-compliant, a CD-ROM drive must be able to

- Read CD-RW disks

- Read packet-written disks (both CD-R and CD-RW)

TABLE 8.1 UDF Disk Compatibility

| Disk type | Playback on | | | |
	CD-ROM or CD player	Multi-Read CD-ROM	CD-R	CD-RW
CD-R	Yes	Yes	Yes	Yes
CD-RW	No	Yes*	Yes*,†	Yes

*A UDF reader utility may be required.
†*If* it reads CD-RW disks.

■ Support the operating system to utilize UDF 1.5

> **NOTE:** *There are some non-Multi-Read CD-ROM drives which can read UDF-formatted CD-R media, but not CD-RW media, using an appropriate UDF reader utility.*

UDF readers

A UDF reader enables Multi-Read CD-ROM drives to read closed-session UDF-formatted CD-R and CD-RW media under Windows 95 and the Macintosh operating system. The UDF reader for Windows is called UDF Reader Driver, and the UDF reader for the Mac OS is called UDF Volume Access. UDF readers are particularly useful if you're using DirectCD to *record* data to a CD-RW disk because you will then be able to read the CD-RW disk in a Multi-Read CD-ROM drive. Without a UDF reader, you could read the UDF disk only in another CD-RW drive using DirectCD. Since UDF is designed to be a cross-platform file format, UDF readers also allow you to interchange UDF-formatted disks between Mac and Windows systems.

Most companies that develop DirectCD software (such as Adaptec) already offer UDF reader utilities free of charge. You can download the Adaptec UDF reader from the Adaptec Web site at *www.adaptec.com*, or specifically from Adaptec's patch/upgrade Web page at *http://www.adaptec.com/support/files/upgrades.html* . For more information, you could also send email to Adaptec at *udfreader@adaptec.com*.

UDF reader compliance

Since UDF is intended to provide a universal file interchange format, any UDF reader utility *should* be able to read all UDF 1.5-formatted media (i.e., media formatted with DirectCD). However, there is no independent third-party organization to test for UDF compliance, so there is no guarantee that all media claiming to be UDF formatted will be readable by every UDF reader under all conditions. If you have trouble reading a UDF disk with one particular reader utility, you might wish to try another reader utility.

UDF and audio CDs

A popular use of CD-R and CD-RW disks has been to record music for playback on an ordinary CD player (i.e., copying old vinyl LPs to CD). While this is a tried-and-true process for CD-R disks recorded under ISO 9660, it will *not* work with UDF disks recorded with DirectCD. Audio files recorded under UDF will *not* work when played back in a commercial CD player. However, audio files played back on a CD-R or CD-RW drive under DirectCD should work normally.

Windows 98 and UDF

While Windows 95 does not provide direct support for UDF, information gleaned from Microsoft and Adaptec suggests that Windows 98 *will* support UDF 1.02 for DVD-ROM and DVD-Video disks. However, preliminary results indicate that Windows 98 may not provide native support for UDF 1.5, so DirectCD software and UDF readers may still be required after Windows 98 is installed.

NOTE: *Mac OS 8.1 already supports UDF 1.02.*

Using DirectCD

There are some simple rules to follow when preparing and working with CD-RW drives. Preparing new disks, writing data, adding data, erasing data, ejecting the disk, and recovering damaged disks are the most typical procedures that you'll need to master. This part of the chapter outlines these essential steps—though you should refer to your CD-RW user's manual for specific information.

Preparing a data CD

Use the following steps to start DirectCD and prepare a blank CD-RW disk for reading and writing data:

■ Start the computer and insert a blank CD-RW disk in the CD-RW drive. After a few seconds, a screen will appear that asks *Please select the type of CD you wish to create.* If the *DirectCD Disk Ready* window appears, the disk has already been prepared, and you can start writing data to it immediately.

> **NOTE:** *If no screen appears after about 15 s, the disk may not be blank, or it may have an unreadable format— or the auto insert notification option may be disabled.*

■ Select the option *Click here to create a data CD that will be accessible through a drive letter* (i.e., as you would use a floppy drive). The *Format Disk* screen appears.

■ If you're formatting a CD-R disk, click *Next* on the *Format Disk* screen.

■ If you're formatting a CD-RW disk, you can choose between two formatting options. Click the *Advanced* button that appears on the *Format Disk* screen. When the next screen appears, select either *Fast Format* or *Full Format* and click *OK*.

> **NOTE:** *It's often easier to select the fast format option, which lets you start writing to the CD-RW disk almost immediately (while the disk is formatted in the background). A full format requires you to wait about an hour until the formatting is complete before you can write to the disk.*

■ When the *Name Your Disk* screen appears, type a name for the disk and click *Finish*. Disk formatting begins. When the *DirectCD Disk Ready* window appears, the formatting is complete.

■ Click *OK*. The DirectCD disk is ready for you to write data to it.

Writing data to a DirectCD disk

Once your CD is formatted as a DirectCD disk, you can write data to it in several different ways:

- "Drag and drop" files from Windows Explorer right onto the CD-RW icon.

- Select *Save As* from a Windows 95/98/NT application *File* menu, and select the drive letter of your CD-RW.

- Use the *Send To* command.

- Use the MS-DOS command prompts from a DOS window in Windows 95/98/NT.

Ejecting a DirectCD disk

DirectCD gives you several formatting options when you eject a DirectCD disk from the CD-RW drive. The options depend on what kind of disk DirectCD detects in the drive, and how you want to use the disk. To eject a DirectCD disk, follow these steps:

- Push the *Eject* button on the front of the CD-RW drive, or right-click on the CD icon on the taskbar and select *Eject* from the drop-down list box—the *Eject Disc* screen will appear.

- Carefully read the text that appears on the screen and (if options are presented) select the option you require.

- Click *Finish* to eject the disk from the CD-RW drive.

Erasing a DirectCD disk

If you are using CD-RW disks, you can actually erase files from the disk and use the recovered space to write new files. However, if you "delete" files from a CD-R disk, the files become invisible to the file system (i.e., Windows Explorer) but the space they occupy is *not* made available for other files. So deleting files from a

CD-R disk will not increase the available free space on the disk. To erase the contents of a DirectCD disk, follow these steps:

- While in Windows Explorer, select the file(s) you want to erase.
- Select *Delete* from the *File* menu.
- Click *Yes* to confirm that you want to erase the files from the disk.
- DirectCD erases the selected file(s) from the disk.

Fixing an unreadable disk

If no window appears on the screen (after about 15 s) when you insert a disk in the CD-RW drive, the disk may have an unreadable format. DirectCD has a ScanDisc application that may be able to recover data on the disk and allow you to write to it and read from it again. Follow these steps to use ScanDisc:

- Double-click the CD icon on the right side of the Windows taskbar. If the disk is unreadable, the *ScanDisc* window will appear.
- Read the text in the window, then click the *ScanDisc* button.
- Wait while ScanDisc repairs the disk. A message will appear on the screen when ScanDisc is finished.

Caring for rewritable CDs

As a rule, rewritable CDs are as rugged and reliable as ordinary pressed CDs. Still, you should observe some rules for the careful handling and storage of rewriteable media:

- *Maintain a comfortable environment.* Don't expose rewritable disks to sunlight or other strong light for long periods of time. Also avoid high heat and humidity, which can damage the physical disk.

Always keep blank or recorded media in clean
"jewel" cases for best protection.

- *Don't write on the disk.* Don't use alcohol-based pens
  to write on disks—the ink may eventually eat
  through the top (lacquer) surface and damage your
  data. Also, don't use ballpoint or other sharp-tipped
  pens because you may scratch right through the
  lacquer surface and damage the reflective gold layer
  (and ruin your data).

- *Don't use labels on the disk.* Don't put labels on disks
  unless the labels are *expressly* designed for
  rewritable CDs. The glue may eat through the lacquer surface just as some inks do, and/or the label
  may unbalance the disk and cause problems in reading it back or recording subsequent sessions. Never
  try to remove a label—you might tear off the lacquer
  and some of the reflecting surface.

- *Watch your media quality.* Many different brands
  of rewritable CD media are now available in the
  marketplace. Quality varies from brand to brand
  (and even from batch to batch within a given
  brand). If you have repeated problems that can be
  traced to the blank media you are using, try using
  a different brand or even a different batch of the
  same brand.

- *Don't use Kodak Photo CDs.* Avoid the use of Kodak
  Photo CDs on everyday CD recorders. Kodak Photo
  CDs are designed to be used only with Kodak Photo
  CD professional workstations. Although the disks
  are inexpensive, they have a protection bit which
  prevents them from being written on many CD
  recorders. When you attempt to write these disks on
  recorders which recognize the protection bit, you
  will receive an error message.

- *Careful for power issues.* If you lose power while
  writing to your CD-RW (or if you exit an application
  or press <Ctrl> + <Alt> + <Del> while writing),

you may be able to salvage your rewritable CD if you follow the steps below:

1. Leave the CD in the drive—do *not* open the tray.
2. Turn the machine off, then turn it back on.
3. Reenter the application you were using.

Once the application tries to access the CD-RW drive, the recovery operation will make it appear that the last session is there. However, only a part of the CD's directory may be there. Your rewritable CD is still usable if you can read that directory. Repeat the entire copy operation to make sure that your files are copied successfully.

CD-RW Installation and Replacement

CD-RW drives are generally easy devices to install or replace. Most are installed as master devices located on the secondary IDE drive controller channel, although a few will coexist as slave devices alongside a hard drive or some other drive device. The most important issue to remember is that the BIOS will not support the CD-RW directly (even if the BIOS identifies the CD-RW at boot time)—you'll need real-mode drivers for the CD-RW under DOS or protected-mode drivers for the CD-RW under Windows. This part of the chapter covers the guidelines needed to install a basic internal IDE-type CD-RW.

Select jumper configurations

An IDE-type CD-RW drive may be installed as a master or a slave device on any hard drive controller channel. These master/slave settings are handled through one or two jumpers located on the rear of the drive (right next to the 40-pin signal cable connector). One of your first decisions when planning an installation should be to decide the drive's configuration:

- If you're installing the CD-RW as the first drive on the secondary drive controller channel, it must be jumpered as the master device.

- If you're installing the CD-RW drive alongside another drive (on either the primary or the secondary drive controller channel), the CD-RW must be jumpered as the slave device.

  NOTE: *Refer to the documentation that accompanies your particular CD-RW drive to determine the exact master/slave jumper settings. If you do not have the drive documentation handy, check the drive manufacturer's Web site for online information.*

Attach cables and mount the drive

- Turn off and unplug the PC, then remove the outer cover to expose the computer's drive bays.

- Attach one end of the 40-pin drive interface cable to the drive controller connector on your motherboard (or drive controller card). Remember to align pin 1 on the cable (the side of the cable with the blue or red stripe) with pin 1 on the drive controller connector.

- Locate an available drive bay for the CD-RW drive. Remove the plastic housing covering the drive bay, then slide the drive inside. Locate the four screw holes needed to mount the drive. In some cases, you may need to attach mounting rails to the drive so that the drive will be wide enough to fit in the drive bay. In virtually all cases, you should mount a tray-driven CD-RW drive horizontally (although caddy-loaded CD-RW drives may be mounted vertically).

- Attach the 40-pin signal cable and the 4-pin power connector to the new drive, then bolt the drive securely into place. Do not overtighten the screws, since this may damage the drive. If you do not have an available 4-pin power connector, you may use an appropriate Y splitter if necessary to split power from another drive (preferably the floppy drive).

■ Attach the small 4-pin CD-audio signal cable from the CD-RW to the CD-audio input connector on your sound card. This connection allows you to play music CDs directly through your sound card. Verify that the CD-audio cable is compatible with your sound card (if it is not, you may need a specialized cable from the sound card's manufacturer).

> **NOTE:** *If you already have a CD-ROM drive in the system that is providing CD audio to the sound card, you may choose to use the CD-RW instead or to leave the CD-ROM's audio cable alone. If your sound card has a second CD audio connector, you may be able to wire the CD-RW's audio to your sound card also.*

Configuring the CMOS Setup

Although the CD-RW does require driver support, recent motherboard designs can identify the ATAPI IDE CD-RW drive in BIOS, so you should configure your computer's BIOS to accept the drive if possible (through the CMOS Setup).

■ Turn the computer on. As your computer starts up, watch for a message that describes how to run the CMOS Setup (e.g., *Press F1 for Setup*). Press the appropriate key to start the CMOS Setup program.

■ Select the *hard drive settings* menu, and choose the drive location occupied by the CD-RW drive (i.e., *primary slave*, *secondary slave*, or *secondary master*, depending on how you've physically jumpered and installed the drive).

■ Select *automatic drive detection* if available—this option will automatically identify the new drive. If your BIOS does *not* provide automatic drive detection, select *none* or *not installed* for the CD-RW, and rely on drivers *only*.

■ Save the settings and exit the CMOS Setup program. Your computer will automatically reboot.

Reassemble the computer

Double-check all of your signal and power cables to verify that they are secure, then tuck the cables gently into the computer's chassis. Check that there are no loose tools, screws, or cables inside the chassis. Now reattach the computer's outer housing(s).

Install the software

In order to complete your CD-RW installation, you'll need to install the software drivers that accompanied the drive on diskette or CD. Windows 95/98 systems will generally detect the presence of the new CD-RW and prompt you for the protected-mode drivers automatically. After you install the drivers and reboot the system, the CD-RW should be ready for use. Before you can write your own CD-RW disks, you'll also need to install the DirectCD and CD authoring software (e.g., Adaptec Easy CD Pro) and other utilities from the drive's installation disk.

> **NOTE:** *Many CD-RW drives will not support real-mode (DOS) drivers, so they will work only under Windows 95/98.*

Upgrading CD-RW firmware

You may be able to update the firmware used in your CD-RW drive. This may be necessary in order to correct bugs or fix drive compatibility problems with the system. The steps below offer a guideline that you can refer to when upgrading CD-RW firmware.

> **NOTE:** *The steps below are based on an internal Plextor SCSI CD-RW drive. You should always refer to the Web page or README file that accompanies the new firmware download. Be sure to download the correct*

*firmware version for your drive—installing the wrong
firmware can permanently disable the drive.*

- Power off your system completely.

- Locate the CD-RW drive and place its "flash" jumper
  in the flash upgrade position.

- Make sure the power cable and the signal cable (i.e.,
  SCSI or IDE) are still connected.

- Power on your system and boot "clean" to a command-line prompt.

- Make sure that the CD-RW appears in program
  mode. For an internal Plextor SCSI CD-RW, you'll
  see that all four LEDs on the front panel of the drive
  are blinking.

- When the system comes up, execute the new
  firmware program (e.g., FIRM412.EXE), which you
  may receive or download from the manufacturer,
  and use the new firmware (*.BIN) file.

- When the .EXE application starts, specify the location of the .BIN file.

- Click the *Update* button to begin the flash process.

- When the *Update* button becomes highlighted
  again, the flash process is complete.

- Power off the system and reset the CD-RW drive's
  "flash" jumper to its original position.

- Power on the system normally.

Troubleshooting CD-RW Drives

Although UDF and CD-RW drives are now well-established industry standards, there are still a number of
compatibility problems and operating issues which
technicians may eventually need to address. This part
of the chapter examines a selection of UDF issues and
CD-RW problems.

NOTE: *For basic CD-related issues, refer to Chapter 6 for CD-ROM troubleshooting information.*

Troubleshooting tips

CD-RW drives are not terribly complicated devices to troubleshoot, but they can present some peculiar problems for technicians and do-it-yourselfers. Before you attempt to troubleshoot a CD-RW issue with your system, take a moment to work through the checklist below:

- Verify that your system meets the minimum requirements for your CD-RW drive. If it does not, the system may fail to run properly (if it runs at all).

- Make sure that the computer is plugged in and that each device has power. Connect any devices that are not receiving power.

- Turn off the computer's power, wait 15 to 20 s, then reboot the system. This can clear some software conflicts.

- Repeat the operation with a different (good-quality) CD.

- Make sure that you are using the right type of CD for the task at hand.

- Check the README file that came with the CD-RW drive for any last-minute compatibility or performance notes that might be present with your system. Also check the CD-RW drive maker's Web site for the latest drivers and firmware upgrades.

- If the problem(s) occur with power management, disable your PCs power management modes.

General symptoms

Symptom 8.1: The CD-ROM drive or CD audio player refuses to read CD-RW disks. This is a common problem that is related to the age of the CD-ROM drive itself.

Older CD-ROM drives (manufactured prior to mid- to late 1997) are probably not Multi-Read/UDF-compatible, and so cannot read UDF-formatted disks at all. CD audio players also cannot read UDF disks. If your CD-ROM is not Multi-Read-compliant, you'll need to either upgrade to a Multi-Read-compliant model or record your disks (especially audio disks) in a conventional ISO 9660 format using the CD-RW or CD-R drive.

CD-ROM drives manufactured after mid- to late 1997 will probably offer Multi-Read capability, but still may not be able to read a UDF-formatted disk without the assistance of a UDF reader utility. In most cases, you can obtain a free UDF reader from the company providing the DirectCD software (e.g., Adaptec).

Symptom 8.2: A backup disk will not run properly. DirectCD is not suitable for making backup copies of game or application disks where the application must run from the CD. This is because DirectCD uses a different method of writing data to disk (a.k.a. packet writing) from that used to write any disks produced with the ISO 9660 format. Packet-written (UDF) disks cannot be read by many standard CD-ROM drives or game machines. The only real way to work around this sort of problem is to use other recording software (such as Easy CD Creator for Windows 95/98 or Adaptec Toast for the Mac) to make a backup copy of the disk to CD-R.

> **NOTE:** *Keep in mind that some games and commercial application disks use forms of copy protection which recording software cannot work around or "break." Also remember that you cannot copy commercial software because of copyright restrictions.*

Symptom 8.3: You cannot see a second session reading a CD-RW disk from a CD-ROM drive. First make sure that you're trying to read the disk on a newer Multi-Read-compatible CD-ROM drive (along with a UDF reader utility, if necessary). Try ejecting the CD and reinsert-

ing it in the drive, then refreshing the screen by selecting *My Computer* from inside Windows Explorer and
pressing <F5>. Finally, try reading the disk from the
CD-RW drive (or from another suitable CD-ROM
drive). If another drive can read the disk, the problem
is likely to be with the suspect CD-ROM drive. If the
disk cannot be read in any drive, the problem is likely
to be with the disk itself (try re-recording the disk).

You cannot read a multisession disk created with
DirectCD under DOS or Windows 3.1x—there are no
drivers to support UDF on these operating systems. If
the disk was *not* recorded with DirectCD (i.e., if it was
recorded with ISO 9660) and you cannot read it under
DOS or Windows 3.1x, make sure that your copy of
MSCDEX (located in the AUTOEXEC.BAT file) is
version 2.23. You can download the latest version
of MSCDEX from the Microsoft Web site at
www.microsoft.com.

**Symptom 8.4: You receive an error such as *CD-RW is not
under DirectCD control.*** You'll typically notice this
problem under Windows 95/98 when you attempt to
erase, format, or copy data to a CD-RW. This type of
problem is most frequently encountered when using a
Ricoh CD-RW drive and Adaptec Direct CD software.
The problem can occur when the CD-RW drive uses
older firmware (i.e., a Ricoh CD-RW drive with version
2.03 firmware or earlier), or if you're using Adaptec
DirectCD 2.0 or earlier. Try updating the drive's
firmware and CD authoring software.

**Symptom 8.5: The CD-RW media cannot be used when the
UDF format is interrupted.** If power is lost while you are
formatting a CD-RW disk, the disk will become unusable in any application and will fail if another format
is attempted. To correct this problem, use the
DirectCD Full Erase feature to wipe the disk, then try
the format operation again.

Symptom 8.6: Files recorded in a second session do not appear. If the files that you recorded in a second session do not appear when you try to read the disk in a CD-ROM drive, try the following tips:

- Try ejecting and reinserting the CD.

- Refresh the file list—select the CD-RW icon in *My Computer* or Windows Explorer, and then press <F5>.

- Check the drive. CD-RW disks can be used only in CD-RW drives or newer Multi-Read CD-ROMs.

- Try reading the CD in other CD-ROM drives. If other drives are able to read the disk, the problem is probably with the original CD-ROM drive.

Symptom 8.7: Your computer lost power while writing a CD-RW disk, and now the disk is inaccessible. If you lose power while writing to your CD (i.e., while the CD-RW's drive light is on) or if you press <Ctrl> + <Alt> + <Del> while writing to a CD, you'll interrupt the disk. But you may be able to salvage your disk. Leave your CD-RW disk in the drive, but don't open the CD tray. Turn your computer off and cycle the power back on. Then restart the utility that you were using.

Once the DirectCD utility tries to access the CD-RW drive/disk again, the recovery operation will make it appear that the last session is there, although actually only a *part* of the CD's directory may be there. Your recordable CD is still usable if you can read the directory. Just repeat the entire copy operation to make sure that your files are copied to the rewritable CD.

Symptom 8.8: You receive a *buffer underrun* error when you're writing in CD-R mode. CD recordable devices require an uninterrupted data stream from the hard drive to write successfully to a CD. A *buffer underrun* message appears when the data stream is interrupted;

this can occur if another program interrupts the writing process (or if the CD-RW drive's write speed is set too high for the speed at which the hard drive is running). Here are some tips for dealing with buffer underrun errors (see Chapter 7 for more detailed information on buffer underruns):

- Use the CD authoring software's Test option to ensure that the write speed is appropriate for your computer.

- Try recording at a lower speed (such as 4×, 2×, or 1×).

- Do not use hard drive compression software—buffer underruns may be caused by this type of software.

- Exit any other background programs before writing data to the CD.

- Disable your computer's power-management feature.

- Run ScanDisk and Defrag on your hard drive— these programs improve access times to the hard drive.

- Do not run other programs that could interrupt the writing process. Log off any networks, and disable fax modem software, screen savers, or other programs (i.e., TSRs) that may automatically send messages to your computer while you are writing data to the CD.

- Make sure that the hard drive has enough temporary directory space—the space free should be at least twice the size of the largest file that you are recording.

- Do not copy empty folders (files with a zero byte size) or files that are in current use.

Symptom 8.9: There is no DirectCD window after a new CD-RW disk is inserted. Verify that the CD-RW drive's DirectCD software and utilities have been installed properly. If the DirectCD window doesn't appear on the screen after you insert a new disk, follow these steps:

- Wait a moment—it can take up to 15 s for the DirectCD window to appear.

- If the rewritable disk is already formatted, you can "force" the window by clicking *Start* on the taskbar, choosing *Programs*, and then selecting *Create a CD*.

- To prepare a CD with Easy CD Creator or DirectCD, the disk must be blank (you may have inserted a disk that is already formatted). Remove the disk and insert a good-quality blank one.

- The disk may have an unreadable format. DirectCD has a ScanDisk utility that *may* be able to recover data on the disk—simply double-click the CD icon on the Windows taskbar. Start ScanDisk and allow the process to run. A message will appear when ScanDisk is finished.

Symptom 8.10: The CD-RW drive doesn't show up in *My Computer or Windows Explorer.* In effect, the drive is disconnected from the rest of the system. There are many possible problems that can cause this kind of behavior.

- *Refresh Windows Explorer.* If the drive doesn't appear in Explorer, click *View* from the top menu, then click *Refresh*. You might also try rebooting the computer (from a cold start) so that the PnP BIOS can recognize the CD-RW drive.

- *Check the drive power.* Make sure that the drive's power connector is attached securely. Test the power by opening and closing the drive tray using the Eject button.

- *Check the signal cable.* Make sure that the drive's SCSI or IDE signal cable is oriented properly and secured between the drive and the drive controller.

- *Check the drive jumpers.* Chances are that you installed the CD-RW as a master IDE device. Verify that the drive jumpers are set properly, and confirm that any other drive on that channel has been rejumpered as a slave drive. If you're using a SCSI CD-RW drive, see that the SCSI ID for the CD-RW is unique and that the SCSI chain is properly connected and terminated.

- *Check the drivers.* Verify that the latest CD-RW drivers and utility software are installed.

- *Replace the drive.* If problems persist, try another CD-RW drive, or reconfigure the drive so that it is alone on its controller channel (i.e., disconnect the slave IDE drive).

Symptom 8.11: The device that is sharing the IDE signal cable with your CD-RW drive no longer responds. In most cases, that other drive was accidentally disconnected or unpowered when the new CD-RW drive was installed.

- *Check the cables.* Turn off and unplug your computer, then make sure that the power cables are securely attached to both drives. You can verify power to the drives by observing their power LEDs or ejecting their disk trays. Also verify that the SCSI or IDE signal cable is oriented properly and connected securely at both drives. When using a SCSI controller, verify that the SCSI chain is properly terminated.

- *Check the IDE jumpers.* The master/slave relationship of the drives may also be an issue. If you installed the CD-RW drive as a slave device, try reconfiguring the devices so that the CD-RW drive is the master. For example, when using a CD-RW drive with a Sony or Goldstar CD-ROM, try configuring the CD-RW drive as the master and setting the CD-ROM as the slave.

- *Replace the suspect device.* Try the suspect drive by itself (disconnect the CD-RW drive). If the suspect drive returns to normal, there may be a conflict between the CD-RW drive and the other device—you may need to separate the two devices to different drive controller channels. If the problem persists, try replacing the suspect device.

Symptom 8.12: You receive an error message when you double-click on the CD-RW icon. There are several possible issues which are typically caused by the drive's inability to read the disk. Here are a few things to check:

- There may be no CD in the CD-RW drive. Insert a good-quality CD and try reading again.

- After inserting a CD, you need to wait a moment to let the CD-RW drive read the disk information. When the LED on the front of the drive stops flashing and stays green, click on the CD-RW drive's icon again.

- The CD may be in the tray upside-down or a little off center. Try reinserting the CD—the disk label should be facing up.

- You may be trying to read from a blank recordable CD. Copy some information to the disk and try reading it again.

Symptom 8.13: You receive an *invalid media error* when trying to boot from the CD-RW. In many newer PC platforms, it is possible to boot from a CD-RW drive rather than a floppy or hard drive. An *invalid media* error from the CD-RW drive generally means that the disk doesn't contain the bootstrap files needed to begin the boot process and load your operating system. Chances are that the disk itself isn't bootable. Use a bootable CD (such as a system rescue disk or an OS disk such as Windows NT).

If you need to work around this problem, simply remove the disk from the CD-RW. During boot, the BIOS will skip the CD-RW and move directly to the next drive in the boot order (i.e., the hard drive). If you want to prevent your system from checking the CD-RW at boot time, go into the system's CMOS Setup and change the boot order so that the CD-RW is not included. For example, you might change the boot order to A:/C: or C:/A:.

Symptom 8.14: You cannot copy directly from a CD-ROM drive to the CD-RW drive.   This is a very common problem which is almost always caused by inadequate hardware capabilities. Here are the major issues to check:

- *Check the source drive.* The source drive (typically a CD-ROM) must support the extremely fast data transfers found in late-model ATAPI EIDE or SCSI-2 drives. If you're copying audio CDs, the source drive must be capable of digital audio extraction (or DAE). It may be necessary to upgrade the source drive or drive controller in order to support faster data transfers.

- *Check the drive arrangement.* If you're using an IDE-type source and a CD-RW drive, make sure that the source and destination drives are *not* on the same IDE controller channel. You may need to reconfigure your drives so that the source and destination drives are on separate controller channels.

- *Check the CD itself.* Some CDs have a copy-prevention feature (or other features) that does not allow a CD-to-CD copy. If that's the case, it may not be possible to copy that particular disk.

  NOTE: *Make sure that you copy only copy material which belongs to you, or that you have written permission to copy. Otherwise, you may be violating international copyright laws.*

Symptom 8.15: Audio from the CD-RW drive is poor or absent. Whenever you have trouble with CD audio from a CD-ROM, CD-R, or CD-RW drive, try listening to the audio using a set of headphones attached to the headset connector on the drive's front panel. If you cannot hear the audio (and volume adjustments don't help), then the drive is probably defective and should be replaced. If you hear the audio normally, the problem is likely to be in the PC's sound system:

- *Check the CD-audio cable.* Make sure that the audio cable is completely plugged into the sound card and into the CD-RW drive. If you already have a CD-ROM or other drive providing CD audio to the sound card, you cannot connect the CD-RW's audio cable unless you remove the current CD-audio cable or use a sound card with more than one CD-audio port.

- *Check the mixer applet.* Make sure that the CD-audio channel is not muted in the mixer software, and verify that the CD-audio level is turned up adequately. You may need to update the sound card's drivers or application software if the sound system is not currently supporting CD audio.

- *Check the sound file quality.* If the problem is with .WAV file playback from the disk, try listening to the .WAV files from your hard drive. If the problem persists, the problem is with poor .WAV recordings (not with the CD-RW drive or the sound card). If the .WAV files sound correct from the hard drive (but not from the CD), the problem may be poor recording to the CD—it may be necessary to re-record the disk using updated recording software.

Symptom 8.16: Video playback from a CD-RW drive is choppy. This is generally *not* a problem with the CD-RW drive, but rather with the system's ability to handle streaming audio/video data from a CD. Your best solution is typically to reduce the system's processing overhead in order to provide more processing power to the video playback software (e.g., Windows Media Player):

- Shut down any background applications, TSRs, or screen savers.

- Reduce the size of your video playback window.

- Download and install the latest versions of DirectX, your video drivers, and your multimedia player (e.g., Windows Media Player).

- Many CD-RW drives tend to be rather slow (i.e., 4×/2×), and this may interfere with data transfers on older systems. Try playing the video from another faster drive, such as your system's CD-ROM drive.

- If problems persist, you may need to make one or more hardware upgrades to improve your system's multimedia playback capability (such as a faster video card, more system RAM, and a faster CPU).

Symptom 8.17: Your CD-ROM drive cannot see a second (or subsequent) session recorded on disks from a CD-RW drive. There are several possible difficulties that can occur when reading multisession disks created on a CD-RW drive with DirectCD software. Try the following:

- *Reinsert the disk*. Start by ejecting and reinserting the disk. This allows the drive to redetect the disk and try reading its sessions once again. You should also try refreshing the display—select the *My Computer* icon in Windows Explorer, then press <F5>.

- *Check the drive*. CD-RW disks can be used only in CD-RW drives or in newer MultiRead CD-ROMs (compatible with the UDF file system). If you're trying to read the disk on an older CD-ROM which is

not MultiRead-compliant, you may need to upgrade
the CD-ROM to a newer version.

- *Check your operating system.* Multisession CDs created with DirectCD cannot be read in DOS or
  Windows 3.x. Make sure that you're in Windows 95,
  Windows 98, or some other UDF-compliant operating system.

**Symptom 8.18: You cannot get an application to find a CD
in the CD-RW drive.** This is almost always a problem
with the application itself rather than with the drive.
Many programs (e.g., CD-based games) look only for
the first logical drive letter assigned to a CD-ROM
drive or CD-RW drive. For example, if a CD-ROM drive
is assigned to D:\ and the CD-RW drive is assigned to
E:\, the program will probably look for the CD *only* in
drive D:\ and will not see the CD in drive E:\. If you
want to use the CD-RW drive with such programs,
reassign the drive letters to make the CD-RW drive
precede the CD-ROM drive:

- For Windows 95/98, click *Start*, highlight *Settings*,
  then click *Control Panel*. Double-click the *System*
  icon. Select the *Device Manager* tab and double-click
  the *CD-ROM* entry.

- Double-click on the CD-ROM drive, then click the
  Settings tab. Under *Reserved* drive letters, select the
  drive letter *after* the existing letter (for both *start*
  and *end* drive letter) and click *OK*.

- Now double-click on the CD-RW drive entry, and
  click the *Settings* tab. Under *Reserved* drive letters,
  select the drive letter *before* the current one and
  click *OK*.

Web Contacts

Hewlett-Packard: *http://www.hp.com/*

Philips: *http://www.pps.philips.com*

Plextor: *http://www.plextor.com*

Smart and Friendly: *http://www.smartandfriend-ly.com*

DVD-ROM Drives

The *compact disk* opened up a whole new world of possibilities for the PC. These simple, mass-produced plastic disks could hold up to an hour of stereo music, or as much as 650 MB of computer programs and data. Software makers quickly found the CD-ROM to be an outstanding medium for all types of multimedia applications, large databases, and interactive games. But today, the CD-ROM is showing its age, and a single CD no longer provides enough storage for the increasing demands of data-intensive applications. A new generation of high-density optical storage called *DVD* is now widely available for the desktop PC (Figure 9.1). The acronym DVD stands for digital versatile disk (because it can hold programs and data as well as video and sound). But whatever you call it, DVD technology promises to supply up to 17 GB of removable storage on your desktop PC. This chapter covers the background and workings of a DVD package, shows you the steps for DVD installation, and offers a series of basic troubleshooting solutions.

The Potential of DVD

The argument for DVD is a compelling one because having gigabytes of removable storage to work with

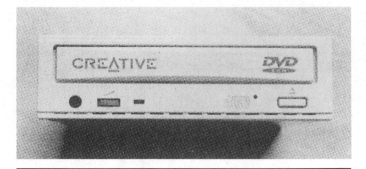

Figure 9.1 A DVD-ROM drive.

opens up some exciting possibilities for entertainment and software development. You'll typically see two designations for DVD: DVD-Video and DVD-ROM. DVD-Video is the approach used to store movies on the disk (analogous to the way audio is placed on CDs). Eventually, DVD-Video is expected to replace video-tape players (and older laser disk players) in home entertainment. DVD-ROM refers to computer-based software, data, and multimedia recorded on the disk. Where audio CDs can be played on CD-ROM drives, DVD-Video disks will be playable on DVD-ROM drives in your PC. Understandably, there are a lot of forces trying to make the most of what DVD has to offer:

- Hollywood has been a major factor in the development of DVD-Video, placing full-length movies, sound tracks, and even multilingual subtitling on a single disk. Since all DVD disks are read by laser, there is no physical contact between the disk and its player. The result is that the disk won't wear out like VHS videotapes, so the image will not degrade with each playback.

- Business presentations, education, and professional training will also benefit from DVD technology. Animations, charts, and interactive applets can be integrated with real-time video. This offers a truly immersive training experience that CD-ROM technology has only scratched the surface of.

- Applications for archiving are limitless. Mapping programs, telephone directories, encyclopedias— any software that now spans several CDs can be concentrated on one DVD disk *and* be dramatically expanded to offer unprecedented detail.

- Any data-intensive computer software (especially three-dimensional and other interactive games) will get a real boost from the sheer storage volume offered by DVD-ROM.

Specifications and Standards

The next step in exploring DVD is to understand the various specifications "on the box" and become familiar with the specifications that make DVD work and what a DVD will support. You don't need a lot of technical details, but you should recognize the most important points that you'll probably run across while reading documentation.

Access time

The *access time* is the time required for the drive to locate the required information on a disk. Optical drives like CD and DVD drives are relatively slow; they can demand up to several hundred milliseconds to access information. For a DVD drive like the Creative Labs (Matsushita) DVD drive, DVD access time is 470 ms (almost half a second), whereas access time for an ordinary CD is 180 ms. The reason DVDs require so much more time is the greater density of data. However, not all drives are this slow. The Toshiba DVD drive bundled with Diamond Multimedia's Maximum DVD Kit quotes a DVD access time of only 200 ms (130 ms for CDs).

Data transfer rates

Once data have been accessed, they must be trans-ferred off the disk to the system. The *data transfer rate* measures how fast data can be read from the disk. There are two typical means of measuring the data rate: the speed at which data are read into the drive's on-board buffer (the *sequential* data transfer rate), and the speed at which data are transferred across the interface to the drive controller (the *buffered* data transfer rate). The Creative Labs (Matsushita) DVD drive offers a *sequential* data transfer rate of 1.35 MB/s, and 900 KB/s for an ordinary CD (about equal to a 6× CD-ROM drive). By comparison, the drive can support *buffered* data transfer rates of 8.3 MB/s (DMA Mode 2), 13.3 MB/s (DMA Mode 1), or 11.1 MB/s (PIO Mode 3). As a result, the DVD-ROM drive is compati-ble with most EIDE (and later) drive controllers in the marketplace today.

Books and standards

CD technology is defined by a set of accepted stan-dards—we have come to know these as "books." Since each CD book was bound in a different color jacket, each standard is referred to by color. For example, the standard that defines CD audio is called Red Book. Similarly, DVD technology is defined by a set of books. There are five books (labeled A through E) which relate to different DVD technology applications:

- *Book A* defines the format and approach used for DVD-ROM (programs and data).

- *Book B* defines DVD-Video.

- *Book C* defines DVD-Audio (this specification is still under development).

- *Book D* defines DVD-WO (write once).

- *Book E* defines DVD-E (erasable or rewritable) and DVD-RAM.

Data formats

All DVD disks must use a data format that describes how data are laid out. Data formats are critical because they outline data structures on the disk such as volumes, files, blocks, sectors, CRCs, paths, records, file allocation tables, partitions, character sets, and time stamps, as well as methods for reading and writing. The format used by books A, B, and C is called the *UDF bridge*. The UDF bridge is a combination of the UDF [Universal Disk Format, created by OSTA (Optical Storage Technology Association)] and the established ISO-9660 format used for CDs. You may see the UDF referred to as standard *ISO/IEC 13346*. The UDF is a very flexible format that has been adapted to DVD and made backward-compatible with existing ISO-9660 operating system software (such as Windows 95). Actual utilization of this format on DVD disks will depend in large part on what Microsoft dictates as the future operating system standard. Standalone DVD movie players are supposed to use UDF. With the release of Windows 98, the UDF bridge has been abandoned in favor of full UDF support.

> **NOTE:** *Refer to Chapter 8 to learn more about UDF and its importance in CD-RW drives.*

Audio and video standards

Even with the huge data capacities offered by DVD, an entire movie's worth of real-time audio and video would never fit on a DVD without some form of *compression*. Both audio and video must be extensively compressed, and MPEG (Motion Pictures Experts Group) compression has been the scheme of choice. *Video compression* uses fixed data rate MPEG-1 (ISO/IEC 1117-2) at 30 frames per second with resolutions of 352×240, or variable data rate MPEG-2 (ISO/IEC 13818-2) at 60 frames per second with resolutions of 720×480. *Audio compression* uses MPEG-1 (ISO/IEC 1117-3) stereo, MPEG-2 (ISO/IEC 13818-3)

5.1 and 7.1 surround sound, or Dolby AC-3 5.1 surround and stereo. MPEG-2 and AC-3 audio compression allow 48,000 samples per second, whereas MPEG-1 allows only 44,100 samples per second. MPEG-2 compression is typically regarded as the preferred scheme for DVD.

> **NOTE:** *The audio designations 5.1 and 7.1 indicate five (or seven) signal channels plus one subwoofer channel.*

Region code control

Motion picture studios want to control the home release of movies in different countries because theater releases are not simultaneous. Therefore, they have required that the DVD standard include codes which can be used to prevent playback of certain disks in certain geographical regions. Each player is given a code for the region in which it's sold. The player will refuse to play disks which are not allowed in that region. This means that disks bought in one country may not play on players bought in another country. Table 9.1 lists the code numbers and the regions each number covers. Keep in mind that region codes are entirely optional, and disks without codes will play on any player in any country.

TABLE 9.1   DVD Region Codes

Code	Region
1	Canada, United States, and U.S. territories
2	Japan, Europe, South Africa, Middle East (including Egypt)
3	Southeast Asia, East Asia (including Hong Kong)
4	Australia, New Zealand, Pacific Islands, Central America, South America, Caribbean
5	Former Soviet Union, Indian subcontinent, Africa (also North Korea, Mongolia)
6	China

CD compatibility

One of the most important aspects of any technology is backward compatibility—how well the new device supports your existing media. This is also true for DVD drives. Since DVD technology was designed as an improvement over existing CD-ROMs, it was designed to *replace* the CD-ROM rather than coexist with it. Ideally, you would remove your CD-ROM and replace it with a DVD-ROM drive. This means that the DVD must be compatible with as many existing CD-ROM standards as possible. A typical DVD-ROM drive will support CD audio, CD-ROM, CD-I, CD Extra, CD-ROM/XA, and Video CD formats. Multisession formats such as Photo CD are not yet supported on all DVD drives.

> **NOTE:** *One format that may* not *be supported by older DVD drives is the CD-R (recordable CD) format. The laser used in older DVD drives could not read the CD-R and, in some cases, could even damage the CD-R disk. However, developments in CD-R disks and DVD drive design have largely overcome this problem.*

Caring for a DVD disk

Like a CD, a DVD disk is a remarkably reliable long-term storage medium (conservative estimates place the life expectancy of a DVD disk at about 100 years). However, the longevity of an optical disk is affected by its storage and handling, and a faulty CD can cause file and data errors that you might otherwise interpret as a defect in the drive itself. You can get the most life out of your optical disk by obeying the following rules:

- *Don't bend the disk*. Polycarbonate is a forgiving material, but you risk cracking or snapping (and thus ruining) the disk.

- *Don't heat the disk*. Remember, the disk is plastic. Leaving it by a heater or on the dashboard of your car will cause melting.

- *Don't scratch the disk*. Laser wavelengths have a tendency to look past minor scratches, but a major scratch can cause problems. Be especially careful of circular scratches (those that follow the spiral track). A circular scratch can easily wipe out entire segments of data which would be unrecoverable.

- *Don't use chemicals on the disk*. Chemicals containing solvents such as ammonia, benzene, acetone, carbon tetrachloride, or chlorinated cleaning solvents can easily damage the plastic surface.

A buildup of excessive dust or fingerprints can interfere with the laser beam enough to cause disk errors. When this happens, the disk can be cleaned easily using a dry, soft, lint-free cloth. Hold the disk by its edges and wipe radially (from hub to edge). *Do not wipe in a circular motion*. For stubborn stains, moisten the cloth with a bit of fresh isopropyl alcohol (*do not use water*). Place the cleaned disk in a caddy or jewel case for transport and storage.

> **NOTE:** *Contrary to popular belief, DVD disks are* not *more sensitive to scratches or dust than ordinary CDs..*

The MPEG-2 Decoder Board

Although the DVD drive requires a SCSI or EIDE drive controller for normal program data, DVD video and audio do *not* use this data path. There are two reasons for this. First, the data required to reproduce real-time video and audio would bog down all but the fastest PCs. Second, video and audio data are highly compressed using MPEG standards, so even if the PC bus wasn't bogged down by the compressed data, the decompression process would load down the system with processing overhead. In order to play DVD audio and video (DVD-Video) as smoothly as possible, DVD-ROM drives require a standalone, hardware-based PCI bus MPEG-2 decoder board which works *inde-*

pendently of the drive controller system, video system, and sound system.

A look at MPEG-2

When the original video source is recorded for DVD, MPEG-2 analyzes the video picture for redundant data. In fact, over 95 percent of the digital data that represent a video signal are "redundant" and can be compressed without visibly harming the picture quality (also referred to as *lossless compression*). By eliminating redundant data, MPEG-2 achieves excellent video quality at far lower bit rates.

MPEG-2 encoding for DVD is a two-stage process. The original signal is first evaluated for complexity, then higher bit rates are assigned to complex pictures, and lower bit rates are assigned to simple pictures. This allows for an adaptive variable-bit-rate process. The DVD-Video format uses compressed bit rates with a range of up to 10 MB/s. Although the "average" bit rate for digital video is often quoted as 3.5 MB/s, the actual figure will vary according to movie length, picture complexity, and the number of audio channels required. With MPEG-2 compression, a single-layer, single-sided DVD disk has enough capacity to hold 2 h and 13 min of video and audio on a 12-cm disk. At the nominal average data rate of 3.5 MB/s, this still leaves enough capacity for discrete 5.1-channel digital sound in three languages, plus subtitles in four additional languages.

Notes on Dolby AC-3

Dolby AC-3 (also called Dolby Surround AC-3 or Dolby Digital) is another method of encoding DVD audio (besides MPEG-2 audio). With five channels and a common subwoofer channel (known as 5.1), you get the effects of three-dimensional surround sound with right, left, center, left ear, right ear, and common subwoofer speakers. AC-3 runs at 384 KB/s. In actual practice, DVD products sold in North America and Japan will include Dolby AC-3 sound on the accompanying MPEG-2 board, while DVD products sold in Europe will probably use the MPEG-2 audio standard.

Decoder board connections

There are five major connections on the MPEG-2 decoder board, as shown in Figure 9.2: an Analog Input jack, an Analog Output jack, a Digital Output jack, a Monitor connector, and a Video Input connector. The *Analog Input* is rarely (if ever) used in normal operations, but it may be handy for mixing in an auxiliary audio signal to the decoder board. The *Analog Output*

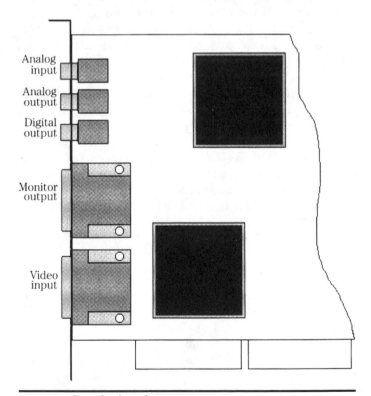

Figure 9.2 Decoder board connections.

signal provides the master audio signal, which is fed to the *Line Input* of your existing sound board. The advantage of using a Line Input is that you don't need a volume control on the decoder board. Instead, you can set the Line Input volume through your sound board's mixer applet. When you play a DVD video, any audio will continue to play through your sound board and speakers. The *Digital Output* is intended to drive an external Dolby Digital device, so you will probably not be using the *Digital Output* in most basic PC setups.

The MPEG-2 decoder board will now drive your VGA/SVGA monitor through the *Monitor* connector. This is important because the decoded video stream is converted to RGB information and fed to the monitor directly; this avoids having to pass the video data across the PCI bus to your video card. The normal output from your video card is looped from your video board to the decoder card, so while the decoder board is idle, your normal video signal is just passed through the MPEG-2 board to the monitor.

Software DVD decoders

While a hardware decoder card is highly recommended, it is not always required—decoding can be accomplished using software applications. The advantage of software decoding is simplicity. DVD upgrades are easier, since you don't need the hardware decoder card. However, considering the amount of processing power required for real-time MPEG-2 decoding, you will need a very fast Pentium II/III platform in order to sustain an adequate DVD-Video frame rate. Slower PCs (or those with other processing overhead, such as running background applications) may not be able to support software-only decoding. This may manifest itself as choppy video, lost frames, and/or distorted audio. Make certain that your PC meets the minimum system requirements (and preferably the recommended system configuration) for DVD decoding software.

If your PC does *not* meet the minimum requirements for decoding software, you may wish to update your video card to a model that offers motion compensation, or other types of DVD playback assistance. For example, various ATI graphics chips (including the Rage 128, Rage PRO, and Rage LT PRO) contain DVD-processing hardware which can assist in decoding DVD without the need for a full-blown hardware decoder card. Still, if you need to consider a video card upgrade, it is often more efficient to leave the video device in place and add a full hardware decoder card instead.

DVD-ROM Installation and Replacement

DVD-ROM drives are generally easy devices to install or replace. Most are installed as master devices located on the secondary IDE/EIDE/Ultra-DMA drive controller channel, though a few will coexist as slave devices alongside a hard drive or some other drive device. The most important issue to remember is that the BIOS will not support the DVD-ROM directly (even if the BIOS identifies the DVD-ROM at boot time)—you'll need real-mode drivers for the DVD-ROM under DOS or protected-mode drivers for the DVD-ROM under Windows. Keep in mind that real-mode (DOS) drivers for DVD-ROM drives are extremely rare, so if you need them, be sure that your particular DVD offers real-mode drivers before making a purchase. This part of the chapter covers the guidelines needed to install a basic internal ATAPI IDE-type DVD-ROM.

> **NOTE:** *Before beginning the installation, be sure to set the Display mode to 640 × 480 × 16 (60-Hz refresh rate) or another default video mode suggested by the DVD maker's installation instructions. Once the DVD drive is installed and running, you can readjust the video mode to an appropriate resolution, color depth, and vertical refresh rate.*

Select jumper configurations

An IDE-type DVD-ROM drive may be installed as a master or a slave device on any hard drive controller channel. These master/slave settings are handled through one or two jumpers located on the rear of the drive (right next to the 40-pin signal cable connector). One of your first decisions when planning an installation should be to decide the drive's configuration:

- If you're installing the DVD-ROM as the first drive on the secondary drive controller channel, it must be jumpered as the master device.

- If you're installing the DVD-ROM drive alongside another drive (on either the primary or the secondary drive controller channel), the DVD-ROM must be jumpered as the slave device.

  NOTE: *Refer to the documentation that accompanies your particular DVD-ROM drive to determine the exact master/slave jumper settings. If you do not have the drive documentation handy, check the drive manufacturer's Web site for online information.*

Attach cables and mount the drive

- Turn off and unplug the PC, then remove the outer cover to expose the computer's drive bays.

- Attach one end of the 40-pin drive interface cable to the drive controller connector on your motherboard (or drive controller card). Remember to align pin 1 on the cable (the side of the cable with the blue or red stripe) with pin 1 on the drive controller connector.

- Locate an available drive bay for the DVD-ROM drive. Remove the plastic housing covering the drive bay, then slide the drive inside. Locate the four screw holes needed to mount the drive. In some cases, you may need to attach mounting rails to the drive so that the drive will be wide enough to fit in the drive bay. In virtually all cases, you should mount a tray-driven DVD-ROM drive horizontally (although caddy-loaded DVD-ROM drives may be mounted vertically).

■ Attach the 40-pin signal cable and the 4-pin power connector to the new drive, then bolt the drive securely into place. Do not overtighten the screws, since this may damage the drive. If you do not have an available 4-pin power connector, you may use an appropriate Y splitter if necessary to split power from another drive (preferably the floppy drive).

■ Attach the small 4-pin digital audio (a.k.a. CD-audio) signal cable from the DVD-ROM to the CD-audio input connector on your sound card. This connection allows you to play music CDs directly from the DVD-ROM through your sound card. Verify that the CD-audio cable is compatible with your sound card (if it is not, you may need a specialized cable from the sound card's manufacturer).

NOTE: *If you already have a CD-ROM drive in the system that is providing CD audio to the sound card, you may choose to use the DVD-ROM instead or to leave the CD-ROM's audio cable alone. If your sound card has a second CD audio connector, you may be able to wire the DVD-ROM's audio to your sound card also.*

Installing the decoder card

Locate an open PCI card slot, and install the PnP MPEG-2 decoder card into the slot. In most cases, you simply need to disconnect the monitor from the video output, attach the monitor to the decoder card's Monitor Output port, then use a short passthrough cable to connect the video output to the decoder card's Video Input connector. This ties the decoder card in with the video system.

NOTE: *If you will be using a software decoder, you may not need to install a hardware decoder card, and this part of the installation may be omitted.*

Configuring the CMOS Setup

Although the DVD-ROM does require driver support, recent motherboard designs can identify the ATAPI IDE DVD-ROM drive in BIOS, so you should configure your computer's BIOS to accept the drive if possible (through the CMOS Setup).

- Turn the computer on. As your computer starts up, watch for a message that describes how to run the CMOS Setup (e.g., *Press F1 for Setup*). Press the appropriate key to start the CMOS Setup program.

- Select the *hard drive settings* menu, and choose the drive location occupied by the DVD-ROM drive (i.e., *primary slave*, *secondary slave*, or *secondary master*, depending on how you've physically jumpered and installed the drive).

- Select *automatic drive detection* if available—this option will automatically identify the new drive. If your BIOS does *not* provide automatic drive detection, select *none* or *not installed* for the DVD-ROM, and rely on drivers *only*.

- Save the settings and exit the CMOS Setup program. Your computer will automatically reboot.

Reassemble the computer

Double-check all of your signal and power cables to verify that they are secure, then tuck the cables gently into the computer's chassis. Check that there are no loose tools, screws, or cables inside the chassis. Now reattach the computer's outer housing(s).

Install the software

In order to complete your DVD-ROM installation, you'll need to install the software drivers that accompanied the drive on diskette or CD. Windows 95 OSR2 and Windows 98 systems will generally detect the presence of the new DVD-ROM (and hardware decoder, if appropriate) and prompt you for the protected-mode drivers automatically. After you install the drivers and reboot the system, the DVD-ROM should be ready for use. Before you can play DVD movie disks, you'll also need to install the DVD Player software (e.g., Zoran SoftDVD) and other utilities from the drive's installation disk.

> **NOTE:** *Many DVD-ROM drives will* not *support real-mode (DOS) drivers, so they will work only under Windows 95/98.*

Upgrading DVD-ROM firmware

You may be able to update the firmware used in your DVD-ROM drive. This may be necessary in order to correct bugs or fix drive compatibility problems with the system. The steps below offer a guideline that you can refer to when upgrading DVD-ROM firmware.

> **NOTE:** *You should always refer to the Web page or README file that accompanies the new firmware download. Be sure to download the correct firmware version for your drive—installing the wrong firmware can permanently disable the drive.*

- Power off your system completely.

- Locate the DVD-ROM drive and place its "flash" jumper in the flash upgrade position. If there is no "flash" jumper, it may not be possible to upgrade the drive's firmware.

- Make sure the power cable and the signal cable (i.e., SCSI or IDE) are still connected.

- Power on your system and boot "clean" to a command-line prompt.

- Make sure that the DVD-ROM appears in program mode. You'll need to refer to the documentation for your particular drive in order to identify the correct program mode.

- When the system comes up, execute the new firmware program (e.g., FIRM412.EXE), which you may receive or download from the manufacturer, and use the new firmware (*.BIN) file.

- When the .EXE application starts, specify the location of the .BIN file.

- Click the *Update* button to begin the flash process.

- When the *Update* button becomes highlighted again, the flash process is complete.

- Power off the system and reset the DVD-ROM drive's "flash" jumper to its original position.

- Power on the system normally.

Troubleshooting DVD-ROM Drives

Even though a DVD-ROM package should install with an absolute minimum of muss and fuss, and run with all the reliability of a CD-ROM, there are times when things just don't go according to plan. Both software and hardware problems can interrupt your DVD-ROM system. The following symptoms cover some of the most common troubleshooting issues.

> **NOTE:** *DVD drives use lasers in normal operation. Although these are very-low-power semiconductor lasers and the chances of injury to your eyes is extremely slight, you should still take the proper precautions and not operate a DVD drive with the protective covers open. Turn off and unplug the PC before opening a DVD drive.*

Initial setup and tips

When installing or correcting problems on a DVD-ROM system, it may help to set the DVD system configuration to a default state using the criteria outlined below:

Video configuration. Regardless of the amount of video RAM provided by your video adapter, try setting the display to 640 × 480 using 16-bit color (the "high-color" mode). You might also try setting the monitor type to "standard VGA."

DirectX installation. If you're not yet using Windows 95 OSR2 (4.00.950 B) and you do not have any Windows 95 games installed, chances are that you don't have DirectX installed (or that you're using a very old version). Though DirectX versions 2.0 and higher should support DVD, using the latest version may increase your system's video performance (since it also included newer DirectDraw drivers for your video card). Check for the latest version of DirectX (i.e., DirectX6.1) at: *http://www.microsoft.com/directx.*

DVD drivers. Drivers are being updated regularly to provide better hardware compatibility, so you should check for the latest Cinemaster drivers and the latest release of DVD Player from Quadrant International at *http://www.qi.com/.*

Video drivers. Many video drivers are also updated regularly for better video performance and compatibility. Check the Web page for your video card vendor for updated video card drivers. This may be especially important if you're using a video card with motion compensation or other DVD video decoding features instead of a full hardware decoder card.

IDE controller compatibility. There is also a lingering issue with the IDE controllers on some motherboards (depending on which version of Windows 95 you're using). If you have trouble with your IDE controllers, check the Intel Developer's Page for more details and fixes at *http://developer.intel.com/design/motherbd/IDEINFUP.HTM.* Late versions of Windows 95 and Windows 98 should have no problems with IDE controller identification and setup.

DVD software and Windows 98

Although Windows 98 is supposed to offer full support for DVD systems, you may find that DVD systems refuse to install properly (or cease working) once Windows 98 is installed. If this is the case, check the

DVD manufacturer's Web site for updated DVD-ROM drivers and software applets.

Microsoft supports DVD disks within Windows 98 using SCSI and ATAPI-compliant DVD-ROM drives. Playing movies (DVD-video) is supported only with the following decoder adapters:

- Toshiba DVD decoder adapters used with Toshiba Infinia DVD systems with either S3 or ATI display adapters.

- Quadrant Cinemaster C rev. 1.2 decoder adapters included with Dell XPS series computers. Note that updated Quadrant Cinemaster decoder drivers are available on the Windows 98 CD-ROM in the *drivers\dvd\quadrant* folder.

The Windows 98 DVD player is designed to work with the Windows 98 decoder drivers, so the option to add or remove the DVD player is not available until a supported DVD decoder adapter is installed and detected.

Once a DVD decoder adapter is detected and the Windows 98 drivers are installed, a shortcut for the DVD player is added to the *Entertainment* menu. The option to add or remove the DVD player becomes available under *Multimedia* on the *Windows Setup* tab (in the *Add/Remove Programs* tool). After being installed, the DVD player software can be removed and reinstalled without your having to reinstall the decoder drivers.

> **NOTE:** *If an appropriate DVD decoder card is used, but it has third-party drivers installed, Windows 98 will not install the Windows 98 drivers or DVD player software until the third-party drivers are removed using* Device Manager.

> **NOTE:** *Other DVD playback software and decoder cards (including other Cinemaster DVD decoder adapters like the Cinemaster S) are not supported, and require the drivers and software provided by the manufacturer in order to function properly.*

**Installation and startup
symptoms**

Symptom 9.1: The DVD drivers refuse to install. This is
almost always because Windows 95/98 is having a problem with one or more .INF files on your driver installation disk(s). Check with your DVD vendor to confirm
whether you need to delete one or more entries in your
OEMxx.INF file(s) (where xx is any suffix). If you're
using an MKE DVD kit, you may also need to delete
one or more entries from a MKEDVD.INF file. The .INF
files are typically contained in the C:\WINDOWS\INF\
OTHER directory. Once you've corrected the appropriate
.INF file(s), you can reinstall the DVD drivers:

- Click *Start*, select *Settings*, then click on *Control
  Panel*. Double-click the *System* icon.

- Click on the *Device Manager* tab, then select *Sound,
  Video, and Game Controllers* or *CD-ROM*.

- Select the DVD driver(s), then click *Remove*.

- Exit the *Device Manager* and reinstall the drivers.

Symptom 9.2: The DVD drive isn't detected. There are
several possible reasons why the DVD drive would not
be detected. Check the power connector attached to the
drive, and make sure that the drive isn't being powered from a Y splitter power cable. Check the signal
cable next. Both SCSI and EIDE signal cables must be
attached securely to the drive. SCSI interfaces are
complicated a bit by termination, so verify that any
SCSI bus is properly terminated. Make sure that the
drive is jumpered properly for its SCSI IDE or EIDE
master or slave relationship. Finally, make sure that
the DVD drivers are installed and running. Check the
drivers under the *Sound, Video, and Game Controllers*
(or *CD-ROM*) entry of your *Device Manager*.

**Symptom 9.3: You see an error message that the drive is
not fully compatible with the software.** You may also see

this as a message that no DVD drive is found. This frequently occurs when installing a DVD-ROM drive in conjunction with ZIP, Jaz, tape, or CD-ROM drives. The DVD drive will need to be the next available drive letter *after* any IDE or SCSI hard drives. Alphabetically, there should be no other drives (i.e., Zip, Jaz, tape, or CD-ROM drives) with drive letters *before* that of the DVD drive.

To change the drive letter assignment in your system, power down and disconnect all the affected drives *except* the DVD drive, then boot to Windows 95/98 safe mode and remove the drives (including the DVD drive) from *Device Manager*. Restart in normal mode; the DVD drive will be reassigned the lowest available drive letter. Next, power down again and reconnect the other drives. Restart the system, and they will automatically be redetected and assigned drive letters *higher* than the DVD drive.

You should also check the version of three Windows 95 files: WINASPI.DLL, WNASPI32.DLL and APIX.VXD. Click on *Start*, *Find*, and select *Files or Folders*. This will open the *Find: All Files* dialog box. Type one of the filenames in the *Named* box (make sure the *Look In* box is referring to the C:\ drive) and press <Enter>. If no files are found, go to Windows Explorer, click on *View*, and select *Options*. Click on the radio button next to *Show All Files*, and finally click on the *Apply* button. Now try to find the files again. Once you've located these files, you should see that each of the files has a timestamp of either 9:50 (for Windows 95 version 0 or A) or 11:11 (for Windows 95 version B).

> **NOTE:** *To check your version of Windows 95, open the* System *applet from* Control Panel. *Below* Microsoft Windows 95, *you should see 4.00.950 followed by one of the above characters, denoting your version.*

If the timestamps are not correct, you'll need to restore the original versions of WINASPI.DLL, WNASPI32.

DLL, and APIX.VXD. First, rename the current versions of the files using an extension of .OEM. For example, APIX.VXD should be renamed APIX.OEM. Next, extract the original files directly from the Windows 95 CD (or copy the files from another system where the files have the proper timestamp). You may also wish to update the system to Windows 98.

Symptom 9.4: You see an error indicating that the DVD device driver could not be loaded. You'll need to check the DVD driver installation or manually install the drivers. To do this, you will need to open the *Control Panel*, open *System Properties*, then select the *Device Manager* tab. In the category of *Other Devices*, select *PCI Multimedia Device* and click on *Properties*. In the *Properties* dialog box, select the *Driver* tab and click on *Change Driver*. Browse to the *DVD Drivers Installation Disk* and click on *OK*. Click on *OK* again, select the proper MPEG board (such as *MKE DVD-AV Decoder Board*), and click on *OK* again. Exit the *PCI Multimedia Device Properties* by clicking on *OK* again, and Windows 95/98 will copy over the proper drivers. You will then need to restart the machine.

Symptom 9.5: You see an error such as *Cannot open <file-name>, video and audio glitches may occur*. This type of error almost always indicates a fault with the driver installation, and you should rerun the setup utility which accompanied your DVD drive product.

Symptom 9.6: There is no audio when you are playing an audio CD. This is a common problem, especially during new DVD-ROM drive installations. Chances are that you did not connect the 4-wire CD-audio cable between the DVD-ROM drive and the sound board. If you did connect the cable, it may be reversed (or defective). Of course, if you're still using your original CD-ROM drive, and the CD-ROM is connected to the sound board, there will be no CD audio from the DVD-ROM drive—there is no way to parallel or gang the sound cable. If the DVD-ROM audio cable is connected to the sound board, make sure that the CD-audio input of your sound board's mixer applet is turned up to a reasonable level.

If you wish to continue using an existing CD-ROM drive as the CD audio drive, you can still use audio from the DVD-ROM drive by using a patch cable to feed the headphone output signal from the drive to the sound card's Line In jack. Then adjust the sound card's Line In mixer so that you can hear audio from the DVD-ROM headphone.

Symptom 9.7: The system will not restart in normal mode after DVD-ROM drive installation. This problem sometimes occurs when you install the DVD on a system with the USB Supplement for Windows 95 (OSR2). You may need to uninstall the USR Supplement.

- *Remove the USB Supplement*. Boot into Windows 95 safe mode and open the *Add/Remove Programs* applet from *Control Panel*. If the *Universal Serial Bus Supplement* is listed, highlight it and click on the *Add/Remove* button. This will uninstall the supplement, and you will be prompted to restart the system.

- *Check the decoder IRQ*. The DVD system's MPEG-2 decoder card should be assigned a unique interrupt request (IRQ). Open the *System* applet from *Control Panel*, click on the *Device Manager* tab, and double-click on *Computer*. Here you'll see a list of IRQs and the name of the device using each IRQ. If the decoder card is not listed (or if its IRQ is being shared with any device other than the IRQ holder for PCI steering), assign a unique IRQ to the card. This can usually be accomplished through the BIOS of your computer, or possibly by moving the decoder card to another PCI slot.

- *Check the decoder memory range*. You may need to change the memory range used by the MPEG-2 decoder card. Open the *System* applet from *Control*

Panel, click on the *Device Manager* tab, then double-click on *Sound, video and game controllers*. Finally, double-click on the MPEG-2 decoder card. Click on the *Resources* tab and remove the check mark next to *Use automatic settings*. Finally, double-click on the *Memory Range* entry and enter `D1000000-D10fffff`. Click on *OK* and restart the PC for your changes to take effect.

Symptom 9.8: You experience error messages or system lockups during DVD software installation. Movies play, but white lines appear randomly on the screen. In virtually all cases, the problem is being caused by an IRQ or memory range conflict.

- *Check the decoder IRQ.* Open the *System* applet from *Control Panel*, click on the *Device Manager* tab, and double-click on *Computer*. Here you'll see a list of IRQs and the name of the device using each IRQ. If the decoder card is not listed (or if its IRQ is being shared with any device other than the IRQ holder for PCI steering), assign a unique IRQ to the card. This can usually be accomplished through the BIOS of your computer, or possibly by moving the decoder card to another PCI slot.

- *Check the decoder memory range.* You may need to change the memory range used by the MPEG-2 decoder card. Open the *System* applet from *Control Panel*, click on the *Device Manager* tab, then double-click on *Sound, video and game controllers*. Finally, double-click on the MPEG-2 decoder card. Click on the *Resources* tab and remove the check mark next to *Use automatic settings*. Finally, double-click on the *Memory Range* entry and enter `D1000000-D10fffff`. Click on *OK* and restart for the changes to take effect.

Symptom 9.9: Your DVD-ROM will not autoconfigure using the automatic configuration utility provided with the drive.

In many cases, this is a problem caused by an unusually high video refresh rate. DVD systems seem to operate best at video refresh rates of 60 Hz or so. Try lowering your video refresh rate to 75 Hz or lower through the video card's *Properties* dialog or *Display* control settings.

Symptom 9.10: You can play DVD-based games (e.g., Wing Commander 4 or Silent Steel), but the system hangs up when you insert a DVD-Video. When the system hangs, either the video windows stays black or the DVD logo comes up—and then the machine freezes. This is often a surprisingly simple issue. Frequently, setting the video adapter's settings to the default values (a.k.a. Initial Setup Recommendations) will correct the problem. Although your current video settings may work wonderfully with static images (even through other player software), the unique demands of your DVD decoder board may cause too much information to be directed at your video card at once. Start with your basic video default settings, then systematically increase resolution and color depth to an acceptable quality level.

As an alternative, you might try setting the drive letter so that the DVD-ROM drive is the *first* CD-ROM in the system. This is a particularly useful tactic when playing back CD-I and VideoCD movies with software (such as Xing), but it also helps the DVD player software utilize the DVD-ROM drive.

Symptom 9.11: Movies appear bright (then dim) when you are watching a DVD-Video from the video card's TV output. This problem occurs only when a VCR is connected between the TV output of the video adapter and the TV set. Video display adapters with TV output capability will enable Macrovision copy protection during DVD movie playback. The Macrovision-encoded video signal will effectively prevent a VCR from recording a watchable movie.

If you videotape a MACROVISION-encoded movie, and then play it back, you'll typically see occasional glimpses of the movie interspersed with 20 to 30 s of no picture (or possibly just a blue screen). Even if you're *not* actually recording, the VCR attempts to compensate for the Macrovision-encoded signal, and this generally leads to the symptom described. To resolve this symptom, simply connect the video card's TV output directly to the TV set, using either the composite or the S-Video connections.

> **NOTE:** *Remember that sound connections are completely independent of video connections, and that if you wish to hear the DVD movie through the TV set, you will also need to connect the audio output of the PC to the TV set.*

Symptom 9.12: When you play DVD-Video, the image appears distorted (often described like a "spaghetti western"). This type of issue is often associated with Matrox Millennium or Mystique video cards, but it can also occur with other types of video cards. In virtually all cases, the trouble is with your video drivers—they may be old or buggy or incompatible with the DVD drivers and video player software at work on your system. Download and install the latest video drivers, and try flashing the video card's BIOS (if possible). If the problem persists, disable DirectDraw for Overlays and resize the screen to the default sizes recommended.

Symptom 9.13: You cannot resize the movie display to full screen (or select any display size other than the default). This is particularly associated with Matrox video cards, but it may also occur with other video cards. These video cards probably don't support the hardware-based video scaling required for DVD. Try upgrading the video drivers, and flash the video card's BIOS (if possible). Otherwise, you have little alternative except to upgrade the video card or to continue using the smaller screen size.

Symptom 9.14: You receive a *display overlay not available* error message when launching the DVD player software. This is a known issue with the ATI DVD player 1.2 software, but similar problems can occur with other players. Chances are that the DVD player software requires additional display adapter memory (beyond what is used by the current display mode). If the current display mode uses most of the display adapter's memory, there's no memory left over for the DVD player, and the error message will occur.

This message is most likely to occur when the display adapter has only 4 MB of display memory, and 1152×864 at 32 bits per pixel (bpp) is selected as the display mode—this display mode consumes almost 4 MB of display memory just to paint the Windows desktop. To resolve this problem, simply select a lower color depth or lower resolution. For example, if you're running at 32 bpp, try 16 bpp; this will consume only half as much display memory and should leave an adequate amount for the display overlay and other DVD functions.

If the error message persists after you reduce the display resolution (and/or color depth), the problem may be the result of interference by other video-related processes. Check for WebTV or WaveTop background tasks—these are normally visible in the taskbar. Right-click the icons for these tasks and select *Pause*, *Suspend*, *Quit*, or *Exit* to disable them, then try the DVD player software again.

Symptom 9.15: You encounter a *card required* error when installing SoftDVD player software. This is a known problem with ATI video cards and Zoran SoftDVD player software *(e.g., ATI AGP card required)*, and is almost always due to inadequate system requirements. The SoftDVD player has several major system requirements:

1. An appropriate video card must be present.

2. AGP support must be enabled at the operating system level.

3. An Intel Pentium II processor is required.

4. Only a 16-bpp color depth (65K colors) is supported.

5. The sound drivers must be DirectX-compliant.

To resolve this problem, ensure that all requirements of the SoftDVD Player are met:

■ *Check the video card.* A PCI video card may not be supported. If you are uncertain which video card is installed, use *Device Manager* to examine the *Display Adapter*. Click the *Status* button on the diagnostics page—the *ASIC Type* entry should include the *AGP* designation.

■ *Check the operating system.* AGP support must be enabled. The following components must be installed on the system to properly enable AGP:

Windows 95 OSR 2 (950b or 950c). Right-click *My Computer* and select *Properties*. You should see *Microsoft Windows 95 4.00.950 B or 4.00.950 C*.

USB supplement. This is available from Microsoft's Web site and on some later Windows 95 CDs. Windows 95 (950C) normally has the USB patch preinstalled. For 950B, check the *Add/Remove Programs* list in *Control Panel* to determine whether the *USB Supplement to OSR2* has been installed.

AGP-to-PCI bridge drivers. This is also known as a "chipset patch" or "PIIX4 patch" and usually comes on a diskette or CD from the motherboard manufacturer. Examine the *Device Manager* and look for *Unknown* or *Other* entries related to the *PCI Bridge*. If any such entries are present, this is an indication that the proper chipset patch is *not* installed. You may need to install such a patch before proceeding.

DirectX5 (or later). This is available from Microsoft's Web site and may also be included with your video card's driver CD. From the *Control Panel*, open *Add / Remove Programs*, and double-click on the *DirectX* entry (if there isn't one, then DirectX is not installed at all). The DirectDraw component should show a version number of 4.05.00.0155 (or later). If it does not, your system is using an earlier version of DirectX, and this will need to be updated to DirectX5.0 or later (i.e., DirectX6 or DirectX6.1).

■ *Check your processor*. The software may demand an Intel Pentium II/III processor. Even if your motherboard uses a compatible Socket 7 processor (such as an AMD K6-2), the software may not operate without a Pentium II/III. Other DVD player software may not be so stringent. Otherwise, you may need to upgrade the motherboard and CPU.

■ *Check the video color depth*. The software may support only limited color depths. Right-click on the desktop, select *Properties*, then select the *Settings* tab. The *Color Palette* entry should say *High Color (16 bit)*—change the setting to this value if necessary.

■ *Check the sound drivers*. In most cases, sound drivers must be DirectX-compliant. From *Control Panel*, open *Add / Remove Programs* and double-click on *DirectX*. Check the listing for *Primary Sound Driver*—it should indicate *Certified*. If the sound driver is not certified or indicates *no hardware support*, check with the sound card manufacturer (or system maker) for updated sound drivers.

Performance/operating symptoms

Symptom 9.16: The DVD motorized tray won't open or close. The most common issue here is the DVD application itself. Some DVD applications (such as DVD-Video player applications) will lock the disk tray closed while a video DVD disk is playing. Try closing all open applications. If the tray still won't open, try restarting the PC. This should clear any software lock. If the tray still refuses to open or close, the drive itself may be defective—you can force the tray open using a straightened paper clip in the emergency eject hole in the front of the drive.

Symptom 9.17: There is no DVD audio while playing a movie or other multimedia presentation. Here's another common oversight during new DVD installations. Check the external audio cable attached between the MPEG-2 decoder board and the Line In jack of your sound board. The cable may be plugged into the wrong jack(s), or the cable may simply be defective. Also check the sound board's mixer applet and verify that the Line In volume control setting is turned up to an acceptable level. If you're connecting the DVD-ROM's CD-audio cable to the sound card, verify that the cable is attached securely, and see that the cable is compatible with the drive and the sound card.

Symptom 9.18: Video quality appears poor. MPEG-2 compression is well respected for its ability to reproduce high-quality images. Problems with poor image quality almost always stem from your video configuration—your color depth or resolution are too low. DVD-Video playback is best at resolutions of 800 × 600 or higher and color depths of 16 bits (high color) or higher (e.g., 24-bit True Color). In most cases, 256 colors will result in a "dithered" image.

Symptom 9.19: The video image is distorted when you try to play an MPEG file. Other video operations probably seem fine. A fully or partially distorted MPEG image can be the result of two problems. First, the video connections on the back of the card could be loose. Verify that all connections to the MPEG-2 decoder card are secure. Another common cause of distorted playbacks is that the refresh rate on your video card is set *too high*—it is recommended that the video refresh rate be kept *below* 85 Hz when running MPEG files. Try adjusting the vertical refresh rate to 72 Hz, or even 60 Hz.

Symptom 9.20: The picture is beginning to occasionally pixelize or "break apart." The audio may also seem periodically distorted. It is highly likely that the DVD disk needs to be cleaned. Clean the DVD disk properly and try it again, or try another disk. Also try closing any unused applications running in the background. If the problem persists with another DVD disk (and both disks are in good condition), try reinitializing the drive by powering down and rebooting the system. If the problem still persists, the internal optics of the DVD-ROM drive may need to be cleaned with a bit of photography-grade compressed air. Otherwise, try replacing the DVD-ROM drive.

Symptom 9.21: You notice the DVD-ROM light flashing regularly without a disk inserted. System performance may be reduced. This is often because the DVD-ROM drive's properties are set for auto insert notification under Windows 95/98. Start the *Device Manager*, highlight the DVD-ROM drive, and click the *Properties* button. You'll see the *DVD-ROM Properties* dialog. In the *Options* area of the *Properties* dialog, locate the check box that says *Auto insert notification*, and uncheck it. Save your changes (you might need to reboot the system). This should stop the drive's constant checking for a disk.

Symptom 9.22: The DVD drive's "busy" indicator flashes slowly once a disk is inserted. The drive is not recognizing the disk. In most cases, the disk is simply dirty. Try cleaning the disk in a radial motion (from the hub to the edge like the spokes of a wheel). Try another disk. If the drive cannot recognize other disks, the drive's optical reader may be dirty—try using a can of photography-grade compressed air to clean any accumulations of dust from the drive. If the drive's "busy" indicator is on all the time (and it doesn't recognize any disks), the drive may be defective.

Symptom 9.23: You see an error message that says *Disk playback unauthorized.* The region code on the DVD disk does not match the code embedded into the drive. There isn't much that can be done when this error occurs. Note that region code limitations are applied only to DVD-Video movie releases—programs and data disks are generally not marked with region codes.

Symptom 9.24: You receive an *authentication error when playing DVD movies with a Zoran SoftDVD player.* The error suggests that the region code for the DVD disk is not supported by the player software. This problem normally occurs when the DVD disk is designed for a region different from that for which the player being used is designed. For example, the error message would appear if you attempted to play a region 2 DVD disk on a region 1 version of SoftDVD software. However, there are rare reports of this error occurring in situations where the DVD region codes are correct. The following suggestions may help to correct region problems with the Zoran SoftDVD player:

- Ensure that the DVD title being played is designed for the appropriate region. Today, the SoftDVD player is designed for the playback of region 1 DVD titles. You may need to upgrade the player software.

- If you're using SoftDVD with a SCSI DVD drive, ensure that the most recent ASPI driver is installed for the SCSI controller.

- Panasonic A01 F/W 1.12 DVD drives will yield authentication errors when attempting to play DVDs with Zoran SoftDVD software. This appears to be an issue with the DVD drive itself, and no solution exists with that specific drive.

- Toshiba SM-M1002 DVD drives using a firmware version *prior* to 3426 should be updated to the current firmware revision.

- For Matsushita SR-852 DVD drives, the following DVD-ROM driver files should be used:

  1. mkeatapi.mpd and mkevsd.vxd (on the SR-8582 installation disk)
  2. mkeupd.vxd (on the SR-8581 installation disk)

Symptom 9.25: You cannot locate the video window when you Adjust the DVD video overlay feature. When adjusting the video overlay, you may have some trouble finding the video window. It often helps to change your background to magenta so that you can see where the video window is. To do this, right-click on your background, and select *Properties*. Select the *Background* tab, and select *none* as both the *Pattern* and the *Wallpaper*. Then select the *Appearance* tab and select *Magenta* as the color of the desktop. Click on *OK* to finish changing your background color to magenta. It should now be easier to locate the video window while adjusting the overlay.

Symptom 9.26: The DVD drive cannot read CD-R or Photo CD disks. This is not an error—most first-generation DVD drives will not read CD recordable or Photo CD (Kodak) disks. In some cases, it is even possible for the laser wavelength and energy used in the DVD drive to damage CD recordable disks. Do not attempt to read CD-R or Photo CD disks in the DVD unless the drive specifications specifically state that the drive *is* compatible with those types of disks. Chances are that you'll need to update the older DVD drive's firmware (or replace the DVD drive completely) in order to correct the problem.

Symptom 9.27: You experience difficulties with a particular DVD movie title, even though others play normally. If most movies play normally, chances are that the problem movie is an older edition (version). Some older DVD-ROM movie releases contained mastering problems which caused playback errors. Try exchanging the movie for a later edition.

If the problem persists (or if you cannot play most movies properly), you may need updated DVD-ROM drivers. Download the latest drivers from the DVD manufacturer's Web site and install them. The following instructions explain a driver upgrade for a Creative Labs DVD-ROM drive:

- Create a directory called DVDNEW in the root directory of the boot drive.

- Download file DVDEW95.EXE into this directory.

- Click on *Start*, *Programs*, and select *MS-DOS Prompt*.

- Change to the DVDNEW directory you created (e.g., C:\DVDNEW), then type DVDEW95 -D and press the <Enter> key.

- The file will extract and create a SETUP subdirectory within C:\DVDNEW.

- Now follow the instructions in the README.1ST file to install the new drivers and programs.

Symptom 9.28: You experience difficulties with the DVD software's Parental Control feature. The Parental Control is not working properly or is causing user problems. This is often because the Parental Control feature is not working properly in the DVD software, and you'll need to uninstall and reinstall the DVD software to *disable* Parental Control.

First, uninstall the DVD software. To do this, open the *Add/Remove Programs* applet from *Control Panel*. Highlight the particular DVD software (i.e., Encore software) and click on *Add/Remove*. After the uninstall is complete, reinstall the software, choosing the option *Custom Install*. Make sure there is *not* a check mark next to *Parental Control* in the select list. This will reinstall the software *without* the Parental Control feature. A later release of the DVD software (or a patch) may address this problem and allow you to resume using the Parental Control feature.

Symptom 9.29: When playing some DVD-Video titles, you encounter a "blue screen" error that mentions Parental Control. You notice that the Parental Control feature is set to "kids" and will *not* retain any other settings. The problem is outdated Quadrant Driver/Player software. This issue has been corrected in the Quadrant Driver/Player software released after December 23, 1997. You must go to Quadrant International's Web site (*http://www.qi.com/*), then download the latest player and the drivers from the S Series 2.x Cinemaster section.

> **NOTE:** *These drivers are only for the S Series 2.3 version of the card. If you have the 2.2 version of the card, use the links which point to the last updates for the 2.2 cards.*

Symptom 9.30: Your screen saver turns on while you are playing a DVD title. Since a screen saver is activated after some period of inactivity, leaving the keyboard/mouse untouched while watching a DVD movie can allow the screen saver to activate. Screen savers do not check for the presence of DVD activity, so you'll need to disable the screen saver before using the DVD-ROM drive to watch movies.

Symptom 9.31: You notice a reddish tint when you play movies with the DVD-ROM drive. This is typically an end-user issue which can easily be corrected by reducing contrast or adjusting the tint setting through the DVD player application software.

Symptom 9.32: You find that MPEG-1 files play back fine on your DVD player software, but there is no sound. However, MPEG-2 files and DVD-Video (movies) play back correctly *with* sound. This is generally a problem with the DVD player software, which may require a patch or upgrade (check with the player software's manufacturer). As a temporary workaround, use a generic MPEG file player (e.g., Windows Media Player) to run MPEG-1 files until the DVD player can be upgraded or replaced.

Symptom 9.33: You cannot play a DVD or CD in the DVD drive, or certain types of disks cannot be read in the drive. There are many possible (often simple) problems that can prevent a disk from playing in an optical drive.

- *Check the disk*. The disk may be placed upside-down in the disk tray, or the disk may be dirty. Recheck the disk orientation, and clean the disk if necessary. If the disk is warped or seriously damaged, it may need to be replaced.

- *Check the drive*. The drive's optical reader may be dirty—this can happen on older drives or drives which are operated in dusty/dirty environments. Use a can of photography-grade compressed air to gently blow dust out of the drive.

- *Check the region code*. DVD movie disks are released with a region code that must correspond to the code contained in the drive—if the codes are different, the DVD disk will not play. You may need to obtain a disk with the correct region code.

Symptom 9.34: When attempting to play a disk, you receive a message such as *Disk does not contain DVD Video data*. DVD player software cannot find the title track and/or information files on the disk. If you're trying to use a DVD disk, the disk may be scratched or damaged—clean the disk if possible, or replace the damaged disk. If you're simply trying to play MPEG video from an ordinary CD, click *OK* to close the error dialog—the disk may still play.

Symptom 9.35: You receive an error message such as *Unable to locate DVD-ROM drive—assume drive D:—Error1.* The DVD drive may not have been properly configured by Windows 95/98, or it may be disconnected.

- *Check the cables.* Verify that the DVD drive is jumpered properly, and see that its power and signal cables are oriented and secured. Try another signal cable if necessary, or try the DVD drive as the only device on the drive controller.

- *Try a manual installation.* Reboot the PC from a cold start and see if Windows will redetect the DVD drive. If it will not, run the Windows 95/98 *Add New Hardware* wizard to force Windows to detect the hardware. If the *Add New Hardware* wizard fails to detect the DVD drive, you may need to specify the drive make and model manually. In all cases, be sure to have the latest DVD drivers on hand.

Symptom 9.36: During the DVD video configuration process, you receive an error such as *Auto Alignment failed.* This error almost always suggests that the hardware MPEG-2 decoder card *cable* may not be properly connected. Check the cable connections on the hardware decoder card (particularly VGA In and VGA Out) and see that the cable is secure. Try another cable if possible. Start the DVD player software, press the *Settings* button, and select *Video Configuration.* Press the *Auto* button to have the video automatically configured.

Symptom 9.37: After you connect an MPEG-2 decoder card, the video image seems blue (or contains a blue tint). This is generally due to improper connection or setup of the MPEG-2 card.

- *Check the loopback cable.* The VGA loopback cable between the video card and the MPEG-2 decoder card may not be connected correctly. Check the loopback cable, and try reseating the connector if possible.

- *Check the video alignment*. The DVD video alignment may not be set correctly. Open the *Video
Configuration* utility and set the video alignment.
Try using the *Auto* button to automatically configure the video. If automatic configuration does not
work, try making minor adjustments manually.

- *Check the color key setting*. Your color key value may
not be set correctly. Change the color scheme of your
Windows 95/98 desktop. Right-click on the Windows
95/98 desktop and click *Properties*. In the *Display
Properties* dialog, click the *Appearance* tab. Then
select *Desktop* in the *Item* list, and select a different
color scheme from the list. Click *OK* to accept the
changes.

**Symptom 9.38: The DVD-ROM drive cannot play a DVD disk
or certain other types of disk media (e.g., CD-plus).** There
are several possible problems that might cause this.

- *Check the drivers*. Make sure that the entire suite of
drivers for your drive has been installed. Check for
the latest drivers, and download any available
patches or updates.

- *Check the player software*. You may not have the correct player software for your drive. Make sure to
download and install the latest version of your player software.

- *Check the format*. Verify that the DVD disk is the
correct format for the type of system that you're
using. For example, a PC should use an ISO
9660–compatible format rather than an Apple/Mac
HFS disk or Unix disk format.

- *Check for viruses*. Your DVD drivers/software may
have been corrupted by a virus. Run a Virus Scan program, then remove/reinstall any damaged software.

Windows-related symptoms

**Symptom 9.39: After you upgrade the video card, DVD
movies will not play.** Chances are that your new video

card is neither defective nor incompatible—instead, the problem is that the link(s) between your video and DVD drivers have been broken. When new video cards are installed, they change entries in the Registry which associate MPEG playback with video card drivers. The new video card's MPEG drivers are probably *not* DVD-compliant, and since they took precedence over the MPEG drivers of the older DVD system, this is likely to be the problem. Try reinstalling the video card from scratch, and then reinstall the DVD drivers and software. This should reinstall the proper DVD MPEG-ready drivers and correct the problem.

Symptom 9.40: DVD-Video movies will play only on the primary monitor. When DVD player software is installed in a multimonitor Windows 98 system, DVD movies will only play on the primary monitor—if the DVD player window is moved to the secondary monitor, no picture appears. This is a limitation of secondary displays under Windows 98. The primary display has a full complement of 3D and video acceleration features, but a secondary display does not. To correct this problem, move the DVD player window back to the primary monitor.

Symptom 9.41: Windows 98 halts or reboots when running a software DVD player designed for Windows 95. This is an issue most frequently associated with the Zoran SoftDVD player, but it may occur with other software products. In most cases, the system halts immediately after you click the *play* button, but it may also halt at other points within the player software, or, in some instances, the system may reboot or report an *Unrecoverable Application Error*. Generally, the SoftDVD player may successfully play a single DVD movie or file, and then report an error (such as *your computer is not configured to start DVD*) when you attempt to play a second movie. Chances are that the subtle design changes between Windows 95 and Windows 98 are causing a problem with the player software (tailored for Windows 95). Try the following:

- Remove and reinstall the DVD player application.

- Check to see if a patch or update is available for your DVD player.

- Experiment with different video resolutions, color depths, and refresh rates.

- Try an alternative or updated video driver.

Symptom 9.42: Even when a DVD system is properly configured under Windows 95, you get no sound from the speakers. This is almost always due to an old (original) release of Windows 95—the use of old Windows 95 drivers was corrected in Windows 95 OSR2 and is not an issue with Windows 98. If you cannot upgrade your operating system to Windows 95 OSR2 or Windows 98, check with the DVD package manufacturer for updated drivers and patches that might correct the problem. Keep in mind that the DVD drive will still read data DVD disks and other CDs properly.

Symptom 9.43: Creative and MKE DVD drives may not work with Windows 98. If you're using a first-generation Creative Labs DVD kit or an MKE DVD kit, the kit may not work properly with Windows 98 (note that newer kits should operate properly). For example, you may no longer be able to read from the drive. These older DVD kits rely on the Compact Disk File System (CDFS), but Windows 98 loads the Universal Disk Format file system (UDF) by default for DVD drives. To work around this incompatibility, disable UDF support for the DVD drives:

- Click *Start*, click *Run*, type `msconfig` in the *Open* box, and then click *OK*.

- Click the *Advanced* option.

- Click to select (check) the *Disable UDF File System* check box, and then click *OK*.

- Click *OK* again. When you're prompted to restart your computer, click *Yes*.

- When your computer restarts, UDF support is disabled, and the DVD kit should work.

Symptom 9.44: You receive a media error when using Windows Explorer to eject a DVD movie. This issue has been reported with Toshiba DVD players. When you use Windows Explorer to eject a DVD movie that is currently being played by a Toshiba DVD player, you receive the following "blue screen" error message:

```
Re-insert the media and press any key to continue.
```

When you insert the DVD movie back into the player and press a key, you may receive the same error message (and the movie may be automatically ejected). This problem may occur if you press a key before the DVD movie is fully spun up. To resolve the problem, insert the DVD movie into the player, but wait to press a key until the light on the Toshiba DVD player is turned off—this indicates that the DVD movie is fully spun up.

Symptom 9.45: You cannot capture a DVD video image with the Print Screen key under Windows 98. If you try to capture a still image of a DVD movie with the <Print Screen> key, then paste the image into a program, only a blue or black box may be pasted into the program. This is the normal design of your DVD system. The DVD data stream is decoded by the DVD decoder card, and then redirected to the video adapter. When the computer uses an external patch cable, the video stream is sent from the video adapter to the DVD decoder card, and then directly to the monitor as an overlay. This is done to improve the playback performance of DVD video by bypassing slower portions of the computer. Since the DVD data stream does not pass through the Windows API layer, the video output cannot be captured; you capture only the playback area in which the movie is displayed.

Symptom 9.46: You encounter problems when using a SoftDVD player under Windows 98. When you view a DVD movie using the SoftDVD player program included with some computers, you may experience various playback problems. In most cases, you can correct these types of problems by modifying the player's .INI file:

- Click *Start*, select *Find*, then click *Files Or Folders*.

- In the *Named* box, type softdvd.ini and then click *Find Now*.

- In the list of found files, double-click the softdvd.ini file.

- Type the following lines in the softdvd.ini file:

```
[dvdfs]

AlignedAccess=0
```

> **NOTE:** *Be sure to type a blank line above and below these two lines.*

- In the *File* menu, click *Save*, then click *Exit*.

- Restart your computer when prompted to do so.

Symptom 9.47: The screen appears clipped when a DVD movie is played. This is a known issue when Cinemaster 1.2 drivers are used under Windows 98—both sides of the screen may appear clipped. This is caused by an aspect ratio bug in the DVD player software. You'll need to contact Microsoft or the maker of your DVD player software in order to obtain the correct patch or software update for your DVD player. For example, Microsoft offers an update for the DVD-PLAY.EXE file (09/29/98, 9:43a, 125,440 bytes) which should correct this aspect ratio problem. Keep in mind that you may also need to update your DirectX components (i.e. you may need the Microsoft DirectX Media 6.0 Run Time module) before you update the DVD player software.

Symptom 9.48: You encounter problems with the DVD/TV tuner unit after upgrading Windows. After you upgrade a Toshiba Infinia 72xx laptop PC to Windows 98, a yellow exclamation point may be displayed next to the *DVD/TV Tuner* device in the *Device Manager*, and your DVD/TV Tuner device may not work correctly (if at all). This problem can occur if your computer is configured to use the Toshiba TV/FM version 2.13B2 device driver—this driver is not totally compatible with Windows 98. Contact Toshiba to obtain an upgraded driver for your PC.

Symptom 9.49: A Creative Labs DXR2 DVD drive will not work under Windows 98. After you upgrade your computer to Windows 98, your Creative Labs Encore DXR2 DVD drive may no longer work correctly. This problem occurs because the Windows 98 Setup process updates the .DLL files used by the DVD drive, and those new files may not be compatible with the Creative Labs DXR2. There are two methods of correcting the problem:

- *Update your drivers*. Contact Creative Labs to obtain updated drivers designed specifically for Windows 98. You can download drivers from Creative Labs at *http://www.soundblaster.com/ wwwnew/tech/ftp/ftp-cd.html*.

- *Replace older .DLL files*. You can try renaming WINASPI.DLL, WNASPI32.DLL, and APIX.VXD, then extracting new copies of WINASPI.DLL, WNASPI32.DLL, and APIX.VXD from your original Windows 98 CD-ROM (the WINASPI.DLL and WNASPI32.DLL files are in the Win98_40.cab file, and the APIX.VXD file is in the Win98_47.cab file.

Symptom 9.50: Windows 98 may lock up if the DVD drive tray is left open at boot time. If your portable computer includes a DVD drive, and the nonmotorized drive tray is left open during and after the Windows 98 startup, you may find that Windows 98 locks up several minutes after Windows is started. This problem is known to occur with the Toshiba Tecra 8000 DVD under Windows 98 and is usually caused because the DVD drive or CD-ROM drive supports Media Event Status Notification (MESN) according to the PC98 specification. Since those portable drives have nonmotorized trays, the trays are not closed automatically when Windows boots, and so Windows fails because of false reporting from the MESN feature.

First, close the drive tray while Windows is starting (or within 1 min after it starts). You should generally keep the DVD drive or CD-ROM drive tray closed except when you're inserting or removing disks. This policy also reduces the risk of drive problems due to dust buildup (or damage from striking the opened tray). Another option is to disable DMA support for the DVD drive or CD-ROM drive:

- Click *Start*, highlight *Settings*, then click *Control Panel*.

- Double-click the *System* icon, then click the *Device Manager* tab.

- Click the *CD-ROM* branch to expand it, click your CD-ROM drive or DVD drive, then click *Properties*.

- Click the *Settings* tab.

- Click the *DMA* check box to clear it, then click *OK*.

- Click *OK*, and then restart your computer when prompted to do so.

Finally, you can try disabling the auto insert notification feature for the DVD drive or CD-ROM drive:

- Click *Start*, highlight *Settings*, then click *Control Panel*.

- Double-click the *System* icon, then click the *Device Manager* tab.

- Click the *CD-ROM* branch to expand it, click your CD-ROM drive or DVD drive, then click *Properties*.

- Click the *Settings* tab.

- Click the *Auto Insert Notification* check box to clear it, then click *OK*.

- Click *OK*, and then restart your computer when prompted to do so.

> **NOTE:** *For more information on Media Event Status Notification, review the SFF8090 (a.k.a. Mt. Fuji) specification available from* ftp://fission.dt.wdc.com/pub/standards/SFF/specs/.

Symptom 9.51: You receive a *fatal exception in CDVSD* when starting Windows 98. When starting the computer, you encounter the following "blue screen" error message:

```
An exception 0E has occurred at 0028:C143EADA in
VXD CDVSD(01) + 00001CFA. This was called from
0028:C18413E8 in VXD voltrack(04)+ 00000A18. It may
be possible to continue normally.
```

This problem is reported to occur with the Agate Technologies AGAATAPI.MPD and Intel IDEATAPI.MPD miniport drivers, and can generally occur if a disk is not in the DVD drive (or when a disk is ejected from the DVD drive) while you're using a third-party SCSI miniport driver. An incorrect communication method is used when an IOS VSD is installed between the CDVSD and SCSIPORT layers *and* the DVD drive supports Group 2 timeout commands. Check with Microsoft (or your DVD drive maker) to see if an updated version of CDVSD.VXD is available.

Web Contacts

ATI: *http://support.atitech.ca/*

Creative Labs: *http://www-nt-ok.creaf.com/mmuk/pcdvd/*

Diamond Multimedia: *http://www.diamondmm.com*

Hitachi: *http://www.hitachi.com/*

Matsushita: *http://www.panasonic.com/PCEC/dvd/index-dvd.html*

Panasonic: *http://www.panasonic.com/*

Toshiba: *http://www.toshiba.com/taisdpd/dvdrom.htm*

10

Removable Media Drives

Perhaps the single most important complaint about hard drives has been that they are not portable—you can't just slide out one drive and pop in a new one. Hard drives are traditionally permanent installations. When a drive fills up, you must physically add another hard drive or replace the existing hard drive with a larger model. Both options require an invasive and time-consuming upgrade procedure (and then the drive must be partitioned and formatted before use). The idea of high-capacity "removable media" drives overcome this limitation—the drive hardware remains in the PC, but the media (or the "disks") can be inserted and removed as needed.

With a removable media drive (such as the Iomega Bernoulli, Iomega Jaz, SyQuest EZ-Flyer, or SyQuest SyJet), you can finally achieve *limitless* storage simply by exchanging data cartridges. If you need to use files on another PC, you can just pop out a cartridge, then take it with you to another PC with a compatible drive. While removable media drives are not quite as fast as hard drives, they are close, and you can usually start programs (or even boot the PC) right from the removable media drive. This chapter highlights a series of troubleshooting procedures for the Iomega Bernoulli and Jaz drives, and also the SyQuest EZ-Flyer and SyJet families.

General Drive Installation and Replacement

Removable media (or RM) drives are generally easy devices to install or replace. Most are installed as master devices located on the secondary IDE drive controller channel, although a few will coexist as slave devices alongside a hard drive or some other drive device. The most important issue to remember is that the BIOS will not support an RM drive directly (even if the BIOS identifies the RM drive at boot time)—you'll need real-mode drivers for the RM drive under DOS or protected-mode drivers for the RM drive under Windows. In most cases, you'll also install a set of software utilities for disk cartridge partitioning, formatting, R/W protection, and so on. This part of the chapter covers the guidelines needed to install a basic internal IDE-type RM drive.

Select jumper configurations

An IDE-type RM drive may be installed as a master or a slave device on any hard drive controller channel. These master/slave settings are handled through one or two jumpers located on the rear of the drive (right next to the 40-pin signal cable connector). One of your first decisions when planning an installation should be to decide the drive's configuration:

- If you're installing the RM drive as the first drive on the secondary drive controller channel, it must be jumpered as the master device.

- If you're installing the RM drive alongside another drive (on either the primary or the secondary drive controller channel), the RM drive must be jumpered as the slave device.

NOTE: *Refer to the documentation that accompanies your particular RM drive in order to determine the exact master/slave jumper settings. If you do not have the drive documentation handy, check the drive manufacturer's Web site for online information.*

Preinstall any software

Some RM drive designs require that you preinstall one or more software utilities prior to installing the physical drive; this ensures that Windows will find the drive after installation. If your particular RM drive suggests that you insert a software CD and install software *prior* to the drive's physical installation, you should handle that software installation now. After the required software is installed, you can power down the PC and begin the actual drive installation.

Attach cables and mount the drive

- Turn off and unplug the PC, then remove the outer cover to expose the computer's drive bays.

- Attach one end of the 40-pin drive interface cable to the drive controller connector on your motherboard (or drive controller card). Remember to align pin 1 on the cable (the side of the cable with the blue or red stripe) with pin 1 on the drive controller connector.

- Locate an available drive bay for the RM drive. Remove the plastic housing covering the drive bay, then slide the drive inside. Locate the four screw holes needed to mount the drive. In some cases, you may need to attach mounting rails to the drive so that the drive will be wide enough to fit in the drive bay. In virtually all cases, you should mount an RM drive horizontally (although some RM drive models may be mounted vertically).

- Attach the 40-pin signal cable and the 4-pin power connector to the new drive, then bolt the drive securely into place. Do not overtighten the screws, since this may damage the drive. If you do not have an available 4-pin power connector, you may use an appropriate Y splitter if necessary to split power from another drive (preferably the floppy drive).

Configure the CMOS Setup

Although virtually all RM drives require real- or protected-mode driver support, recent motherboard designs can identify the ATAPI IDE RM drive in BIOS, so you should configure your computer's BIOS to accept the drive if possible (through the CMOS Setup).

- Turn the computer on. As your computer starts up, watch for a message that describes how to run the CMOS Setup (e.g., *Press F1 for Setup*). Press the appropriate key to start the CMOS Setup program.

- Select the *hard drive settings* menu, and choose the drive location occupied by the RM drive (i.e., *primary slave*, *secondary slave*, or *secondary master*, depending on how you've physically jumpered and installed the drive).

- Select *automatic drive detection* if available—this option will automatically identify the new drive. If your BIOS does *not* provide automatic drive detection, select *none* or *not installed* for the RM drive, and rely on drivers *only*.

- Save the settings and exit the CMOS Setup program. Your computer will automatically reboot.

Reassemble the computer

Double-check all of your signal and power cables to verify that they are secure, then tuck the cables gently into the computer's chassis. Check that there are no loose tools, screws, or cables inside the chassis. Now reattach the computer's outer housing(s).

Since the operating system will assign a drive letter only to a partitioned and formatted disk cartridge, you should be sure to insert an appropriate disk cartridge into the drive before rebooting the system. If you do not insert a disk cartridge, the drive may not receive a drive letter at boot time.

Install the software

In order to complete your RM drive installation, you'll need to install the software drivers and utilities that accompanied the drive on diskette or CD. If you've pre-installed any software prior to installing the drive, you'll probably need to complete the software installation now. Windows 95/98 systems will generally detect the presence of the new RM drive and prompt you for the protected-mode drivers automatically. After you install the drivers and reboot the system, the RM drive should be ready for use.

Iomega Bernoulli and Jaz drives

The Bernoulli disk is a variation of fixed disk technology. Conventional hard drives rotate rigid disks, and the read/write heads ride on the resulting cushion of air. In contrast, the Bernoulli disk uses a *flexible* platter which is forced to flex beneath a fixed read/write head. At a casual glance, you probably would not notice the difference between a fixed-platter cartridge (such as a SyQuest or Iomega Jaz cartridge) and a Bernoulli cartridge.

Bernoulli disks have been around for years, and have been through 20-, 35-, 44-, 65-, 90-, 105-, 150-, and 230-MB incarnations. The Iomega Bernoulli 230 drive will operate with all of the previous disk sizes (except 20 and 44 MB) with only a negligible performance hit. Bernoulli drives are traditionally SCSI devices, but Iomega offers a parallel-port-to-SCSI adapter to allow operation with a PC parallel port. On a SCSI system, you can use the Iomega PC2x, PC4x,

PC90, PC800, PC1600, and PC1616 SCSI adapters. Other SCSI adapters can also be used as long as they are ASPI-compatible and an ASPI driver is provided by the adapter vendor.

By contrast, the Iomega Jaz family uses more conventional rigid disks which suspend the read/write heads under a thin layer of air (the same approach used in hard drives). The Jaz is also a more recent development, offering faster drive performance and storage capacities of 1 and 2 GB per cartridge.

Read/write-protecting Jaz disks

Read/write protection prevents data from being written to (or read from) the disk. Jaz disks are protected electronically rather than by a traditional mechanical write-protect tab. Jaz disk protection is available from Iomega SCSI utilities 2.2 for DOS and in the Windows version of Iomega Tools. Protection features include four options:

- Write protection
- Read/write protection
- "Unprotect" until ejection
- Remove protection

Note that password protection is optional for write protection, but is *required* for read/write protection. When read/write protection is set, the password *must* be used to access the disk (or change protection options). Keep in mind that no one can recover data from a read/write protected disk should you forget the password. If the password is forgotten, you'll have to reformat the Jaz disk using a "surface verify" option. Reformatting the disk will destroy all the data on it. You cannot use DOS format (or any other type of disk management software) to remove the password protection. To unprotect a Jaz disk, you must run the Iomega SCSI utilities (or use the Iomega Tools program):

- Double-click the *My Computer* icon.

- Read/write-protect the Iomega disk by right-clicking on the disk icon and choosing the *Protect* option (if a disk is not inserted in the drive, the *Protect* option will not be available).

- Use the same processes to remove the read/write protection.

Unprotecting the Jaz software disk

During a normal successful installation from the Jaz Tools disk, the unused partition is removed and the disk becomes formatted for the platform that the software is installed on. Until this process is performed (or the software reclaims the disk), the disk will remain write-protected. Use the following steps to remove the write partition and reclaim the disk. To reclaim the Tools disk, double-click on the *My Computer* icon, then double-click the Jaz drive icon. In the Jaz drive folder, open the *W95STUFF* folder, then run *RECLAIM*. Once the disk is reclaimed, the write protection should be removed. If this does not reclaim the disk properly, try the following DOS procedure:

- Start the PC to the *Startup* menu.

- From the *Startup* menu, choose *Command Prompt Only*.

- Place the Jaz software floppy disk into your A: drive.

- At the C:\ prompt, type A:\GUEST and press <Enter>.

- Once GUEST assigns a drive letter, insert the Tools disk into the Jaz drive.

- Type X: (where X is the drive letter for the Jaz drive) and press the <Enter> key.

- At the X:\ prompt, type cd\dosstuff and press <Enter>.

- Finally, type `Reclaim` and press `<Enter>` to reclaim the Tools disk.

Removing Iomega Tools from the Startup group

Programs located in the *Startup* folder are automatically executed when Windows is loaded. During installation, Iomega Tools places several programs in this group. If a program icon is moved or deleted from the Startup group, the program will no longer start automatically when Windows starts (the program will have to be started manually). To move or remove items from the Startup group:

- Open the *Iomega Tools* folder by double-clicking on it from *My Computer*.

- Click on *Start*, highlight *Settings*, and then click on the *Taskbar* entry.

- Choose the *Start Menu Programs* tab, and then click the *Advanced* button.

- Click on the (+) symbol next to *Programs*, then double-click on the *Startup* folder.

- To move the contents, highlight all the icons to be moved, then drag them to the open *Iomega Tools* folder. To delete the icons instead, highlight the icons and press the `<Delete>` key.

  NOTE: *Once icons have been removed from the* Startup *folder, the Iomega Tools software must be reinstalled in order to reinsert them into the Startup group.*

Uninstalling Jaz Tools software

You may need to remove the Jaz software in order to upgrade it or to resolve possible software/driver conflicts. Use the following steps to remove the Iomega Tools software under Windows:

- Click *Start*, point to *Settings*, and click *Control Panel*.

- From the *Control Panel*, open the *Add/Remove Programs* wizard.

- Highlight *Iomega Tools for Windows 95/NT* and click on *Add/Remove*.

- Restart your computer when prompted to do so.

If you need to remove Iomega Tools software under DOS:

- From the C:\ prompt, type edit autoexec.bat and press <Enter>.

- Remove the following lines:

```
@SET SCSI_DRIVER=C:\IOMEGA
@SET SCSI_UTILITY=C:\IOMEGA
```

- From the *File* menu, select *Exit* and save the changes when prompted.

- From the C:\ prompt, type edit config.sys and press <Enter>.

- Remove the following lines:

```
DEVICE=C:\IOMEGA\SCSICFG.EXE
DEVICE=C:\IOMEGA\SCSIDRVR.SYS.
```

- From the *File* menu, select *Exit* and save the changes when prompted.

- From the C:\ prompt, type deltree iomega and press <Enter>.

- Reboot the computer.

Bernoulli drive troubleshooting

Symptom 10.1: The Bernoulli drive has a floppy icon in Windows 95/98. This is usually the result of running a real-mode driver to support the Bernoulli drive and adapter under Windows 95/98. Check the Bernoulli driver—you may need to disable the real-mode driver (i.e., in CONFIG.SYS) and install the protected-mode driver under Windows 95/98. The Iomega software bundle typically provides protected-mode drivers for Jaz Jet, Zip Zoom, PC1600, PC1616, PC800, PC2x, PPA-3, and parallel-port devices. If you are using a different drive adapter, you may need to upgrade and update the driver accordingly. If you are using a non-Iomega adapter (such as a SCSI adapter), you will need protected-mode drivers from the particular SCSI adapter vendor (such as Adaptec). However, Windows 95/98 does have a comprehensive library of protected-mode drivers already available.

Symptom 10.2: A Bernoulli SCSI drive does not have a drive letter in Windows 95/98. The drive does not appear to respond. In virtually all cases, the SCSI driver has failed to load.

■ *Check the SCSI driver.* Open the *Device Manager* and expand the *SCSI Controllers* entry, then check the *Iomega Adapter* line beneath it. If there is a yellow symbol with an exclamation mark on it, the Windows 95/98 driver did not load. Highlight that *Iomega Adapter* line and select *Properties*. Click on the *Resources* page, then verify that your I/O Range and IRQ options are set correctly—they must match the jumper settings on your SCSI adapter board. If you must update the resource settings manually, make sure the *Automatic Settings* box is not checked. Remember to save any changes. If you allocated new resources, you may have to shut off the PC and change jumper settings on the controller to match the resources allocated in the *Device Manager*. Restart the computer—once the system reboots, the Windows 95/98 driver should load normally.

■ *Check the connections.* If the driver checks out properly, you'll need to check the device connections. Check the SCSI signal connector first, and make sure that the SCSI cable is intact and connected to the drive properly.

- *Check SCSI termination and ID assignments.* If problems persist, your SCSI adapter is probably installed correctly, but the bus may be terminated improperly. See that you terminate both ends of the SCSI bus properly. Finally, make sure that the SCSI ID for your drive does not conflict with the IDs of other SCSI devices in the system.

Symptom 10.3: The Bernoulli drive takes over the CD-ROM's drive letter in Windows 95/98. You may simply need to switch drive letters between the Bernoulli drive and the CD-ROM drive:

- Open *Device Manager* and double-click on the *Disk Drives* entry.

- Highlight the *Iomega Bernoulli* drive entry and click on *Properties*.

- Click on the *Settings* page.

- In the *Reserved Drive Letters* section, there is a *Start Drive Letter* and an *End Drive Letter* setting. Enter the desired drive letter for the Bernoulli drive in both the start and end drive entries (be sure to use the same drive letter for both start and end). Click on *OK*.

- Double-click on the *CD-ROM* entry.

- Highlight your *CD-ROM Drive* entry and click on *Properties*.

- Click on the *Settings* page.

- In the *Reserved Drive Letters* section, there is a *Start Drive Letter* and an *End Drive Letter* setting. Enter the desired drive letter for the CD-ROM drive in both the start and end entries (be sure to use the same drive letter for both the start and end). Click on *OK*.

- Click on *OK* to close *Device Manager*, then shut down and restart the computer.

Symptom 10.4: You encounter an *Invalid Drive Specification* error after installing an Iomega SCSI drive. Your system automatically boots into Windows, and it will not return to the installation program. The error occurs when you try to access the Iomega drive. In most cases, you need to install the Iomega SCSI software from the DOS prompt. Boot the system from a clean diskette, then try installing the Iomega SCSI software again.

Symptom 10.5: You encounter SCSI communication problems. In virtually all cases, SCSI problems can be traced to hardware problems or driver issues. Check the power connector first, and see that power is provided to the drive (the drive power light should be on). Make sure that the SCSI cable is intact and connected securely between the drive and the SCSI adapter. Try a new signal cable if possible. Termination may also be a problem. Both ends of the SCSI bus must be terminated properly. Make sure that terminators are installed in the correct places on your SCSI chain. The Bernoulli SCSI drive must be assigned to a SCSI ID that is not in use by any other SCSI device. Finally, check the drivers. Make sure that the drivers for your SCSI adapter and drive are correct and use the right command-line switches, and verify that you're using the very latest versions. Also check for conflicts between SCSI drivers and other drivers in the system.

Symptom 10.6: Your IDE Bernoulli drive receives two drive letters. Your plug-and-play (PnP) BIOS is detecting the Bernoulli drive as a fixed drive and assigning one drive letter, but the Iomega drivers detect the Bernoulli drive *again* and assign a second drive letter. PnP support for the Bernoulli drive may be a problem. Enter your system CMOS Setup and disable the PnP support for the Bernoulli drive. Save your changes and reboot the system. If you cannot disable BIOS support for the Bernoulli drive, power up the system with the Bernoulli disk *removed*—this causes BIOS to overlook the drive, but the Iomega drivers will still assign the drive letter properly.

Symptom 10.7: The compressed removable media drive(s) are not automatically mounted on startup. This problem can occur under Windows 95 if the computer has two floppy disk drives and the following settings exist in the DRVSPACE.INI file:

```
MaxRemovableDrives=2
AutoMount=1
```

To resolve this issue, you'll need to increase the value of the MaxRemovableDrives= setting to match the total number of removable media drives in the computer. For example, if your computer has two floppy disk drives and a double Bernoulli drive, use MaxRemovableDrives=4 (two floppy disk drives plus two Bernoulli drives). Edit the DRVSPACE.INI file as follows:

- Locate the DRVSPACE.INI file using Windows Explorer (it should be in the root directory). Right-click the file, then click *Properties*.

- Click the *Read-only* check box to clear it, then click *OK*.

- Double-click the *DRVSPACE.INI* file to open it.

- Change the value of the MaxRemovableDrives= setting to match the total number of removable media drives, or set the AutoMount= entry to the drive letters assigned to the removable media drives. For example, if you have a double Bernoulli drive with drive letters D and E assigned to the drive, use the setting AutoMount=DE.

■ Save and close the file, then reboot Windows 95.

> **NOTE**: *When you use an Iomega RCD driver with a double Bernoulli drive, you may receive a* General Failure *error message the first time you access the second drive. This causes automatic activation and automatic mounting to fail. Use an Iomega OAD or SCSI driver to resolve the problem.*

Jaz/Bernoulli adapter troubleshooting

Symptom 10.8: You encounter an error such as *chipset error 0x8* when using a Jaz Jet PCI card. When you start the computer, you find that the Jaz Jet PCI card will display the error, and the computer may lock up. This error is usually caused by a bad connection in the PCI slot.

■ *Check the PCI card.* Make sure the SCSI adapter card is seated properly. Shut down your computer, and disconnect the power supply. Disconnect the Jaz drive from the Jaz Jet SCSI adapter card. Remove the case from your computer and locate your SCSI adapter card. Reinsert the card in the *same* slot, pressing firmly on the edge of the card to ensure proper connections. Be sure to bolt the card securely into place. If the error disappears after you restart the computer, you may reconnect the Jaz drive and continue using it normally.

■ *Exchange the slot or card.* If the error persists, try the card in another slot. If this corrects the problem, then the slot is defective. This will not damage the card, but you may need to replace or upgrade the motherboard at some point in the future. If the card still refuses to work in another slot, the card may be defective, so try another card.

Symptom 10.9: Using an Iomega PC2X 8-bit Bernoulli controller may cause the system to crash. According to

Iomega, PC2X 8-bit Bernoulli controller cards may not function properly on 486/33-MHz and faster computers. For Windows 95 Setup, you may need to run Setup with the ignore hardware detection parameter, such as

```
SETUP /I
```

To correct this problem, you'll need to use the controller on a slower computer (rarely a practical option) or install a better Bernoulli controller card in the existing system.

Symptom 10.10: The parallel-port adapter (PPA-3) does not have a drive letter in Windows 95/98.   Parallel-port drive problems can almost always be traced to faulty connections, port configuration issues, or driver problems.

- *Check the power/signal connections*. Parallel-port drives are powered externally, so ensure that the power pack is working, and see that the power cable is connected properly to the drive. If the drive does not appear to power up, try a different power pack or drive. Also make sure that you are using a good-quality, known-good parallel-port cable which is attached securely at the PC and the drive.

- *Isolate the parallel port*. Remove any other devices on the parallel port. Parallel-port drives are often very sensitive to devices such as copy protection modules (or dongles) and other pass-through devices. Try connecting the drive *directly* to the parallel port. Also disconnect any printers on the parallel port.

- *Check the CMOS Setup*. The parallel port's setting may not be compatible with the drive. Reboot the PC and enter CMOS Setup. Check to see that the parallel port is configured in EPP or bidirectional mode.

- *Check the SCSI controller*. There is a known incompatibility between the Bernoulli drive and the Adaptec 284x adapter—the Iomega PPA-3 driver does not work with the Adaptec 284x controller. Check with Iomega for an updated SCSI driver. You can also try contacting Adaptec for updated drivers.

■ *Check the SCSI drivers.* Open the *Device Manager* and find the *SCSI Controllers* entry (even though this is a parallel-port device). If there is no such entry, the driver is not installed. If you expand the *SCSI Controllers* section, there should be an entry for the *Iomega Adapter*. If there is not, the driver is not installed. If the *Device Manager* entry for the *Iomega Adapter* has a yellow circle with an exclamation mark on it, the interface is configured improperly and is conflicting with other devices in the system.

■ *Check the host adapter configuration.* Highlight the *Iomega Adapter* entry, click on *Properties*, then select the *Settings* page. Find the box marked *Adapter Settings*, then type

```
/mode:nibble /speed:1
```

Save your changes and reboot the system.

■ *Try reinstalling the host adapter drivers.* Highlight the *Iomega Adapter* and select *Remove*. Then reinstall the drivers from scratch.

■ *Check/replace the drive.* Try the drive on another PC. If the drive works on another system, the parallel port is incompatible (or the PPA-3 is not configured properly). If the drive does *not* work on another PC, try a new Bernoulli drive.

Symptom 10.11: You encounter an *Invalid Unit Reading Drive <x>* error.   Software drivers appear to load properly, and the Bernoulli drive is assigned a drive letter as expected. This often occurs under Windows 3.1x or DOS. In virtually all cases, there is a problem with the SMARTDRV statement in AUTOEXEC.BAT.

- *Check the drive controller BIOS*. There may be a conflict with the BIOS on your PC1616 controller card. If you are *not* booting from the PC1616, try disabling the PC1616 BIOS with the ISACFG.COM utility accompanying the PC1616 adapter (you can also obtain the utility from Iomega at *www.iomega. com*). Reboot the PC—the error should be corrected.

- *Check for SmartDrive*. If you *are* booting from the PC1616 controller (the Bernoulli drive), leave the controller's BIOS *enabled*, but try loading SMARTDRV high (i.e., into the upper memory area). If you cannot load SMARTDRV high, disable its command line in AUTOEXEC.BAT and reboot the system, then load SMARTDRV from the DOS command line once the PC initializes. If problems persist, try the new GUEST program from Iomega (make sure you're using the latest version). Once you install the GUEST.EXE and GUEST.INI files to your PC, enter the path and command line for GUEST near the end of AUTOEXEC.BAT (before Windows starts), such as

```
c:\zinstall\guest.exe
```

If these solutions fail to correct the error, then SMART-DRV *cannot* be loaded and will need to be REMarked out of the AUTOEXEC.BAT file entirely.

> **NOTE**: *If you use the GUEST program, you cannot compress the disks using DISKSPACE. Also, GUEST does not support PC80 or PC90 adapter cards.*

Symptom 10.12: You encounter problems using the parallel-port interface (PPA-3) with a Bernoulli drive. Problems with the PPA-3 are usually related to installation issues, but drivers can also prevent the PPA-3 from responding.

- *Check the power/signal connections*. The external device *must* be turned on *before* you power up the computer. If the device refuses to power up, check the power pack and its connection to the Bernoulli drive. Make sure that the signal cable is the proper length and is connected securely to the drive and the system. Unusually long cables may cause read/write errors.

- *Isolate the parallel port*. Try disconnecting the printer or other parallel-port devices from the system, and try the PPA-3 as the only parallel-port device attached to the parallel port.

- *Check the drive termination*. The PPA-3 board is terminated, and the last drive attached to the PPA-3 cable must also be terminated. If the Bernoulli drive is the last device attached to the PPA-3, make sure it is terminated properly.

- *Check the driver installation*. You need either OAD 1.3 (or higher) or Iomega SCSI 2.0 (or higher) to use the PPA-3 board. Once the drivers are installed, you should see several lines in CONFIG.SYS, such as

```
REM OAD 1.3 or later:
DEVICE=C:\OADDOS\ASPIPPA3.SYS /L=001
DEVICE=C:\OADDOS\DOSCFG.EXE /M1 /V /L=001
DEVICE=C:\OADDOS\DOSOAD.SYS /L=001
```

or

```
REM Iomega SCSI 2.0 or later:
DEVICE=C:\IOMEGA\ASPIPPA3.SYS /L=001
DEVICE=C:\IOMEGA\SCSICFG.EXE /V /L=001
DEVICE=C:\IOMEGA\SCSIDRVR.SYS /L=001
```

Try some ASPIPPA3.SYS command-line options. The ASPIPPA3.SYS driver provides several important command-line options (Table 10.1) that can be employed to streamline its operation. If the ASPIPPA3.SYS command line generates any errors, you can decipher the errors with Table 10.2.

TABLE 10.1   Command-Line Options for ASPIPPA3.SYS

`/MODE=n`

`/MODE=1` is the most compatible mode.

`/MODE=2` is the bidirectional transfer mode—your PC must have a bidirectional parallel port.

`/MODE=3` is enhanced mode, which requires an Intel SL series microprocessor (i.e., 80386SL, 80486SL, or 82360SL).

`/SL360=Yes/No`
This tells the ASPIPPA3.SYS driver whether or not the computer uses an Intel SL microprocessor chipset. If you're not sure (or if a divide overflow occurs during loading), set to `/SL360=No`.

`/SPEED=n`
Values 1 to 10 are available. Start by setting `/SPEED=1`. If that solves the problem, continue to increase the value until the problem recurs, then use the highest value that functioned properly. If you are still not sure which value to use, set `/SPEED=1`.

`/SCAN`
This forces the ASPIPPA3.SYS driver to check all parallel-port addresses. There are three addresses possible: 278h, 378h, and 3BCh.

`/Busy_Retry=Yes`
This option forces the driver to retry several times when a device is busy (instead of just reporting an error).

`/Port=<Address>`
This is used to manually specify the port address of the parallel port.

TABLE 10.2   ASPIPPA3.SYS Error Messages

Error code	Possible cause
4001	Command-line syntax error
4002	Adapter initialization failed—possible problem with the adapter or the parallel port
4003	User specified a port address and there was no adapter there
4004	No adapter found
4005	User pressed both SHIFT keys to bypass this driver
4006	Current DOS version is not supported by this driver
4100	Conflicting port address was detected in command line
4107	Improper speed value; acceptable range is 0 to 10 decimal
4108	Bad value—value outside limits

Symptom 10.13: The Iomega PPA-3 locks up on installation. Chances are that the ASPIPPA3.SYS driver is causing the computer to lock up or is causing a divide by zero overflow error.

- *Check the power/signal connections.* The external device *must* be turned on before you power up the computer. If the device refuses to power up, check the power pack and its connection to the Bernoulli drive. Also make sure that the signal cable is the proper length and is connected securely to the drive and the system. Unusually long cables may cause read/write errors.

- *Check the drive termination.* The PPA-3 board is terminated, and the last drive attached to the PPA-3 board must also be terminated. If the Bernoulli drive is the last device attached to the PPA-3, make sure it is terminated properly by setting the termination switch on the back of the drive to I. If the switch is set to O, turn off the drive, set the switch to I, turn the drive on, and reboot the PC. Update the ASPIPPA3.SYS driver. Try adding the /SL360=NO switch to the command line, for example,

```
DEVICE=C:\IOMEGA\ASPIPPA3.SYS /SL360=NO
```

Save your changes to CONFIG.SYS and reboot the computer.

- *Isolate PPA-3 problems.* Try the PPA-3 board and Bernoulli drive on another PC. If they work on another system, the original parallel port is probably incompatible. If the PPA-3 and drive do not work on another system, try another set of cables. If problems persist, try the Bernoulli drive directly on a SCSI adapter. If the drive works directly, the PPA-3 has probably failed. If the drive still does not work, it has probably failed.

Jaz drive troubleshooting

Symptom 10.14: You have problems when running Iomega Jaz Tools under Windows 95. When Iomega Tools for Windows 95 is installed on your computer, the system may crash (or you may receive an error message referencing the IOMEGA.VXD file) when you attempt to use the Iomega Jaz Tools. This occurs most frequently under FAT32 partitions of OSR2. Chances are that you're using an older version of Jaz Tools for Windows 95 (earlier than version 5.0). Earlier versions of Jaz Tools are *not* compatible with FAT32 (OSR2). You'll need to uninstall the Jaz Tools package, then install version 5.0 or later, which is FAT32-aware.

Symptom 10.15: The system runs in DOS compatibility mode when booting from a removable media drive. When your PC is configured to boot from a removable media drive, the *Performance* tab in *System* properties may show that the computer is using DOS compatibility mode for virtual memory. This is known to be a frequent problem under Windows 95 and OSR1, and it is known to occur with Zip drives, Jaz drives, and SyQuest EZ drives (and may also occur with other IDE or SCSI removable media drives). This problem does *not* occur with Windows 95 OEM Service Release 2. To avoid this problem, configure Windows 95 so that the Windows swap file is located on a nonremovable disk:

- In *Control Panel*, double-click *System*.

- Click the *Performance* tab, and then click *Virtual Memory*.

- Click *Let me specify my own virtual memory settings*, click a *Nonremovable* disk in the *Hard Disk* box, click *OK*, and then click *OK* again.

Symptom 10.16: The Jaz drive isn't detected when it is connected through a SCSI adapter card. In many cases, this is a software problem. Boot clean (from a bootable floppy disk) and then run your GUEST software from the Jaz installation disk by typing

```
a:\guest
```

If the drive *is* detected using the GUEST utility under DOS, then the problem is software-related. Try removing the Jaz drivers and software utilities, then reinstalling the latest software version from scratch. If the problem is *not* resolved, then the trouble is hardware-related. Verify that there are no other devices using the same IRQ as your SCSI adapter. Also make sure that your Jaz drive is correctly terminated and is *not* using the same SCSI ID as another SCSI device. Check all power connections to the Jaz drive. If the Jaz drive doesn't respond and the power connections are secure, the drive is probably defective and should be replaced.

Try the Jaz drive on a different computer. If the drive is detected properly on a different computer, there may be a problem with the first computer's configuration. If the Jaz drive is *not* detected on another computer, the Jaz drive may be defective.

Symptom 10.17: The Jaz drive isn't detected when it is connected through a Jaz Traveler. In many cases, this is a software problem. Boot clean (from a bootable floppy disk) and then run your GUEST software from the Jaz installation disk by typing

```
a:\guest
```

If the drive *is* detected using the GUEST utility under DOS, then the problem is software-related. Try removing the Jaz drivers and software utilities, then reinstalling the latest software version from scratch. If the problem is *not* resolved, then the trouble is hardware-related. The Jaz drive must be connected directly to the parallel port—the Jaz drive will not work properly if it is connected through a switch box, dongle, or software key. Also verify that no other device is using IRQ 7. Check all power connections to the Jaz drive. If the Jaz drive doesn't respond and the power connections are secure, the drive is probably defective and should be replaced.

Try the Jaz drive on a different computer. If the drive is detected properly on a different computer, there may be a problem with the first computer's configuration. If the Jaz drive is *not* detected on another computer, the Jaz drive may be defective.

Symptom 10.18: The PC locks up (or does not finish booting) when connected to a SCSI Jaz drive. Make sure that you're powering on the Jaz drive and your computer at the same time (try connecting both the computer and the Jaz drive to a power strip and powering the system from the power strip).

Try removing the Jaz drive and SCSI card from your computer. If the computer still won't boot, there may be a problem with your system's configuration. Try the Jaz drive on a different computer. If the system boots after you remove the Jaz drive, the drive may be defective. If the Jaz drive works properly on another computer, you may need to reconfigure the system (or the SCSI adapter card).

If the computer locks up, boot clean and run the GUEST utility from the Jaz installation disk by typing

```
a:\guest
```

If the drive *is* detected using the GUEST utility under DOS, then the problem is software-related. Try removing the Jaz drivers and software utilities, then reinstalling the latest software version from scratch. Try isolating any conflicting software. Open the *Close Program* dialog box by pressing the <Ctrl> + <Alt> + <Del> keys at the same time. Close open programs by highlighting a program and then clicking the *End Task* button (do not close Explorer). Remember to close one application at a time, then try your Jaz drive again. Repeat this process until the problem is resolved. Once the problem is resolved, the last application that was closed is the one that is causing the conflict.

If the problem is *not* resolved, then the trouble is hardware-related. Verify that there are no other devices using the same IRQ as your SCSI adapter. Also make sure that your Jaz drive is correctly terminated and is *not* using the same SCSI ID as another SCSI device. Check all power connections to the Jaz drive. If the Jaz drive doesn't respond and the power connections are secure, the drive is probably defective and should be replaced.

Try the Jaz drive on a different computer. If the drive is detected properly on a different computer, there may be a problem with the first computer's configuration. If the Jaz drive is *not* detected on another computer, the Jaz drive may be defective.

Symptom 10.19: An incorrect icon appears for a Jaz drive. Ideally, the icon should be a green Jaz drive, so the actual problem depends on the icon that *is* shown in Windows Explorer.

First, the Jaz icon may appear like a floppy or hard disk drive icon. Chances are that there's a real-mode terminate and stay resident program (TSR) or driver interfering with the Jaz drive. Restart your computer. When you see the message *Starting Windows XX...*, press the <F8> key. From the *Startup Menu*, choose *Step-by-Step Confirmation*. As each step is processed, answer *Y* to every entry except *Process your startup device drivers (CONFIG.SYS)* and *Process your startup command file (AUTOEXEC.BAT)*. This will prevent real-mode drivers from loading at startup. If the incorrect Jaz icon is now replaced with the correct green Jaz icon, there is a driver conflict in either your AUTOEXEC.BAT or your CONFIG.SYS file. You'll need to systematically disable each real-mode command line until you identify the offending command line. If the Jaz icon is not the correct green Jaz icon, then there is a Windows driver causing the problem. You may need to remove the Jaz drivers and other software, then update/reinstall that software from scratch.

If the Jaz icon takes any other form, there may be a problem with Imagicon software. Open the *Close Program* dialog box by pressing the <Ctrl> + <Alt> + <Del> keys simultaneously. Highlight the *Imagicon* entry and then click the *End Task* button. Click on *Start*, point to *Programs*, *Startup*, and then click on *Iomega Disk Icons*.

If the problem persists, reboot your computer and run ScanDisk. Correct any file system problems indicated by ScanDisk. If the problem still continues, delete and then reinstall the Iomega Tools software.

Symptom 10.20: The system locks up while installing Jaz Tools software. In most cases, you'll notice lockups when the Iomega setup software is launched. This is usually caused by a conflict with another driver that is loading during Windows 95/98 startup. To determine which file is causing this conflict, close all open programs.

- Open the *Close Program* dialog box by pressing the <Ctrl> + <Alt> + <Del> keys simultaneously.

- Close open programs by highlighting a program and then clicking the *End Task* button (do not close Explorer).

- Close one application at a time, then try your Jaz drive again.

- Repeat this process until the problem is resolved. Once the problem is resolved, the last application that was closed is the one causing the conflict.

- Once you have determined which application is causing the conflict, you should discontinue the use of that application when using your Jaz drive or obtain an updated version of that software.

Symptom 10.21: You receive an *insufficient disk space* message when writing to the Jaz disk under DOS. This error message may be caused if the disk is full, if it exceeds the file limit imposed by your operating system, or if the disk is defective.

- *Check the disk space*. Verify that the disk has enough space available to hold the files you wish to copy.

- *Check the operating system*. Make sure that you do not exceed the file limit of your operating system. DOS will not allow you to include more than 511 files in the root directory. Switch to the drive letter of your Jaz drive. From the drive prompt, type `dir` and press <Enter>. The number of files in the root directory should be less than 511. If it is not, you'll have to move individual files into other directories to reduce the number of files on the root directory.

- *Try cycling power*. If the error persists, try shutting down the computer (and Jaz drive), then restarting the system from a "cold" start.

- *Try several different disks*. If the error message occurs on only *one* disk, try reformatting that disk (formatting the disk will remove all data from the disk). If reformatting the disk doesn't help, discard the disk and use a fresh one. If you're receiving the error message with *more* than one disk, the drive may be defective.

Symptom 10.22: There are no drives on your system supported by Iomega Tools in DOS. Boot the system clean, and then run GUEST from the Jaz installation disk by typing `a:\guest`. If the drive *is* detected using the GUEST utility under DOS, then the problem is software-related. Try removing the Jaz drivers and software utilities, then reinstalling the latest software version from scratch. Try isolating any conflicting software. Open the *Close Program* dialog box by pressing the <Ctrl> + <Alt> + <Del> keys at the same time. Close open programs by highlighting a program and then choosing the *End Task* button (do not close Explorer). Remember to close one application at a time, then try your Jaz drive again. Repeat this process until the problem is resolved. Once the problem is resolved, the last application that was closed is the one causing the conflict.

If the problem is *not* resolved, then the trouble is hardware-related. Verify that there are no other devices using the same IRQ as your SCSI adapter. Also make sure that your Jaz drive is correctly terminated and is not using the same SCSI ID as another SCSI device. Check all power connections to the Jaz drive. If the Jaz drive doesn't respond and the power connections are secure, the drive is probably defective and should be replaced.

Try the Jaz drive on a different computer. If the drive is detected properly on a different computer, there may be a problem with the first computer's configuration. If the Jaz drive is *not* detected on another computer, the Jaz drive may be defective.

Symptom 10.23: The GUEST utility cannot locate the Jaz Tools disk. Verify that the Jaz Tools disk is in your Jaz drive. If the Jaz Tools disk is already inserted into your Jaz drive, eject and then reinsert the Jaz Tool disk. You may also wish to try another Jaz Tools disk. Next, verify that your Jaz drive is assigned a drive letter. Double-click the *My Computer* icon—there should be an icon representing the Jaz drive. If your Jaz drive is *not* assigned a drive letter, you'll need to connect the drive properly.

Close all open programs. Open the *Close Program* dialog box by pressing the <Ctrl> + <Alt> + <Del> keys simultaneously. Close open programs by highlighting a program, then clicking the *End Task* button (do not close Explorer). Close one application at a time, then try your Jaz drive again. Repeat this process until the problem is resolved—the last application that was closed is the one causing the conflict. Once you've determined which application is causing the conflict, discontinue the use of that application while using your Jaz drive (or obtain an updated version of the software).

Symptom 10.24: No drive letters were added for the Jaz drive in DOS. Boot the system clean, and then run GUEST from the Jaz installation disk by typing a:\guest. If the drive *is* detected using the GUEST utility under DOS, then the problem is software-related. Try removing the Jaz drivers and software utilities, then reinstalling the latest software version from scratch. Try isolating any conflicting software. Open the *Close Program* dialog box by pressing the <Ctrl> + <Alt> + <Del> keys at the same time. Close open programs by highlighting a program and then clicking the *End Task* button (do not close Explorer). Remember to close one application at a time, then try your Jaz drive again. Repeat this process until the problem is resolved. Once the problem is resolved, the last application that was closed is the one causing the conflict.

If the problem is *not* resolved, then the trouble is hardware-related. Verify that there are no other devices using the same IRQ as your SCSI adapter. Also make sure that your Jaz drive is correctly terminated and is not using the same SCSI ID as another SCSI device. Check all power connections to the Jaz drive. If the Jaz drive doesn't respond and the power connections are secure, the drive is probably defective and should be replaced.

Try the Jaz drive on a different computer. If the drive is detected properly on a different computer, there may be a problem with the first computer's configuration. If the Jaz drive is *not* detected on another computer, the Jaz drive may be defective.

Symptom 10.25: You see an error indicating that the Jaz disk in the drive is not formatted. First verify that you're using a PC-formatted disk (a Mac-formatted Jaz disk will not work in a PC). Try several different Jaz disks. If the error message occurs on only *one* disk, try reformatting that disk (remember that formatting the Jaz disk will remove all data from that disk). If you cannot format the suspect Jaz disk, it may be defective and require replacement. If you're receiving the error message with *any* Jaz disk (or if the disk will not format on your drive), the drive may be defective and need to be replaced.

Symptom 10.26: You encounter a *general failure reading drive* message in DOS. In many cases, this is a disk problem. First check your connections and confirm that the Jaz drive's signal and power cables are attached properly. Verify that you're using a PC-formatted disk (a Mac-formatted Jaz disk will not work in a PC), and compare results with several different Jaz disks. If the error message occurs on only *one* disk, try reformatting that disk (remember that formatting the Jaz disk will remove all data from that disk). If you cannot format the suspect Jaz disk, it may be defective and require replacement. If you're receiving the error message with *any* Jaz disk (or if the disk will not format on your drive), the drive may be defective and need to be replaced.

Symptom 10.27: You get a *disk full* error even though there is still space on the Jaz disk under Windows 95/98. In virtually all cases, you've exceeded the file limit imposed by the operating system (although in a few cases, a defective disk may cause this error message). Verify that the Jaz disk has enough room available to contain the files you wish to copy. The number of files you see when you first open your Iomega drive cannot exceed the limit imposed by your operating system (typically 511 files under DOS and Windows 95/98). If the number of files exceeds this limit, you will have to move individual files into another folder (usually on your hard drive) to temporarily reduce the number of files, and make a new folder on your Jaz disk. You may then move the files back to your Iomega disk:

- Click on *Start* and select *Windows Explorer*.
- Make a new folder on your hard drive by clicking *File*, *New*, and selecting *Folder*.
- Type a name for the new folder.
- Move two or more files from the root directory of your Jaz disk into the newly created folder.
- Move the new folder from your hard drive to your Jaz drive.
- Move other files from the root directory of your Jaz drive to this new folder to make additional space.

If the problem persists with a certain disk, compare results with several different Jaz disks. If the error message occurs on only *one* disk, try reformatting that disk (remember that formatting the Jaz disk will remove all data from that disk). If you cannot format the suspect Jaz disk, it may be defective and require replacement. If you're receiving the error message with *any* Jaz disk (or if the disk will not format on your drive), the drive may be defective and need to be replaced.

Symptom 10.28: When backing up, you receive an error indicating that *disk linking is not supported under Windows 95/98*. This is a problem with Microsoft Backup—it does not support disk linking over multiple Jaz disks. Instead, you should remove Backup and install Iomega's 1-Step Backup for Zip and Jaz software (part of the Iomega Tools software bundle).

To install Iomega Tools for Windows 95/98, put the Jaz installation floppy in the A: drive. Click *Start* and select *Run*. In the *Open* box, type a:\guest95 and click *OK*. Put your Jaz Tools disk into the Jaz drive. Double-click on the *My Computer* icon, then double-click on the Jaz drive icon. You should see a folder called *W95stuff*. Double-click on the *W95stuff* folder, and then double-click on *setup95.exe*. Follow the screen instructions to complete the installation. Now try backing up with the Iomega software.

Symptom 10.29: You encounter a *fatal exception* error when using the Copy Machine software for your Jaz drive. In virtually all cases, the problem is caused by the Auto Spin-down/Eject feature in the Iomega Copy Machine software. You'll need to disable the feature under Windows 95/98. Start the Iomega Copy Machine software by clicking its icon in the *Iomega Tools* folder. Select *Options* and then choose *Runtime*. Deselect the *Auto Spin-Down/Eject* option by clearing the check box. Finally, choose *OK* to accept the changes.

Symptom 10.30: You see an error such as *program performed an illegal operation*. Try rebooting the system first (make sure to cycle power to the drive also). Close all open programs to clear possible conflicting software. Open the *Close Program* dialog box by pressing the <Ctrl> + <Alt> + <Del> keys simultaneously. Close any open programs by highlighting a program, then clicking the *End Task* button (do not close Explorer). Close one application at a time, then try your Jaz drive again. Repeat this process until the problem is resolved. Once the problem is resolved, the last application that was closed is the one causing the conflict. You may be able to patch or update the offending program. As an alternative, you may be able to uninstall and reinstall the Iomega Tools software.

Symptom 10.31: You receive a DOS error such as *Cannot create or replace: make sure the disk is not full or write protected*. You may also see this as a *General failure writing to drive* error or a *Drive does not exist* error. In most

. cases, the Jaz disk is formatted improperly, or the disk is defective. Start by checking the disk format—you must use a PC-formatted disk (a Mac-formatted disk will not work on a PC). Try several different disks. If the error message occurs on only *one* disk, try reformatting that disk (remember that formatting the disk will remove all data from the disk). A defective disk should be replaced. If you're receiving the error message with *any* disk (or if the disk will not format on that drive), the drive may be defective. Try another drive.

Symptom 10.32: You receive an error such as *ASPI for Win32 not installed* when working with a SCSI Jaz drive. This error message is known to occur while you are trying to install the IomegaWare software and is caused by a conflict with the MSWHEEL application (which is part of the Microsoft IntelliMouse Pro). The MSWHEEL software controls the functionality of the wheel on the mouse. Start by closing the MSWHEEL application:

- Open the *Close Program* dialog box by pressing <Ctrl> + <Alt> + <Del> simultaneously.

- Highlight the MSWHEEL application by clicking on *Mswheel*.

- Click on the *End Task* button to close the application.

Now manually install the Iomega SCSI driver in Windows 98/95:

- Insert the IomegaWare CD into your CD-ROM drive. If the installation begins automatically, *cancel* the installation process.

- Click on *Start*, highlight *Settings*, then click on *Control Panel*.

- Double-click on *Add New Hardware* from the *Control Panel*.

- Click on the *Next* button to start the installation process.

- If you're prompted to have Windows search for new hardware, choose *No*.

- Choose *SCSI Controllers* from the *Hardware Types* list, then click on *Next*.

- Choose *Have Disk* from the next screen.

- From the *Install from disk* prompt, click on the *Browse* button.

- From the *Drives* drop-down list, choose the drive letter of your CD-ROM drive.

- From the *Folders* list, double-click on the `w9xstuff` folder and select *OK* twice.

- In the *Models* list, choose the driver for the Zip or Jaz drive you are installing as shown below.

If you're using	*Use this driver*
Jaz or Zip drive with a PCMCIA card	Iomega Jaz & Zip Card PCMCIA SCSI Host Adapter
Jaz drive with a Jaz Jet ISA card	Iomega Jaz Jet ISA SCSI Host Adapter
Jaz drive with a Jaz Jet PCI card	Iomega Jaz Jet PCI SCSI Host Adapter
Zip parallel-port drive	Iomega Parallel Port Interface
Zip SCSI drive with a Zip Zoom PNP card	Iomega Zip Zoom PNP SCSI Host Adapter
Zip SCSI drive with a Zip Zoom card	Iomega Zip Zoom SCSI Host Adapter

- After highlighting the driver, select *Next* and click *Finish*.

- Restart your computer.

Finally, install the IomegaWare software manually:

- Click on *Start*, then *Run*.

- Click on *Browse*. In the *Browse* dialog box, highlight your CD-ROM drive by clicking in the *Look in* drop-down box.

- Highlight the file *setup.exe* and click on the *Open* button.

- In the *Open* box (after the path and filename), type a space, then /N—this will prevent GUEST from running during the installation.

- Follow the prompts to complete the installation of your IomegaWare software.

Symptom 10.33: You receive an *INST30* error with your Jaz disk under Windows 95/98. When you attempt to install IomegaWare software, you may receive the following error message: *ISINST30—this application performed an illegal operation and will be shut down*. In virtually all cases, the problem is due to a software conflict or corruption. Start by closing any background software. Open the *Close Program* dialog box by pressing the <Ctrl> + <Alt> + <Del> keys simultaneously. Close each application (one at a time) by highlighting an application, then clicking on the *End Task* button. Remember not to close Explorer. If the error disappears, the last program to be closed was responsible for the error. You may need to stop using that software while installing the Iomega software (or the Jaz drive). In some cases, you may be able to patch or update the offending software. If the problem persists, you may need to remove and/or reinstall the IomegaWare software from its installation CD.

Symptom 10.34: You get an error such as *Disk not in the drive* when using IomegaWare 2.0 under Windows 95/98. If you receive the error message *Disk not in the drive* when a disk is actually inserted in the drive, it may be that the disk has been read/write-protected. Double-check your Jaz drive to be sure that a Jaz disk is inserted. Eject the disk and reinsert it to ensure that it is positioned properly. Also try several different disks. If no disks are detected, the drive may be defective. If only one disk is causing the problem (and the steps below don't help), then the disk itself may be defective.

If the problem persists, check the read/write-protection status on the Jaz disk. If the disk is protected, it may not respond until it is unprotected. Make sure that the Jaz disk is inserted properly in the drive. Locate the Iomega drive icon where the disk is inserted, then click on it. If you don't have an IomegaWare shortcut on your desktop, click *Start*, select *Programs*, select *Iomega*, then double-click on the IomegaWare icon. From the pop-up menu, choose *Properties*, located at the bottom of the list. In the dialog area labeled *Disk* is a padlock symbol, which will indicate whether the disk has been protected or locked. If the padlock is displayed as closed (or locked), the disk has been protected using the read/write-protection tool.

> **NOTE**: *If you have forgotten the password, you will be given the option to perform a long format on the disk. Performing a long format on the Jaz disk will erase all information.*

If the Jaz disk *is* protected, you'll need to unlock the read/write-protected disk now. Locate and click on the Iomega drive icon where the disk is inserted. If you don't have an IomegaWare shortcut on your desktop, click *Start*, select *Programs*, select *Iomega*, then double-click on the IomegaWare icon. From the pop-up menu, select *Properties*, located at the bottom of the list. Click on the *Change* button in the *Disk* section. In the *Unprotect* window, type the password for the disk and click *OK*.

> **NOTE**: *There is an option within the* Unprotect *window, which allows you to remove the read/write protection* temporarily. *Checking this option will allow you to access the disk in that session, but once the disk is ejected, it will be read/write-protected again.*

Symptom 10.35: The Jaz drive fails to spin up. This is a surprisingly common problem that can have three causes. First, check the drive's power connections. If the drive is not receiving adequate power, it will not spin up a Jaz disk. If the drive is external, you may need to replace the Jaz drive's power adapter. The disk itself may also be at fault. Make sure that the disk is inserted properly and securely (you may need to eject and reinsert the disk). Also try a new disk. If a new disk works, the original disk may be damaged or defective. Finally, boot the system clean from a floppy diskette and try the drive/disk again from the GUEST utility under DOS. If the problem clears, there may be some DOS (or Windows) utility software that is conflicting with the disk. If a clean boot fails to clear the problem, the Jaz drive itself may be defective.

Symptom 10.36: The Jaz drive will not format a disk. In many cases, this occurs when the Jaz disk is read/write-protected, so you'll need to verify that the disk is *not* protected. Double-click the *My Computer* icon, then right-click on the Jaz drive. From the dropdown menu, select the *Protect* option. In the *Disk Protect Options* dialog, choose *Remove Protection*. If the disk *is* password-protected, you must supply the password used to initially write-protect the disk in order to remove the protection.

If the disk is *not* protected, you should try several different disks. If other unprotected Jaz disks format normally, the original disk is probably defective. If the problem continues with more than one disk, try a clean DOS boot and enable the drive using the GUEST utility. If problems disappear with other disks, you're probably getting software interference from one or more TSRs or drivers on the system. If the problem persists with any disk (even after you boot the system clean), the Jaz drive may be defective.

Symptom 10.37: The computer locks up after running parallel-port accelerator software. This problem may occur if you install the parallel-port driver and then run the Parallel Port Accelerator utility. Running the Parallel Port Accelerator utility will sometimes cause the drive not to work (or even cause the system to lock up during boot). Turn off the PC, disconnect the drive, and try rebooting the computer with the drive's signal cable disconnected. The system will almost certainly boot normally. Now remove the system changes made by your parallel-port accelerator software:

- Right-click the *My Computer* icon on your desktop.
- Select *Properties* from the menu.
- Click on the *Device Manager* tab.
- Click on the plus sign (+) next to *SCSI controllers*.
- Double-click on *Iomega Parallel Port Interface*.
- Click on the *Settings* tab.
- Remove all the information from the *Adapter Settings* box.
- Click *OK*, then click *OK* again.
- Click *Yes* when prompted to restart your computer.

Symptom 10.38: You cannot long-format a 1-GB Jaz disk in a 2-GB Jaz drive. The internal read/write heads on a 2-GB Jaz drive are different from those on a 1-GB Jaz drive. A short format will work correctly on the 1-GB Jaz disk, but a long format will fail. Use only a 1-GB Jaz drive to perform a long format on a 1-GB Jaz disk.

Symptom 10.39: The Jaz drive makes a grinding noise when reading or writing to a disk. This is a very serious symptom that may indicate a mechanical problem with the drive. Carefully eject and reinsert the Jaz disk. Do not try another disk in the drive—if the drive is defective, it may cause damage to other Jaz disks. Immediately eject the disk if the grinding noise begins again. If the noise returns, try the disk on another Jaz drive. If the disk is readable on another Jaz drive (and there is no grinding nose), chances are that the original Jaz drive is defective and should be replaced.

SyQuest EZ-Flyer and SyJet Drives

SyQuest is another drive manufacturer which has capitalized on the popularity of removable media drives. Rather than using the flexible disk media of Bernoulli technology, SyQuest chose to employ the rigid platter/floating head approach used by more conventional hard drives. Like Iomega Jaz drives, SyQuest drives are a bit closer to being real hard drives than Bernoulli drives. The traditional 44- and 88-MB SyQuest drives of years past have been replaced by products such as the EZ-Drive (135 MB), EZ-Flyer (230 MB), and SyJet (1.5 GB) drives.

> **NOTE**: *As of April 1999, SyQuest has sold virtually all of its resources to Iomega and changed its name to SYQT. It is unlikely that SYQT will continue to provide substantial support for its products, and drive failures may require upgrading to another make and model. The last information available on SYQT is SYQT, Inc., Suite 222, 21060 Homestead Road, Cupertino, CA 95014, email: info@syquest.com. You can learn more about the situation at http://www.syquest.com/infaqans.html.*

Ejecting a "powered" SyQuest cartridge

- Verify that the power LED glows green.
- Exit all applications that use the cartridge, and close all open files on the cartridge.
- Software-unlock the cartridge (if you use Windows 3.1x, OS/2, or DOS only).

  Press the *Eject* button on the front of the drive.

  Remove the cartridge and place it in its protective case.

NOTE: *If you remove or eject the cartridge, you must pull it out halfway or more* before *you can reinsert it. This built-in feature prevents partial insertion.*

Ejecting an "unpowered" SyQuest cartridge

■ Wait for 45 to 60 s after power is turned off.

■ Open the drive door and remove the cartridge.

■ Return the cartridge to its protective case for storage or transport.

NOTE: *Never manually eject a cartridge while the power is on—this can damage the drive.*

SyQuest drive and cartridge tips

■ *Never* eject a cartridge without the system's knowing about it. *File Share* opens a hidden file. If this file is not closed properly, the directory of that cartridge may be damaged and inaccessible until the system is restarted.

■ Do *not* load multiple SyQuest drivers if you can avoid it.

■ *Never* optimize a data cartridge without a backup.

■ It is better to place the cartridge in its protective case when it is not in use (instead of partially inserting the cartridge in the drive).

■ Do *not* turn off power to the drive in order to remove the cartridge. If power has been turned off, wait at least 45 s before removing the cartridge. Removing the cartridge *before* it has stopped spinning may result in damage to the recording surface and read/write head.

■ *Never* disconnect or connect the drive and the computer while power is on.

■ *Always* remove the data cartridge *before* moving the drive or the computer.

- Do *not* apply cleaners or lubricants of any kind to the drive or the cartridge.

- To keep the cartridge free of dust or contamination (and to protect it from shock damage), always store it in its protective case when it is not installed in a SyQuest drive.

- *Never* open the cartridge. Opening the cartridge door may result in contamination of the recording surface, possible damage to the cartridge, and loss of data.

- Use only cartridges that are at room temperature. Allow the cartridge to stabilize at room temperature *before* using it (e.g., if you have moved the cartridge from a cold car into a warm room, or from a warm car into an air-conditioned room).

- Do *not* use a bulk tape eraser to erase the cartridge. The cartridge has magnetic calibration information written on the recording surface which bulk erasing will remove—this *cannot* be restored.

- Do *not* expose the cartridge to magnetic fields. Note that the x-ray machines at airports will *not* affect the data stored on SyQuest cartridges.

- Use only the cartridge label provided. Do not apply cartridge labels that will interfere with the operation of the drive or the cartridge door.

- Do *not* write on cartridge labels with a graphite pencil—the graphite dust from the pencil could contaminate the recording surface.

- Place only *one* cartridge label on the cartridge at a time—more than one label may interfere with the insertion and ejection of the cartridge.

General SyQuest drive tips

- *Make the system safe.* Turn off and unplug the PC (and drive, if it's external).

- *Check your cabling*. Verify that the striped or colored edge of the EIDE cable attaches to pin 1 of the
EIDE devices and the EIDE controller port. For
most EIDE devices, the striped edge of the cable
should be nearest to the dc power connector. Make
sure that all ribbon-cable connectors fully engage 40
pins and that no pins are bent. See that all power
connectors to the EIDE devices are fully seated. If
you're using a parallel-port drive, see that the external cable is attached securely at both ends.

- *Check the jumper settings*. Verify that the drive is
jumpered as a master or slave device, as appropriate. For SCSI drives, the drive should have its own
SCSI ID. If the drive is cabled with other devices,
check their jumpers as well.

- *Check the CMOS Setup*. Restore power to the system and drive and go into the CMOS Setup. Select
the setup screen that lets you manage hard drives.
Locate the SyQuest entry (i.e., SyJet EIDE) and
identify it as the *primary master*, *primary slave*, *secondary master*, or *secondary slave*. If the BIOS does
not detect the SyQuest drive automatically, you'll
need to enter the drive geometry manually:

Logical block addressing (LBA) mode: Yes
Multiple sector read/write: 2, 4, 6, 8, or 16 sectors at
 a time
Fast programmed I/O mode: 0 through 4
Cylinders: 2906
Heads: 16
Sectors per track: 63

> **NOTE**: *SyQuest drives ignore Write Precomp and
> Landing Zone entries. You may enter any valid number
> for these parameters.*

- *Reboot the computer*. If the drive still does not
appear, use the *Add New Hardware* wizard to detect
and install the SyQuest drive.

SyQuest drive troubleshooting

Symptom 10.40: Your EIDE SyQuest SparQ or SyJet drive doesn't work properly under a Phoenix 4.0 (version 6.0) BIOS. In most cases, you find that your system locks up while loading Windows 95/98 or when attempting to access the drive while some EIDE removable cartridge hard drives (over approximately 500 MB) are attached to your computer. The solution to this problem is almost always to perform a BIOS upgrade, so contact your system or motherboard maker to see if there's an update available. If there is no BIOS update available, consider upgrading your drive controller with a model offering its own on-board BIOS.

Symptom 10.41: Windows 95/98 locks up with a SparQ 1.0-GB drive attached. The computer will lock up while loading Windows (or when attempting to access the drive) when the following three conditions are met:

1. You have a SparQ drive with firmware revision SA_0032 or SA_0033.

2. You have a computer that has a 1997 or 1998 release of Phoenix BIOS.

3. Windows DMA support for the SparQ drive is enabled.

To correct this problem, you'll need to turn off the DMA support for the drive. SyQuest recommends that you perform this using the SyQuest DMA wizard:

- Restart your computer. When the *Starting Windows* message is displayed, press <F8>.

- Select the *Safe Mode* option and press <Enter.

- While in safe mode, run the SyQuest DMA wizard by double-clicking its icon.

- Follow the on-screen prompts to disable Windows DMA support for the drive.

■ When the wizard finishes, restart your system for the changes to take effect.

> **NOTE**: *Other SyQuest drives and other versions of the SparQ firmware do not have this problem.*

Symptom 10.42: A SparQ parallel-port drive doesn't work when you install Windows 98. You'll generally see a *Fatal error* message during the hardware detection phase of Windows 98 Setup (or Windows 98 simply will not recognize the drive). This is known to be a driver problem. Replace the SyQuest EPATHD.MPD driver, located in the \Windows\System\Iosubsys folder. One option is to download the files PI_355_1.EXE and PI_355_2.EXE (*www.syquest.com*). These contain an updated version of EPATHD.MPD. Now reinstall your drive using these new files.

Symptom 10.43: Your EZ-Flyer 230 or EZ-135 drive does not work after you upgrade to Windows 98. You'll generally see a *Fatal error* message during the hardware detection phase of Windows 98 Setup (or Windows 98 simply will not recognize the drive). This is known to be a driver problem. Replace the SyQuest EPATHD. MPD driver, located in the \Windows\System\ Iosubsys folder. One option is to download the PI_352_2A.EXE file (*www.syquest.com*). This contains an updated version of EPATHD.MPD. Now reinstall your drive using these new files.

Symptom 10.44: You encounter an error indicating *invalid media*. You cannot copy files to the SyQuest cartridge. This is almost always caused by a media mismatch (i.e., you're probably using a Mac-formatted cartridge in a PC). To correct the problem, you'll need to partition and format the cartridge from scratch using FDISK and FORMAT. You can also run the SyQuest Format Utility, which partitions and formats the cartridge automatically.

Symptom 10.45: There is no drive letter assigned to your SyQuest SCSI drive. You notice that the drive doesn't have an icon in *My Computer*. This is often a problem with the SCSI adapter itself. Check the SCSI host adapter to verify that it's installed properly, and see that any necessary SCSI drivers are installed:

- Right-click on *My Computer*.

- Select *Properties*, then select *Device Manager*.

- Now double-click on *SCSI Controllers*.

If there isn't an entry for your SCSI controller, you'll have to use the *Add New Hardware* wizard to install your SCSI adapter under Windows 95/98. Update your Windows 95/98 drivers for the SCSI adapter if possible. If your adapter is not responding (or is not compatible with Windows 95/98), replace the SCSI adapter with another model.

If your SCSI controller is present and operating properly in the *Device Manager*, there are a few more checks that you can make. Verify that power is applied to your SyQuest SCSI drive. The SCSI cable must be properly connected from the controller to your SyQuest drive. The SyQuest drive must also be properly terminated (if it's the last drive in the SCSI chain).

Symptom 10.46: Your modem stops responding after installation of a SyQuest parallel-port EZ-135 or EZ-Flyer 230 drive. You'll typically notice that this happens under Windows 95/98 when you are using SyQuest driver version 3.42 (or later). But you'll almost always find that this occurs on systems with a VL bus IDE controller. Check to see that your modem and the SyQuest drive are not *both* assigned to the same IRQ— the SyQuest drive normally uses IRQ 7. You might also try adding the /DE switch to your existing driver:

- Right-click on *My Computer*.

- Select *Properties* from the pop-up menu.

- Select *Device Manager*, then double-click on *SCSI Controllers*.

- Double-click on *SyQuest Parallel Port Device*.

- Select *Settings*.

- Enter /DE into the *Settings* window.

- Select *OK*, then shut down Windows.

- Cycle the power to your computer.

If the steps above don't solve the problem, you may need to replace your current driver with the version 3.41 (or higher) driver. You need the EPATHD.MPD file from your version 3.41 SyQuest diskette 2, or download the latest driver version from the SyQuest Web site.

Symptom 10.47: The SyQuest parallel-port drive works in DOS but not in Windows. Your SyQuest EZ-135 or EZ-Flyer 230 parallel-port drive is not recognized by Windows 95, but it works fine in MS-DOS mode using VISIT. Check for hardware conflicts in the *Device Manager*. If your *SyQuest Parallel Port Device* (under your *SCSI Controllers* entry) is marked with a yellow exclamation mark, you may have an IRQ conflict. SyQuest drives connected to LPT 1 use IRQ 7, but many sound cards default to using IRQ 7. Use an IRQ other than 7 for your sound card. If you have a second parallel port (LPT 2), connect your SyQuest drive there instead of to LPT 1. If that fails, try adding the driver setting /di to your existing driver:

- Right-click on *My Computer*.

- Select *Properties*, then select *Device Manager*.

- Double-click on *SCSI Controllers*.

- Double-click on *SyQuest Parallel Port Device*.

- Select *Settings*.

- Enter /di into the *Settings* window.

- Select *OK*, then shut down Windows.
- Cycle the power to your computer.

If the problem persists, you may have to run the SyQuest parallel-port drive in DOS compatibility mode. Edit the CONFIG.SYS file by adding the following two lines at the bottom of the file:

```
device=C:\SYQUEST\SQATDRVR.SYS
device=C:\SYQUEST\EPATSYQ.SYS
```

You may need to make a directory called C:\SYQUEST, then add SQATDRVR.SYS and EPATSYQ.SYS to that directory.

Symptom 10.48: You cannot use your floppy drive(s) after installing your SyQuest EZ-135 or EZ-Flyer 230 parallel-port drive. You'll typically notice that this happens under Windows 95/98 when using SyQuest driver version 3.42 (or later). But you'll almost always find that this occurs on systems with a VL bus IDE controller. You might try adding the /DE switch to your existing driver:

- Right-click on *My Computer*.
- Select *Properties* from the pop-up menu.
- Select *Device Manager*, then double-click on *SCSI Controllers*.
- Double-click on *SyQuest Parallel Port Device*.
- Select *Settings*.
- Enter /DE into the *Settings* window.
- Select *OK*, then shut down Windows.
- Cycle the power to your computer.

If the steps above don't solve the problem, you may need to replace your current driver with the version 3.41 (or higher) driver. You need the EPATHD.MPD file from the version 3.41 SyQuest diskette 2, or download the latest driver version from the SyQuest Web site.

Symptom 10.49: After you change a data cartridge, the new cartridge is not recognized. If you just reformatted a Mac-formatted cartridge using the FORMAT utility from DOS or Windows, it may not be recognized by your system (Mac cartridges need to be partitioned before they're formatted). Partition and format the cartridge using the SyQuest utilities—the format option automatically partitions the cartridge before formatting it. Enable *Removable and Int 13 support* for the SyQuest drive. FDISK (partition) the cartridge, and then format it with FORMAT.

- Right-click on *My Computer*.
- Select *Properties*.
- Select *Device Manager*.
- Double-click on *Disk Drives*.
- Double-click on the SyQuest drive.
- Select *Settings*.
- Click on the Int 13 check box.
- Click on the *Removable* box.
- Close any open windows, then restart Windows.

Symptom 10.50: You cannot remove or reinstall SyQuest utilities. Download and install the latest version of the SyQuest utilities. It cleans out any traces of previous installations and installs the new version. If your object was to remove the utilities, you can now do so cleanly, using the uninstall feature. There are three installation versions available; download the version that's appropriate for the drive interface that you're using:

- IDE interfaces—use the W95Innn.EXE file
- Parallel-port interfaces—use the W95Pnnn.EXE file

- SCSI interfaces—use the *W95Snnn.EXE* file

The term *nnn* denotes a driver version. You can download the latest driver version from the SyQuest site at *http://www.syquest.com/support/ftp.html*.

Symptom 10.51: The SyQuest EZ-Flyer 230 parallel-port drive appears in *My Computer,* but is not detected by SyQuest Windows 95/98 software. In virtually all cases, the computer is using a VL bus IDE controller, and Int 13 support is *not* enabled. Int 13 support *must* be enabled; this can be accomplished automatically by updating the drivers to the latest version. You can also try enabling Int 13 support manually:

- Right-click on *My Computer*.
- Select *Properties*, then select *Device Manager*.
- Double-click on *Disk Drives*.
- Double-click on the SyQuest drive.
- Select *Settings*.
- Click on the *Int 13* check box—a check mark should appear in the box.
- Save your changes, then shut down and restart Windows.

Symptom 10.52: After shutting down to DOS mode, your EZ-135 or EZ-Flyer 230 parallel-port drive cannot be accessed. This is probably because there are no real-mode (DOS) drivers installed for the drive. You'll need to add DOS drivers—edit your DOSSTART.BAT file to load the drivers when you enter MS-DOS mode. Edit C:\WINDOWS\DOSSTART.BAT adding the following three lines at the bottom of the file:

```
PATH=C:\SYQUEST;%path%
SQLOAD C:\SYQUEST\SQATDRVR.SYS /P
SQLOAD C:\SYQUEST\EPATSYQ.SYS /DE
```

Save your changes to DOSSTART.BAT. Remember that you may need to make the directory C:\SYQUEST if it doesn't already exist, then use your version 3.45 SyQuest diskette 3 to copy the files SQLOAD.COM, SQLOAD.INI, SQATDRVR.SYS, and EPATSYQ.SYS to that directory. The next time you exit Windows to DOS mode, your SyQuest parallel-port drive should be available.

Symptom 10.53: You receive a *read capacity* error when writing to your SyQuest drive. You may also find that your SyQuest Windows 95/98 utilities don't work. This is almost always due to a driver configuration error, so try adding the /DE switch to your SyQuest driver:

- Right-click on *My Computer*.

- Select *Properties*, then select *Device Manager*.

- Double-click on *SCSI Controllers*.

- Double-click on *SyQuest Parallel Port Device*.

- Select *Settings*, then enter /DE into the *Settings* window.

- Save your changes, then shut down Windows.

- Turn your PC off, then turn it back on again.

Symptom 10.54: Your SyQuest EZ-135 or EZ-Flyer 230 parallel-port drive cannot be accessed (or shows errors) while running Seagate (Arcada) Backup software, version 1.1. This is a known problem between the backup software and SyQuest drives. You'll need to update the Seagate/Arcada Backup software, or disable it and use Microsoft Backup.

Symptom 10.55: You cannot print through the printer passthrough port of an EZ-135 or EZ-Flyer 230 drive. This problem frequently occurs when you are using an advanced printer that requires an enhanced capabilities port (or ECP). Hewlett-Packard 820 printers are just one example of printers that may have trouble. Chances are that the computer's parallel port is configured for standard or compatibility mode. Check the computer's printer port in the CMOS Setup and verify that the port is set for ECP or EPP mode.

Symptom 10.56: While the system is copying data, the drive's orange Activity indicator flashes, and Windows 95/98 freezes. This is almost always due to problems with the data cartridge. Reboot the system if necessary, then run ScanDisk and/or format the cartridge. The EZ-Flyer 230 parallel-port drive does extensive error recovery that can take several minutes. If new errors are discovered each time you run ScanDisk, the cartridge may need to be replaced.

Symptom 10.57: The SyQuest drive's printer passthrough works only intermittently. Sometimes printing works fine, but at other times it's impossible to print. In virtually all cases, the printer needs to be "refreshed":

- Double-click on *My Computer*.
- Double-click on *Printers*.
- Highlight the printer that needs to be refreshed.
- **Press the** <F5> function key to refresh the printer.

If the problem persists, you may need to remove and reinstall the printer's driver.

Symptom 10.58: Windows 95 may change from 32-bit to 16-bit mode after installation of SyQuest IDE drive. The SyQuest drive may appear as a nonremovable hard drive (e.g., the D: drive) instead of as Removable Disk D:. You may note that there is a loss of drive performance or access speed. You may also see no drive letter at all for the SyQuest drive. In most cases, this is due to a Registry problem caused by a NOIDE entry. Check the NOIDE entry:

- Click *Start* and then click *Run*.
- In the *Run* box, type REGEDIT and press <Enter>.
- In the Registry Editor utility, go to the *Edit* menu and select *Find*.
- In the *Find* box, type NOIDE, and click *Find Next*.
- If NOIDE is *not* found in the Registry, close REGEDIT and check/replace the SyQuest drive.

If NOIDE is found in the Registry, you will need to remove it. Back up your Registry first:

- Run the REGEDIT program as shown above.
- From the *Registry* menu, click *Export Registry File*.
- In the *File Name* box, type C:\REGBACK.REG and click *Save*.

Now locate the NOIDE entry again and correct it:

- Go to the *Edit* menu and select *Find*.
- In the *Find* box, type NOIDE and click *Find Next*.
- Highlight and remove each occurrence of NOIDE. If there is a DEFAULT VALUE NOIDE, it may refuse to be removed. Ignore this entry if it occurs.
- Close the REGEDIT program.
- Open the SYSTEM.INI file (found in the Windows directory) and check to make sure that the RemovableIDE=TRUE entry is present in the [386enh] section.
- Reboot the computer.

This should fix the problem. If Windows 95 experiences any significant problems (e.g., video resolution changing or icons distorted), or if it reports a registry error, then run the REGEDIT program and restore the original Registry:

- From the *Registry* menu, click *Import Registry File*.

- In the *File Name* box, type C:\REGBACK.REG and click *Open*.

- After the Registry information has been loaded, restart the computer.

Symptom 10.59: There is no drive icon assigned to your SyQuest drive under Windows 95. First, be sure to boot with a cartridge in the drive—Windows 95 declares the drive nonfunctional if it can't read from it at boot time. Second, check for a LASTDRIVE statement in your CONFIG.SYS file. If it is set too low, you can increase it. If you're using Windows 95, you can REMark out the statement entirely.

Symptom 10.60: Your SyQuest DOS software won't install. During installation, you receive a message such as *Missing COMMAND.COM* or *insufficient memory*. This is due to a shortage of conventional memory. You need 500 KB of free memory to run the install routine. Use the MEM /C feature to see how much free conventional memory you have available. If you have less than 500 KB, you'll have to REMark out TSRs or device drivers in your CONFIG.SYS and/or AUTOEXEC.BAT file (at least temporarily) to perform the installation. After the SyQuest software is installed, remove the REMs that you added.

Symptom 10.61: Iomega's ToolBox utility takes over the SyQuest EIDE drives. This is a problem with the Iomega software, and you'll need to download and install the latest version of that software from *http://www.iomega.com/software* in order to correct the problem. SyQuest EIDE drives and Iomega drives *can* coexist on the same system, but the updated Iomega ToolBox utility must be loaded.

Symptom 10.62: Your SyQuest Windows software won't install. In virtually all cases, this is due to interference from other Windows software operating on your system. Some programs impede the installation sequence and need to be disabled until your drive and software are installed. Disable the troublesome program(s), perform your SyQuest installation, then reenable the program(s). The following programs typically have to be disabled to perform an installation:

- Norton Antivirus
- Flexicd
- QuickRes

Symptom 10.63: You encounter problems with removable media IDE drives in Windows 95. There are several potential problems, such as

- The removable drive is not detected (or not accessible) within Windows 95.
- Media changes (i.e., removing a disk and inserting a new disk) are not detected.
- The removable drive appears as a nonremovable hard disk in Windows Explorer or *Device Manager*.

This happens because removable media IDE drives are not fully supported by the IDE drivers included with Windows 95. You'll need to install the following patch files for Windows 95: ESDI_506.PDR (version 4.00.1116 dated 8/25/97 or later) and VOLTRACK.VXD (version 4.00.954 dated 3/6/96 or later). Both of these files can be found in the REMIDEUP.EXE file, available from the Microsoft Software Library (*www.microsoft.com*). Once it has been downloaded, find the file in Windows Explorer and double-click on it, then follow the on-screen instructions. The new files will be patched to the \Windows\System\Iosubsys directory.

> **NOTE**: *The VOLTRACK.VXD file is installed on Windows 95a computers only—this file is not installed on computers running OSR2.*

Symptom 10.64: You encounter problems with SyQuest drives and Future Domain SCSI adapters. Although SyQuest drives should perform properly with Future Domain SCSI adapters, there are some issues that may cause problems. Inspect the SCSI ID first. Future Domain SCSI adapters install drives from the highest SCSI ID (6) to the lowest (0)—this is opposite to the practice of the majority of HBA manufacturers, which assign drives from ID 0. Make sure that any hard disk drives have a higher SCSI ID number than the SyQuest drives when you install a removable drive on the SCSI bus. That way, the hard drives will be assigned the lower DOS drive letter (e.g., C: then D:).

Future Domain controllers will not allow the SyQuest drive to serve as a boot device. If you must make the SyQuest drive bootable, contact Future Domain for a firmware upgrade. Cartridge preparation can also be a problem. Future Domain PowerSCSI software works with cartridges prepared and used on the same PC. When you exchange the cartridge for one of a different format, size, or partition, the PowerSCSI driver will not handle the new cartridge properly. You may need different SCSI drivers. Check your SCSI drivers. In order for the SyQuest utilities to work properly with Future Domain adapters (and handle nonnative cartridges), the CONFIG.SYS file must contain the following drivers:

```
DEVICE=C:\PWRSCSI!\DCAM18XX.EXE

DEVICE=C:\PWRSCSI!\ASPIFCAM.SYS

DEVICE=C:\SYQUEST\SCSI\SQDRIVER.SYS
```

The correct CAM.EXE driver for your particular adapter must be used in the CONFIG.SYS file (such as CAM950.EXE). Do not use FDBIOS.SYS or INT4BCAM.SYS with SQDRIVER.SYS (only one driver can be used to control the SyQuest drive). The SyQuest DOS formatting program SQPREP will partition and format DOS cartridges with Future Domain

adapters if the drivers are correctly installed in CON-
FIG.SYS as shown above.

**Symptom 10.65: You encounter problems with SyQuest
drives and NCR SCSI adapters.** SyQuest drives are
reported to work well with NCR (now part of AT&T
Global Systems) adapters, but you must be using version 3.12 or later of the SyQuest utilities. The SCSI
drivers may be causing problems. To make the
SyQuest cartridges removable under DOS, the following three entries must be present in CONFIG.SYS:

```
DEVICE=C:\SDMS\DOSCAM.SYS       (10-08-93 or later)

DEVICE=C:\SDMS\ASPICAM.SYS      (10-08-93 or later)

DEVICE=C:\SyQuest\SCSI\SQDRIVER.SYS
```

If you choose to use the NCR driver SCSIDISK.SYS
instead of SQDRIVER.SYS, the ability to remove cartridges and use nonnative cartridges will be lost. Make
sure that the two drivers are *not* loaded together, or
data corruption will result. Also suspect an issue with
the SCSI ID. Typical NCR SCSI priority is from lowest
(0) to highest (6), and the NCR adapter is SCSI ID 7.
The SyQuest DOS partition and format utility
(SQPREP) works well with NCR adapters as long as
the drivers are loaded in CONFIG.SYS as shown
above.

**Symptom 10.66: You encounter problems with SyQuest
drives and Rancho Technology SCSI adapters.** SyQuest
SCSI drives are reported to work properly with Rancho
Technology SCSI adapters, but there are some issues
that you must be aware of. First, Rancho Technology
SCSI BIOS requires that a cartridge be installed in the
SyQuest drive at *boot time* (older Rancho Technology
BIOS versions may hang if no cartridge is installed
and the drive is ready). SCSI drivers can also be
an issue. SyQuest utilities will work through the ASPI-
CAM driver supplied with Rancho Technology

adapters. To make the cartridges removable under DOS, the CONFIG.SYS file must have drivers loaded in this order:

```
REM For the Rancho Technology 1600:

DEVICE=C:\RT1600\DOSCAM.SYS      (12-14-94 or later)

DEVICE=C:\RT1600\ASPICAM.SYS     (12-14-94 or later)

DEVICE=C:\SyQuest\SCSI\SQDRIVER.SYS
```

or

```
REM For the Rancho Technology 1000:

DEVICE=C:\RT1000\RTASPI10.SYS    (01-26-93 or later)

DEVICE=C:\SyQuest\SCSI\SQDRIVER.SYS
```

If you choose to use the Rancho Technology driver SCSIDISK.SYS instead of SQDRIVER.SYS, the ability to remove cartridges and use nonnative cartridges will be lost. Make sure that the two drivers are *not* loaded together, or data corruption will result. Check the SCSI ID—typical Rancho Technology SCSI priority is from lowest (0) to highest (6), and the Rancho Technology adapter is SCSI ID 7. The SyQuest DOS partition and format utility (SQPREP) works well with Rancho Technology adapters as long as the drivers are loaded in CONFIG.SYS as shown above.

Symptom 10.67: You encounter problems with Packard-Bell multimedia PCs and SyQuest drives. Packard Bell systems often use unusual IRQ assignments which may interfere with the default settings of many SCSI adapters. Check the hardware settings—many Packard Bell PCs use IRQ 11 and IRQ 12 for the CD-ROM drive, sound board, and mouse. When you install a SCSI adapter, make sure to use IRQ 10 and the I/O address of 340h. However, if there is any other 16-bit card (especially a network card) in the system, use IRQ 15 instead.

Symptom 10.68: You encounter problems using BusLogic SCSI adapters and SyQuest drives. The BusLogic ASPI driver (BTDOSM.SYS) will operate with the SyQuest device driver SQDRIVER.SYS, but the order of installation can be very important. Install the BusLogic driver *first*, then install the SyQuest software. Once the drivers are installed, the CONFIG.SYS file should be in this order:

```
DEVICE=C:\BUSLOGIC\BTDOSM.SYS /D
DEVICE=C:\SYQUEST\SCSI\SQDRIVER.SYS
```

Remove the BusLogic disk driver BTMDISK.SYS:

```
REM DEVICE=C:\BUSLOGIC\BTMDISK.SYS
```

Relocate any other BusLogic device drivers *after* SQDRIVER.SYS. Reboot the system after making any changes to CONFIG.SYS. Finally, check the driver dates. Make sure that you are using SQDRIVER.SYS version 7.72 or higher, or the SyQuest software release 3.12 or higher (1/27/95 or later).

Symptom 10.69: You encounter problems using Qlogic SCSI adapters and SyQuest drives. While SyQuest SCSI drives are reported to operate properly with Qlogic SCSI adapters, there are some issues that can cause problems. First, Qlogic FastSCSI software does not support SyQuest cartridge exchange without your installing the SyQuest SQDRIVER.SYS driver. Install the two Qlogic drivers, *then* install the SyQuest drivers. Make sure that the QL00DISK.SYS driver is *not* installed in CONFIG.SYS. A typical CONFIG.SYS file will appear; for example,

```
DEVICE=C:\QLOGIC\QL41DOS.SYS
DEVICE=C:\QLOGIC\QL00ASPI.SYS
DEVICE=C:\SyQuest\SCSI\SQDRIVER.SYS
```

Make sure to use the correct QLxxDOS.SYS driver for your particular Qlogic SCSI adapter. CorelSCSI software is often shipped with Qlogic SCSI adapters. If a CorelSCSI driver is installed to support a SyQuest drive, do *not* install the SQDRIVER.SYS driver. Finally, disable or REMark out the QL00DISK.SYS driver if it is entered in the CONFIG.SYS file. If the QL00DISK.SYS driver is allowed to coexist with SQDRIVER.SYS, data corruption will result.

Symptom 10.70: You encounter problems using an IBM MicroChannel SCSI controller and a SyQuest drive. This note applies to the /A and /2A MicroChannel SCSI adapters. The IBM ASPI driver (ASPI4B.SYS) will operate with the SyQuest driver SQDRIVER.SYS only under DOS—*not* under Windows. The MSDRVR.ZIP shareware has been known to circumvent this incompatibility. For current pricing and availability, contact the shareware maker:

Micro Staff Co., Ltd.
1-46-9 Matsubara, Setagaya-ku, Tokyo, Japan 156
Tel: 011-81-3-3325-8128
Fax: 011-81-3-3327-7037
CompuServe ID: 100157,1053

Symptom 10.71: You encounter problems using Data Technology Corporation (DTC) SCSI adapters and SyQuest drives. The DTC SCSI adapters will operate with SyQuest drives, but there are several points that can cause problems. Install the DTC ASPI driver first, *then* install the SyQuest utility software. Once all the drivers are installed, the CONFIG.SYS file should appear in this order:

```
REM For the DTC 3280AS ISA version and the DTC
3290AS EISA version:

DEVICE=C:\DTC\ASPI3xxx.SYS

DEVICE=C:\SYQUEST\SCSI\SQDRIVER.SYS
```

Remember to remove the DTC device driver ASCSI. SYS in the CONFIG.SYS file:

```
REM DEVICE=C:\DTC\ASCSI.SYS
```

Also remove it from the AUTOEXEC.BAT file:

```
REM C:\DTC\ASCSI.EXE
```

Load any other DTC device drivers after SQDRIV-ER.SYS, or

```
REM For the DTC 3130 PCI version:
DEVICE=C:\DTC\DOSCAM.SYS
DEVICE=C:\DTC\ASPICAM.SYS
DEVICE=C:\SYQUEST\SCSI\SQDRIVER.SYS
```

Remember to remove the DTC device driver SCSIDISK.SYS in the CONFIG.SYS file:

```
REM DEVICE=C:\DTC\SCSIDISK.SYS
```

Load any other DTC device drivers *after* SQDRIVER. SYS. Remember to reboot the PC after making any changes to your CONFIG.SYS or AUTOEXEC.BAT files. Finally, check the driver dates. Make sure that you are using SQDRIVER.SYS version 7.72 or higher, or the SyQuest software release 3.12 or higher (1/27/95 or later).

Symptom 10.72: The lights on the SyQuest drive are blinking in a regular pattern. The drive has suffered a fault and generally must be replaced. Use Table 10.3 to find the specific error code. In most cases, you will have to replace the drive outright.

TABLE 10.3 SyQuest Error Codes for SQ555, SQ5110C, and 5200C Drives

Green flashes	Amber flashes	Problem	Action
0	3	Microprocessor problems	Replace drive
1	1, 2, 3	PCBA (drive circuitry) failure	Replace drive
2	1, 2, 3, 4, 5, 6	PCBA (drive circuitry) failure	Replace drive
3	0, 3	Microprocessor problems	Replace drive
3	1, 2, 4, 5	PCBA (drive circuitry) failure	Replace drive
4	1, 2, 3	Drive motor problem	Replace drive
4	4, 5	Drive motor speed problem	Replace cartridge
4	6	Cannot find servo	Reinsert cartridge
5	1	Power failure	Check power supply
5	2	Drive motor speed problem	Replace cartridge
5	3, 4, 5, 6, 7, 8, 9	Power-up initialization incomplete	Reinsert cartridge
			Replace cartridge
6	0, 1, 2, 3	PCBA (drive circuitry) failure	Replace drive
6	4	Drive motor speed problem	Replace cartridge
6	5	Excessive runout failure	Reinsert cartridge
			Clean spindle motor
			Replace cartridge
6	6	Incompatible cartridge	Use proper cartridge
6	7	PCBA (drive circuitry) failure	Replace drive
7	1, 2, 3, 4, 5	PCBA (drive circuitry) failure	Replace drive
Off	Solid on or flashing light	Power fault	Replace drive
		Defective cartridge	Replace cartridge
		Head loading failure	Replace drive
Solid on	Solid on	Microprocessor problem	Reinitialize the drive
			Replace the drive

Web Contacts

Iomega: *http://www.iomega.com*

SyQuest: *http://www.syquest.com*

Exabyte: *http://www.exabyte.com*

Index

About the Author

Stephen J. Bigelow is the founder and president of Dynamic Learning Systems, a technical writing, research, and publishing company specializing in electronic and PC service topics. Bigelow is the author of more than 14 feature-length books for TAB/McGraw-Hill and over 100 major articles for mainstream electronics magazines such as *Popular Electronics, Electronics NOW, Circuit Cellar INK,* and *Electronic Service & Technology.* Bigelow is also host of the DLS Video Lecture Series, and editor and publisher of **The PC Toolbox**—a premier PC service newsletter for computer enthusiasts and technicians. You can contact the author at:

Stephen J. Bigelow
Dynamic Learning Systems
PO Box 402
Leicester, MA 01524-0402 USA
http://www.dispubs.com
sbigelow@cerfnet.com